RACE AND LIBERTY IN THE NEW NATION

›RACE AND LIBERTY IN THE NEW NATION‹

Emancipation in Virginia from the Revolution to Nat Turner's Rebellion

EVA SHEPPARD WOLF

LOUISIANA STATE UNIVERSITY PRESS BATON ROUGE

Published by Louisiana State University Press
Copyright © 2006 by Louisiana State University Press
All rights reserved
Manufactured in the United States of America
Louisiana Paperback Edition, 2009

DESIGNER: Michelle A. Garrod
TYPEFACE: Adobe Caslon Pro
TYPESETTER: G&S Typesetters, Inc.

LIBRARY OF CONGRESS CATALOGING-IN-PUBLICATION DATA

Wolf, Eva Sheppard, 1969–
  Race and liberty in the new nation : emancipation in Virginia from the Revolution to Nat Turner's Rebellion / Eva Sheppard Wolf.
  p. cm.
  Includes bibliographical references and index.
    ISBN-13: 978-0-8071-3194-7 (cloth : alk. paper)
    ISBN-10: 0-8071-3194-6 (cloth : alk. paper)
  1. Slaves—Emancipation—Virginia—History—18th century. 2. Slaves—Emancipation—Virginia—History—19th century. 3. Virginia—History—1775–1865. 4. Virginia—Race relations—History—18th century. 5. Virginia—Race relations—History—19th century. 6. Slavery—Virginia—History—18th century. 7. Slavery—Virginia—History—19th century. 8. African Americans—Virginia—History—18th century. 9. African Americans—Virginia—History—19th century. I. Title.
E445.V8W65 2006
975.5'00496073—DC22

2006010526

ISBN-13: 978-0-8071-3417-7 (pbk.)

The paper in this book meets the guidelines for permanence and durability of the Committee on Production Guidelines for Book Longevity of the Council on Library Resources. ∞

To my parents, Ann and Asher Sheppard, who launched me

Contents

Preface ix

Acknowledgments xvii

Abbreviations xxi

1. "Are we willing to grant this liberty to all men?":
Ambivalence in the Revolutionary Era 1

2. "The liberty of Emancipating their Slaves":
The Practice of Manumission, 1782–1806 39

3. "Deep-rooted Prejudices":
Race and the Problem of Emancipation, 1782–1806 85

4. "White negroes" and "inchoate freedom":
Life after Manumission 130

5. A "contest for power":
Slavery and Emancipation Become Political Issues in the 1820s 162

6. The "most momentous subject of public interest":
The Public Debate over Slavery and Emancipation, 1831–1832 196

Epilogue: Virginia and the Nation 235

Appendix A: Religion of Manumitters in Deeds of Manumission Whose Religious Affiliation Could Be Identified 239

Appendix B: Petitions Regarding Slavery, Emancipation, and Colonization Sent to the House of Delegates in 1831–1832 242

Bibliography 249

Index 273

Preface

About the year 1775, in the midst of revolutionary upheaval, a mulatto boy named Sam was born into slavery in Virginia. We do not know precisely where or when or to whom he was born—it is the nature of slavery to obscure the facts of biography—but we do know that in 1802 he made an agreement with his owner to purchase his freedom, an arrangement facilitated by the Revolutionary-era Virginia manumission law that allowed owners to free slaves without the legislative approval that had been necessary previously. After a decade's hard work Sam achieved his goal, his success evident in the 1812 act of emancipation by which he became free and took the name Samuel Johnson. When he died in 1842 Johnson was illiterate and impoverished and had achieved nothing great aside from his own liberty. So he has remained unknown to history, simply one of the thousands of enslaved Virginians who found freedom in the decades after the American Revolution.[1]

The changes brought by the Revolution in Virginia also allowed John Cropper Jr., a Revolutionary War hero, slaveholder, and Accomack County leader, to alter the role he played in Virginia's slave society. In the light of that revolution he looked at the people he held as slaves and saw that they deserved liberty. More than that, he took action, emancipating sixteen people in 1794 because he was "impressed with the belief that all men by Nature are equally free and independent and that the Holding of Man in a State of Slavery is unjust and oppressive."[2]

---

1. Sam's petition, 1812, Legislative Petitions, Fauquier County; *Fauquier County, Virginia Register of Free Negroes* (for evidence of Johnson's age); Richard Brent deed, 2 Aug. 1812, Fauquier County Deeds, 18 (1809–13), Library of Virginia, Microfilm Collections; Samuel Johnson will, 11 Mar. 1836, recorded 22 Aug. 1842, Fauquier County Wills, 17 (1840–42), ibid. All deed books and will books cited below are from Library of Virginia, Microfilm Collections.

2. John Cropper Jr. deed, 31 Dec. 1794, Accomack County Deeds, 8 (1793–97).

Some members of the Ketocton Association of Baptist congregations, in northern Virginia, also contemplated the morality of slaveholding in the post-Revolutionary years, asking in 1796 whether slavery could be supported "by scripture and the true principles of a republican government." When the association agreed the next year that slavery violated divine law, it drew up an emancipation plan, which the member churches promptly rejected, declaring that emancipation was the business of government, not the church.[3]

By examining these and other accounts of how ordinary, often obscure Virginians thought and acted in the face of the vexing issue of racial slavery in a society dedicated to universal liberty, this book attempts to sharpen our picture of liberty, slavery, emancipation, and race in Virginia from the American Revolution to the slavery debates that followed Nat Turner's rebellion. A number of historians have seen the Old Dominion and its leaders, men such as Thomas Jefferson, James Madison, James Monroe, Ferdinando Fairfax, and St. George Tucker, as relative moderates on the question of slavery, and the apparent number of enslaved people who were freed in the late eighteenth century has suggested to several observers that enough white Virginians sympathized with antislavery views to make a general emancipation possible. That Virginia remained a slave state would then seem a failure of leadership and not a reflection of Virginia culture in general. By moving our attention away from the elite, though they remain in the scene, we allow a different understanding of how Virginians responded to the challenges of the early national period to emerge.[4]

Clues left behind in various public and organizational records and in contemporary newspapers indicate that although the Revolutionary period did bring challenges to slavery in Virginia, on the whole white Virginians remained committed to the institution throughout the late eighteenth and

---

3. *Minutes of the Ketocton Baptist Association. Thumb Run,* 4; *Minutes of the Ketockton Baptist Association, Held at Frying-Pan,* 4–6; *Minutes of the Ketocton Baptist Association, Continued at Broad-Run Meeting-House,* 5.

4. Gary Nash, in *Race and Revolution,* articulates particularly clearly the argument that the Revolutionary period made abolition in Virginia possible and that a failure of leadership (mostly in the North) accounted for the persistence of slavery. William Freehling also focuses on the moderate stance of many Virginians in *The Road to Disunion.* On the other side of the argument Robert McColley, in *Slavery and Jeffersonian Virginia,* emphasizes the strength of slavery in Virginia, focusing mostly on the elite (and on the weakness of their opposition to slavery) to explain slavery's persistence and expansion.

early nineteenth centuries. Perhaps most important, a statistical and textual analysis of deeds and wills of manumission reveals that even the act of freeing slaves was not necessarily—and after the early 1790s not usually—motivated by antislavery sentiment sprung from Revolutionary fervor. It was not true, as Gary Nash and others have assumed, that all manumitters thought slavery "immoral and unnatural," although some, such as John Cropper Jr., did. Other slaveholders, however, used manumission to help control their slaves and even to support rather than undermine the slave system. Data derived from manumission documents also show that previous estimates of the number of people emancipated in Virginia after the Revolution based on the size of the free black population are wrong: many fewer people were freed than has been thought. Other evidence in Revolutionary-era legislative proceedings, court cases, newspaper articles, and church debates confirms the notion that white Virginians, though sometimes disturbed by the existence of slavery, remained generally convinced of slavery's importance to their society as well as of the inferiority of the black people who were enslaved. White Virginians' qualms about slavery made them sound potentially liberal, but their continuing unwillingness to abandon slavery in the late eighteenth century demonstrated the strength of their conservative reflexes.

This study also traces the transition from the Revolutionary to the antebellum period, often ignored in works that focus on either the late eighteenth century or the years after 1830. One exception is William Freehling's *Road to Disunion: Secessionists at Bay, 1776–1854*, which argues that the history of the South from the Revolution to the Civil War is best understood as one in which proslavery extremists created one South out of many southern states. In Freehling's account they slowly but surely gained the upper hand over more moderate and even reform-minded thinkers through a series of consequential events and crises. Especially important among those reform-minded thinkers were the "Conditional Terminators," such as Thomas Jefferson, who "would nudge his class toward termination [of slavery], assuming conditions seemed safe." Freehling emphasizes the persistence of this tradition in the upper South even after the Missouri Crisis of 1819–21 and the Virginia debates of 1831–32.[5]

---

5. Freehling, *Road to Disunion*, quotation on 122. Dillon, *Slavery Attacked*, also addresses the transitional period as part of a survey of challenges to slavery from the colonial period to the Civil War.

When we focus exclusively on Virginia and move our attention from the elites to more ordinary folk, we see a substantially different story. Rather than there being an ongoing battle between extremists and moderates stemming from the Revolution, discrete pro- and antislavery blocs crystallized in Virginia only in the late 1820s. True, some Virginians had defended slavery before that time as others, particularly religious radicals, had attacked it. Sporadic debate over slavery in Virginia took place from the years of the Revolution forward. Indeed, debate over slavery is a theme of this book. But it was only when antislavery sentiment became tied to the achievement of distinct political ends that attacks on slavery carried enough weight to spark a sustained and coherent response.

Demographic, economic, and political changes in the late eighteenth and early nineteenth centuries together promoted the development of an antislavery bloc as nonslaveholding white farmers in western Virginia grew more numerous and began to demand political rights equal to those of the eastern slaveholding elite. In response, eastern conservatives, fearing an attack on slavery, held back from granting westerners the proportional representation and universal white manhood suffrage they demanded. Their intransigence brought about the very opposition they feared as westerners' quest for power turned to an attack on the basis of the eastern elite's supremacy, slavery. This dynamic grew more intense during the Virginia Constitutional Convention of 1829–30 and then again after Nat Turner's rebellion of 1831, which gave westerners greater cause to see both slaves and the slaveholding regime as a distinct threat to their own (white) liberty. The fusion in the 1820s and early 1830s of the issue of white Virginians' rights and power with the problem of slavery created a threat to Virginia slavery greater than the one posed by Revolutionary ideology in the late eighteenth century.

In this way, Virginia's history mirrored national developments, since the national political antislavery movement that began in 1819 with the Missouri Crisis proved more perilous to the Union than the antislavery movement that had accompanied the Revolution. And Virginia's fate in the 1860s also paralleled the nation's as the state split in two over the issue of slavery. As much as Virginia's story is unique, it also tells us much about the America of the early national period.

The approach taken here, focusing on ordinary Virginians more than on political and intellectual leaders and looking at the Virginia experience over a span of two generations, yields a complex portrait because the behavior of white Virginians often conflicted with their stated beliefs, with legislative trends, and with judicial decisions and because black Virginians also played a role in shaping the debate over emancipation in Virginia. Always present amidst that complexity, however, was white Virginians' fear of black people, especially *free* black people. Racial fear played a pivotal role in any consideration of emancipation in Virginia.[6]

Indeed, race was at the center of the problems of slavery and liberty in the Revolutionary and early national years. For opponents of slavery race defined the limits that even the most imaginative and liberal among them placed on their dreams of abolition. From the 1780s onward emancipation schemes proffered by elite Virginians always included plans for colonizing freed slaves to some other land because their authors could not conceive of a society in which free whites and blacks lived peacefully together. Seeking to end slavery, the emancipation plans nevertheless endorsed Virginia's racial system. By 1832 racial fears—whites' conviction that all blacks whether enslaved or free threatened their safety—had become the impetus for emancipation-colonization schemes that had as their goal an all-white, all-free society. The shift among emancipationists from being limited by racial fears to being motivated by them mirrored the change in antislavery thinking in Virginia from a concern for black rights to a concern for white rights.

But in another way white Virginians' engagement with race changed little since, as Edmund Morgan and Kathleen Brown have shown, race and liberty were entwined from the colonial period when the reduction of Africans' freedoms helped make possible greater equality and liberty among whites. From that time through the Civil War and beyond, the majority of white Virginians, like many of their fellow Americans north and south, understood liberty as a racial concept: liberty was white, even when white people did not share its blessings equally and even—especially—where the existence of free blacks threatened the racial basis of freedom.[7]

---

6. This is in contrast to scholarship, some of it recent, that deemphasizes race in the formation of American political philosophy. See, e.g., Ericson, *Antislavery and Proslavery Liberalism;* and Bruce, *Rhetoric of Conservatism.*

7. Morgan, *American Slavery, American Freedom;* Brown, *Good Wives.* Another essential work is Winthrop D. Jordan's seminal study, *White over Black.* Critical Race Theory scholars such as Derrick Bell argue that the pattern Morgan found, in which black slavery helped define white liberty and mute class tensions among European colonists, still obtains. Bell writes, "Even those whites who lack wealth and power are sustained in their sense of racial superiority by policy deci-

The construction of liberty in Virginia as white occurred, then, not at a single moment but repeatedly and with extra vigor when political and social changes made possible some new arrangement. In part, the problems inherent in racializing liberty, problems evident in the fuzzy language of Virginians who tried to explain what race meant, necessitated the repetitive process. White Virginians also found it necessary to insist repeatedly on the privileges of whites over blacks because over time more and more people of African descent came to resemble free white Virginians in status, manners, and even appearance.[8]

Additional explanation is necessary regarding the term *race*. As used in this book the word refers to the idea that people are intrinsically different by virtue of birth into distinct human groups, and more specifically that people of African descent are different from those with European forebears. Although recent scholarship in both the biological and social sciences has shown otherwise, almost all white Virginians of the late eighteenth and early nineteenth centuries accepted as a premise that peoples were in fact different—that race existed. Many white Virginians viewed Africans and their descendants as naturally and enduringly inferior well before the rise of scientific racism in the nineteenth century. That view held fast despite the popularity in the late eighteenth century of "environmental" views of race, which held that the environment shaped differences between people and so those differences were not permanent. *Race* is a problematic term, though, because early national Virginians used it differently from the way we do. While they did sometimes

---

sions that sacrifice black rights." Bell, "Racial Realism after We're Gone," 7. Viewing the polity and nation as white, closely tied to seeing freedom as white, was a broadly American phenomenon. In New England, according to Joanne Pope Melish in *Disowning Slavery*, whites resisted "coming to terms with the concept of free persons of color as a new class requiring a new set of relations" and continued to conceive of their society as a white one in which free blacks were "permanently degraded 'aliens and outcasts in the midst of the people'" (88, 237). As Brown has shown, gendered notions of freedom and power coincided with racial ones; though not a major theme of this book, the role of gender does figure into its discussions.

8. I am grateful for Jan Lewis's comments at the Organization of American Historians meeting in 1999, which helped me crystallize my ideas. In response to papers written by Anthony Iaccarino and me, Lewis suggested the existence of "a dynamic, . . . a constant attempt to reinscribe and reinforce racial difference because the difference is always being eroded. . . . [W]e might hypothesize that doctrines of racial difference are asserted most loudly at just those moments when racial boundaries are being breached."

refer to "races" of people such as the Irish, the Germans, or Africans, they did not generally speak of distinctions between people as distinctions of "race." White Virginians of the period wrote instead of "national characters" whose "discriminating characteristicks" lay in the structure of "organs, passions, and appetites"; of the "difference of Hair, Features and Colour" between slaves and their owners; and of the "real distinctions which nature has made." They wrote that freedom for slaves would "mongrel the nation and destroy our celestial complexion" and that intermixture would lead to a "mixed mongrel of mulattoes, of whites and blacks, bays, chestnuts, sorrels, and skewbalds." Clearly they saw the differences between themselves and their slaves as physical ones that arose from belonging to different groups, whether those groups were defined as national or natural. But the language they used varied. In the absence, then, of a consistent contemporary equivalent, I use the word *race* to refer to ideas white Virginians held about inherent differences between the descendants of Europeans and the descendants of Africans.[9]

The moment between slavery and liberty—emancipation—provides the organizing principle for this book, which is arranged both chronologically and thematically. Chapter 1 examines the emergence of the question of emancipation in the 1770s as Quakers and other antislavery radicals urged Virginians to abandon slavery in order to fulfill the promise and meaning of the Revolution and as Virginia's Revolutionary leaders grew cognizant of the conflict between the liberty they declared universal and the slavery in which they held so many among them. The legacy of the Revolution was ambivalent, including on the one hand clear definitions of citizenship and the body politic in Virginia as white and on the other the 1782 Virginia statute that eased restrictions on manumission. Chapter 2 focuses on how ordinary citizens, including John Cropper Jr., wrestled with the question of emancipation from the passage of the 1782 manumission law to the 1806 statute that again restricted the freeing of slaves. Analysis of the deeds and wills of manumission recorded in eight Virginia counties from 1782 to 1806 reveals the meaning manumission held for those involved on both sides of the contract and the factors that promoted or

---

9. *Virginia Gazette and Weekly Advertiser* (Richmond), 14 Sept. 1782; antislavery petition, 8 Nov. 1785, Legislative Petitions, Miscellaneous Legislative Petitions; Jefferson, *Notes on the State of Virginia*, 132; *Virginia Independent Chronicle* (Richmond), 23 Jan. 1788; *Virginia Gazette and Weekly Advertiser*, 31 Aug. 1782.

impeded manumission. Although acts of private manumission did not always spring from antislavery ideals, the freeing of slaves continually provoked questions about emancipation as a moral and social problem. The way in which the evangelical movements most associated with antislavery ideas addressed those questions, discussed in chapter 3, demonstrates the limitations that existed not only on evangelical antislavery activity in Virginia but on all pro-emancipation activity in the state. Especially after the Haitian Revolution began in the 1790s and after the discovery of Gabriel's plot in 1800, whites' attitudes toward emancipation hardened, leading to legislative restrictions on free blacks and manumission, particularly the 1806 law barring subsequently freed people from remaining in the state. Chapter 4 examines the consequences of manumission for people such as Samuel Johnson and the ambiguities of freedom after 1806—the complex social position of free African Americans; the continuing and, especially after about 1820, increasingly difficult quest for liberty; and the new language needed to describe "free people of color." As liberty for Afro-Virginians became more tenuous in the 1820s, tensions among whites highlighted the issue of slavery and made it more a political problem than an ideological one. That process, traced in chapter 5, occurred through Virginia's response to the Missouri Crisis, the rise and decline of the American Colonization Society in Virginia, the development of a coherent western antislavery constituency in the state, and the debates of the 1829–30 Virginia Constitutional Convention. The final chapter shows that changes already in place by 1830 shaped how white Virginians discussed the future of slavery in their state in the wake of Nat Turner's insurrection of 1831. The public and legislative debates of 1831–32, which were mainly a battle between two sections by then referred to as "East" and "West," put the question of emancipation to rest: those who opposed it had won. As the Old Dominion's leaders began to support and defend slavery more vocally in the years after 1832, the question of emancipation in Virginia largely disappeared from public forums.

Acknowledgments

This project has a long history, and there are many people to thank for their assistance. I am especially sad that two who were there at the beginning will not be able to read these words. I do not think Jim Kettner, my undergraduate adviser at UC Berkeley, ever realized how important a role he played in the genesis of this project. When I told him that I wished to write my senior paper on the conflict between Revolutionary ideology and slaveholding in the United States, he suggested that I investigate the Virginia jurist St. George Tucker's *Dissertation on Slavery*. Working on that paper inspired me to pursue history as a profession, and I went to graduate school intent on exploring more deeply the themes I had uncovered in Tucker's work. At Harvard my adviser, William Gienapp, asked critical questions at key moments, provided keen editorial advice, and never flagged in his loyal support of me and the work I was doing. I hope that this book will serve as a tribute to both of them.

The research for this work took me several times to Virginia, where I found a host of wonderful, welcoming, helpful people. In particular, the crew at the Library of Virginia have been since I first met them uniformly helpful and interested in my work. I want especially to thank Chris Kolbe and Minor Weisiger, the archivists without whose help I would have missed many important documents, and Brent Tarter, John Kneebone, John Hopewell, and Paul Shelton, all of whom provided particular pieces of advice as well as general support. James Baird, Tony Iaccarino, Michelle Krowl, Blair Pogue, Phil Schwarz, Beth Schweiger, and Tatiana van Riemsdijk, who were working at the library while I was there, provided both social and intellectual stimulation and influenced my work in subtle ways. At the Virginia Historical Society, where I held a Mellon Fellowship, Nelson Lankford, Frances Pollard, and Janet Schwarz made me feel welcome and helped me find the documents and collections I needed. I also consulted collections at the Virginia Baptist

Historical Society, the University of Virginia, the University of North Carolina, Chapel Hill, and Duke University, and I am grateful for the help of the archivists at all those places. One of the most delightful trips I made was to the Eastern Shore, where the local historians of Accomack County welcomed me and provided much useful information. I want to thank especially Miles Barnes, of the Eastern Shore Public Library, who guided me toward the treasures located there, particularly Methodist church records that greatly informed chapter 2 and appendix A. No one supplied more comfort than Barbara Smith, who welcomed me into her warm and cozy Church Hill home during two of my research trips and was always supportive.

Many others helped as well. I was fortunate to be able to enlist Bernard Bailyn as a second reader for the dissertation upon which this book is based. His advice and encouragement at many stages helped me to "press on" with the project and finally to see it in print. Andy Coopersmith, Sarah Curtis, Gavin Jones, Paul Longmore, Barbara Loomis, Philip D. Morgan, Rich Newman, Judy Richardson, Jules Tygiel, Chris Waldrep, Susan Wyly, and the members of the Bay Area Seminar in Early American history (among whom Robin Einhorn and Jennifer Spear were particularly helpful) read portions of the work either in its early draft stages or as it neared completion, and all provided useful suggestions for improvement. Susan Wyly also generously passed along primary sources when in the process of her own research she came across items pertinent to my work, and conversations with her about our common interests helped me refine my thinking. Ira Berlin, David Brion Davis, Douglas Egerton, Jan Lewis, Robert McColley, Marcy Sacks, and Deborah Van Broekhoven commented on portions of this work that I presented at academic conferences. Their comments have been incorporated into the present version in subtle but important ways. Editorial credits at various stages go, with great appreciation, to Barbara Loomis, Sven Wolf, Abe Sheppard, and Asher Sheppard, whose help with the preface was invaluable. Anne Curi Preisig explained to me the legal definition of *consideration*, which was crucial to my understanding of the manumission documents, and a conversation with William Fisher, of Harvard Law School, aided my analysis of some of the legal materials. Chatting with my then office mate, Bill Issel, alerted me to the necessity of defining how I used *race* in the manuscript. A few hearty souls, in addition to my advisers, read the entire manuscript. Their general observations and specific suggestions helped me sharpen the work. I am happy to thank members of my spring 2005 graduate seminar at San Francisco State; Dan

Singal, who epitomizes what it means to be a good colleague and who made many trenchant and helpful comments; two anonymous readers whose many suggestions I incorporated to great benefit; and Christopher Curtis, whose careful and critical reading forced me to confront a tension in the manuscript regarding how race in Virginia operated and to construct what is, I hope, a better and more truthful analysis than the one he read.

Turning the manuscript into a book required the help of several people and institutions. Sylvia Frank Rodrigue brought me to Louisiana State University Press, and Rand Dotson has seen the process of publishing the work to completion. Rand also provided much encouragement and useful advice. I am grateful for the careful copyediting of Joanne Allen. Mary Lee Eggart drew the map of Virginia counties both well and with good cheer.

Finally, I want to express my gratitude to those who helped more indirectly but in important ways nonetheless by providing space, time, and encouragement. A one-course release in the spring semesters of 2003 and 2006 through the auspices of San Francisco State's Affirmative Action Award gave me much-needed time to work on the manuscript. Sven Wolf, my husband, supports me unwaveringly and makes it possible for me to be a scholar, a mother, a wife, and a teacher all at more or less the same time. In the house we share I have a room of my own, but for a woman writer who is also a mother that is not enough. I am deeply grateful to Klaus Wolf, Doris Wolf, Valentina Shestyuk, and Yakov Rakhlin for watching over little Matthew in the final stages of this project. Matthew's good cheer and delightful being sustain me. The Schlesingers, Sheppards, Wolfs, and Zimmers will be happy, I am sure, that they can finally stop asking how the book is going. I doubt they fully understand how much their love and encouragement over the years have meant.

Abbreviations

JHD	*Journal of the House of Delegates*
LP	Legislative Petitions, House of Delegates, Archives Division, Library of Virginia
LVA	Library of Virginia, Richmond
VBHS	Virginia Baptist Historical Society, Richmond
VHS	Virginia Historical Society, Richmond

RACE AND LIBERTY IN THE NEW NATION

I

"Are we willing to grant this liberty to all men?"

AMBIVALENCE IN THE REVOLUTIONARY ERA

> Whilst we are spilling our blood and exhausting our treasure in defence of our own liberty, it would not perhaps be amiss, to turn our eyes towards those of our fellow men who are now in bondage under us. We say, "all men are equally entitled to liberty and the pursuit of happiness" but are we willing to grant this liberty to all men?
>
> "A FRIEND TO LIBERTY," *Virginia Gazette and Weekly Advertiser,* 25 May 1782

THE TENSION BETWEEN LIBERTY and slavery in Virginia presented itself nowhere more clearly than in the Revolutionary leaders' discussions about how to draft a founding document that championed natural rights without threatening the institution that held two hundred thousand black Virginians in bondage. It was spring 1776 when they met in Williamsburg to declare their independence from King George and write a state constitution. Like constitutions in other states, the Virginia constitution included a declaration of rights that laid out the fundamental principles of government and the basic rights governments ought to respect. The original version, authored largely by George Mason and a major inspiration to Thomas Jefferson when he drafted the nation's Declaration of Independence a few weeks later, asserted, "That all Men are born equally free and independant, and have certain inherent natural Rights, of which they can not by any Compact, deprive or divest their Posterity; among these which are the Enjoyment of Life and Liberty, with the Means of acquiring and possessing Property, and pursueing and obtaining Happiness and Safety." But as some of Virginia's slaveholding leaders themselves noticed, "their execrable system [of slavery] cannot be reared on such foundations." Even if one could argue that the original enslavement of Africans had been legitimate under the rules of war, the principle Mason articulated—that men cannot "divest their Posterity" of "natural Rights"—invalidated Virginia's system of hereditary enslavement, in which the children of female slaves were also enslaved for life.[1]

That system had become part of colonial Virginia's economy, society, and laws in the seventeenth century, and by 1776 it was one of the new state's defining features. As many observers have pointed out, slavery in Virginia and in America generally was more than a system of labor. Because slaves were brought from Africa and were visually as well as culturally distinct from Europeans, American slavery became tied to a system of race that long outlasted the system of bondage. To some extent race—not a biological category but a social one that reflected and supported power relationships—preceded slavery as well. Decades before Africans replaced English indentured servants as the majority of laborers on tobacco plantations in the late seventeenth century, that is to say, well before slavery became central to Virginia's economy, the colony's leaders passed laws that began to codify race. Early statutes created a separate, lower status for Africans even if they were free. Kathleen Brown notes the 1643 "tax levied on African women" as the "earliest distinctive and clearly unfavorable treatment of African people," since it defined African women as "tithables" who performed taxable labor, in contrast to European women, who were not counted as laborers. Other important laws that helped create both race and slavery included a 1667 statute that recognized black slavery as a perpetual and hereditary condition not affected by baptism (traditionally European slavery had been reserved for non-Christians) and a 1670 law that prevented freed slaves, whether black or Indian, from purchasing Christian indentured servants so that no dark-skinned person could have control over whites. The commonwealth's first slave code, passed in 1705, prescribed that enslaved men who raped white women would be dismembered (castrated), though rape was only a high misdemeanor when committed by a white man. The different and unequal punishments and the absence of any statute defining the rape of a black woman emphasized that not only were blacks in Virginia slaves but they were treated as lesser people with lesser rights. The rape provision also signaled white Virginians' fears of race mixing, especially the despoliation of white women by black men, and highlighted how race was shaped by and helped shape gender. These laws and the attitudes that accom-

---

1. Rutland, *Papers of George Mason*, 1:274–91; the phrase "execrable system" is from Thomas Ludwell Lee to Richard Henry Lee, 1 June 1776, in Rowland, *Life of George Mason*, 1:240.

panied them had been in place so long by the time of the Revolution that for many white Virginians they seemed to represent the natural order of things, an order suddenly threatened by the declaration that "all Men are born equally free and independant."[2]

It was not only the systems of slavery and race that American Revolutionary ideology threatened. The meaning of freedom was also at stake, for just as slavery in colonial Virginia had been made black, freedom had been made white. The whiteness of freedom was marked especially by laws addressing emancipation and free blacks, whom white Virginians from the late seventeenth century onward considered an anomalous and undesirable population. So determined were white Virginians by the end of the seventeenth century to keep free blacks outside their society that in 1691 Virginia's colonial legislature, the House of Burgesses, required subsequently emancipated slaves to leave the colony within six months. Although the burgesses justified banning free blacks on the grounds that they might cause disruption by luring slaves away from their owners, by "receiving stolen goods, or being grown old bringing a charge upon the country," the law had a deeper purpose: exiling free blacks preserved the concomitance of skin color and other racial markers with slave or free status. In 1723 the burgesses further limited individual emancipation, or manumission, to slaves who had performed a "meritorious service" and who gained the approbation of the governor and council. By design this law allowed for the reward of slaves who had done some special, notable deed that aided the white community, particularly informing about slave conspiracies, but it made such a reward difficult to attain and consequently rare. As a result of these laws, at the time of the Revolution there were only several thousand free blacks in Virginia, about 1 percent of the population. Most of the Revolutionary-era free black population probably descended from those liber-

---

2. For an introduction to the debate over the precise relationship between the development of racism and the development of slavery see Handlin and Handlin, "Origins of the Southern Labor System"; Morgan, *American Slavery, American Freedom;* Jordan, *White over Black;* Davis, *Problem of Slavery in Western Culture,* chap. 15; Berlin, *Many Thousands Gone,* intro. and chap. 5; and Brown, *Good Wives,* quotation on 116. Historians' redefinition of race as a social and not a biological category is now commonplace. For an influential essay on the subject see Fields, "Slavery, Race, and Ideology"; and see also "Constructing Race." The discussion of the legal history of slavery in Virginia in this and subsequent paragraphs is taken from Higginbotham, *In the Matter of Color,* chap. 2; Morris, *Southern Slavery and the Law;* Morgan, *American Slavery, American Freedom;* St. George Tucker, *Dissertation on Slavery;* and Jordan, *White over Black,* 71–82.

ated before 1691, and they remained at the bottom of the social order, their lives circumscribed by laws regarding free "negroes and mulattoes." Since the time of the 1705 code, which defined a mulatto as "the child of an Indian, and the child, grandchild, or great grandchild of a Negro," free colored people had held a legal status distinct from and lower than that of other free people. In 1723, for instance, colonial leaders barred free "negroes and mulattoes" from bearing arms unless they were "householders or licensed frontier dwellers," excluded them from the militia, and disfranchised them. It did not need to be so. In most slave societies, as Orlando Patterson has pointed out, manumission existed alongside slavery without conflict, and in many places in the contemporary Atlantic world free colored people formed a sizable and important part of the population. Often, freed slaves became clients of their former owners, maintained allegiance to them, and served as a buffer between slaves and masters. The North American dualism between black and white, slave and free, was distinctive—even if the existence of free colored people and of mixed-race slaves demonstrated that the dualism was not as sharp in reality as in theory—and it had important consequences for how the intertwined notions of slavery and freedom evolved.[3]

Since George Mason's draft of the Virginia Declaration of Rights threatened the whole web of white Virginians' understandings about slavery, race, and freedom and since enslaved Virginians constituted two-fifths of the state's population and performed labor central to its plantation-based economy, Virginia's leaders had to find a way around the obvious inconsistency the draft pointed up. Edmund Pendleton, who in the near future would aid Thomas Jefferson and George Wythe in the radical task of devising an abolition proposal, was here the voice of conservatism. He suggested that it be made clear that the rights enumerated by the declaration devolved only to people in society, that they were inherent *social* rights rather than inherent *natural* rights. Slaves, by traditional definition outside society, could be excluded, while the rights of free white people retained their integrity.[4]

Following Pendleton's suggestion, the new first item in the Declaration of Rights as adopted by the convention began, "That all men are by nature equally free and independent, and have certain inherent rights, of which, *when*

3. Brown, *Good Wives*, 215, 219; St. George Tucker, *Dissertation on Slavery*, 70; Patterson, *Slavery and Social Death*, 247, 259–61. On the pre-Revolutionary population of free blacks see below, chapter 2; for an insightful comparative perspective see Degler, *Neither Black nor White*.

4. Rutland, *Papers of George Mason*, 1:289.

they enter into a state of society, they cannot, by any compact, deprive or divest their posterity." It was a clever resolution to the problem, because at first glance the phrase "when they enter into a state of society" seemed consonant with the original version, but the amendment changed the meaning of the sentence fundamentally because it excluded a large class of people and, without actually using the word *white,* racialized the rights Virginians declared to be the basis of their government. If any question remained about whether free blacks could be counted among those in society, Virginia legislators answered it clearly a few years later when they defined Virginia citizens as "all *white* persons born within the territory of this commonwealth, and all who have resided therein two years." Virginia's Revolutionary-era leaders consciously and purposefully declared citizenship, the Declaration of Rights, and the government of Virginia to be for whites only. They responded to the tension between liberty and slavery with two equally sincere impulses, affirming the abstract right to liberty that lay at the heart of American Revolutionary ideology while simultaneously protecting the twin institutions of slavery and race. They were, in a word, ambivalent.[5]

In part that ambivalence reflected the inner impulses and sentiments of many leading Virginians, but it was also shaped by their understanding of the society in which they lived and their sensitivity to the feelings and interests of those who voted for them, most of whom were slaveholders. Indeed, the logic of this book rests on the idea that Virginia's political elite spoke and acted with attention to how their words and deeds would be understood by their constituents. To the extent that ordinary citizens and voters considered the problems of slavery and liberty, they, like their more visible and prominent spokesmen, responded in a number of different and sometimes contradictory ways, but slaveholders almost always wanted to protect their property in slaves. As James Madison in 1791, then in the House of Representatives, explained his decision not to introduce a Quaker petition against the national slave trade, "Those from whom I derive my public station are known by me

---

5. Ibid., 1:287, emphasis mine; Hening, *Statutes,* 10:129 (1779), emphasis mine; for the passage of the citizenship bill see *JHD* (begun May 1779), 63, 67–68. The legislature modified the definition of citizenship in the years after the Revolution. Acts of 1783 and 1786 repealed the 1779 one and defined citizens as "all free persons, born within ... this commonwealth," henceforth allowing free blacks born in Virginia to be citizens. These acts did not specify whether emancipated slaves would be citizens, and other laws barred free blacks from voting. Hening, *Statutes,* 11:323, 12:261.

to be greatly interested in that species of property [slaves], and to view the matter in that light."[6]

The ambivalence that was so much a part of the Revolutionary era has led to conflicting interpretations of it by historians. For some, the radical potential of the Revolution evident in Mason's original draft of the Virginia Declaration of Rights is most significant. They see several indications that it was possible to end American slavery in the late eighteenth century: during the war years and also in the decade that followed, Quakers, Methodists, and Baptists all decried slavery; in the northern states members of these groups, along with their secular allies, pressed for and won a gradual end to slavery, leaving only the states from Delaware southward as homes to slavery after 1804; and those who viewed slavery as wrong came to include even some prominent southerners, including Virginians who published editorials against slavery or proposed schemes to lessen or eliminate the number of slaves in their commonwealth. If Virginia, which was in a number of ways the most important state in the Union, with both the largest enslaved and white populations and a disproportionate share of national leaders, had joined the northern states in emancipating its slaves, the effect would have been profound. Several Revolutionary-era Virginia laws seemed to signal a shift toward anti-slavery policies that could have led to universal emancipation: in 1778 the law-makers prohibited the importation of slaves into the commonwealth; in 1782 they eased restrictions on manumission; and the following year they freed slaves who had fought for the Revolutionary cause.[7]

But this chapter, which focuses on developments up to 1783, reminds us that the limits constraining radicalism and the opposition met by antislavery advocates are just as important to the story of Revolutionary Virginia. It yields a complex picture of countervailing forces that neither indicated Virginia's readiness for the gradual abolition of slavery, as some have argued, nor pointed to the commonwealth's inability to change. The complexity of the picture and the ambivalence felt by many thinking Virginians toward slavery persisted for more than a generation, because until the third decade of the nineteenth century ambivalence, hesitance, and cautiousness regarding the problems of

---

6. Madison to Robert Pleasants, 30 Oct. 1791, quoted in McColley, *Slavery and Jeffersonian Virginia*, 187. About half of all white families in Virginia owned slaves in the 1770s, and those slaveowners almost certainly formed the majority of those who held land sufficient to qualify for voting.

7. Nash, *Race and Revolution*, 10–20, 35–50; Freehling, *Road to Disunion*, chap. 7.

slavery and emancipation proved useful to white Virginians who struggled to reconcile ideals and reality and who wished other Americans to see them as truly committed to the values of the Revolution. What is significant about the Revolutionary period in Virginia, particularly the period from 1775 to 1783, is that in highlighting the related problems of race and liberty it created turbulence and disarray out of a much more settled and ordered colonial world. And out of that turmoil came new, often contested notions of how the American experiment in republicanism should run.[8]

THE EMERGENCE OF ANTISLAVERY IDEAS AND ACTIVITY IN THE REVOLUTIONARY AGE

When Virginia's "aristocrats," as Thomas Ludwell Lee described them, noticed in 1776 that their "execrable system" of slavery could not be "reared" on a creed declaring all men equal and deserving of liberty, they merely voiced what had by then become apparent to a number of Americans. The antislavery movement in America had begun before the Revolutionary period, largely among the Quakers, and the Revolution and its Enlightenment ideology propelled it forward. By the 1770s members of the small but growing Methodist and Baptist sects, some of Virginia's elite, and slaves themselves were denouncing and acting against slavery. These groups presented a potentially powerful but ultimately limited challenge to Virginia's long-entrenched system of bondage.[9]

The Quakers' challenge to slavery had its origins in the seventeenth century, when the early Quaker leader George Fox suggested that terms of bondage for Barbadian slaves be limited to thirty years. The Friends' antislavery sentiment sprang in part from their emphasis on each individual's relationship to the Holy Spirit and on the guiding principle of the Golden Rule. But during nearly all of the colonial period Quakers did not have any compunction about holding slaves, and most members of the Society of Friends in Virginia did not begin to consider antislavery policies until several Quaker activists began visiting Quaker meetings in the late 1750s to preach against the institution. When the antislavery leader John Woolman went to Virginia in 1757 he found Virginia's Quakers not yet sufficiently concerned with the well-

---

8. Thus, while this analysis agrees in large measure with Robert McColley's, it differs significantly from his by tracing change over time and following the story to the 1830s. See McColley, *Slavery and Jeffersonian Virginia*.

9. Thomas Ludwell Lee to Richard Henry Lee, 1 June 1776.

being of their slaves. He also disapproved of their willingness to buy slaves for their own use, although the Virginia Yearly Meeting had barred its members from participating in slave trading, an act always considered worse than slaveholding itself. After the 1765 visit of John Griffith, another antislavery Friend and activist, Virginia Quakers discussed whether to ban all purchases of slaves, even for their own use, but found themselves "divided in their sentiments." Considering the importance of slavery to the Virginia economy and the fact that many of Virginia's Quakers lived in tobacco-growing regions along the James River, it should not be surprising that some Quakers were reluctant to deny themselves the possibility of purchasing more of what was, after all, a valuable economic resource.[10]

The resistance of Virginia's slaveholding Quakers to antislavery ideas diminished, however, as the religious call from within their community coincided with the expression of natural-rights philosophy in the colonies' struggle with England. Likewise, as natural-rights philosophy became a more important part of American political discourse in the 1760s, it grew larger in the Quaker message as well. In the wake of the Stamp Act crisis of 1765–66 the prominent Quaker antislavery activist Anthony Benezet noted the shift, stating that the "general rights and liberties of mankind" had become "much the subjects of universal consideration." Benezet used the opportunity to focus attention on his cause, arguing that the "Advocates of Liberty" who fought the Stamp Act ought to take notice of those who were "kept in the most deplorable state of slavery." Another writer of the era similarly pointed out the inconsistency of the slave trade with American pleas for liberty, asking, "With what consistency can an American-Captain, trading upon the Guinea Coast for slaves, open his mouth and plead for liberty, as his natural rights?" About the same time, Virginia Quakers gradually moved toward an antislavery policy, frequently emphasizing the importance of educating slaves and caring well for them and banning in 1768 all further purchases of slaves. In the 1770s, as Quaker writers referred more directly to the ideas of Locke and Montesquieu and began to call for the abolition of the Atlantic slave trade, some Virginia Quakers suggested that they eliminate slavery altogether among themselves, even discussing the matter of emancipation with members of the General As-

---

10. Davis, *Problem of Slavery in Western Culture*, 304; Weeks, *Southern Quakers and Slavery*, chap. 5 and appendix (for location of Quaker meetings), 200–204. For the progress of antislavery ideas in the Philadelphia Yearly Meeting see Soderlund, *Quakers and Slavery*.

sembly. In 1773 the Yearly Meeting encouraged Virginia Quakers to "minister justice and judgment" by freeing their slaves. The deeds of manumission that many Quakers drafted as a response to this call reflected the fusion of Quaker and secular ideas that had driven them to action. James Williams, for example, manumitted his slave Sarah in 1783, mentioning first the natural-rights philosophy of the Revolution, that he was "persuaded that Freedom is the Natural right of all mankind," and then the biblical Golden Rule, that "it is my duty to do unto others as I would desire to be done by in the like Situation." Though individual manumission of slaves before 1782 was not legal unless each act had the specific sanction of the legislature (probably the reason Williams waited until 1783), some Quakers freed their slaves before that date, and according to the Quaker Robert Pleasants, "a considerable number" of enslaved Virginians had been emancipated by 1777.[11]

The growing intensity of the Quaker antislavery commitment in Virginia in the 1770s and 1780s spurred some Virginia Quakers to try to persuade those outside their society of slavery's evils. The two most effective activists were Warner Mifflin and Robert Pleasants, and their communications with Virginia leaders probably helped push some legislators toward a bolder antislavery stance. For Warner Mifflin, born in Virginia but by the 1770s a Delaware resident, antislavery belief resulted from a powerful conversion he experienced when God finally "arouse[d] me to greater vigilance, by his terrors for sin." Mifflin put his beliefs into action by freeing his own slaves, persuading his father, Daniel, to do the same, and working in his local Quaker meeting to show other Friends the inconsistency of slavery with their precepts. There his efforts met great success, and "in a little time, most of our members liberated their slaves." The Declaration of Independence, which resonated so well with Mifflin's own beliefs about the equality of all people, helped inspire him to broaden his campaign. Mifflin lobbied several state legislatures in favor of laws allowing emancipation, hoping that eliminating slavery might "remove one cause of impending judgment" on the new nation. Robert Pleasants also worked to encourage emancipation generally as well as in Quaker societies. He presided over the Virginia Society for Promoting the Abolition of Slavery in 1790 and wrote letters calling for abolition to important Virginia leaders,

11. Benezet, *Caution and Warning to Great Britain*, 3; [Appleton], *Considerations on Slavery*, 18; James Williams deed, 9 Sept. 1783, Mecklenburg County Deeds, 6 (1779–86); Weeks, *Southern Quakers and Slavery*, 202–5; Pleasants, "Some account of the first settlement of Friends," 14.

including Patrick Henry, George Washington, and James Madison. Pleasants also considered petitioning the legislature to enact a plan of general emancipation in 1791, but James Madison advised against it. For his own part, Robert Pleasants freed eighty slaves, and as early as 1777 treated his slaves as free people, allowing them to benefit from their own labor. He also pursued a precedent-setting court case to obtain freedom for his father's slaves, emancipated by a 1771 will that predated the law allowing such manumissions.[12]

The antislavery impulse also activated a number of Methodists and Baptists, who shared with the Quakers a commitment to spiritual equality. In contrast to the Quakers, however, both the Methodist and Baptist organizations were in their infancy in the Revolutionary years, which limited their ability to spread the antislavery message. Methodism had been associated with antislavery ideas since 1743, when its founder, John Wesley, included a rule against slave trading in the General Rules of the Methodist movement within the Church of England. In 1774, influenced in part by the Quaker Anthony Benezet's writings, Wesley published *Thoughts on Slavery*, reiterating the Enlightenment argument against slavery, that "Liberty is the right of every human creature." While Wesley's plea for an end to slavery was not based primarily on religious arguments but on secular ones, his *Thoughts on Slavery* resonated powerfully with Methodist theology, which, as Donald Mathews puts it, focused on the goal of spreading "scriptural holiness," a form of Christian ethics that included sobriety, peacefulness, and caring for the less fortunate members of one's community. Elsewhere, Wesley identified slaves as "outcasts of men" who characterized the kind of humility true believers sought. As outsiders, "outcasts" like the Methodists themselves in the 1770s, slaves were a class of people with whom the Methodists could sympathize. When they established the Methodist Episcopal Church of America in 1784, Methodist leaders forbade church members from holding slaves but gave them a grace period in which to comply. The new church's antislavery rules required that all members

---

12. Justice, *Life and Ancestry of Warner Mifflin*, 140; *Virginia Gazette and Petersburg Intelligencer*, 8 July 1790; Finnie, "Antislavery Movement in the Upper South"; McColley, *Slavery and Jeffersonian Virginia*, 158–59, 187; Weeks, *Southern Quakers and Slavery*, 214. The Virginia Society for Promoting the Abolition of Slavery was organized in 1790 and according to its constitution was to meet twice yearly, in October and April. The society seems to have had little impact, however, on the public discourse about emancipation and appears little in the historical literature on Virginia. I came across very few references to the society in my research. For more on the Pleasants court case, see below, chapter 4.

who owned slaves draw up legal instruments guaranteeing their adult slaves freedom within five to ten years and their minor slaves freedom at age twenty-five and also barred members from buying or selling any slaves except for the purpose of emancipating them. Local church leaders or "assistants" were to enforce the emancipation rules and to ban members who did not comply within one year. Attempting to mediate between their conviction that slavery was wrong and their understanding that Virginia was a slave society, the church rules gave "our brethren in Virginia" more time, two years instead of one, to "consider the expedience of compliance or non-compliance with these rules." As with the Methodists and the Quakers, antislavery sympathies among the Baptists arose in part from egalitarian strains within their doctrine and from their commitment to righteous living. A few Baptists, notably David Barrow, became outspoken antislavery leaders, and in the Revolutionary era Virginia's Baptist General Committee asked member churches to examine the righteousness of slavery. The Baptists, however, never tried to force members of their church to free their slaves. (As discussed further in chapter 3, Methodists' and Baptists' Revolutionary-era antislavery activity proved short lived, particularly in slaveholding areas. Methodists repealed their antislavery rules less than a year after they had agreed to it, and most Baptists had accommodated themselves and their religion to slavery by the 1790s.)[13]

During the turbulent years of the War for Independence dissenting (non-Anglican/non-Episcopalian) religious groups such as Methodists and Baptists posed what conservative Virginians felt was a significant danger to an already fragile society, in part because dissenters sought out slaves as converts. Citizens from Cumberland County, about thirty miles upriver from Richmond, complained to the legislature in 1777 that dissenting religious groups promoted ideas "subversive of the morals of the people, and destructive of the peace of families, tending to alienate the affection of slaves from their masters, and injurious to the happiness of the publick." They cited in particular "nightly meetings of slaves, to receive instructions of these [religious] teachers, without the consent of their masters, which have produced very bad consequences." Although their reputation as a danger to slavery thus dated from the 1770s, the main thrust of Methodist and Baptist antislavery activity in Virginia came in

13. John Wesley, *Thoughts on Slavery*, in *Works of the Rev. John Wesley*, 504; Mathews, *Slavery and Methodism*, 5–6; Essig, *Bonds of Wickedness*, 32–35, 49; Bennett, *Memorials of Methodism*, 129–31, 213–15; Daniel, "Virginia Baptists," 65. Essig argues that persecution strengthened some evangelicals' commitment to antislavery principles.

the next decade, so the two groups had little effect on the major Revolutionary-era legislation regarding slaves and slavery.[14]

The contrast between the antislavery words and deeds of religiously inspired activists and those of Virginia's secular elite is instructive, for while a number of Virginia's leaders wrote against slavery, their main concern was subtly but importantly different from that of the Quakers, Methodists, and Baptists. Arthur Lee, a member of the large and genteel Lee family, exemplified the impulses of early secular antislavery thinkers. In 1767 Lee published his *Address on Slavery* in the *Virginia Gazette,* in which he declared slavery "a violation both of justice and religion." While this sounded much like the contemporary Quaker critique, a closer look at Lee's argument reveals that his reasoning rested on the baneful effects that slavery had on white society: the fact that slavery "is dangerous to the safety of the community in which it prevails; that it is destructive to the growth of arts and sciences; and lastly, that it produces a very fatal train of vices, both in the slave, and in his master." The possibility of a slave revolt was his greatest concern. The mere existence of slaves put the masters at risk, for "slavery, wherever encouraged, has sooner or later been productive of very dangerous commotions." Lee's message, though focused on slavery's effect on white people, was still radical in 1767. It predated by more than a decade the main thrust of Revolutionary antislavery ideas, and in the eyes of contemporaries the mere mention of insurrection, which they feared might encourage slaves to rebel, made the essay incendiary. The publishers of the *Virginia Gazette* refused to print the sequel to Lee's *Address,* and in later reprints the most descriptive parts of the section on slave rebellions were excised.[15]

Following Lee, others among Virginia's elite also came to oppose slavery in

14. *JHD* (1777), 36. For more on the persecution of the dissenting denominations see Essig, *Bonds of Wickedness,* 45–49; Andrews, *Methodists and Revolutionary America,* 55–59; Heyrman, *Southern Cross,* 15–22 and passim; and Isaac, *Transformation of Virginia,* 146–54, 172–77, 192–93. Isaac's view of evangelicals' low social status has been challenged recently, as noted below in chapter 3. My sense is that dissenting religions did provoke anxieties among established elites in the mid-eighteenth century, but more because of their views and passions than because of their social station.

15. Lee, *Extract from an Address in the Virginia Gazette,* 1, 4; MacMaster, "Arthur Lee's 'Address on Slavery,'"; Anthony Benezet to Robert Pleasants, 8 Apr. 1773, in Brookes, *Friend Anthony Benezet,* 301. Benezet wrote, "When I reprinted Doctr. Lee's Address & added it to my last Book, I left out the most striking expressions least I should raise a prejudice agst. my Book particularly where he tells them: 'On us, or on our Posterity, the inevitable blow must, one day fall.'"

the Revolutionary era, among them George Mason, James Madison, Patrick Henry, George Washington, and Thomas Jefferson, but their own dependence on slavery limited their willingness to act against it, and their sense of how the public would respond to ideas that threatened valuable slave property kept them, for the most part, from condemning slavery in public forums. Mason, like Lee, focused primarily on slavery's effect on whites, not blacks, including the danger of slave rebellion. Recalling classical history, Mason commented to George William Fairfax and George Washington that "perhaps the primary Cause of the Destruction of the most flourishing Government that ever existed was the Introduction of great Numbers of Slaves—an Evil very pathetically described by the Roman Historians." Others were more concerned with the inconsistency between natural-rights philosophy and the keeping of slaves. Patrick Henry, for example, told a correspondent in 1773 of his repugnance toward the slave trade, "an abominable practice," but admitted that he was "the master of slaves of my own purchase" and was "drawn along by the general inconvenience of living here without them." Henry looked to a future time "when an opportunity will be offered to abolish this lamentable evil," but he suggested that if that day did not come, one should at least treat the "unhappy victims with lenity." Despite their antislavery feelings, both Mason and Henry later opposed the U.S. Constitution, in large measure because they thought the national compact would threaten slave property.[16]

Thomas Jefferson did make his views public, though in a manner carefully tailored to serve the cause of revolution. In his *Summary View of the Rights of British America* (1774) Jefferson condemned King George for "preferring the immediate advantages of a few African corsairs to the lasting interests of the American states, and to the rights of human nature, deeply wounded by this infamous practice [of slave trading]." In his original draft of the Declaration of Independence (but not in the final version approved by Congress) Jefferson repeated his denunciation of the king for "captivating & carrying them [Africans] into slavery in another hemisphere" and for "keep[ing] open a market where *Men* should be bought & sold." While Jefferson did oppose both slavery and the slave trade because they violated what he understood to be the basic rights of humanity, he aimed his high-blown rhetoric in the *Summary View*

---

16. Enclosure with a letter from George Mason to George William Fairfax and George Washington, [23 Dec. 1765], in Rutland, *Papers of George Mason*, 1:61–62; Mason on the Constitution in ibid., 1:1065–66, 1086–87; Patrick Henry, letter of 18 Jan. 1773, in William Wirt Henry, *Patrick Henry*, 1:152–53; Einhorn, "Patrick Henry's Case against the Constitution."

and in his draft of the Declaration not at slavery but at the king. He attacked the slave trade because it served his larger purpose in justifying rebellion, just as other political leaders publicly attacked slavery or the slave trade when it coincided with their political ends.[17]

Jefferson also typified the Virginia political elite in his cautious approach to antislavery legislation. Though he favored the interdiction of the slave trade and supported a voluntary manumission law and even the gradual abolition of slavery, Jefferson did not himself submit proposals to effect these goals. In 1769 he convinced his cousin Richard Bland to act on his behalf; Bland introduced into the House of Burgesses a bill that would have allowed slaveholders to free their slaves without special legislative consent, but the bill did not pass. Jefferson favored a law banning slave imports in 1778 but played no direct role in introducing or drafting the act. Although he, George Wythe, and Edmund Pendleton considered including an abolition amendment with their revisal of Virginia's laws (1776–79), in the end they decided to withhold it, fearing that the public would not receive it well. Jefferson also drafted, but never submitted, a gradual abolition proposal in 1783 (the plan was part of a proposed state constitution, but no constitutional convention was called).[18]

If Virginia's leaders pursued their antislavery goals rather feebly and if dissenting religious leaders were not in a position to affect the larger society as much as they would have liked, enslaved people themselves acted unequivocally and sometimes to great effect in favor of freedom. Thousands of slaves, encouraged by British promises of freedom, waged their own war for inde-

---

17. Jefferson, *Summary View of the Rights of British America*, 16–17; Wills, *Inventing America*, 377.

18. Miller, *Wolf by the Ears*, 5, 17, 22; Peterson, *Thomas Jefferson and the New Nation*, 44, 152–53; Jefferson, *Notes on the State of Virginia*, 131–32, 193, 197–98; Iaccarino, "Virginia and the National Contest over Slavery," 8–9; *JHD* (begun Oct. 1778), 12–23. According to Merrill Peterson, Bland took the lead in proposing a law ameliorating slavery in 1769 because he was the senior member. Anthony Iaccarino says that the Quaker Edward Stabler pushed for a manumission law in 1769 and that it is probable that "Stabler, not Jefferson, was the guiding forces [sic] behind the Bland notion." Peterson also notes that Jefferson claimed authorship of the anti-importation law, but the legislative journals do not mention him in connection with the statute. For further discussion of Jefferson's ideas about emancipation and the abolition plan, see chapter 3, below, and also Duncan Macleod's discussion of the abolition proposal in *Slavery, Race, and the American Revolution*, 128–30. The revised code, which did not include the abolition proposal, was not actually passed until 1785.

pendence by running from their owners toward British troops. Their actions weakened slavery directly and implicitly challenged the notion that slaves were content with their lot. Opportunities for enslaved Virginians to act against slavery appeared even before British Royal Governor Lord Dunmore made his famous proclamation in November 1775. The previous spring, Dunmore had threatened to emancipate slaves if the American rebels harmed any senior British official or raised troops against the royal governor. In response, some slaves fled toward the royal governor's residence to offer "their Service." Several months later, Dunmore's November 1775 proclamation called for slaves and servants to fight on behalf of loyal forces in exchange for freedom. Only a few hundred people managed to join Dunmore and help form his "Ethiopian Regiment," but the event set a precedent. Enslaved Americans in Virginia and elsewhere came to see the British as a refuge. As a consequence, hundreds flocked to British ships in the Chesapeake Bay; "about 300" slaves from Virginia's Northern Neck counties boarded a single ship in 1777, and several hundred more found their way to a British fleet in 1779. Benjamin Harrison reported in 1783 that he had lost thirty of his "finest slaves" during the war, and other individual slaveholders reported that similarly high or even higher numbers of slaves had left. In June 1779 the commander in chief of the British forces in America made official what had become widespread practice when he issued a proclamation promising that enslaved Americans who ran away from rebel masters to the British army could pursue the occupations of their choice while with the British troops. In total, many thousands of Virginia slaves fled to the British, though some were taken involuntarily by British troops or treated as spoils of war. But running toward freedom was risky since runaways could be taken up by Virginia officials and put to work in the lead mines or sold abroad.[19]

Together these various forms of antislavery rhetoric and behavior posed the first real challenge to American slavery since Virginians had introduced the institution in the seventeenth century. But only the Quakers entirely eliminated slaveholders from among their ranks, and only the Quakers re-

---

19. Quarles, *Negro in the American Revolution*, 28, 31, 113–18; Frey, *Water from the Rock*, 150–60, 211; Holton, *Forced Founders*, 144–48, 154–61; *JHD* (1777) (for evidence of runaways sent to the lead mines). Quarles estimates that about eight hundred slaves succeeded in reaching the British in response to Dunmore's proclamation. Benjamin Harrison's statement is from Harrison to George Clinton, 19 Dec. 1783, cited in Quarles, *Negro in the American Revolution*, 118.

mained dedicated to antislavery ideas after other white groups had abandoned them. The reasons for the unusual success of Quaker antislavery activity are significant, for they shed light on why other Revolutionary-era antislavery movements failed. One was that the Quakers were uncompromising, preferring to see people who could not comply with their rules leave their society rather than remain among them, an impulse at odds with the Methodists' and Baptists' desire to enlarge their following. Another was the primacy in their tradition of the Golden Rule to do unto others as one would have others do unto oneself. That rule, cited frequently in Quaker manumission documents, created an empathy with African Americans that moved Quakers to action. The Quakers emphasized that all humans were "of one Blood," establishing a bond between black and white people that made enslavement especially repugnant. The Quaker activist Warner Mifflin, for example, challenged his fellow Americans to empathize with African slaves when he asked in his 1796 pamphlet, "Is there a white man among thousands, who, if captured by the Algerines, should not embrace his liberty, should the opportunity present?" The transcendence of race through empathy was the radical center of the Quakers' antislavery philosophy, and while it impelled them to free their own slaves, it did not resonate with most other white Virginians and was largely absent from secular antislavery thought. But because Quakers were such a small group in Virginia, their actions had little effect on the society as a whole, in contrast to the situation in Pennsylvania or Delaware, for example, where Quaker efforts helped spur widescale manumissions.[20]

THE BEGINNING OF A DEBATE: THE PROSLAVERY RESPONSE

Even if Quakers' actions—freeing their own slaves and in some cases lobbying for a general emancipation provision—did not greatly reshape slavery in Virginia, their arguments against slavery, along with arguments advanced by others and the actions taken by slaves themselves, prompted immediate response. One way, of course, to answer the charges against slavery was to sidestep them, as the writers of Virginia's Declaration of Rights did. Another was to respond directly by both attacking the notion of abolition and defending slavery, a challenge several newspaper essayists took on. Often overlooked, these Revolutionary-era writers advanced proslavery arguments that had much in common with the proslavery defense of the antebellum era, justifying slavery

---

20. Justice, *Life and Ancestry of Warner Mifflin*, 77–101. For Delaware see Williams, *Slavery and Freedom in Delaware;* and for Pennsylvania see Nash and Soderlund, *Freedom by Degrees*.

through perceived racial differences between blacks and whites. Racial defenses of slavery, in other words, were no post-Revolutionary invention but had existed all along and were available for use whenever slavery came under attack.[21]

Early proslavery newspaper essays suggest that many Americans in the late eighteenth century understood differences between people as inborn and God-given and even doubted whether blacks were fully human, evidence that is at odds with historians' understanding that Americans in the Revolutionary era viewed race primarily in terms of environmentalism, the theory that differences between groups arose from differences in the environment. As early as 1769 a "Southern Man" from a "Southern Province" wrote to the *Pennsylvania Chronicle* to "prove the improbability of Negroes having souls" and to assert that "Southern Men" were not so "totally blind to our ease and interest, as to set our slaves at liberty, when the certain consequence would be that we must work ourselves." The Southern Man thought it clear that "keeping a few thousands of soul less slaves in bondage" was surely preferable to giving up the "joys and pleasures of life" made possible by slavery. Another early example of how defenders of slavery dehumanized Africans also first appeared in a Pennsylvania paper and was reprinted in late 1773 in the *Virginia Gazette*. The anonymous author wrote in order "to silence those Writers who insist upon the African belonging to the same Species of Man with the white People." God, he asserted, had given Adam and his posterity dominion "over the Negroes of Africa," who were not fully human. Rather, "God formed them in common with Horses, Oxen, Dogs &c, for the Benefit of the white People alone, to be used [by] them either for Pleasure, or to labour with their *other* Beasts." The viciousness of this depiction is striking. On the one hand it can be read, like the claim that Africans were soulless beings, as a tactical maneuver, a way to deflect calls for universal liberty by placing Africans below the level of humanity. But on the other, it hints at the way many slaveholders must have viewed their slaves even before challenges to the institution arose. Beings who were in most instances considered property and who worked under the whip like animals could easily appear to be subhuman to those who owned and whipped

---

21. Duncan Macleod, for example, emphasizes the Revolution as a turning point that "promoted a real concern over the nature and significance of slavery; and that out of that concern grew a consciously racist society." Drew Faust and William Jenkins note, by contrast, that proslavery ideology had its roots in the colonial period. Macleod, *Slavery, Race, and the American Revolution*, 8; Faust, *Ideology of Slavery*, 3–4; Jenkins, *Pro-Slavery Thought*, 46–47.

them. The fact that these pieces, one written by a self-described southerner, appeared first in Pennsylvania papers probably reflects the strength of Quaker antislavery activism there—they were meant to counter Quaker arguments—and also hints at the scale of the debate: the conflict between slavery and freedom was a broadly American one, and ideas, pamphlets, and letters moved among the colonies and, later, the new states with relative ease.[22]

Virginians had their own internal debates as well and argued with one another over the extent to which Revolutionary ideology necessitated freeing slaves. One exchange occurred in 1782 when "A Friend to Liberty," clearly influenced by religious beliefs and probably a Quaker (a Friend), published a passionate denouncement of slavery in the *Virginia Gazette and Weekly Advertiser*. Although the battle of Yorktown had been won and only sporadic skirmishes continued, A Friend to Liberty attacked the inconsistency between fighting for liberty and holding slaves. He (almost surely not a she, as women rarely contributed to public discourse in the Revolutionary era) began, "Whilst we are spilling our blood and exhausting our treasure in defence of our own liberty, it would not perhaps be amiss to turn our eyes toward those of our fellow men who are now in bondage under us." He remarked that God was just and that if Americans did not free their slaves in the spirit of that justice, "how can we expect he [God] will decide in our favor?" It was for that reason—to avoid "divine retribution"—that Virginians ought to "release our slaves from bondage," not gradually as Pennsylvania had done in its 1780 emancipation act (which freed slaves born after 1 March 1780 once they had reached the age of twenty-eight) but immediately, since justice ought not be delayed.[23]

Two Virginians responded with defenses of slavery surprising in their detail and range of arguments, since historians usually consider coherent proslavery defenses to belong to the generation before the Civil War. The first, "A Holder of Slaves," did not directly attack A Friend to Liberty's central argument, that slavery was wrong, but offered several reasons why emancipation would be harmful. First, it would be difficult to take away "the greatest part of the property of thousands of our best citizens, most of whom have acquired their slave property at the expence of much labour or risk." Even greater than

22. *Pennsylvania Chronicle*, 6–13 Mar. 1769; *Virginia Gazette* (Williamsburg: Purdie & Dixon), 2 Dec. 1773. On similar arguments in the 1840s and 1850s see Fredrickson, *Black Image in the White Mind*, chap. 3. On environmentalism in the Revolutionary era see Jordan, *White over Black*, 287–94; and Dain, *Hideous Monster of the Mind*, chap. 1.

23. *Virginia Gazette and Weekly Advertiser*, 25 May 1782. For the Pennsylvania act see Nash, *Forging Freedom*, 62.

the problem of compensation to owners for emancipated slaves was the problem of how free Africans could coexist peacefully with free whites. If settled in a separate "place or tract of country" near Virginia, freed slaves might find retribution for slavery by banding together, "taking up arms and waging war with their former masters." If the free blacks remained among white Virginians, society would be doomed to an even worse fate: not only would blacks steal from whites but they would be "ravishing and cohabiting with our white women, and in a century or less, our offsprings would be a mixed mongrel of mulattoes, of whites and blacks, bays, chestnuts, sorrels, and skewbalds." Describing mixed-race children with words more appropriate for horses than for people, especially *skewbald*, which means "marked with patches of white," indicated that Virginia slaveholders commonly viewed Africans as beastly. Moreover, it seemed to A Holder of Slaves, blacks did not want freedom: "in a vast number of instances last year, wherein negroes had left their masters [for the British] . . . those negroes chose rather to come back and serve their masters in the place of their nativity and amongst their connections." As if these arguments against emancipation were not enough, A Holder of Slaves asked why a man should plow his own field when he could have a slave do it, leaving the white man time to cultivate his mind in the "state-house, school house, or pulpit . . . to the great advantage of . . . the state in general."[24]

Another anonymous author, styled "A Scribbler," largely agreed with A Holder of Slaves but went further in his defense of slavery by attacking the idea that slavery was morally wrong. He noted at the outset of his essay that slavery was a "practice founded on the general principles of war and commerce, and sanctioned by the concurrence of all nations, even those we enslave." In addition, whatever was "generally usefull," including slavery, was right, "for general utility is the basis of all law and justice, and on this principle, is the right of slavery founded." Having rejected the notion of universal natural rights with this utilitarian argument, A Scribbler turned to his central concern, racial differences. He argued that all "national characters" had "their discriminating characteristicks," due not to climatic variation as some had "erroneously" argued but to differences in physiology, in the structure of "organs, passions, and appetites." Savagery was biological, not environmental; Europeans had tried to educate Indians and Africans, but "American [Indian] and African organs have proved impenetrable, and the savages still remained savage." Africans, as

---

24. *Merriam-Webster Collegiate Dictionary*, 10th ed., s.v. "Skewbald"; *Virginia Gazette and Weekly Advertiser*, 31 Aug. 1782.

savages, could not change and "therefore must appear incapable of any thing among civilized people, but the state of slavery in which they have for a great length of time been held by us, with as much general happiness to themselves, as they seem susceptible of." To A Scribbler, any emancipation scheme thus consisted of the "delusive idea of encreasing happiness where no misery exists." Echoing A Holder of Slaves's argument that slavery promoted whites' achievements, A Scribbler cited as examples of civilized slave societies Greece and Italy, "which in greatness and wealth surpassed all the nations that ever existed," and contended that America's position as the wealthiest nation on the continent resulted from the existence of slavery there.[25]

In appealing as much as possible to practical rather than moral reasons for retaining slavery—a distinctive characteristic of many Revolutionary and early national defenses of slavery—A Holder of Slaves and A Scribbler typified their own era. But in suggesting that Africans were inferior to whites and suited to slavery, that black slavery therefore existed in accord with God's natural order, and that it allowed whites to achieve a greater degree of sophistication, culture, and even republicanism than they could without the institution, they presaged the later argument that slavery was, in John C. Calhoun's words, a "positive good." It should not be surprising that proslavery arguments based on the perceived inherent differences between blacks and whites would arise so easily among a people who since the late seventeenth century had defined their own freedom in terms of black slavery and who amidst the challenges of the Revolutionary era now needed to defend their way of life.[26]

If in the 1770s and 1780s writers could conceive and articulate proslavery defenses generally associated with the 1830s, 1840s, and 1850s, why did they not do so more often? One answer may be that the dominance of Revolutionary rhetoric forced most people to shy away from direct challenges to the ideal of universal liberty. Another reason may be that few slaveholders felt the need to defend slavery vigorously because from Virginia southward they did not perceive the Revolution's rhetoric, the activities of Quakers, abolitionist movements in the northern states, or even the behavior of runaway slaves to

25. Ibid., 14 Sept. 1782.

26. The evidence presented here would modify Jan Lewis's claim that "Americans of the Revolutionary generation apparently were neither willing nor able to perceive" the relationship between slavery and freedom "and explain it in republican terms." Lewis, "Problem of Slavery in Southern Political Discourse," 266. Calhoun made his famous statement in his "Speech on the Reception of Abolition Petitions," 6 Feb. 1837. See McKitrick, *Slavery Defended*, 12–16, quotation on 13.

pose any serious danger to the institution since no widespread and politically active organization dedicated to ending slavery in the South then existed. A Friend to Liberty's warning of damnation was unusual fare for Virginia newspapers, and his essay inspired unusually spirited defenses. The tone taken by slavery's defenders supports the notion that even though they were riled to defend slavery, they did not perceive A Friend to Liberty's words to be a grave threat. They wrote with disdain for his plan, annoyed that anyone should dare to publish such a poorly thought out, unwise, and impolitic scheme as immediate and universal emancipation. A Scribbler referred sarcastically to the possible "phrensy" of "renouncing property valuable to ourselves, and useful to the state," and A Holder of Slaves chided A Friend to Liberty for thinking his arguments "unanswerable" and accused him of acting not from noble motives but from "self-interest." This tone of irritation is significant, for it suggests that Virginia slaveholders saw the antislavery writers of the 1770s and early 1780s more as noisome mosquitoes to be shooed away than as menacing foes to be engaged in battle.

ENDING THE IMPORTATION OF SLAVES TO VIRGINIA

Virginia slaveholders also remained relatively secure in the face of ideological and actual challenges to slavery during the Revolutionary years because even the political leaders who were uncomfortable with slavery bowed to the feelings and interests of their slaveholding constituents. One apparent exception to this rule is the effort Virginia's legislators made to stop the importation of slaves to their commonwealth. Because so many people at the time viewed ending the slave trade as a first step toward ending slavery, it seems logical to view the ban on slave trading as part of a larger antislavery program, as some historians have done. In fact, however, the 1778 law barring the importation of slaves to Virginia arose more from the economic interests of eastern Virginia's elites than from the ideals of the Revolution. The origins of that law demonstrate how self-interest could merge with Revolutionary rhetoric to create the appearance, if not the reality, of a Revolutionary antislavery statute in Virginia.[27]

Concerns that the slave trade injured Virginia's white citizens predated the

27. Gary Nash, for one, argues that "such disgust [with the tyranny of masters over slaves] was strong enough to produce a ban of further slave importation." Nash mistakenly dates the ban to the Virginia 1776 constitution, however. Nash, *Race and Revolution*, 12. For arguments similar to mine, see Holton, *Forced Founders*, 66–72; Miller, *Wolf by the Ears*, 9; and Macleod, *Slavery, Race, and the American Revolution*, 38–40.

Revolution by a number of years and were distinct from calls for the abolition of slavery. George Mason, for instance, opposed the slave trade because he thought it hindered Virginia's economic growth. Mason wrote in a 1765 letter that because of the immigration of slaves rather than free people "one Half of our best Lands in most Parts of the Country remain unsetled, & the other cultivated with Slaves; not to mention the ill Effect such a Practice has upon the Morals & manners of our People." Richard Henry Lee explained the situation similarly, stating that colonies without slaves were more advanced because "with their whites they import arts and agriculture, whilst we, with our blacks, exclude both." In later years, after the cotton boom, slaveholders would defend the economic viability of slavery, and Jeffersonian Republicans would champion agriculture and dispersed settlement over industrialization and metropolitan growth. But in the 1760s and 1770s, before Americans had recast their colonial inferiorities into national strengths, their rural backwardness into republican virtue, many Virginians feared that slave-based plantation agriculture impeded progress toward a more densely settled and sophisticated society. In part they were reacting to the late-eighteenth-century decline in eastern Virginia's economy, which occurred as soil exhaustion devastated the tobacco farms that had been the source of earlier wealth. As more and more farmers picked up and moved west to new lands, they left behind them a landscape that looked increasingly barren. To some observers, the problem was slavery itself, since they noticed that slave agriculture was associated with dispersed settlement and the declining economy. Furthermore, they understood that Virginia's slaveholding farmers traded their staple crop, usually tobacco, for finished goods, which created a trade imbalance that Virginians viewed as detrimental to their economic interests. Ending the slave trade, they thought, would slow the growth of slavery and rectify these ills. While Robert McColley has argued convincingly that slavery was not economically moribund before the rise of cotton, to slaveholders such as Mason and Lee it appeared to be so. Their objections to the slave trade, but not necessarily to slavery itself, arose partly out of that understanding.[28]

28. Enclosure with a letter from Mason to Fairfax and Washington, [23 Dec. 1765]; Richard Henry Lee, ed., *Memoir of the Life of Richard Henry Lee, and his Correspondence...*, 2 vols. (Philadelphia, 1825), 1:17–19, quoted in Brown and Brown, *Virginia*, 72; McColley, *Slavery and Jeffersonian Virginia*, 3–4, 30; McCoy, *Elusive Republic* (on Madisonian and Jeffersonian agrarianism). Those who comment on how colonial insecurities were transformed into national strengths include Bailyn, *Ideological Origins*, 160; and Wood, *Creation of the American Republic*, 103.

In fact, at least from the 1760s Virginia leaders tried to curtail the slave trade in order to strengthen their economy. According to Woody Holton, the trend actually began as far back as the 1710s, when the burgesses imposed high duties on slaves in order to raise the price of tobacco (by curtailing production through a reduction of the labor force). Henry Lee's 1767 bill to increase the tax on slaves was probably aimed, in a similar way, at limiting their importation. Though Lee's act passed, the crown disallowed it and also blocked a similar 1769 act that set a duty of 15 percent on slaves from Africa and 20 percent on slaves from other states. The proposed 1769 tax was so high that one English factor stationed in Alexandria considered it prohibitive, even though duties at the same rate had existed in earlier years, and it provoked protest from English merchants engaged in the slave trade, who thought the law would diminish the "number of Negroes" imported. The House of Burgesses tried to enact another high tax on slaves in 1772 but this time made their motives clearer. The burgesses wrote an address to King George III arguing that the slave trade "greatly retards the settlement of the Colonies with more useful inhabitants, and may, in time, have the most destructive influence." Once again the royal authority disallowed the tax, but the burgesses were not deterred. They considered another bill imposing prohibitive duties in 1774 but did not pass it before Governor Dunmore, trying to maintain British control in the midst of growing colonial rebelliousness, dissolved the House of Burgesses in May of that year.[29]

Thus, when in the summer of 1774 Virginians denounced the slave trade in their county resolves, documents drawn up to protest the Coercive Acts and other British policies, their position was neither new nor inspired by Revolutionary ideals. As stated by the freeholders of Prince George County, "the African Trade is injurious to this Colony, obstructs the Population of it by Freemen, prevents Manufacturers and other useful Emigrants from Europe from settling among us, and occasions an annual increase of the Balance of Trade against this Colony." The language of the Revolution did, however, help them reframe their opposition to the slave trade in moral terms. The Fairfax County Resolves, authored by Mason, announced a freeze on the importation of slaves and further condemned the slave trade, pleading for a permanent end to "such a wicked cruel and unnatural Trade." Citizens of Hanover, Caroline, Nansemond, and Princess Anne generally agreed, and the Association of the Virginia Convention, made up of representatives from the counties, barred

29. Holton, *Forced Founders*, 66–70, 67n; St. George Tucker, *Dissertation on Slavery*, 36–44; Miller, *Wolf by the Ears*, 9; MacMaster, "Arthur Lee's 'Address on Slavery.'"

the importation of slaves from Africa in August 1774, though the ban did not become law in Virginia until 1778.[30]

Because it grew from economic concerns, the issue of banning slave importations was also a sectional issue, a contest between eastern and western farmers. Support for ending the slave trade came especially from those in the Tidewater region, the lowlands of the coastal plain. The wealthy planters of the Tidewater had numerous slaves, descendants of those purchased by the planters' fathers and grandfathers in the earlier part of the century. Some even had surplus slaves, since the number of slaves in Virginia had been growing naturally for a couple of generations and since when farmers there turned from tobacco to wheat in the mid- to late eighteenth century they needed fewer workers. Those surplus slaves, who might profitably be sold to farmers to the west who were opening up new lands, were made less valuable by the continual importation of new slaves from Africa. Even if the Tidewater planters did not wish to sell, the importation of slaves depressed prices, which consequently lowered the net worth of planters whose main wealth was in their chattels and limited their opportunity to obtain credit. For the Tidewater leaders the fear of slave rebellion buttressed economic interests, since insurrection seemed more likely in those areas where slaves were a large proportion, even a majority, of the population. By contrast, families starting out on new farms in the Piedmont, the gently hilly region that rose from the Tidewater toward the Appalachian Mountains, had much less fear of a slave uprising and, moreover, desired cheap slaves to make their ventures profitable. According to Governor Fauquier in 1760, western farmers consequently favored importation to keep slave prices low.[31]

Once Virginia had effectively become independent of England in 1776, legislators could follow through on their earlier efforts to curtail the importation of slaves into the commonwealth. In June 1777 Patrick Henry, the former Quaker Isaac Zane, and other delegates were ordered to prepare and introduce a law that would ban the importation of slaves into Virginia. It was one thing to denounce Great Britain for disallowing high duties on slave imports, or to condemn King George for permitting the "wicked" and "unnatural" slave trade, and quite another actually to end the importation of the people upon

---

30. Prince George County Resolves, as printed in the *Virginia Gazette* (Williamsburg: Purdie & Dixon), 30 June 1774; Rutland, *Papers of George Mason*, 1:192n, 210n. Rutland argues that Mason authored the Prince William County Resolves, as well as the Fairfax Resolves.

31. Brown and Brown, *Virginia*, 71–72.

whose labor much of Virginia's wealth rested. The prospect seems to have engendered some reluctance, as Henry and the others failed to complete their assigned task. No bill was considered until the next legislative session, when Henry was again appointed to a committee to author a bill "to prohibit the importation of slaves." The bill drafted by the committee was introduced in November 1777 and sent to the Committee of the Whole House, where lawmakers discussed matters of especial importance. The Committee of the Whole House never considered the bill. Their procrastination suggests deep discomfort: on Saturday, 22 November, the House resolved to form a Committee of the Whole House to consider the bill the following Wednesday, and on Wednesday they put it off again until the next Tuesday. When Tuesday, 9 December, came around they further postponed action on the bill for another week, with delays continuing into January, when the delegates finally resolved to consider the bill again on 1 March, by which time they were not in session. Several months later, in the fall of 1778, legislators who favored banning the importation of slaves began the legislative process anew. This time the House made quicker progress, considering the bill in the Committee of the Whole House on 19 and 20 October and approving it on 22 October, nearly a year and a half after first addressing the issue.[32]

Although the delays in passing the "act for preventing the farther importation of Slaves" betrayed hesitation about cutting off the importation of a valuable economic resource, the provisions of the 1778 law demonstrated the seriousness with which legislators viewed their larger goal of limiting the growth of the enslaved population in Virginia and in the absence of other records are our best window into the minds of the legislators. First, the law took effect immediately after its passage and put an end to both the foreign and the domestic trade of slaves into the state by prohibiting them to be brought in "by sea or land." Another indication of the lawmakers' intent was that the penalty for transgressing the law was high, a fine of £1,000 for each violation and the liberation of any illegally imported slaves. The freedom provision could easily be interpreted as evidence of Virginia leaders' commitment to liberty. After all, freeing illegally imported slaves placed a premium on liberty over bondage in as clear a manner as possible. Indeed, the original law only allowed ten days for immigrants to take an oath before the county court that allowed them to

32. *JHD* (1777), 98; *JHD* (begun Oct. 1777), 16, 41, 75, 84, 88, 93, 97; *JHD* (begun Oct. 1778), 12, 19–21, 23. For evidence of Zane's Quaker past see Moss, "Isaac Zane, Jr."

bring in slaves for their personal use (not for sale). If they failed to take the oath, the slaves could sue for freedom, which they sometimes did.[33]

But subsequent amendments to the law, starting in 1780, indicated that legislators had meant for the freedom provision not so much to create free blacks as to discourage illegal importation of slaves. The 1780 amendment allowed South Carolina and Georgia slaveholders fleeing the fighting in their home states to bring their slaves with them to Virginia and even to sell them if they needed the cash, which certainly violated the spirit of the 1778 anti-importation statute. In 1788 the legislature began granting extensions and amnesty to immigrants who had brought slaves into the state but had failed to take the oath required by law, first to settlers in Kentucky (still a part of Virginia) and then to immigrants throughout Virginia. The 1788 law regarding Kentucky settlers prevented any subsequent suits for freedom by slaves whose masters had previously failed to take the required oath. Laws passed in 1789 and 1790 granting further extensions suggest that new residents frequently ignored the anti-importation act, since "many persons" who were "strangers to the laws of this state, at the time of such removal" had "failed to take the oath within the time prescribed." Ironically, it was George Mason, himself opposed to the importation of slaves, who penned the petition that prompted the 1789 extension, for while Mason disapproved of the slave trade, he greatly respected the property rights of slaveowners. Again in 1793 the legislature modified the freedom provision. In the same law that barred free "negroes and mulattoes" from entering Virginia, legislators made sure that slaves illegally brought in from Africa or the West Indies—seen as more likely to rebel, especially if they had witnessed the revolution in Saint Domingue—would be transported out

---

33. Hening, *Statutes*, 9:471–72 (1778). The act also allowed importation of slaves devised by will or marriage, as well as importation of slaves owned by Virginians but kept in another state. The oath required by immigrants read, "I, A.B. do swear, that my removal to the state of Virginia was with no intention to evade the act for preventing the farther importation of slaves within this commonwealth, nor have I brought with me, or will cause to be brought, any slaves, with an intent of selling them, nor have any of the slaves now in my possession been imported from Africa, or any of the West India islands, since the first day of November, 1778. So help me God." County records regarding slavery at the Library of Virginia include a number of signed copies of this oath, indicating that this aspect of the law was at least sometimes put into practice. County records also point to several successful suits for freedom arising from this provision, especially by slaves who lived near Virginia's border with Maryland and were transported back and forth across state lines. For more on freedom suits see below, chapter 2; and Nicholls, "Squint of freedom."

of Virginia rather than freed and allowed to remain in the commonwealth. Finally, in 1806 the legislature rescinded the provision of freedom for any illegally imported slave. The following year, they passed a further amendment granting Virginians, but only for a six-month period, the right to bring into Virginia any slaves owned as of 25 January 1806 but kept in another state. Peter Albert's analysis of the patterns of voting on the 1807 bill demonstrates that the importation of slaves remained a sectional issue, with westerners generally in favor of easier importation and easterners opposed to it.[34]

In spite of the exceptions made for Americans from other states who wished to bring their slaves to Virginia, the anti-importation law seems effectively to have ended the slave trade to the commonwealth. The importance of that step was great, even if it did not cause the diminution of Virginia's slave population. Ending the importation of slaves symbolically cut Virginia slaveholders off from the process of enslavement, from the horrific images drawn by antislavery writers of innocent people torn from their families, treated brutally by their captors, and sold in markets like animals. The age of the Revolution made a number of Virginia slaveholders sensitive to that horror. Although opposition to the slave trade had originally sprung from economic concerns, by 1774 Virginians referred to it publicly as a "wicked" commerce.

But in separating themselves from that wickedness, Virginia slaveholders made it easier to view their brand of slavery as a different creature altogether from the one attacked by antislavery writers. If the slave trade was evil, slaveowning itself was, recalling A Scribbler's words, a longtime Virginian institution in which slaves were held in "general happiness." The double vision allowed Virginians a generation later to condemn South Carolina for reopening its slave trade, a "horrible" and "diabolical traffic," even as Virginians were further restricting the laws regarding manumission, slaves, and free blacks

34. Hening, *Statutes*, 10:307 (1780), 12:713 (1788), 13:62 (1789), 13:121 (1790); Rutland, *Papers of George Mason*, 1:1175–77; Shepherd, *Statutes at large of Virginia*, 2:239, 3:251–52, 290 (1806–7); Albert, "Protean Institution," 126–29. Another weakness of the law in its original form was that it failed to define importation clearly. An 1807 amendment addressed that failure when it allowed citizens of other states to use slaves as porters to carry produce out of or into Virginia and when it clarified that slaves born in Virginia could be moved back and forth across state lines without coming under the purview of the law. Michael L. Nicholls offers an analysis of the law similar to mine, stating that the legislators "may have seen the freeing of an illegally imported slave as such a severe penalty that it would not have to be imposed" and noting that the law provided no mechanism for enacting the freedom. Nicholls, "Squint of freedom," 51.

in their own state, measures that received no such public criticism.[35] Ironically, then, banning the importation of slaves into Virginia may have helped strengthen some slaveholders' commitment to slavery there. And Virginians who denounced those who participated in the Atlantic slave trade seem to have conveniently ignored Virginia's central role in exporting slaves to the Southwest in the domestic slave trade. Clearly, a willingness to end the foreign importation of slaves should not be confused with a willingness to end slavery or slave trading, and especially not with a willingness to subordinate property rights to universal liberty.

TOWARD THE MANUMISSION ACT OF 1782

During the same month in which the legislature finally passed the anti-importation law, the House of Delegates received a petition from an enslaved man named George begging for freedom. George stated that he, "a negro man, late the property of John Thornton, Esq., deceased, . . . received repeated assurances from his late master that he would set him free at his death, from a sense of his having discharged his duty as a domestic servant with unremitted assiduity." George requested that "an act may pass for that purpose" in accord with the spirit of the colonial law that required the governor's and the council's assent for every act of manumission in Virginia. Importantly, Thornton's heirs endorsed George's request for freedom, which probably never would have reached the legislature otherwise. It is also worth noting that as a domestic servant, George was the sort of favored slave most likely to be emancipated in many slave societies, including Virginia. In response to George's petition, the legislators took the surprising step of reconsidering the 1723 manumission law. Though no new general manumission law arose from George's efforts in 1778 and no specific law regarding George was enacted that year, the House of Delegates did pass a manumission act four years later after considering three possible statutes. In fact, it seems that by the end of the war a subtle shift had occurred in the legislature; by 1782 lawmakers showed a greater liberality toward slaves, perhaps a result of the Revolutionary-era challenge to slavery. The legislative history of what became the 1782 manumission law is useful in tracing that small but important shift, as well as in illuminating Virginians' attitudes toward emancipation more generally.[36]

---

35. *Virginia Argus* (Richmond), 3 Jan. 1806 ("horrible traffic"); *Petersburg Republican*, 19 Dec. 1805 ("diabolical traffic").

36. *JHD* (begun Oct. 1778), 56, 67.

The decision to instruct the committee considering George's petition to broaden George's case into a general manumission law appears to have been a spontaneous one and raises the question of why in 1778 the legislators desired an act "for emancipating any slave or slaves that the proprietor may think proper, under certain circumstances." One possibility is that the rhetoric of the Revolution, its emphasis on freedom and self-determination, spurred legislators to reconsider the 1723 statute. Another is that Quakers, who were putting pressure on some Virginia leaders, including Patrick Henry, to act against slavery, were already having some effect. It is also possible that the lawmakers simply wanted to streamline the process of manumission in order to ease the procedural burden of having to decide on each case of manumission individually, although only a few petitions for freeing slaves were recorded during the war years and that burden does not appear to have been very high.[37]

The 1778 emancipation bill itself made clear that the motive certainly was not to encourage the growth of the free black population, since, following the precedent from 1691, it required freed slaves to leave Virginia within six months or else be returned as slaves to their previous owners. But creating a more liberal slave code *was* on the lawmakers' minds, as the bill stated that it was "consistent with Justice and Humanity that owners of such Slaves which have served with fidelity and diligence" should be able to free them under certain circumstances. Like George's owner, the legislators viewed freedom for slaves as a reward for loyalty and hard work and not as a natural right. The legislators who drafted the bill—William Fleming and John Taliaferro (pronounced *Toliver*), who came from the black-majority counties of Powhatan and King George, respectively—also viewed manumission as an act that occurred within the context of an interested community. The bill delegated the responsibility of authorizing manumissions to county courts and required the owner or the owner's executor (if the owner was deceased) to take the slave to two court sessions and announce his intention to free the slave. In a third appearance at court the manumitter could finally effect the act of manumission, but only after the slave had "declare[d] in open Court" his "willingness to be emancipated." Requiring the approbation of the enslaved person, as well as the tacit agreement of the county residents, made sense to those who understood slavery not merely as a relationship between owner and owned but as a public

---

37. See Finnie, "Antislavery Movement in the Upper South"; McColley, *Slavery and Jeffersonian Virginia*, 158–59, 187; Weeks, *Southern Quakers and Slavery*, 214; Iaccarino, "Virginia and the National Contest over Slavery," 10.

relationship affecting the character and form of the community. Revolutionary-era republicanism, which promoted acting for the communal good, probably also contributed to this provision of the bill. Before drawing up freedom papers, the justices were to inspect the manumitted slave, and if they found him or her "likely to become chargeable for maintenance within seven years," they were to note that on the documents of manumission so that if the freed slave became indigent, he or she could be turned over to the former owner and "not to the Parish for a maintenance." This was a bizarre stipulation considering that the newly freed people were also supposed to leave Virginia, in which case they would be too far away for the county to worry about having to support them. Its inclusion again underscores the lawmakers' sensitivity to how manumission might affect the white community as a whole.[38]

Although the bill passed the House of Delegates on 8 December 1778, it did not become law. The Senate proposed an amendment (no longer extant) to the House version, which likely addressed the cumbersome and self-contradictory procedures outlined in the bill. Before the House and Senate could work out an agreement, the legislative session ended and the bill died. The failure of the 1778 manumission bill was a fortunate turn of events for enslaved Virginians and for those who wished to emancipate them, since the manumission bill enacted several years later was much less restrictive.[39]

Since the General Assembly had not passed the 1778 bill and the 1723 law remained as the guiding statute, legislators had to approve individually the subsequent requests of masters who wished to free their slaves. While these requests were not significant for their volume, they set important precedents upon which the legislators would build when drafting a general manumission law in 1782. Responding to petitions that cited the exemplary behavior of the slaves rather than natural-rights philosophy or Revolutionary ideals as justifications for emancipation, the legislature freed five slaves between 1778 and 1782. In one case the legislature itself took the initiative to free an enslaved man, Kitt, who had exposed a counterfeiting ring.[40]

38. *Return of the Whole Number of Persons* (1791); "An Act Concerning Emancipation," 14 Dec. 1778, Rough Bills, House of Delegates, LVA, Archives Division.

39. "An Act Concerning Emancipation," 14 Dec. 1778.

40. *JHD* (begun Oct. 1778), 107, 109; *JHD* (begun May 1779), 42, 47, 55, 59, 62. The legislature heard of Kitt's case, sequestered him to protect him from the people he had informed on, and eventually freed him, paying his owner £1,000 in compensation. It seems that the owner did not receive the money, for he petitioned for it several years later. Petition of Hinchia Mabry, 22 Nov. 1786, LP, Brunswick County.

Probably following from colonial practice, the emancipating acts of the war years carefully protected the property rights of any people, other than the slaves' manumitters, who might have an interest in the emancipated slaves, such as creditors or part owners. A 1779 law, for example, emancipated three slaves owned by three different people, stating that "John Hope, otherwise called Barber Caesar, William Beck, and Pegg, . . . are hereby respectively declared to be free. . . ; saving to all and every other person, his or their heirs, executors, or administrators . . . any right, title, or claim they may have to the said negroes, as if this act had never been made." While it is not surprising that an act of emancipation would be restricted by the claims of third parties in this way—opening the possibility, for instance, that a person who thought himself free could be seized as payment for a loan taken out by his former owner—it is significant in highlighting the sources of Virginians' ambivalence toward slavery and emancipation. To a large extent, that ambivalence grew out of the central tension within slavery itself: slaves were persons whom owners might wish to reward with freedom even if they did not view freedom as a natural right for blacks, and at the same time slaves were valuable property in a society that viewed protecting property rights as one of the highest functions of the law. Considerations of slaves as property perhaps also shaped evolving thought about manumission since the right to free slaves could be seen as one of the rights of ownership, rights lawmakers strengthened in the late 1770s as they regarded land tenure. The tension between the view of slaves as persons and the view of slaves as property would influence discussions of emancipation from the Revolutionary period through the Civil War and would be one of the main issues in the slavery debate of 1832.[41]

Meanwhile Quakers, unencumbered by such ambivalence and guided by the moral certitude that Africans were people toward whom one should act as one expected to be treated, continued to free slaves in deeds and wills without any legal sanction to do so, eventually forcing the lawmakers to respond.

41. Hening, *Statutes,* 10:211 (1779), 10:372 (1780); Curtis, "Jefferson's Chosen People," 60–63. As described by Christopher Curtis, the Land Act of 1779 made land ownership allodial, or absolute, rather than held at the pleasure of the sovereign. Another measure of the reconsideration of slaves as property was in the 1792 slave code, which reclassified slaves as personal rather than real estate. This affected how slaves were treated in issues of inheritance and marriage, in some cases diminishing women's claims to slave property. See Shepherd, *Statutes at large of Virginia,* 1:122–30 (1792). For the inherent tension in slavery see Davis, *Problem of Slavery in Western Culture.* For discussions of property rights versus natural rights in the 1832 debate see below, chapter 6.

Robert Pleasants explained that some Quakers felt that the commonwealth's new Declaration of Rights, with its pronouncements in favor of liberty—"that all men are by nature equally free and independent"—gave them the authority to emancipate, apparently unaware of the care taken to ensure that the Declaration of Rights implied no such thing. By 1779 Quakers who had not freed their slaves were under a great deal of pressure to do so. In local societies members were sent out to cajole slaveholders into compliance with the Quaker discipline, although those who retained their slaves could still remain within the society. Many who did free their slaves worried that illegal emancipations might do "freed" slaves more harm than good; blacks whose freedom was in question could be taken up by "wicked men" who might reduce them "again to a State of Slavery." In fact, such events had occurred. To address this problem, a committee of Quakers drew up a petition in 1780 asking the legislature to validate, ex post facto, the manumissions the Friends had effected and to authorize future emancipations. The petition evoked the ideals of the Revolution, explaining that Quakers had freed slaves because they were "solicitous to act up to the great principle, that freedom is the natural rights [sic] of all mankind." Their request also displayed the Quakers' sensitivity to the prevailing culture, in which fear of both emancipation and black people figured large, asking that manumission be authorized "in such manner as will prevent injury to the community."[42]

The Quaker petition of 1780 spurred a second attempt to pass a law allowing individual manumission, and lawmakers again backed away from endorsing emancipation more broadly. The House of Delegates' Committee of Propositions and Grievances, to which the petition had been referred, drew up three resolutions regarding the Quakers' request. The first two stated that slaves already manumitted in last wills and testaments and in other documents "under the hand and seal of their respective owners" should be declared free. But the third resolution rejected the proposal that "a general license may be granted to the society of Quakers, for emancipating their slaves." The bill drawn up in accord with the first two resolutions reflected the concern of the legislature that freed slaves might become a burden on society. The bill al-

42. Pleasants, "Some account of the first settlement of Friends," 14–15; *JHD* (begun May 1780), 32. See also Robert Pleasants to Governor Patrick Henry, 28 Mar. 1777, quoted in McColley, *Slavery and Jeffersonian Virginia*, 158, in which Pleasants asked for Henry's support against "meddling people" who threatened that slaves who had been emancipated without the proper legislative authorization would be seized.

lowed the future emancipation of slaves only if they had already been promised freedom in a will or deed and were healthy adults of sound mind and body. Children, those over sixty years, and the infirm could not be freed unless the manumitter gave the court security for their maintenance. In addition, the bill reserved the property rights of third parties who claimed interest in the freed slave. In a departure from the previous bill, the 1780 bill did not, however, include any provision for the removal of freed slaves beyond Virginia, perhaps because they had already been emancipated with the expectation they would remain in the commonwealth. This was a significant change both in itself and because it defined a more liberal stance that would be incorporated into the manumission law as finally passed two years later. In the end, the 1780 measure was neither passed nor defeated but simply blocked by postponement. And while they were hesitant to act on the Quakers' petition, the legislators were sympathetic to those who wished to free their slaves: in the same legislative session they endorsed principles of freedom by refusing to consider two requests from petitioners who wanted to prevent the emancipation of slaves they would otherwise inherit.[43]

Quaker activists did not give up, and it was because of their efforts that the legislature considered a third, at last successful manumission measure, one more liberal than the previous failed bills. Warner Mifflin and other Quakers appeared before the Virginia General Assembly to promote a law allowing emancipation in 1782, which, according to Mifflin, "was attended with great satisfaction, having a set of liberal-spirited members to deal with." Aside from Mifflin's account, other facts point to the importance of the Quakers. The scant legislative records that remain include notice of a petition from Quakers, and notations on the petition itself indicate that legislative action was taken in response. Although the Quakers' 1782 petition did not ask specifically for a manumission law, it did decry slavery and complain about county officials who had seized illegally emancipated slaves as payment for debts owed by the slaves' (former) owners. The persistent presence of Quakers at the capital probably helped push the 1782 bill to passage on 10 June; one contemporary wrote that Warner Mifflin and several others spent fifteen days in their

---

43. "A Bill for granting freedom to Slaves in certain cases," 8 Dec. 1780, Rough Bills, House of Delegates, LVA, Archives Division; *JHD* (begun May 1780), 38, 42, 43, 49. The requests they refused to consider were the petition of James Moorman and others asking that Charles Moorman's application for the manumission of his slaves be blocked and the petition of Anne Bennet asking the legislature not to allow the manumission of a slave freed by the will of her grandmother.

lobbying efforts. That victory encouraged Mifflin to continue his work in other states "in order to remove legislative obstacles from those who are disposed to liberate their slaves, and to protect those who are set free."[44]

As one would expect from an act written largely by slaveholders elected by fellow slaveholders, the 1782 "act to authorize the manumission of slaves" protected the safety and interests of white society, especially property rights, as the previous bills had done. First, the law, which allowed individual owners to free their slaves without explicit legislative approval, specified the age at which slaves could be emancipated as above eighteen for females and twenty-one for males, which were the ages of majority for whites, and under forty-five; and like the 1780 bill, it required that former owners financially support any freed slaves judged not to be of sound mind or body. Also following precedent, the 1782 law stated that manumission did not negate any right or title to the slave that any person other than the emancipator might hold, such as a creditor, part owner, or heir. The legislators, anxious to keep slave status clear so that runaway slaves could not easily pass as free persons, required written proof of freedom. All manumissions had to be written down and recorded in court, and freed people had to carry copies of those manumission documents if they traveled out of their locality. Finally the law underscored that freedom for blacks did not impart the same rights as it did for whites: freed slaves who failed to pay their taxes could be confiscated by the state and hired out to cover the cost of their liability, an indignity no white person could suffer.[45]

Though it was almost certainly not intended to do so, the 1782 law authorizing manumission subtly but significantly reshaped Virginia slavery and Virginia society in ways to be explored more deeply in subsequent chapters. In brief, the manumission law allowed Quakers to enforce their proemancipation policy more rigorously, so that by 1788 they agreed that none of them should own any slaves. (A considerable number of Quakers were in fact expelled from

---

44. Warner Mifflin, *Defence of Warner Mifflin against Aspersions, cast on him on account of his Endeavors to promote Righteousness, Mercy and Peace, among Mankind* (Philadelphia: Sansom, 1796), in Justice, *Life and Ancestry of Warner Mifflin*, 79, 84, 94, 96, 101; Minutes of the House of Delegates, 6 May 1782 to 2 July 1782 (manuscript), 56, House of Delegates, LVA, Archives Division; Quakers' petition, 29 May 1782, LP, Miscellaneous Legislative Petitions; Davis, *Problem of Slavery in the Age of Revolution*, 197n51; Iaccarino, "Virginia and the National Contest over Slavery," 12–13. The legislative journal for 1782 was never printed and has not been found. The only record available is the clerk's minute book, along with the Quaker petition itself.

45. Hening, *Statutes*, 11:39–41 (1782).

the society on those grounds, including thirteen people of a single local meeting. Even among Virginia's most pious citizens slaveholding proved difficult to abandon.)[46] It also paved the way for hundreds of enslaved African Americans to buy themselves out of slavery and for thousands of other Virginians to free their slaves out of religious, humanitarian, practical, or personal motives. As a result, there grew a larger, more vibrant, and more conspicuous population of free blacks in Virginia than had existed previously, a development with its own important consequences.

Although the 1782 manumission law was in many ways a conservative piece of legislation, careful to restrict manumission in accord with white interests, it nevertheless marked a meaningful break from the past, especially because it did not require freed slaves to leave Virginia. At the heart of the law was the liberal assumption that an owner's right to free his slave, if not a slave's right to liberty, took precedence over society's interest in controlling the black population by keeping all Africans servile. The law represented perfectly the way that the Revolution affected slavery in Virginia, combining liberal impulses with conservative reflexes. One measure of how radical many Virginians viewed the law to be was the statute's relatively short life, ended effectively in 1806 when legislators a generation removed from the fervor of revolution reclaimed the idea that only whites should be free in Virginia by stating that any subsequently freed slaves must leave the commonwealth.

THE AMBIVALENCE OF THE REVOLUTIONARY ERA

The complexity and ambivalence of white Virginians' attitudes toward slavery and freedom revealed themselves in several other laws passed in the early 1780s. One showed the Revolution's potential to reshape ideas about slavery and black people, while two others expressed white Virginians' desire to return to the colonial order that had been upset by the turmoil of war and revolution.

In 1783 the legislature directed "the emancipation of certain slaves who have served as soldiers in this state." As Benjamin Quarles describes, and as the text of the law indicates, some slaveowners, wishing to avoid army life, had illegally substituted slaves for their own service. Although it was legal to employ substitutes and free blacks were allowed to enlist, enslaved men

---

46. Weeks, *Southern Quakers and Slavery*, 205, 210–13. One finds in Hinshaw, *Encyclopedia of American Quaker Genealogy*, that a sizable number of Virginia Quakers were dismissed (expelled) from the society for continuing to hold slaves. For an account of Quaker ambivalence toward emancipation in Pennsylvania see Soderlund, *Quakers and Slavery*.

were barred from the military. A number of slaveowners had lied when they declared their slaves to be free blacks who were eligible to serve in their place, and worse yet, many of the owners wished to reenslave them once the war was over. Such behavior was, according to the text of the law, "contrary to the principles of justice, and their own solemn promise." Perhaps as punishment for such dishonorable actions, the law did not provide for payment to owners for the financial loss they would suffer when the enslaved veterans were freed, in contrast to the usual compensation the state made to owners whose slaves were taken by the state (executed) in punishment for a crime. While the words of the law cast slaveowners poorly, they described the black soldiers glowingly as men who "contributed towards the establishment of American liberty and independence" and who "should enjoy the blessings of freedom as a reward for their toils and labours." The language is remarkable, for most statutes avoided overt philosophical statements or literary devices. Moreover, the use of the words *liberty* and *blessings of freedom* points to the specific influence of Revolutionary-era rhetoric, which was rare in legal documents. Here, both war and revolution had eroded property rights in slaves by liberating without compensation to their owners slaves who had served as soldiers.[47]

By contrast, other laws passed as the war came to a close had as their object the reestablishment of the bond between owner and owned. An act passed just after the manumission statute became law tried to bring slaves back under the control of their masters by banning slave self-hire. There were many "inconveniences," the law noted, that had "arisen from persons permitting their slaves to go at large and hire themselves out." To discourage the practice, which was especially irksome at a time when so much else seemed disordered, the statute punished the owners severely: those who allowed their slaves to hire their own time would forfeit the slaves, who would be sold by the county sheriff at auction. The implicit message here, as in the law freeing slaves who had served as soldiers, was that slaveowning involved responsibilities to the community at large and that society could punish irresponsible slaveholders by depriving them of their slaves. In that sense, even this law undercut the idea that there existed an absolute *right* to own other people. But at the same time, slaveowners who did act responsibly (as defined by their contemporaries) deserved the community's aid in enforcing slave discipline. That was reflected in another

---

47. Quarles, *Negro in the American Revolution*, 69; Hening, *Statutes*, 11:308–9 (1783). This law also freed one slave, Aberdeen, for his meritorious work in the lead mines and similarly failed to compensate Aberdeen's owner.

1782 statute, "for the recovery of slaves, horses, and other property, lost during the war." The main purpose of the statute as it concerned slaves was to provide a mechanism for the capture and return of runaways, but by treating slaves and horses together in one law the legislature revealed that Revolutionary ideology had *not* changed their view that slaves and horses were merely two different species of the same legal category. The law provided that county justices of the peace could confine to jail any slaves found wandering the countryside and directed that county officials take actions to return them to their rightful legal owners, including advertising in the *Virginia Gazette*. The law made no provision for determining whether African Americans who were "wandering about" were indeed enslaved and did not allow captured "slaves" to attempt to prove their freedom. In view of the fact that the legislature was in the same session considering the manumission law (although the bill had not yet been read on the floor when the slave recovery act was passed), their failure to allow blacks any chance to claim freedom is striking. It suggests that white Virginians did not see blacks simultaneously as persons *and* property but saw them alternately as persons *or* property: persons, perhaps, when physically close (as a domestic servant), and loyal, and obviously human; and property when distant (runaways, field slaves), or disloyal, or abstracted as an asset.[48]

In sum, just as the years from the beginning of the War for Independence to the signing of the Treaty of Paris brought challenges to slavery that modified some of the laws and ideas of the colonial era, the events of the Revolutionary period also spurred slaveholders, who dominated the legislature and much of the public discourse, to recommit themselves to the institution in Virginia. In liberalizing the procedures for manumission and in freeing black soldiers, lawmakers showed their receptiveness to new, potentially radical ideas, but in declaring whites only to be citizens of Virginia, enforcing the return of runaways without providing for a method by which free blacks might prove their status, and allowing freed slaves to be taken as payment for former owners' debts, they underscored their dedication to preserving slavery, the rights of slaveholders, and the racial basis of society. Even the anti-importation law, which had been passed less to end slavery than to stimulate the economy, probably had the effect of shoring up slavery within Virginia and perpetuating

48. "A Bill for the recovery of Slaves lost during the Invasion," 28 May 1782, Rough Bills, House of Delegates, LVA, Archives Division; Minutes of the House of Delegates, 6 May 1782 to 2 July 1782, 59–61; Hening, *Statutes*, 11:23–25, 59 (1782).

its hereditary nature. A Holder of Slaves and A Scribbler demonstrated that an articulate justification for racial slavery lay ready in response to any vigorous attack on the institution in Virginia and that the main themes of the antebellum proslavery argument—that slavery was appropriate for Africans by virtue of their inherent difference from and inferiority to whites and that it benefited whites because it freed them from the drudgery of hard labor and allowed them to cultivate their minds and their republican institutions—were already in place. It was the fact that such arguments were only rarely proffered in the 1780s that indicated that the Revolution's challenge to slavery in Virginia had been more superficial than deep, failing to stimulate the kind of organized, elaborate, and oft-repeated defenses of slavery that marked the later era and certainly falling short of any move toward the kind of general emancipation that occurred in northern states. In the absence of a sense of real threat to the institution of slavery, slaveholders in the legislature and in the population at large could open themselves to new possibilities, the most important of which was the possibility of manumission.

2

"The liberty of Emancipating their Slaves"

THE PRACTICE OF MANUMISSION, 1782–1806

[F]or and in consideration of the sum of fourty pounds Current money to me in hand paid ... also for and in consideration of the services heretofore rendered me by negroe Fanny commonly called Fanny Davis heretofore held as my slave. I the said Enock Foley do by these presents manumit, free and set at liberty the said negro named Fanny.

DEED OF ENOCK FOLEY, 22 December 1800

TWO DISTINCT PHASES NOT heretofore noticed by historians occurred in Virginia's experiment with manumission from 1782 to 1806, and each served to alter the institution and practices of slavery in the commonwealth and to call earlier conceptions of both race and liberty into question. First, in the 1780s and early 1790s a small number of antislavery manumitters rejected the morality of holding black people in bondage, a direct challenge to Virginia's slave-race system. Then, starting in the mid-1790s manumission took on a significantly different form as owners began to understand that the possibility of freedom could serve as a carrot to hold out to slaves in order to motivate them to work and as enslaved and free blacks figured out how to obtain manumissions for themselves and their families. The enlargement through manumission of the number of free blacks in Virginia also challenged the traditional system. By 1800 Virginia had begun to look more like other slave societies in the world where, in the absence of a two-race structure, manumission coexisted with slavery and even worked to support rather than to weaken slavery's stability.[1]

The clearest window onto the several functions of manumission and into

1. Patterson, *Slavery and Social Death,* chap. 8.

the lives of those involved in the years 1782–1806 is the body of documents by which enslaved blacks were freed and the patterns revealed by those instruments of emancipation. Here we examine 260 deeds and 99 wills from eight counties, the main units of local government and community, which frequently coincided with Episcopal parishes. The eight counties chosen for this study comprise the range of economies and cultures in Virginia and represent its four major geographic subregions.[2] Half of them lay in the Tidewater region, where colonial Virginians had first settled and where plantation agriculture had first taken hold in the seventeenth century. These include Chesterfield and Charles City counties, both on the James River; Lancaster County, on the Northern Neck, the strip of land between the Potomac and York rivers; and Accomack County, on the Eastern Shore, the southern part of the Delmarva Peninsula, separated from most of Virginia by the Chesapeake Bay. Reflecting the Tidewater's place as the traditional home of Virginia's social and economic elite, these counties included among their residents some of the most prominent colonial Virginia families—the Carters, Harrisons, Lees, and Custises. And typical of the economic fortunes of the Tidewater in the eighteenth century, they saw a decline in tobacco farming and diversification of agriculture in that period, largely due to soil exhaustion. As a consequence, in the last decades of the eighteenth century these counties had stable or declining slave populations.

By contrast, the Piedmont saw an increase in both people and plantations in the late eighteenth century. The two Piedmont counties examined here are Mecklenburg County, in the Southside region, the land between the James River and the North Carolina border; and Fauquier County, in the northern Piedmont, not far from Alexandria and Washington, DC. Colonists had largely avoided the Southside in the early colonial period because it contained no large rivers reaching to the coast and was in places swampy, but in the 1770s and 1780s the region looked appealing because it offered fresh soils. So, too, did the northern Piedmont. The rolling hills of Fauquier County typified the northern Piedmont, as did its mixed economy. Farmers there supplemented tobacco fields with fields of wheat, barley, and other grains, and they also raised livestock for profit, selling butter, eggs, pork, wool, and other animal

---

2. In choosing the counties I also wanted to complement rather than replicate Peter Albert's earlier study of manumission in Albert, "Protean Institution," chap. 7.

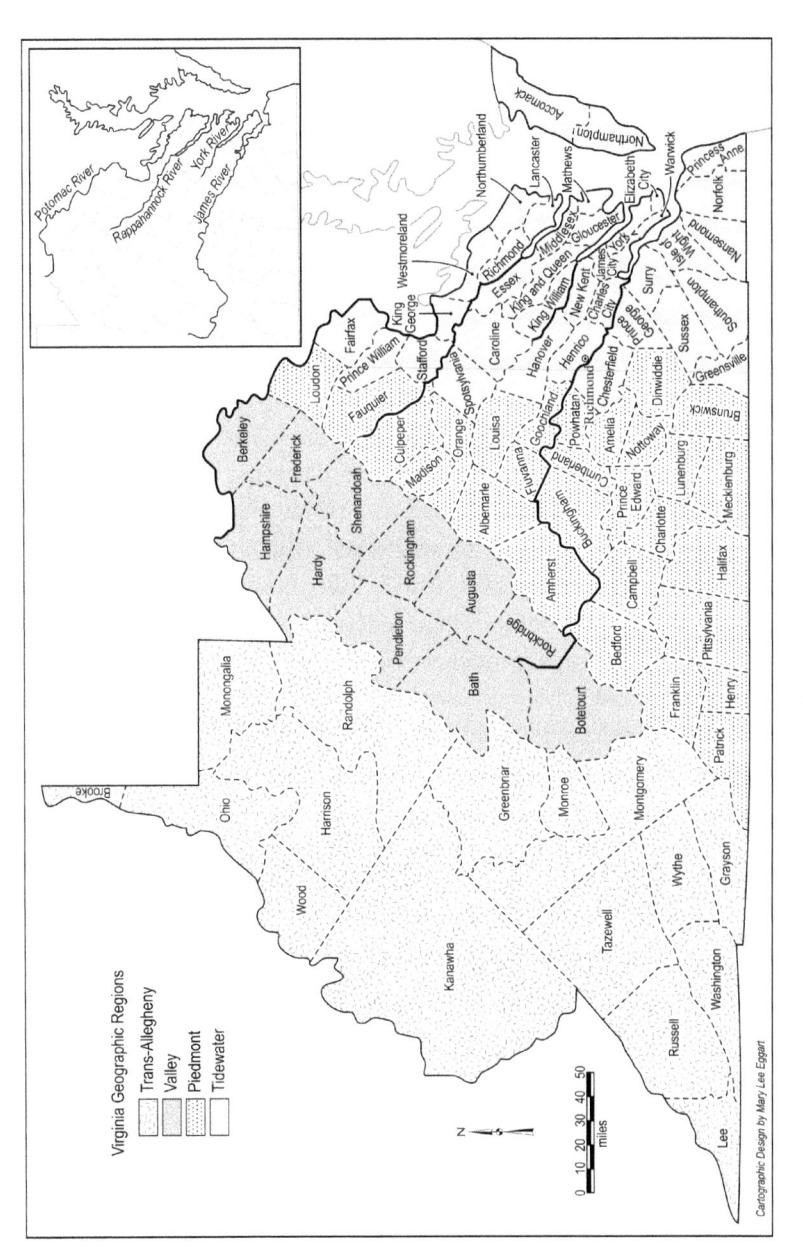

Virginia in 1800

products in cities such as Alexandria. Together the Tidewater and Piedmont made up what Virginians understood as the eastern part of their state.[3]

Past the Blue Ridge Mountains was the west, which included the Valley and Trans-Allegheny regions, both sparsely settled but rapidly growing at the end of the century. Besides the facts that the western regions were never centers of plantation agriculture and that their populations always contained a smaller proportion of slaves than did those of the east, they also had a distinct culture since, in contrast to the mostly English background of whites in eastern Virginia, "60 percent of the European population" of the "southern backcountry as a whole" was "from northern Ireland, Scotland, and northern England" at the end of the eighteenth century.[4] The Valley, running southwest to northeast between the Blue Ridge and Shenandoah-Allegheny ranges, is represented in this study by Botetourt County, many of whose settlers had come from Pennsylvania as part of a southern migration down the Shenandoah Valley. In part because of geographic constraints—narrow plots of fertile land near the river bottoms and a shorter growing season than on the coast—but also because of the culture brought by settlers, Valley counties such as Botetourt were dotted with small farms growing a variety of crops, such as hemp, wheat, and corn, rather than large plantations. The Trans-Allegheny region, though it had few whites and only a very few slaves in the period from 1782 to 1806, is nevertheless included in this study with Wythe County, which separated from Montgomery County in the year 1790.

One indication that these eight counties can serve as a case study for Virginia as a whole is that the percentage of slaves and free blacks in them in 1800 was quite close to the proportion in the entire state (see table 1). But because the eight-county sample includes the Eastern Shore county of Accomack, which saw an extraordinarily large number of emancipations, the study probably overrepresents the total number of manumissions statewide. Just as important as aggregate numbers are individual cases, which provide detail and lend texture to our understanding of manumission. Here, the variety among the counties represents Virginians quite well. Living in them were political leaders, Quakers, newly converted Methodists, struggling immigrant farmers, and a host of anonymous, ordinary white citizens and free and en-

---

3. Beeman, *Evolution of the Southern Backcountry*, 14–16; Fauquier County Bicentennial Committee, *Fauquier County*, 97.

4. Fischer and Kelly, *Bound Away*, 121.

TABLE 1. Slave and free black population of the eight counties in 1800 compared with the total population of Virginia

County	Slaves, 1800	Free blacks, 1800	Total county population, 1800	Percent slaves	Percent free blacks	Number of slaves freed, 1782–1806 (approx.)[a]
Tidewater						
Accomack	4,429	1,541	15,693	28.2%	9.8%	809
Charles City	3,013	398	5,365	56.2	7.4	90
Chesterfield	7,852	319	14,488	54.2	2.2	149
Lancaster	3,126	159	5,375	58.2	3.0	18
Piedmont						
Fauquier	8,754	131	21,329	41.0	0.6	53
Mecklenburg	8,676	553	17,008	51.0	3.3	76
Valley						
Botetourt	1,343	116	9,825	13.7	1.2	31
Trans-Allegheny						
Wythe	831	11	6,380	13.0	0.2	3
Total in the 8 counties	38,024	3,228	95,463	39.8	3.4	1,229
Total in Virginia	346,968	20,507	886,149	39.2	2.3	8,000–11,500[b]

SOURCES: *Return of the Whole Number of Persons* (1800); deed and will books for the eight counties, 1782–1806.
[a] The numbers are approximate because wills of emancipation do not always detail the number of slaves freed; the given numbers are probably within 3 percent of the actual number freed.
[b] The estimate of 8,000–11,500 is significantly lower than the figure of 15,000, arrived at by Theodore Babcock. Babcock extrapolated from the number of manumissions in six counties from two discrete time periods, 1782–95, and 1802–6. Babcock, "Manumission in Virginia," 21.

slaved African Americans. Because individuals shaped manumission as much as larger historical forces did, it is only by examining both individual stories and aggregate patterns that we can understand the meaning of manumission in Virginia.

Looking at manumission in this way, through both zoom and wide-angle lenses, we see that several assumptions about manumission are incorrect. The first is that manumission always sprang from antislavery sentiment, that, as Gary Nash has written, "there was in every manumitter, we might suppose, strong sentiment that slavery was immoral and unnatural." If we were to examine manumission only in the period from the 1780s to the early 1790s, this assertion would be largely persuasive. But because after the mid-1790s manumission usually resulted from something other than whites' antipathy toward slavery—an enslaved person's desire to be free, achieved by purchasing his or her own freedom, or a slaveholder's wish to reward a single favorite slave—it mischaracterizes what manumission signified on the whole. In fact, because more slaves were freed from the mid-1790s to 1806 than in the previous decade, the majority of manumissions in Virginia appear *not* to have been a function of antislavery sentiment. More important, perhaps, is that when owners granted slaves freedom as a reward for loyal behavior, manumission reinforced rather than challenged the values, assumptions, and discipline of slavery. On these occasions manumission was precisely the opposite of what Nash assumed, an assertion of the slaveholder's power over his slave rather than a recognition of the natural equality between them.[5]

A closely related conclusion has been that the "rapid growth of the free black population in the upper South thus gives a final, if rough, indication of antislavery sentiment."[6] But there are two reasons *not* to interpret the growth of the free black population this way. First, because manumission did not necessarily arise from white antislavery sentiment, the growth in the number of free blacks cannot be read as a measurement of that sentiment. Second, estimates of the growth in the free black population based on the difference be-

5. Nash, *Race and Revolution*, 18. Ira Berlin notes of the upper South that "manumission at times had nothing to do with antislavery principles, [but] equalitarian ideals motivated most manumittors in the years following the Revolution," which is an accurate description of the period up to but not after the early 1790s. Berlin, *Slaves without Masters*, 30.

6. Nash, *Race and Revolution*, 18. Nash also says that "in Virginia, where a census in 1782 revealed 1,800 free blacks, the number swelled to nearly 13,000 in 1800." It is possible that Nash has confused Tucker's estimate with a formal census; he has also mistaken the 1790 census figure for the 1800 number, since the free black population in 1800 was actually about 20,000. In addition to Nash, others suggest that the rise in the free black population signified antislavery sentiment. Douglas Egerton writes, "The fact remains that the rapidly rising number of freed blacks gave new hope to those who saw the law of 1782 as only the first step toward a general emancipation. . . . [The law] was an accurate barometer of gentry unease with a suddenly peculiar institution." He also notes, however, that the "rise of this free black caste . . . did not indicate that most gentrymen envisioned an end of slavery." Egerton, *Gabriel's Rebellion*, 11–12, 17. Ira Berlin refers twice to "manumission fever" in the upper South, suggesting a rapid and intense movement toward freedom, in *Slaves without Masters*, 31, 35.

tween the 1810 census figure of 30,570 and St. George Tucker's guess that there were 1,800 free blacks in Virginia before the Revolution are probably wrong. The present study indicates that about 10,000 slaves gained their liberty in deeds or wills of emancipation between 1782 and 1806. One reason for the discrepancy between the findings of this study and estimates based on population growth might be that not all acts of manumission were recorded. But because free blacks who did not have the written proof of their status required by the 1782 law were subject to treatment as slaves, it seems unlikely that very many manumitters would have failed to file a deed or will. To account, then, for the rise in the free black population in the late eighteenth century, this study, along with Peter Albert's, indicates either that Tucker's estimate was low or that the number of African Americans who managed to gain liberty during the War for Independence or through illegal Quaker manumissions before 1782 was higher than historians have previously appreciated. As discussed in the previous chapter, Quakers were reluctant to enact illegal manumissions and lobbied for the 1782 law largely for that reason, so it is unlikely that Quakers freed thousands of slaves before 1782 and left no record of their actions, such as filing the deeds after 1782. In fact, few acts of manumission were recorded before 1790, when the statewide free black population stood at 13,000 (see table 2 for the number freed each year). It is probable that a significant portion of those 13,000 free African Americans, possibly as many as 5,500, were already free before 1782, descendants of the small colonial free black population.[7]

Considering that the number of slaves freed in post-Revolutionary Virginia was lower than often presumed, that the majority of the acts of manumission by which those slaves were freed probably did not reflect whites' commitment to antislavery ideals, and that manumission never threatened the growth of the slave population, it is hard to agree with William Freehling that manumission

7. Albert, "Protean Institution," 268–69; St. George Tucker, *Dissertation on Slavery*, 70. According to my calculations, if there were 5,500 free blacks in Virginia in 1781, the number growing at a natural rate of 3 percent per year and including an additional 400 newly freed slaves per year (giving a total of 10,000 freed from 1782 to 1806), the population in 1800 would have been 20,392, very close to the actual number. See also Stevenson, *Life in Black and White,* which discusses the colonial free black population in Loudoun County and also finds that no manumissions were recorded in that county before 1790 (258–61, 264, 409). An example of a Quaker manumitter who acted before 1782 is Daniel Mifflin, who freed numerous slaves in 1775 and promptly filed the deeds of manumission with the county court once the 1782 law was in place. Daniel Mifflin deeds, 8 Apr. 1775, Accomack County Deeds, 5 (1777–83). Few others recorded deeds dated before 1782.

TABLE 2. Slaves freed by deed and by will in eight counties, 1782–1806

Year of document	Slaves freed by deed	Number of deeds	Average number freed per deed	Slaves freed by will (approx.)[a]	Number of wills	Average number freed per will	Total slaves freed	Total number of emancipating documents
1782	55	4	13.75	1	1	1.00	56	5
1783	12	3	4.00	0	0		12	3
1784	0	0		0	0		0	0
1785	16	5	3.20	4	2	2.00	20	7
1786	4	1	4.00	1	1	1.00	5	2
1787	97	6	16.17	0	0		97	6
1788	31	10	3.10	4	3	1.33	35	13
1789	49	12	4.08	9	1	9.00	58	13
1790	129	30	4.30	1	1	1.00	130	31
1791	34	13	2.62	8	3	2.67	42	16
1792	16	5	3.20	20	6	3.33	36	11
1793	54	13	4.15	18	7	2.57	72	20
1794	28	9	3.11	7	3	2.33	35	12
1795	12	3	4.00	20	8	2.50	32	11
1796	35	12	2.92	8	4	2.00	43	16
1797	10	8	1.25	13	6	2.17	23	14
1798	10	10	1.00	10	3	3.33	20	13
1799	17	6	2.83	17	7	2.43	34	13
1800	32	12	2.67	14	6	2.33	46	18
1801	10	5	2.00	22	7	3.14	32	12
1802	10	6	1.67	20	6	3.33	30	12
1803	27	16	1.69	17	6	2.83	44	22
1804	26	13	2.00	17	5	3.40	43	18
1805	56	17	3.29	32	9	3.56	88	26
1806	177	41	4.32	19	4	4.75	196	45
Total	947	260	3.64	282	99	2.85	1,229	359

SOURCES: Deed and will books for Accomack, Botetourt, Charles City, Chesterfield, Fauquier, Lancaster, Mecklenburg, and Wythe counties, 1782–1806.
[a] See note a of table 1.

and the growth of the free black population left a "Revolutionary legacy" that "weakened the institution [of slavery] in the Northern slave states," including Virginia. While manumission and the ending of slavery were related phenomena in northern states such as New York and Pennsylvania, such was not the case in the Old Dominion. In fact, slavery in Virginia proved resilient and flexible, able to accommodate manumission without being weakened by it, just as in other slave societies throughout the world. What Virginia's experiment with manumission did challenge was white Virginians' construction of race as a marker of slave or free status. It was ultimately that threat that proved most disconcerting to white Virginians and spurred them to curtail manumission in 1806.[8]

IDEAS ABOUT SLAVERY AND FREEDOM IN DEEDS OF MANUMISSION

If manumission did not always indicate antislavery sentiment, what it did mean to the Virginians who practiced it—and by implication what slavery meant as well—reveals itself most clearly in the words and form of the commonest type of emancipating document, deeds of manumission. Far from being highly stylized and formulaic, deeds of manumission were often individual and idiosyncratic, partly because private manumission was novel in late-eighteenth-century Virginia and manumitters, lawyers, and clerks were working out how to construct emancipation papers, and partly because some manumitters took the opportunity to express their feelings on the important event a deed of manumission signified. The legislature's dictate that manumission be effected by deed or will did, however, create broad similarities among the documents since both deeds and wills were common and familiar legal forms. Like other deeds, deeds of manumission transferred property from one party to another in exchange for valuable consideration, a quid pro quo that completed a contract and made the transfer binding. For example, a deed transferring land

---

8. Freehling, "Founding Fathers and Slavery," quotation on 90. Stephen Whitman's study of manumission in Baltimore finds manumission to be "another arena in which masters and slaves contended" and notes that "only in the late antebellum years did manumission there operate solely as a slaveholder's exit from slavery." Before that period, "gradual manumission helped *spread* slavery among craftsmen and at first strengthened slavery in Baltimore." Whitman, *Price of Freedom*, 93, 118. In New York and Pennsylvania the passage of gradual emancipation laws caused the number of manumissions to increase, even though manumission was not necessarily an indication of antislavery sentiment in those states either. Nash, *Forging Freedom*; White, *Somewhat More Independent*.

might read, "[I]n consideration of the sum of £150, I do hereby grant the following tract of land...." In the case of deeds of manumission, however, the property value of the slave was transferred to the slave himself, sometimes in exchange for intangible consideration. Richard Ames's deed of manumission to Luke read, "[B]y Considerations of right Justice and Duty [I] do hereby manumit liberate and set free my negroe man Slave Luke." When an owner manumitted a slave in exchange for money, the transfer of the property value from the owner to the slave became more explicit, such as when Jesse Ward freed James in exchange for sixty pounds, saying that he did "grant bargain and Sell to the said negro man James all my right title Interest and demand of and belonging to the said Negro man James as my slave." The form of deeds of manumission therefore underscored the legal reality that slaves did not own themselves but free people did. Both legally and metaphorically, manumission meant that a slave took possession of himself and his body in order to become free. A slave was possessed, a free person self-possessed.[9]

The transition from slavery to freedom marked by a deed of manumission was so profound that it could only exist as a matter of legal fiction. How could a nonperson (slave) be party to a contract (deed of manumission) in which he or she received his or her own freedom, his or her own self? Only legal persons, excluding, for instance, minor children, could engage in contracts, devise wills, or own property. As a matter of judicial tradition, slaves were not recognized as having the rights of legal persons and were denied all those abilities. But in deeds of manumission slaves *were* effectively treated as legal persons even before becoming free. Only as a party to a contract could a slave receive his freedom, yet by the terms of that same contract the slave became a legal person only *after* the deed of manumission was completed. The law had no logical way to make a person out of a nonperson, to make a slave both party to and object of a deed. The problem remained unresolved.[10]

As a consequence, some of the authors of deeds of manumission, aided often but not always by trained attorneys or clerks, engaged with this conundrum

---

9. Richard Ames deed, 31 Apr. 1806, Accomack County Free Negro and Slave Records, Manumissions, 1783–1814, LVA, Archives Division; Jesse Ward deed, 4 June 1798, Accomack County Deeds, 9 (1797–1800).

10. Orlando Patterson discusses the "formal contractual mode" of manumission as one of several possible modes of manumission in slave societies. Other modes include the adoption of slaves into the family and the freeing of slave concubines by law. Patterson, *Slavery and Social Death*, chap. 8.

and articulated what they thought it meant to become free. Implicitly, too, deeds of manumission defined both slavery and freedom, since the main function of the deed was to create one out of the other. The primary definition of slavery in deeds of manumission was as a legitimate relationship of possession, in part because deeds were legal documents relating to property. But Virginia slaveowners held a more specific concept of what it meant to possess another human being than that expressed in the common legal phrase "right, title, and interest" and a more visceral understanding than that revealed, for instance, in St. George Tucker's learned discussion of whether slaves fit more into the category of personal or real estate. For George Herndon, who emphasized in his deed of manumission that he was "legally possessed" of his three slaves, whom he then freed in exchange for one hundred dollars, relinquishing ownership meant "quit[ting] claim unto . . . their *persons* as well as their *Services* and *estate*." First, slavery was literal ownership of another person's body. With the body came labor or services. And because slaves were themselves owned, they could not own anything nor have any estate. Defined against slavery, freedom was ownership of one's body, one's labor, and one's own property.[11]

Slaveowners also understood slavery in terms of control. When Enock Foley freed Fanny Davis, he gave up possession of her and further released his "controul . . . over the said Fanny," a power that, along with ownership, he claimed to have had "under the laws of Virginia." Significantly, Fanny was a member of the Broad Run Baptist Church who bought her freedom from Foley for forty pounds; had she, by force of personality and perhaps with the aid of the Baptists' egalitarian theology, shown Foley that she could and would control herself? Other manumitters also saw slavery and freedom as questions of control. Thomas Crippen, for instance, implicitly defined enslavement as being controlled when he outlined the conditions of freedom for his emancipated slaves; he set his slaves "to be at their own Disposal and liberty to act for themselves as any other free People without the [least] hindrance or molestation of me or any other person." As Crippen understood it, enslavement was an all-encompassing restriction of one's actions, the ever-present possibility, even probability, that someone else—not just one's owner but "any other person" (presumably white and free)—might hinder one. Indeed, this view accurately reflected slave patrol laws that made most of white male society part of the police force. Caleb Bradford, who apparently did not employ a lawyer

---

11. See St. George Tucker, *Blackstone's Commentaries*, vol. 3, n. E; George Herndon deed, 17 Mar. 1806, Fauquier County Deeds, 16 (1804–7), emphasis mine.

or clerk to draft a deed of manumission for his slave Annes, also linked property rights to personal control. In 1802 he wrote awkwardly, "Annes Negro the *property* of me Caleb Bradford I this Day Mancipates her and Declares her to be a free woman and that I have no *Command* of the sd Negro from this the 27th day of December 1802."[12]

In addition, manumitters recognized that slaves existed outside of society, and so the act of freeing them marked their entrance into the social body. When William Chilton, for example, freed his slave George "in consideration of . . . [his] general good conduct," he released his claim over George and sent him out into the world, "recommend[ing] him to the publick as an honest Sober and well disposed person." Other slaveowners, especially in Accomack County, marked the transition from enslaved person to free member of society by giving their manumitted slaves surnames. As Bridgett James explained, "[T]he Introduction of the above Mentioned Negron [Liddia] into Society, Make a Sec'd Name Necessary for the distinction from the Negrons, who have been or may be hearafter Liberated." To emphasize that freed blacks had undergone a deeply meaningful transition, some manumitters bestowed symbolic surnames on the enslaved people they liberated, such as Joy, Jubely, Planter, or Godfree. As in places such as contemporary Philadelphia or New York City, slaves had, took, or were given surnames that differed from their manumitter's last name. Furthermore, at least some former slaves changed their names after their emancipation, asserting their independence by choosing surnames different from the ones imposed by their former masters.[13]

---

12. Enock Foley deed, 22 Dec. 1800, Fauquier County Deeds, 14 (1798–1801); Thomas Crippen deed, 2 Nov. 1782, Accomack County Deeds, 5 (1777–83); Caleb Bradford deed, 27 Dec. 1802, Accomack County Deeds, 10 (1800–1804), emphasis mine. Fanny is listed as a member of Broad Run Baptist Church in Broad Run Baptist Church, Fauquier County, Minute Book, 1762–1873, LVA, Microfilm Collections, misc. reel 472. On the development of slave patrol laws see Hadden, *Slave Patrols*, 26–31.

13. Elizabeth Bayly deed 23 Dec. 1790, Accomack County Free Negro and Slave Records, Affidavits and Certificates about Slavery, LVA, Archives Division, emphasis mine; and William Chilton deed, 24 Apr. 1804, Fauquier County Deeds, 15 (1801–4). The name Planter is from John Teackle deed, 24 Sept. 1787, Accomack County Deeds, 6 (1783–88); Godfree is from George Corbin deed, 25 Sept. 1787, ibid.; Jubely is from Thomas Ames deed, 8 Jan. 1793, Accomack County Deeds, 7 (1788–93); and Joy is from Thomas Cropper deed, 25 Dec. 1792, ibid. Orlando Patterson, in his study of slavery worldwide, *Slavery and Social Death*, defined slavery similarly as social death. For name changes after manumission in Pennsylvania and New York see, respectively, Nash, *Forging Freedom*, 79–81; and White, *Somewhat More Independent*, 192–94.

Finally, the transition from slave to free was an essential change, an alteration of basic nature rather than a simple change in role. Many natural-rights philosophers believed that no person could ever give up his inborn liberty, that slavery was a violation of this axiom, and that emancipation consequently marked only a return to one's inborn, natural right. Virginia manumitters, by contrast, viewed enslavement to be inborn and therefore just as natural as liberty. Frequently, when manumitters or their lawyers could come up with no other definition of the freedom being granted to slaves, they simply declared them "to all intents and purposes free as if they were born free." Benjamin Branch pronounced Beckey "as free as if she had been freeborn, and had never been in slavery or bondage," and Thomas Goode declared George "to be from henceforth and forever free in as full and effectual a manner as if he had been born free." Because most manumitters did not see emancipation as restoring slaves to their original state of liberty but as altering their natal status, deeds (and wills) of emancipation generally turned rather than *re*turned slaves into free people.[14]

If anyone were to challenge the legitimacy of these tenets—that slaves were persons who had been born unfree, outside society, and were first and foremost objects of possession over which owners had ultimate power—it would be those people who actually freed their slaves. If manumission as practiced by individual slaveowners were primarily a response to the Enlightenment ideals embodied in the ideology of the American Revolution, we might expect manumitters to reject the notion that the individuals they were freeing were or ever had been rightfully slaves. It seems that manumitters should have expressed distaste or discomfort with their ownership of other human beings, or with the unfettered and complete control they had over slaves under the law, asserting instead the basic human equality of their slaves and their consequent natural right to liberty. Some manumitters did this. George Parker, for example, was "well aware that all men are by nature free and independent," and so he "discharged... the following Black Men and Women." Reubin Howard, himself formerly enslaved, declared that he was "fully Satisfyed that liberty is the birthright of all persons whatsoever" when he manumitted his

---

14. Richard M. C. Chichester deed, 29 Apr. 1806, Fauquier County Deeds, 16 (1804–7); Benjamin Branch deed, 8 July 1805, Chesterfield County Deeds, 17 (1805–8); Thomas Goode deed, 10 Nov. 1803, Chesterfield County Deeds, 16 (1802–5). Kathleen Brown discusses how the development of race in the seventeenth century made slavery appear natural. Brown, *Good Wives*, chap. 4.

wife and son, "a Negroe Woman Slave named Minta Howard & her Child Named Reubin," whom he was "at present possessed of."[15]

Most manumitters, however, saw the basic premises of slavery as legitimate, and like slaveholders generally they did not find the idea of owning other people troublesome. The exceptions, such as George Parker, Reubin Howard, and other African American manumitters, proved the rule. Parker freed "Black Men and Women"; Howard freed "a Negro Woman Slave" he was "at present possessed of"; and Frank Jenkins, also a free black man, liberated "a certain negroe woman who I have for a wife."[16] In contrast, the vast majority of white manumitters asserted possession of their (soon-to-be former) slaves without apparent thought. Over and over again in their deeds of manumission slaveowners referred to the people they were freeing as "my negro woman," "my negro man," or "my several negroes." Even in the very act of setting them free, of giving up possession, most manumitters still unreflectively called their slaves "mine." The possessive word could persist even after slaves had been emancipated. In 1790 Ezekiel Tatham freed "my negro woman Mathew," but a year later in his will he called her "my negro Mathew that once was a slave to me but is now free," giving her "five acres of land," as well as a cow and a calf. Although convinced that "for the sake of doing Justice to Humanity" Mathew should be free, and in spite of the concern he showed for her by giving her valuable property in his will, he was apparently unable to liberate himself from the mind-set of slaveholding. Tatham continued to think of Mathew as a possession and an object, referring to her by means of the impersonal pronoun "that" and continuing to call her "my negro."[17]

The ease and unselfconsciousness with which slaveowners possessed other people is striking and highlights the cultural distance between the slave societies of early America and present-day American society. For most manumitters and nearly all slaveowners it was neither illogical nor bizarre to own other human beings and their children forever. Speaking of other people as "mine" was simply a reflex, built into the physiology of a slave society. In that context,

---

15. George Parker deed, 30 Dec. 1793, Accomack County Deeds, 8 (1793–97); Reubin Howard deed, 11 Jan. 1799, Botetourt County Deeds, 6 (1796–99).

16. Frank Jenkins deed, 26 Apr. 1803, Accomack County Deeds, 10 (1800–1804).

17. Ezekiel Tatham deed, 20 July 1790, Accomack County Deeds, 7 (1788–93); Ezekiel Tatham will, 27 Jan. 1791, Accomack County Wills, 1788–94.

manumission was an unusual and sometimes radical act, even if most manumitters did not challenge the legitimacy of owning slaves in general.

MANUMISSION'S FIRST DECADE

As stated above, the era in which manumission in Virginia most reflected radical impulses was the first decade or so after the passage of the 1782 law. In those years antislavery beliefs usually motivated manumitters and compelled them to free all of their slaves as soon as they could, generally through deeds of manumission, which took immediate effect, rather than through wills, which did not operate to free slaves until after the owner died. Delayed manumission, in which an owner set the date of liberty significantly after the date of the deed, occurred in a number of cases, but usually when manumitters wished to liberate enslaved children, who by the terms of the 1782 law could not be freed until they reached the age of majority. In nearly 70 percent of all acts of manumission by deed from 1782 to 1793 manumitters freed all of their slaves, as determined by comparing the number of slaves freed with the number held in the years before and after the manumission was enacted. Many manumitters did not specify in their deeds why they were freeing their slaves, but when they did, nine times out of ten the reasons were framed in terms of secular or religious antislavery ideas. Altogether, antislavery deeds made up about half of all deeds of manumission from 1782 to 1793. Abel Teackle in 1791, for example, looked to "the Laws of Religion" and those of "Morality" to determine that "God Originally distributed equally to the Human race the unalienable right to the enjoyment of Personal Liberty." Martin Baker explained in 1789 that "God has created all Men equally free," and because Baker had a "clear Conviction of the Injustice and Criminality of depriving my fellow Creatures of their natural Rights," he freed his three slaves, their liberty to take effect at Christmas of that year. But even given these strong antislavery feelings and the work of Quakers to enforce antislavery principles in the 1780s, there was no rush to emancipate slaves after the manumission law was passed. As it happened, in 1782 only four individuals in the eight counties wrote deeds of manumission, and only one drafted a will freeing a slave, and the annual number of people freeing slaves rose only slowly after that, peaking in 1790 (see table 2).[18]

18. Abel Teackle deed, 1 Jan. 1791, Accomack County Deeds, 7 (1788–93); Martin Baker deed, 10 Sept. 1789, Chesterfield County Deeds, 11 (1779–91). From 1782 to 1793 57 percent of slaves freed

Though they were not overwhelming in number, the antislavery deeds of the 1780s and early 1790s were impressive for the radical sentiments they evinced, particularly feelings of fellowship between blacks and whites, which contrasted sharply with Virginia's codified separation of the races. Emphasizing the common humanity of all people, the Quaker Thomas Durham Madkins, of Mecklenburg County, wrote in 1782 that he was "fully persuaded that freedom is the natural Right of all mankind & that it is my duty to do unto others as I would desire to be done by in the Like Situation." Others avowed the basic human equality of the races even more explicitly. James and Matilda Ashby, of Accomack County, freed their slaves Peter, Parris, and Pleasant in 1796, declaring "freedom from a state of Slavery the natural & proper right of the black people as well as white." Several others in the county expanded on that idea in subsequent years, asserting that "God of one blood made all nations of men and that it is his wish that the Black People should be free as well as the White people in society." This pronouncement, found in five emancipating documents written in the years 1800–1806, emphasized that it was not enough to declare people spiritually equal; they ought to have equal standing in the social world as well. In defining blacks and whites as "nations," the manumitters suggested that differences between people had more to do with geography and political organization than with inborn characteristics, a starkly different view from that of contemporaneous proslavery writers, who described slaves as naturally inferior and even animalistic. Manumitters thus helped define one end of the spectrum of Virginians' ideas about race and slavery, and acts of manumission driven by egalitarianism and antislavery ideals, though most common in the 1780s and early 1790s, persisted through the first years of the nineteenth century.[19]

---

received their freedom immediately. Of those whose freedom was delayed only 16 out of 92 (cases in which I could determine the age at freedom) were held past the age of majority. Since so many deeds did not give specific reasons, explicitly antislavery deeds accounted for only 47 percent of all deeds in this period.

19. Thomas Durham Madkins deed, 12 Aug. 1782, Mecklenburg County Deeds, 6 (1779–86); James Ashby and Matilda Ashby deed, 13 Nov. 1796, Accomack County Deeds, 8 (1793–97). For the clause "Black people should be free as well as the White people," see Littleton Townsend deed, 1806, Accomack County Free Negro and Slave Records, Manumissions, 1783–1814; Thomas Bagwell deed, 25 Apr. 1806, ibid.; Susanna Upshur deed, 23 Jan. 1800, Accomack County Deeds, 9 (1797–1800); Nanny Melson, Noah Melson, and William White deed, 1 Jan. 1804, Accomack County Deeds, 10 (1800–1804); and Thomas Bagwell deed, 11 Feb. 1806, Accomack County Deeds, 11 (1804–7). See also Isaac Dix deed, 13 Jan. 1804, Accomack County Deeds, 10 (1800–

As the examples above suggest, when people freed slaves out of a conviction of slavery's immorality, they often did so in the context of specific antislavery communities, usually religious communities but occasionally secular ones as well. A large proportion of the manumitters in the early years were Quakers, Methodists, or occasionally Baptists, often living in Tidewater counties where their antislavery sentiment coincided with economic conditions that lowered objections to manumission. The Quaker community of the Eastern Shore county of Accomack serves as a good example of how members of the Society of Friends encouraged one another to manumit slaves and perhaps also how they influenced those who were not Quakers. One of the first Accomack residents to free his slaves was Daniel Mifflin, father of the Quaker activist Warner Mifflin, who was present for the great occasion and witnessed his father's deed. Daniel liberated his ninety-one slaves in 1775, even before it was legal to do so, declaring it an "injustice" to hold "my fellow Creatures in bondage." He recorded the act at the Duck Creek Monthly Meeting of Friends, held north of Accomack in Kent County, Delaware, and after the 1782 manumission law passed he recorded the two deeds—one for the adults and one for the children—with Accomack's county clerk as well. Mifflin's act of manumission was impressive not only for its early date but because he freed so many people. Having established himself as a leader in the cause of manumission, Mifflin was invited, or invited himself, to serve as a legal witness to a number of the deeds of manumission Accomack's residents effected in the subsequent years. Mifflin witnessed the deeds of Thomas Crippen to his thirty-three slaves in 1782, John Booth to his slave Abraham in 1783, Adruaner Michael to his slave Teackle in 1785, Levin Bell to his nine slaves in 1787, James Smith to his seven slaves in 1788, and John Bell to his two slaves that same year. Some of these men continued the tradition of supporting other manumitters by witnessing their deeds. Levin Bell witnessed John Bell's and James Smith's deeds the year after freeing his own slaves, and John and Levin Bell together witnessed William Spiers's 1790 deed of manumission to his slave Peter. (It appears that Spiers only waited until 1790 to free Peter because it was that year that Peter reached the age of majority, twenty-one.) While Thomas Crippen and Daniel Mifflin condemned slavery in their deeds of manumission, others, per-

---

1804), which states that "liberty is the natural and Proper right of the black people as well as the white people in society." The link among these manumitters is probably Methodism, as James Ashby was a Methodist and he witnessed Littleton Townsend's, Susanna Upshur's and Isaac Dix's deeds (Matilda Ashby also witnessed Upshur's).

haps not all of them Quakers, simply freed them "for divers good Causes." In other counties, Quakers' deeds shared a distinct phraseology. Many Quaker manumitters declared themselves "fully persuaded that freedom is the natural right of all mankind" and were "desirous of doing to others as I should be done by."[20]

Common ties to Methodism explain other clusters of manumission, especially where antislavery Methodist ministers took the lead, even after the national church had repealed the antislavery rules of 1784–85. Ministers provided examples by freeing their own slaves, witnessed deeds of manumission drafted by others, and in some communities preached against slavery. Their ardent desire to do good in the world had a particularly Christian meaning, and their deeds of manumission sometimes invoked God more explicitly than those of Quakers. The Methodist minister Edward Mitchell was one of those deeply religious antislavery men. As he explained in a 1794 letter to the itinerant preacher Stith Mead, "I hope to live and die a Methodist and Christian." For Mitchell, Methodism required paying special attention to his own heart and his behavior toward other people. He examined the degree of his brotherly Christian love and found that he was "convinced I do Enjoy it in a Measure both to my great & good master & friend and to his Creatures, but more Especially to his Children, & still in a higher degree to his Labourers." He had proved his Christian love to God's laborers by setting his own fourteen slaves free in 1790 because, as he put it simply, "it is contrary to the Principals of Christianity to hold our Fellow Creatures in Bondage." In addition, Mitchell probably influenced two others of his community, including his own brother,

---

20. Daniel Mifflin deeds, 8 Apr. 1775, Accomack County Deeds, 5 (1777–83) (not counted in the manumission study because of its early date); Thomas Crippen deed, 2 Nov. 1782, ibid.; John Booth deed, 25 Mar. 1783, ibid.; Adruaner Michael deed, 5 Nov. 1785, Accomack County Deeds, 6 (1783–88); Levin Bell deed, 25 June 1787, ibid.; James Smith deeds, 29 July and 26 Aug. 1788, Accomack County Deeds, 7 (1788–93); John Bell deed, 23 Apr. 1788, ibid.; William Spiers deed, 8 Mar. 1790, ibid.; Samuel Hargrave deeds, 21 Jan. 1791, 15 Jan. 1795, and 21 Jan. 1796, Charles City County Deeds, 4 (1789–1802). Eleven deeds in my study used the phrase "freedom is the natural right of all mankind and that it is my duty to do unto others as I would be done by in the like situation." Three were from Mecklenburg County, and eight were from Charles City County, the eleven representing the acts of eight individuals (Thomas Madkins wrote two deeds of manumission, and Samuel Hargrave three). I have been able to verify seven of these individuals as Quakers. In addition, Laurence Stephens, the lone manumitter in Wythe County, used a similar phrase. Probably nine of nineteen deeds of manumission filed in Charles City County were written by Quakers.

to free their slaves in 1791 and 1805, and Reubin Howard, whom Mitchell emancipated in 1790, had by 1799 purchased and liberated his wife and child. These four acts of manumission, all apparently springing from the actions of Edward Mitchell, accounted for nearly half of the nine manumissions by deed recorded in that county. In Lancaster County, in the northern Tidewater, the Methodist minister John Dogget seems to have been successful in persuading at least a couple of others to free slaves. In 1790 John Degges freed his enslaved woman Susannah on the same February day that Dogget emancipated his two slaves Samuel and Winney, and two other people manumitted slaves later that year, which stands out because manumission in that county was infrequent. Dogget also witnessed one other deed in 1798. Aside from the five acts of manumission probably influenced by Dogget, only seven other individuals emancipated slaves in Lancaster (three others by deed and four by will) in the entire generation from 1782 to 1806. Although the Methodist ministers Benjamin Dancy and John Bowry, of Charles City County, seem not to have inspired others to manumit those they held as slaves when they did so in 1793 and 1794, their failure seems more the exception than the rule. Perhaps simply a coincidence, nearly half of all the manumitters who could be identified as preachers (five of eleven) freed slaves in the single year of 1790, which helps explain the spike in the number of manumissions in that year.[21]

Among Baptists, too, identifiable individuals promoted manumission. When the Baptist minister George Layfield freed his three slaves in May of

21. Edward Mitchell to Stith Mead, 20 Mar. 1794, Stith Mead Letterbook, 57–58, VHS; Edward Mitchell deed, 25 Oct. 1790, Botetourt County Free Negro and Slave Records, Emancipation Papers, LVA, Archives Division; James Wright deed, 13 Sept. 1791, Botetourt County Deeds, 4 (1788–93), which shares similar language to Mitchell's deed; Samuel Mitchell deed, 31 Dec. 1805, Botetourt County Deeds, 9 (1805–9); Reubin Howard deed, 11 Jan. 1799, Botetourt County Deeds, 6 (1796–99); John Dogget deed, 15 Feb. 1790, Lancaster County Free Negro and Slave Records, Emancipation Deeds, LVA, Archives Division; John Degges deed, 15 Feb. 1790, ibid.; Jesse C. Ball deed, 19 July 1790, ibid.; William Cannan deed, 10 Oct. 1790, ibid.; William George deed, 17 Jan. 1798, Lancaster County Deeds, 25 (1803–12); Benjamin Dancy deed, 19 Sept. 1793, Charles City County Deeds, 4 (1789–1802); John Bowry deed, 16 Oct. 1794, ibid. Why so many ministers should have freed their slaves in 1790 remains a mystery. Nothing I have read in the secondary literature or in primary sources makes 1790 a particularly important year for religious antislavery activity. That was the year the Baptist General Committee urged Baptists to "make use of every legal measure, to extirpate the horrid evil from the land," but Baptists seem not to have taken heed of this message, as discussed below in chapter 3. *Minutes of the Baptist General Committee . . . 1790* (Richmond, n.d.), quoted in Daniel, "Virginia Baptists," 66.

1790 "for Divers good Causes," Levin Dix, a Baptist minister in later years, witnessed the deed and perhaps also approved granting the freed slaves the symbolic surname Ishmael. (Like Layfield's slaves, Ishmael had been cast out of his native land.)[22] A month later, no doubt encouraged by Layfield, Dix freed his own three slaves, "fully assured, that the Divine Author of the Universe, in his Justice, ordained, that Each and every one of the Human Species should have the Compleat Enjoyment of Personal Liberty." John Parker, a second witness to Preacher Layfield's deed, seems to have been similarly inspired by example; he also freed slaves that year, and may also have been a Baptist.[23]

The clusters of manumission around religious leaders who liberated the men and women they held in slavery and who encouraged others to do likewise reveal how much more important than ideas people were in promoting antislavery manumission. Membership in a community that contained individuals who passionately opposed slavery, who freed their own slaves, and who urged others to do the same could be a powerful impetus to action. Especially because manumitters who emancipated all their slaves were giving up so much—valuable property and the status that accompanied that wealth—community pressure, cajoling, and example were often necessary to help slaveholders translate antislavery ideals into the act of manumission. The links among manumitters, evident in the fact that they often served as witnesses to and borrowed language from one another's deeds, demonstrated the extent to which manumission was an event that took place in the context of an interested community, as the legislators had understood when they drafted the failed 1778 manumission bill. In contrast to the evident importance of com-

---

22. In Genesis 21 Sarah tells Abraham to cast out Ishmael, Abraham's son by his Egyptian servant Hagar, because she does not want Ishmael to be an equal heir to her son Isaac. Abraham is distressed by the idea until God tells Abraham that God will make a nation of Ishmael as well as of Isaac. His conscience eased, Abraham sends Hagar and Ishmael out into the desert. Layfield likely saw his slaves as both outcasts and part of a separate nation, so that the name Ishmael would be meaningful and fitting. George Layfield deed, 6 May 1790, Accomack County Free Negro and Slave Records, Affidavits and Certificates about Slavery, LVA, Archives Division.

23. Ibid.; Levin Dix deed, 14 June 1790, Accomack County Deeds, 7 (1788–93); John Parker deed, 29 April 1790, ibid. Layfield was identified as a "preacher the Gospel" in Accomack County tax records contemporary with his deed of manumission. Dix was an ordained minister by 1817, according to Accomack Association, Minutes, 1815–24, VBHS. It is not clear whether he was a Baptist minister in 1790, when he freed his slaves, because no records from that era remain. His association with Layfield makes it likely that he was by that time a member of the church.

munity in promoting manumission, there is no evidence that the several newspaper essays decrying slavery directly inspired Virginia slaveholders to free their slaves; there were no discernible spikes in the number of manumissions after such articles appeared, and there is no evidence of language borrowed from those essays except the general language of natural rights.

Overall, about 40 percent of the people who freed slaves in deeds of manumission could be identified as members or probable members of a particular religious community (see appendix A). Surprisingly, only one-sixth of those were Quakers, and most of them lived in three of the eight counties: Charles City, Mecklenburg, and Accomack. Perhaps relatively few Quaker manumitters appear in the records because they had already liberated their slaves before 1782, but this is not a fully convincing explanation because, as argued above, Friends knew that it was illegal to free slaves before 1782 and that any illegal emancipation could be challenged in court. The relatively small number of Quaker manumitters is more likely a reflection of the small number of Quakers resident in post-Revolutionary Virginia. The Friends were never a large group in Virginia, and their numbers diminished during the Revolutionary era with their strictures against military service and slaveholding.[24] By the mid-nineteenth century there were few Quakers and Quaker meetings left in the commonwealth. An even smaller number of manumitters could be identified as Baptists, and most of those were ministers whose names were found in surviving Baptist Association records and secondary sources. Other Baptist manumitters may go unidentified because Baptist church records of the period are scanty and rarely include full membership lists. The predominance of ministers among identified Baptists, however, is probably not just an artifact of the remaining evidence. Because the Baptist Church did not force its members to free their slaves, those who did so were among the most religious and most devoted members of the church. A much larger group of religious manumitters, about half of those whose religious affiliation could be identified, were members of the Methodist Church, many of them in Accomack County. Because Accomack had both more Methodists and more manumitters than other counties, evidence from that region may not be representative. Even so, it is clear that antislavery sentiment remained strong among some Methodists well after the national church backed away from its antislavery stance and that

24. Hinshaw, *Encyclopedia of American Quaker Genealogy*, shows that a number of young men were dismissed from the society because of their participation in the Revolutionary War and others because they refused to give up their slaves.

in other counties too, particularly Mecklenburg and Botetourt, Methodists formed a significant proportion of manumitters.

More surprising is that in Accomack County, which had the highest number and proportion of freed slaves among all the counties studied, there existed a strong secular antislavery community as well. There, some of the most prominent and well-connected citizens of the county freed large numbers of slaves. For example, Charles Stockly, a judge on the county court, freed the entirety of his slave property, thirty-three people, in September 1787. On the same day, Colonel William Parramore and John Teackle, also judges on the court and at different times members of the Episcopalian vestry, freed their slaves. They were joined by one other prominent Accomack citizen, George Corbin. Together the four men emancipated eighty-seven slaves in a single day. They all cited natural-rights philosophy in their deeds of manumission, declaring "the Equal right of Human Nature to Personal liberty."[25]

Parramore, who was active in the Methodist Church, was probably the instigator, influencing his friends and peers, who in turn witnessed additional deeds of manumission and were related to other emancipators, many of whom do not appear to have been Methodists. Corbin, for example, may have persuaded his nephew, John Cropper Jr., to free his sixteen slaves in 1794. Cropper was one of Accomack County's Revolutionary War heroes and a county leader in his own right. Later he became a general, a Federalist delegate to the Virginia House of Delegates, a state senator, and member of the Episcopalian vestry. Cropper's deed of manumission expressed his belief that "all men by Nature are equally free." His commitment to those ideals stretched back at least to his days as a soldier in the Revolutionary army. In 1777 Cropper explained why he intended to remain in the army rather than return to Accomack, which he sensed his wife and friends desired. His first motive, he wrote with emphasis, was his "love for *liberty* and the *rights of mankind*." He

---

25. John Teackle deed, 24 Sept. 1787; George Corbin deed, 25 Sept. 1787; William Parramore deed, 24 Sept. 1787; and Charles Stockly deed, 27 Sept. 1787, all in Accomack County Deeds, 6 (1783–88). Though the deeds were written on different days, they were all entered in court on 27 September 1787. Parramore was a member of the vestry of the then Anglican church in 1780, but a few years later he played host to Francis Asbury on his 1783 tour of the Eastern Shore. So it seems that by the time he freed his slaves Parramore was a Methodist. St. George's Parish, Accomack County, Vestry Book, 1763–87, LVA, Archives Division, photostat; Mariner, *Revival's Children*, 21. John Teackle was a member of the Episcopal vestry in 1810. St. George's Parish, Accomack County, Records, 1793–1841, 22, Eastern Shore Public Library.

expressed his commitment to the ideals of the Revolution in his support of education as well as emancipation: he was among the founders of Accomack County's first academy, established because its supporters believed that "the most effectual Means to transmit to Posterity the blessing of Freedom & the late glorious Revolution, is to enlighten the Minds of the rising Generation with knowledge and virtue." Judging from the words and items he left behind, Cropper was a religious and deeply thoughtful person, as well as an ardent patriot and Federalist. His estate included two pictures of George Washington (after whom he had named his son John Washington Cropper) and one each of Alexander Hamilton and the Massachusetts Federalist Fisher Ames.[26]

Others in Cropper's circle also freed slaves. Cropper's cousin by marriage John S. Ker, a wealthy merchant whose large Federal-style mansion currently serves as home to the Eastern Shore of Virginia Historical Society, freed all twenty-eight of his slaves shortly before his death. For years, he said, his mind had been "much exercised on the Subject" of the "evils of Slavery." Thomas Evans, also a friend of General Cropper's and like Cropper a Federalist delegate to the Virginia House of Delegates, freed three slaves in 1791. Thus, connections to a community, and not necessarily a religious community, were a crucial part of manumission in Accomack. The connections among manumitters and the number of shared last names is impressive: there were 93 last names for 147 manumitters (by deed). Many of the manumitters had served in the army or navy during the Revolution, and the politicians among them were Federalists. Because freeing slaves was accepted and even encouraged by some of that county's most powerful men, there existed in Accomack, as nowhere else in Virginia, a true culture of manumission.[27]

26. John Cropper to George Abbot, 24 May 1777, John Cropper Papers, photocopies from collection at Smith College, VHS, emphasis in the original; petition of Accomack and Northampton counties for an academy on the Eastern Shore, 6 Dec. 1786, LP, Accomack County; inventory of John Cropper's estate, Accomack County Wills (1824–25), 72–73. The academy was eventually called Margaret Academy, after Cropper's first wife. Cropper's estate also included a biography of Washington, a copy of Jay's treaty, two histories of Quakers, Montesquieu's *Spirit of the Laws*, a family Bible, and his gold epaulets.

27. John S. Ker deed, 4 Mar. 1806, Accomack County Free Negro and Slave Records, Manumissions, 1783–1814. Ker's cousin was Cropper's second wife. Anthony Iaccarino suggests that Federalists were more able to support manumission because they envisioned society hierarchically, with different classes having different degrees of privilege; Republicans, by contrast, with their emphasis on equality, could not imagine welcoming blacks into that equal world. Iaccarino, "Virginia and the National Contest over Slavery," 56–57, 99.

Something unusual happened on Virginia's Eastern Shore: the ideals of the Revolution, devotion to liberty and the equal rights of all people, took deep root. Economic conditions, of course, provided the basis for the culture of manumission that evolved there. The relatively small percentage of slaves in the county and their nonessential role in an economy no longer dependent on plantation agriculture made it easier for slaveowners to free them. But economic factors were not sufficient in themselves to foster manumission: Lancaster County, with a similar economy, did not see many emancipations. Another obvious influence on manumission in Accomack was the spread of Methodism there and the influence of Quakers, including the Mifflins. But Methodists in other places did not free as many slaves as in Accomack, and the number of Quakers in the county was relatively small. The experience of fighting for liberty seems also to have spurred manumission in Accomack. John Cropper Jr.'s participation in the War for Independence, for example, affected his daily life, shaped his values, and encouraged him to emancipate his slaves. But in other counties Revolutionary War veterans and local elites, such as George Hancock in Botetourt County (the future father-in-law of the explorer William Clark), did not usually manumit all their slaves. Hancock freed only two of his eleven slaves, and he did so not because he recognized their right to freedom but because his father had intended to liberate them "in consideration of their faithful services." If neither economy, religion, nor Revolutionary War experience alone accounted for Accomack's high rate of manumission, the combination of those factors, together with the fortuitous collection of powerful personalities, such as Cropper, Corbin, and Ker, *did* create a unique environment that fostered emancipation. It is also possible that Accomack's unique post-Revolutionary history had its roots in the midseventeenth century, when free blacks in Accomack County could achieve a status more or less equal to whites', though it is difficult to draw any direct connection between the two eras. If historians want to find in Virginia a society where manumission indicated a society moving away from slavery, they should look to the Eastern Shore, which, separated by the Chesapeake Bay from the rest of Virginia, followed a path distinct from that of the mainland. But even there, as discussed below in chapters 3 and 4, resistance to manumission ran high.[28]

28. George Hancock deed, 15 Dec. 1797, Botetourt County Free Negro and Slave Records, Emancipation Papers, LVA, Archives Division; Botetourt County Personal Property Tax Records, 1796, LVA, Microfilm Collections. On Hancock see Stoner, *Seed-Bed of the Republic*, 296; on Accomack in the seventeenth century see Breen and Innes, *Myne Owne Ground*.

MANUMISSION AT THE TURN OF THE CENTURY

In most of Virginia, and in most of the period during which manumission was feasible, things were quite different. For the majority of white manumitters at the turn of the century liberating slaves served as a way to reward one or two favored individuals for their good service rather than as a way to enact deeply held convictions that slavery was wrong. In slightly more than half the manumissions by deed enacted from 1794 to 1806 emancipators freed slaves in exchange for money or good service or in accordance with a will or the terms upon which the slave had been acquired. In total, fewer than a quarter of all deeds of manumission written from 1794 to 1806 included antislavery statements.[29] In addition, slaveholders usually delayed the date of effective freedom in this period, and in contrast to the pattern in the earlier period they did so not simply to comply with the law that barred emancipation of children; about 40 percent of those who awaited delayed emancipations would be past the age of majority when they acquired their liberty (in cases in which the age of the slave at freedom could be determined).[30] Another indication of the shifting meaning of manumission is that from 1794 to 1806 slightly fewer than 40 percent of manumitters (by deed) liberated all their bondspeople, compared with the 70 percent who had done so in 1782–93. Increasingly, slaveowners waited until their own death to set their slaves at liberty rather than manumit slaves during their lifetime, so the number of emancipations by will increased as a proportion of all acts of emancipation (see table 2), and as a general rule slaveholders who freed slaves in their wills were less likely to liberate all of them than those who emancipated slaves by deed.[31] In addition, starting in the

---

29. The proportion of antislavery deeds among all the documents, including those that gave no reason for freeing slaves, was 23 percent from 1794 to 1806. James Sidbury, in *Ploughshares into Swords,* found that in Richmond and in Henrico County about 35 percent of slaves freed from 1782 to 1806 were liberated by manumitters who "probably rejected slavery," while the rest were probably freed for other reasons (210–11). See also Stevenson, *Life in Black and White,* 264.

30. Fifty-five percent of the slaves freed from 1794 to 1806 would not receive their freedom immediately. In 121 cases of delayed manumissions from this period I could determine the age at freedom, and in 46 of those cases the age was greater than twenty-one. For more on delayed manumission see below.

31. Just over one-third of those who emancipated slaves in their wills—27 out of 75 documents in which the evidence was clear—freed the entirety of their slave property. Overall, about half of the cases of manumission by deed (72 out of the 142 documents for which I was able to make a determination) represented the slaveholder's total divestiture from slavery.

mid-1790s, African Americans played a larger role in effecting manumissions. More enslaved people purchased their own freedom, and several free blacks, mostly men, purchased and manumitted family members.

It is important to note that this second stage in which manumission was not primarily an antislavery act involved more slaveowners than the first and probably would have persisted were it not for the change in the law in 1806. Even though manumission may have been affected by news of the Saint Domingue revolution, since there was a decline in the total number of slaves freed in 1791–92, the overall pattern of manumission at the end of the century was stable: a few slaveowners freed a few slaves each year for often personal and singular reasons. William Ball, for example, freed Luke, "the late Stage Driver," for his "many faithful services," and William Chilton similarly freed George "in consideration of the honesty and general good conduct of my negro man Slave George." Sevére Gallé, "Merchant of the County of Lancaster," liberated "my Negroe fellow Duke" in consideration of Duke's "uniform good conduct and behavior" but also in "consideration of Forty pounds Virginia currency to me in hand paid." Hardyman Irby emancipated Eliza because he had promised to do so when he bought her; his deed noted that "part of the consideration of which purchase is that the said slave is to have her freedom at the end of five years from this date together with all her future increase." Many others freed slaves for "divers good causes and Considerations," as Gideon Johnson did when he emancipated Judy Patience.[32]

These examples hint at the ways enslaved Virginians helped shape manumission and also at how the possibility of manumission might have modified slaves' and masters' behavior toward each other. It is likely that at some point before they were manumitted Luke and George perceived that they might be freed if they were honest and true and that they then behaved accordingly or made more of a show of how loyal and faithful they were. Almost certainly Duke had made an agreement with Gallé years or months before his emancipation and knew that he would be liberated if he continued his "good conduct" and paid Gallé forty pounds. And surely Eliza understood from the time she was purchased by Irby that liberty was in her future. Those manumitted for "divers good causes and considerations" probably also had an inkling

32. William Ball deed, 27 Nov. 1802, Chesterfield County Deeds, 16 (1802–5); William Chilton deed, 24 Apr. 1804, Fauquier County Deeds, 15 (1801–4); Sevére Gallé deed, 16 Aug. 1796, Lancaster County Deeds, 23 (1793–1803); Hardyman Irby deed, 23 Nov. 1797, Charles City County Deeds, 4 (1789–1802); Gideon Johnson deed, 26 Mar. 1800, Fauquier County Deeds, 14 (1798–1801).

that liberty might be theirs if through loyal service and upright behavior they persuaded their owners that they deserved it. The expectation or hope of freedom thus altered the relationship between master and slave. Not only might enslaved Virginians like Eliza and Luke be more compliant, knowing that freedom was coming, but masters might be more flexible and more trusting of their slaves' loyalty, figuring that a slave who looked forward to his or her manumission would be less likely to take freedom illegally by running away. Perhaps, too, knowing that one's slave would soon be free changed a master's view of his or her slave from a chattel to a potential member of the community. Manumission could be humanizing even before it took effect, and that certainly shaped how owners treated enslaved people and how enslaved people expected to be treated by their soon-to-be former owners.

Deep ironies and contradictions lay in rewarding excellence in slavery with freedom from slavery. Why would one expect a person so good at being subservient to succeed at being free and independent? If slavery was a good institution, why was emancipation the reward for being a good slave? Of special significance to the history of manumission in Virginia was that manumission or its promise could encourage enslaved people to behave well, thus strengthening rather than weakening the master's hold over his slave, at least in the period before the emancipation took place. And the example provided to other enslaved people might encourage them to seek manumission through loyal and good service to their masters. Freedom could support slavery.

Richard Drummond Bayly, an Accomack County delegate to the House of Delegates who freed his slave Caleb in 1805, understood this fact and argued passionately that manumission was important and even necessary to a stable slave system. It would be unjust, he wrote, to "forever shut the door of the hope of freedom against this unfortunate portion of the human species, To say that no Servant however meritorious his conduct may be shall be freed by a master." Moreover, if manumission were not possible, slaves would have little reason to try to satisfy their masters' wishes. Would not, he asked, "the servants relax in their endeavour to please when they know that the great Reward which probably prompts them to the faithful discharge of their duty can never be bestowed upon them?" Bayly knew that emancipation was rare, but he also understood that a distant hope could still have a powerful effect. "Is it not Sir the idea of being at some future period free (althou' the hope frequently proves elusive) which makes them [slaves] in some measure contented with their condition and proves a security for the peace of families?" Furthermore, the lack of any legitimate possibility of freedom would put pressure on the slave system, perhaps causing that fragile vessel to explode. Manumission could be seen as a safety valve, releasing pressure and thus preventing violence and insurrection. As Bayly put it, "[W]ill not the withdrawing of this only hope from their minds instead of returning or of preventing accelerate & bring forth all the horrors of domestic insurrections? Freedom is the ardent wish of all mankind." Since the discipline of slavery could be enforced through reward as well as punishment, and since "freedom is the ardent wish of all mankind," liberty was the ultimate promise one could make to a slave in order to extract dutiful and loyal service. As time passed, more and more slaveowners in Virginia began to view manumission in that light, which explains why more people freed slaves, especially in their wills, in the 1790s than in the 1780s. Like so many slaveholders in other slave societies, they had come to understand that manumission played an integral role in maintaining a secure system of slavery and could benefit masters by encouraging good behavior in their slaves.[33]

As slaveowners were figuring out how to use manumission as a tool to promote slave discipline, enslaved and free blacks were also learning how the new law could work to their advantage even when slaveowners did not seem favorably disposed to manumit their chattels. After the mid-1790s an increasing number of African Americans like Duke managed either to buy their own freedom or to purchase and liberate members of their family, suggesting that it took a decade or so after the passage of the manumission law for the members of Virginia's African American community to develop the resources, networks, and knowledge necessary to free themselves and others. Altogether, enslaved Virginians who purchased their own freedom and free blacks who emancipated friends and family members accounted for 14 percent of the deeds of manumission filed in the eight counties from 1782 to 1806 and in the years 1794–1806 they accounted for 18 percent, nearly one-fifth of all acts of manumission by deed. Clearly it is a mistake to view manumission as a reflection only of whites' feelings about slavery since blacks' desire to be free and their ability to help one another realize that desire were responsible for a significant portion of the emancipations that took place in the generation after the Revolution, especially in the late 1790s and early 1800s.

33. Richard Drummond Bayly to John Cropper, 6 Jan. 1805, John Cropper Papers. Caleb bought his freedom for eighty pounds, which was secured to Bayly by bond. Bayly trusted Caleb to raise the funds at some future date. Richard D. Bayly deed, 19 Nov. 1805, Accomack County Deeds, 11 (1804–7).

In the counties examined here, twenty-two enslaved people purchased their own freedom (not counting those freed for token payments only), although occasionally the money was delivered through another party, as in the case of James, who paid one hundred dollars "through his wife Dority Hill" (see table 3). Acts of manumission by self-purchase account for about one-twelfth of all the acts of manumission by deed in the eight counties from 1782 to 1806 and for about one-eighth of the manumissions by deed from 1794 to 1806. Judging from information contained in the deeds of manumission, as well as other evidence, the enslaved people who bought their freedom shared certain characteristics. They were independent and willful, yet respectful of their masters. Many were skilled and in violation of the law against slave self-hire had probably been allowed to hire themselves out and earn their own wages. Reflecting the greater earning power of men and the greater likelihood that they would be allowed to hire themselves out, more than three-quarters of the slaves who bought their freedom were male. Often the amounts they paid for their freedom were substantial, ranging from forty to one hundred pounds. Because slave prices varied widely according to age and skill level, factors not revealed in the surviving documents, it is difficult to compare their self-purchase price with their market price, but at least one slave bought himself for more than his estimated worth. Solomon, who had been valued at seventy-five pounds in Abel West's estate, purchased himself a few months later for eighty-eight pounds.[34]

It appears to have been more difficult for African Americans to liberate others, since probably only ten free men of color and one free woman of color were able to wrest friends and family members from bondage either by purchasing and then manumitting them or by paying substantial sums to their owners,

---

34. Thomas Leatherbury deed, 26 Nov. 1805, Accomack County Deeds, 11 (1804–7); "Valuation of Abel West's estate," 6 Aug. 1804, Accomack County Wills, 1804–6. It is possible that three others purchased their freedom, although the documents indicate that white men paid to have them freed. Perhaps the owners would not accept money from the enslaved people themselves (recognizing that slaves could not, strictly speaking, purchase anything) and demanded it from others, or perhaps the payers (about whom I was not able to discover more) were philanthropists. See John Heveningham deed, 11 Sept. 1797, Chesterfield County Deeds, 14 (1795–1800) (freeing Holly for £80); John Heaveningham deed, 9 Jan. 1800, Chesterfield County Deeds, 15 (1800–1802) (freeing Fanny for £37); and Robert Pitt deed, 25 May 1790, Accomack County Deeds, 7 (1788–93) (freeing Durham for £14). James Sidbury found a similar proportion of Richmond City and Henrico County manumissions enacted by free blacks and also discusses the practice of slave self-hire in *Ploughshares into Swords*, 192, 211.

TABLE 3. Manumission by self-purchase

Year of deed	Manumittee	Sex	Amount paid	Manumitter	County
1787	Derry	M	£50	John and Mary McEntire	Botetourt
1796	Duke	M	£40	Sevére Gallé	Lancaster
1796	Tom Jessup	M	£50	Thomas Gaskins	Lancaster
1797	Frank	M	£40	William Silverthorn and Joseph Wagonman	Accomack
1798	James	M	£60	Jesse Ward	Accomack
1799	Sancho	M	$50	Martin Pickett	Fauquier
1800	Fanny	F	£40	Enock Foley	Fauquier
1801	Thomas Kirk	M	£60	Anne Eustace and Hancock Eustace	Fauquier
1802	Solomon Downing	M	£40	John Downing and Robinson Savage	Accomack
1803	Robin	M	£75	William Justice	Accomack
1803	Patty	F	$100	Cornelius Buck	Chesterfield
1804	Solomon	M	£88	Henry Parker	Accomack
1805	Caleb	M	£80	Richard D. Bayly	Accomack
1805	Chriss Laws	F	$100	Doddridge Chichester of Fairfax County	Lancaster
1806	James	M	£100	Thomas Leatherbury	Accomack
1806	Davy	M	£70	Thomas Chilton	Fauquier
1806	Westley, Lewis, and William	M	$100	George Herndon	Fauquier
1806	Nace Pile	M	£73 15s 4d.	William Mann	Fauquier
1806	Hannah	F	$50	Joseph Hale	Fauquier
1806 (or 1805)	Betty Parker	F	$200	George Pickett	Fauquier

SOURCES: Deed and will books for Accomack, Botetourt, Charles City, Chesterfield, Fauquier, Lancaster, Mecklenburg, and Wythe counties, 1782–1806.

who then drafted deeds of manumission.[35] (The total number is "probably" eleven because free blacks were not always identified as African American on

35. Not counted here or in the study as a whole—because no extant document records her manumission and she is not listed in *Fauquier County, Virginia Register of Free Negroes*—is the somewhat unusual case of Moll, purchased by her husband, Sancho, in 1792, while he was still himself enslaved, and presumably freed by him after she helped him pay for his own liberty. See

the available documents, but other evidence points to that conclusion.) Three of the free black manumitters, including Reubin Howard, mentioned above, had themselves been manumitted several years earlier and subsequently purchased their wives and children. Howard had been freed in 1790, and it took him nearly a decade, until 1799, to be able to buy and free his wife and son. His deed reflected his continuing relationship with his former owner, Edward Mitchell, who witnessed it, and it indicated his own humble station and lack of literacy, as it was signed only with his mark. When Caesar Maddison, a free African American, liberated his slave Nancy the following year, he was probably acting similarly, although he left his relationship to Nancy unstated. Mary Griffin, "a free woman" in Accomack, purchased Cyrus Rose Arrow in November 1804 and freed him a few days later in a deed of manumission. The deed was witnessed by two men who, like Griffin, signed with their marks, which was unusual for white men of that era but common for former slaves. While the evidence is sparse, it is almost certain that Mary Griffin and the two witnesses were all free people of color and that they worked together to effect Cyrus Arrow's liberty and to welcome him to Accomack's growing free black community.[36]

More rarely, African Americans gained manumission through a suit for freedom. The two cases in this study in which slaves sued their owners and consequently prompted them to draw up deeds of manumission both took place in Accomack County, probably because travel back and forth across the border with Maryland could provide the grounds for a successful suit according to the anti-importation law of 1778. Such was the case for George, who worked for more than a year in Virginia after his arrival there from Maryland, where his owner, Thomas Wood Potter, resided. Perhaps he learned of his right to freedom under the 1778 law from fellow African Americans, or perhaps he learned of it from some of the antislavery Quakers or Methodists in the area.

Martin Pickett deed, 8 Jan. 1799, Fauquier County Deeds, 14 (1798–1801); and certificate of sale of slave to husband, ibid., 874.

36. Edward Mitchell deed, 25 Oct. 1790, Botetourt County Free Negro and Slave Records, Emancipation Papers, LVA, Archives Division; Reubin Howard deed, 11 Jan. 1799, Botetourt County Deeds, 6 (1796–99); Caesar Maddison deed, 23 July 1800, Fauquier County Deeds, 14 (1798–1800); Thomas M. Bayly deed, 5 Nov. 1804, Accomack County Deeds, 11 (1804–7); Mary Griffin deed, 16 Nov. 1804, ibid. It is clear that Mary Griffin was African American, or else there would have been no reason to identify her as free. See also Sidbury, *Ploughshares into Swords,* 211; and Stevenson, *Life in Black and White,* 260–64.

After George sued Potter in the Virginia courts, Potter manumitted him in 1794, "alas to prevent further Litigation concerning his claim to freedom," and further wished that George might have "all the Happiness of Freedom." Similarly, Major gained his liberty when in 1800 his owner, Anna Maria Andrews, liberated him "in consequence of a Suit in the District Court . . . instituted by major for his freedom against me."[37]

When enslaved people bought or sued for their freedom and when free blacks bought and emancipated family members, white people facilitated the process, demonstrating that even slaveowners who remained committed to the institution of slavery often sympathized with the desire of enslaved people to be free. Aid might be minimal, allowing a slave to purchase his or her freedom—one did not have to agree to such a scheme—or agreeing to sell a slave to a party who intended to free him or her. White attorneys provided more direct help when they represented enslaved people in suits for freedom, and slaveowners sometimes made manumission by self-purchase easier by extending their slaves credit and emancipating them before the full fee was paid. Every so often other white members of the community provided aid by giving enslaved men and women money or loans. Tom Jessup, in Lancaster County, had the assistance of several white members of the neighborhood who raised a subscription to help him purchase his freedom in 1796. Perhaps Jessup held a special status in the county, since he shared his name with a Thomas Jesop (his father or grandfather?) who was freed in 1751, one of the few slaves liberated in mid-eighteenth-century Virginia.[38]

Two other types of manumission also revealed the complexity of the relationships between masters and slaves and underscored that manumission did not necessarily evince white antislavery sentiment. On occasion slaveowners freed their slave mistresses. This form of manumission was rare in Virginia and thus contrasted sharply with the practice of manumission in many slave societies, especially in the Islamic world, where freedom commonly devolved to concubines who gained legitimacy through emancipation. In Virginia the law prohibited interracial marriages, and the racial orthodoxy predicated against

37. Thomas Wood Potter deed, 7 Jan. 1794, Accomack County Deeds, 8 (1793–97); Anna Maria Andrews deed, 4 Nov. 1800, Accomack County Deeds, 10 (1800–1804). For more discussion of freedom suits see Nicholls, "Squint of freedom." For a discussion of the 1778 law see chapter 1, above.

38. Thomas Gaskins deed, 17 Apr. 1796, Lancaster County Free Negro and Slave Records, Emancipation Deeds, LVA, Archives Division; Jonathan Steptoe deed, 7 June 1751, ibid.

a man's admitting in a deed or will of manumission that his slave was also his mistress and the mother of his children. Alexander Banks, for example, did not state that Nancy Fraction and her light-skinned children were his kin when he freed them in his 1806 will "in consideration of the true, faithful, and honest manner" in which they had conducted themselves. Only the circumstances of his act of emancipation point to that conclusion. Banks directed that the three boys, who took his surname rather than that of their mother, be taught to "read, write and cypher, and that they be bound out at the age of Fourteen to some good man to learn the Carpenter's trade." Alexander Banks was not simply a humanitarian; he also directed in his will that his five remaining slaves be sold. Furthermore, the free black register of Chesterfield County, where they lived, suggests that the father of Nancy's children was white since she was labeled "brown" and her sons George Banks and Thomas Banks were called "Yellow" and "mulatto," respectively. While the evidence is not so pointed, it is difficult to understand why Jesse Withers would have bought Sarah from Edward Burgess only to turn around and free her "in Consideration of the Services Rendered me by Negro Sarah" unless he and Sarah had developed a close, probably sexual relationship.[39]

In contrast to these apparent bonds of affection, some manumitters acted very uncharitably and contrary to the intention of the law when they freed their elderly slaves in order to be rid of the responsibility of feeding and clothing them. Samuel and William Goodson said that they freed James Walles, whom it seems they had known since childhood, "for the special value and regard they bear towards a negroe man slave named or called James Walles." But freeing Walles may not have been the generous act they portrayed it to be, since at the time Walles was forty-five years old and had recently been given to Samuel and William by the terms of their mother's will. At his age James was of little financial value to the Goodson brothers, so it was no great economic sacrifice for them to liberate him, and they failed to comply with the law's provision to guarantee his support. While the Goodsons' motives regarding James Walles remain unclear, that nearly one-eighth of the slaves whose ages

39. Patterson, *Slavery and Social Death*, 228–32; Alexander Banks will, 4 June 1806, and codicil, 17 July 1807, probated 14 Dec. 1807, Chesterfield County Wills, 3 (1774–85); Chesterfield County Register of Free Negroes, No. 1, 1804–30, LVA, Microfilm Collections, entries 565, 533, and 485; Jesse Withers deed, 25 Feb. 1799, Fauquier County Deeds, 14 (1798–1801). For more on interracial relationships and the impropriety of admitting them openly despite their frequency see Rothman, *Notorious in the Neighborhood*.

were given in both deeds and wills were forty years or older suggests that a significant minority of manumitters freed slaves only when the slaves were worth little to them and had perhaps become a burden. Furthermore, almost no manumitters promised in their instruments of emancipation to support aged slaves according to the terms of the law.[40]

In 1805 and 1806 the ways Virginians utilized manumission changed again as the number of emancipations swelled in response to anticipated amendments to the manumission law; legislative discussions of those years even suggested manumission might be banned altogether. So slaveowners wishing their slaves to be free acted before the new statute took effect. Most of the manumissions of those years, however, set the actual date of freedom at some point months, years, or even decades into the future. While as a society Virginians made the decision to limit the number of free blacks and to try to exclude them from the commonwealth with the 1806 amendment, in their local communities individual Virginians chose otherwise. This disjunction between legislative action and community response demonstrated again white Virginians' ambivalence about emancipation and their failure to make coherent sense of slavery in the post-Revolutionary period, just as the practice and uses of manumission underscored the complexity of master-slave relationships and the various, sometimes contradictory meanings manumission could have. It is almost certain that had there been no 1806 law, there would have been no spike in the number of manumissions in 1805–6 and that manumission would have continued in Virginia as it had since the 1790s, a relatively fixed, if uncommon, aspect of an entrenched and secure institution.

ECONOMIC CONSIDERATIONS AND EMANCIPATION

One of the great questions concerning manumission is to what extent economic factors shaped the practice. In part this question arises out of a desire to test the assumption that where the local economy was moving away from the staple-crop agriculture associated with slavery, slaveholders began to manumit slaves more often and to adopt attitudes less favorable to slavery. More broadly, historians have been interested in investigating the extent to which slaveholders were businesspeople responding rationally to the dictates of the marketplace or premodern, "precapitalist quasi-aristocratic land-

---

40. Samuel S. and William G. Goodson deed, 14 Apr. 1806, Chesterfield County Deeds, 17 (1805–8).

owners" whose "acquisitive spirit" was channeled into honor and status more than the accumulation of money for its "own sake," a thesis famously formulated by Eugene Genovese in *The Political Economy of Slavery* (1965) and debated ever since.[41] As the examples above indicate, manumission in early national Virginia was often a personal act, arising out of convictions that slavery was wrong, out of special relationships between masters and slaves, or out of enslaved and free blacks' love of liberty, so in many cases economic calculations were minimal. On the other hand, the number of slaves freed who were over forty years of age suggests that slaveowners did respond in part to economic factors. Additional data on the age and sex of slaves at emancipation, which varied between rural and urban areas, on differences in manumission among different regions, and on the frequency of delayed manumission also point to the subtle and complicated influence of economic factors on manumission in Virginia.

The age of slaves at the time of their emancipation, which correlated to their value since young adults were considered the best workers, indicates that most manumitters did not free slaves only when they were worth little. On average, manumitted slaves were about twenty-six years old when freed, still prime hands and valuable property. Furthermore, this study found no discernible difference between the average age at which slaves were freed in the Tidewater, where tobacco production was generally in decline, and the average age at which they were freed in the Piedmont, where tobacco production and plantation agriculture were increasing in the 1790s. Men, generally the most expensive slaves, tended to be slightly older at the time of their emancipation than women, 26.8 versus 25.1 years old for slaves freed by deed, but this is probably an artifact of the different ages of majority for males and females—21 for males and 18 for females—since many slaves were freed when they reached adulthood.[42]

The predominance of men over women among freed slaves is also at odds with the notion that slaveholders generally freed their least valuable slaves. On the whole, 56 percent of the slaves freed in the eight counties were men or boys—57 percent of those freed by deed, 54 percent of those freed by will,

---

41. Genovese, *Political Economy of Slavery*, 23, 28.

42. Peter Albert did find a difference in the age at freedom between the Tidewater and the Piedmont in "Protean Institution" but concluded that overall, "economic factors seem to have placed no significant role in encouraging manumission" (288–89).

where sex could be determined—and the sex ratio seems to have changed little, if any, over time. The higher number of men among freed slaves resulted partly from the fact that more men than women were able to purchase their own freedom. Especially in rural areas, enslaved men had greater access to skilled and paid employment than did women and were more frequently able to accrue the cash with which to liberate themselves. Males' greater capacity for self-purchase accounts, however, for only part of the sex imbalance among freed slaves. One possibility is that enslaved men proved more difficult for masters to control than women—evidence shows that they ran away more often—and that masters might consequently have agreed to free them after a certain number of years of good service. Stephen Whitman provides evidence that masters in neighboring Maryland sometimes promised their slaves freedom at a future date directly in response to the slaves' efforts to liberate themselves by running away. Another reason more enslaved men than women found their way to freedom probably had to do with manumitters' judgments about which of their slaves could support themselves if emancipated. Almost certainly, men were seen as better able to care for themselves, especially in rural areas, where survival often depended on being able to work the land. Enslaved women, by contrast, were doubly dependent—as women and as slaves—so it was more difficult to imagine them as self-supporting and free.[43]

The opposite held true in cities, where more than half of the freed slaves were female and where the urban economy provided better conditions for manumission than did the countryside. It was usually in urban areas that slaveowners allowed their enslaved workers to hire out their own time and keep a portion of their earnings, which made it easier for slaves there to purchase their freedom. The frequent use of hired slaves by urban employers reflected the needs of the relatively fluid, cash-based, market-oriented economies of cities like Richmond. For women, urban centers provided paid work that did not exist in the countryside, especially domestic service and laundry work, which may have promoted their emancipation in two ways. First, urban enslaved women had opportunities to do extra work on their "own" time in ex-

43. In my study men made up 55 percent of the slaves freed during the years 1782–91 and 58 percent of those freed in 1792–1806. The pattern was similar for the counties studied by Albert in "Protean Institution," 289–90. Gerald Mullin shows in *Flight and Rebellion* that in eighteenth-century Virginia men ran away more often than women. For the Maryland pattern see Whitman, *Price of Freedom*, chap. 3. For one (female) slave's attempt to obtain legal freedom in exchange for returning to her master see the account of Ona Judge in Wiencek, *Imperfect God*, 40, 321–34.

change for money with which they could then buy their freedom, which may have been the case for Patty, who resided in the town of Manchester and raised the impressive sum of one hundred dollars to buy her liberty in 1803. Second, the availability of employment for city women might have encouraged masters to free female slaves, confident that those women could support themselves once liberated, a logic similar to that which might have promoted manumission for men in the rural areas. It is also important that in urban centers a relatively high percentage of emancipators were free blacks, many of whom had migrated there to find work. The decisions made by urban free people of color accounted in large measure for the patterns of manumission in those areas, and it seems that given the choice, free African Americans preferred to free women since slave status followed the condition of the mother and a free woman's children were thus guaranteed their liberty, while a free man's were not.[44]

If the urban economy fostered manumission, and especially manumission for women, frontier conditions predicated against it. In general, a greater proportion of slaveholders freed slaves in older counties, and a smaller proportion freed slaves in newly settled regions. About 10 percent of slaveholders freed slaves in the Tidewater counties of Accomack, Charles City, and Chesterfield over the twenty-five-year period 1782–1806 (see table 4). In the more recently settled counties of the Piedmont, Valley, and Trans-Allegheny regions between 1 percent and 4 percent of slaveholders freed slaves in that twenty-five-year period. Peter Albert found similar regional variations, with rising numbers of emancipations in the larger towns after the 1780s, high numbers of manumissions in the southern Tidewater, slightly lower numbers in the

44. Albert found that between 54 percent and 61 percent of the slaves freed in the four urban areas he examined were women. Tommy Bogger, Suzanne Lebsock, and James Sidbury also found more women freed in Virginia's urban areas: Bogger found that 62 percent of the adults manumitted in Norfolk were women; Lebsock found that about three-fifths of the adults freed by whites in Petersburg were women; Sidbury found that "just under 54% of the slaves manumitted between 1782 and 1810 in Richmond and Henrico were women." Albert, "Protean Institution," 290; Bogger, *Free Blacks in Norfolk*, 13; Lebsock, *Free Women of Petersburg*, 95; Sidbury, *Ploughshares into Swords*, 224n. Patty was freed in Cornelius Buck's deed, 28 July 1803, Chesterfield County Deeds, 16 (1802–5). My own study includes the towns of Manchester, in Chesterfield County, and Warrenton, in Fauquier County, but there were so few emancipated slaves in those two towns that my data are inconclusive. On the preference for freeing women of childbearing years see also Stevenson, *Life in Black and White*, 262–63.

TABLE 4. Manumitters as a proportion of all slaveholders, 1782–1806

County	Number of deeds of manumission	Number of individuals who freed slaves by deed[a]	Number of individuals who freed slaves by will	Approximate number of slaveholding heads of household in county[b]	Proportion of manumitters (by deed) to slaveholding households	Proportion of manumitters (by will) to slaveholding households	Proportion of all manumitters to slaveholding households	Approximate annual rate of manumitting
Chesterfield	32	29	13	410 (1790)	7.1%	3.1%	10.2%	0.41%
Accomack	149	146	64	2,025 (1800)	7.2	3.2	10.3	0.41
Charles City	19	17	6	249 (1795)	6.8	2.4	9.2	0.39
Botetourt	9	10	2	284 (1787)	3.5	.7	4.2	0.18
Lancaster	8	8	4	305 (1790)	2.6	1.3	3.9	0.16
Fauquier	28	31	4	946 (1800)	3.3	0.4	3.7	0.15
Mecklenburg	14	12	6	724 (1790)	1.6	0.8	2.4	0.10
Wythe	1	1	0	200 (1810)	.5	0	.5	0.002
Total	260	254	99	5,143	4.9	1.9	6.7	0.27

SOURCES: Botetourt County Personal Property Tax Records, 1787; Chesterfield County Personal Property Tax Records, 1790; Lancaster County Personal Property Tax Records, 1790; Mecklenburg County Personal Property Tax Records, 1790; Charles City County Personal Property Tax Records, 1795; Fauquier County Personal Property Tax Records, 1800; *Return of the Whole Number of Persons* (1800); *Aggregate amount of each descriptions of Persons*; deed and will books from the eight counties, 1782–1806.

[a] Some people freed slaves on several occasions, and sometimes several people (co-owners) signed a single deed.

[b] The year chosen for slaveholding heads of household depended on available data from census enumerations or tax lists. Census data were preferable to tax data because after 1789 slaves under twelve were not taxed and did not appear on tax lists. If I had a choice, I chose the year with fewer slaveholding heads of household. Any error will thus overestimate the proportion of people who freed slaves, strengthening my point that the percentages (even if overestimated) were small. Chesterfield: 67% of 612 families, 1790 tax list; Accomack: 45% of 4,500 households (sampling method used), 1800 census; Charles City: households with slaves over sixteen, 1795 tax list; Botetourt: approximate number of slaveholding households from 1787 tax list; Lancaster: count from 1790 tax list; Fauquier: 43% of about 2,200 households in 1800 taxes (sampling method used); Mecklenburg: approximate number of households with slaves over sixteen, 1790 tax list; Wythe: approximate number of slaveholding households from 1810 census (sampling method used).

northern Tidewater, "and still less in the fall zone and Piedmont." The relatively low number of manumissions in the Piedmont reflected the fact that since slaves there were of increasing economic importance few people were willing to part with them. Certainly that seems to have been the case in the Piedmont county of Mecklenburg, where the tobacco economy was rising and where those who did manumit their slaves were usually associated either with the Methodists or with the Quakers, who were guided more by ideological than by economic concerns. The higher number of manumissions in the Tidewater resulted not only from the declining importance of slavery there but also from the social conditions of Virginia's oldest region, where cohesive community networks, especially religious communities, both encouraged manumission and could help integrate freed slaves into society. By contrast, the slaveholders west of the Blue Ridge, in places such as Botetourt and Wythe counties, lived a more isolated existence often beyond the reach of communities that could encourage manumission. Perhaps of equal importance, the slaveholders who had trekked westward had brought their slaves with them for a purpose—to help them build farms and roads out of thick forests—and were unlikely to liberate them even though the economy in those regions did not depend on staple-crop agriculture.[45]

But it would be wrong to assume that the connection between the character of the local economy and the number of manumissions was a neat one and that manumission always occurred more often in the Tidewater, where slavery was stagnating or declining, and less often in the Piedmont, where slavery was expanding. Though the number of manumissions in the Piedmont county of Mecklenburg, where slavery was on the increase, was relatively low compared with the number in Tidewater Accomack County, it was still higher proportionately than in Tidewater Lancaster, a county that was actually losing slave population, indicating a weak slave economy that ought to have promoted manumission. One might also guess that the large number of manumissions in Accomack was associated with an overall decline in the number of slaves there, but that is not the case (see table 5).[46]

45. Albert, "Protean Institution," 293.
46. Peter Albert came to similar conclusions in ibid., 280–82. Also, it is important to note that areas with declining slave populations did *not* necessarily see rises in the free black population. Tidewater Chesterfield, for example, actually lost free black population from 1790 to 1810, probably because the county was close to Richmond and freed slaves could migrate there

TABLE 5. Change in the slave population compared with the number of manumissions

County	Slaves, 1790	Slaves, 1800	Slaves, 1810	Slaves freed, 1782–1806	Change in slave population, 1790–1810	Percentage change in slave population, 1790–1810
Tidewater						
Accomack	4,262	4,429	4,542	809	+280	+ 6.6%
Chesterfield	7,487	7,852	6,015	149	-1,472	-19.7
Charles City	3,141	3,013	3,023	90	-118	-3.8
Lancaster	3,236	3,126	3,112	18	-124	-3.8
Piedmont						
Mecklenburg	6,762	8,676	10,264	76	+3,502	+51.8
Fauquier	6,642	8,754	10,361	53	+3,719	+56.0
Valley						
Botetourt	1,259	1,343	2,275	31	+1,016	+ 80.7
Trans-Allegheny						
Wythe[a]	828	831	1,157	3	+329	+39.8

SOURCES: *Return of the Whole Number of Persons* (1790); *Return of the Whole Number of Persons* (1800); *Aggregate amount of each description of Persons;* and for the column showing slaves freed from 1782 to 1806, deed and will books for the eight counties, 1782–1806.
[a] Wythe was separated from Montgomery Company in 1790 but not counted separately in the census. The 1790 figure is from Montgomery Company.

In Virginia unpredictable factors such as the power of individual personalities to promote or to suppress emancipation in a particular community governed manumission more than did economic ones. Precisely because the number of slaves freed was small, a few exceptional individuals in each county could have a big effect on the total number of acts of manumission there. So while Lancaster slaveholders apparently preferred to sell their unneeded slaves, accounting for the decline in slave population in that county, Accomack residents rather frequently manumitted their bondspeople even as the number of slaves in the county continued to grow.

easily. Historians must be careful in extrapolating from the number of free blacks in a locality to measure the incidence of manumission, since the free black population did not necessarily correspond to the number of manumissions in a county.

DELAYED MANUMISSION

Economic considerations did, however, encourage white manumitters to delay the effective date on which their manumitted slaves would actually become free. About one-half of the slaves freed by deed and nearly two-thirds of those freed by will did not actually attain their liberty until months or years after their owners had drafted the emancipating documents. The average (mean) length of delayed emancipations by deed was just over nine years. Frequently—probably more than two-thirds of the time—delays resulted simply from compliance with the law that children could not be emancipated, particularly, as noted above, in the period 1782–93.[47] For example, Benjamin Dancy emancipated his eleven slaves in 1793 out of a "sense of its being my duty." Six of the slaves were children, ranging in age from three months to fourteen years old. He set them free, "reserving the service of those of them that are under age, until they arrive at age, the Males to twenty one years of age, the Females to Eighteen years of age." But in other cases owners retained adult slaves for several years after they drew up instruments of emancipation. Although Samuel Holmes wrote his deed of manumission to Lucy, Rachel, and Ned in 1803, he did not free them then. The deed specified that Rachel, an adolescent in 1803, would be freed in 1814, when she would be twenty-five. Lucy would remain Holmes's slave until 1812, by which time she would be thirty-six years old. And Ned had to serve Holmes for eleven more years, to be freed on Christmas of 1814, when, if he survived, he would be thirty-four.[48]

Most likely, manumitters such as Holmes saw delayed manumission as a reasonable compromise between their antislavery leanings and their need for laborers. Even when they were genuinely uncomfortable with owning slaves, they could not afford to be without them. This seems to have been the case for some of the manumitters in Accomack County. There, Methodist Quarterly Meetings required their members to produce certificates of emancipation for their slaves even after the national church had rescinded its emancipation rule.

---

47. Uncertainty arises from the fact that the age at freedom was not always specified.

48. Benjamin Dancy deed, 19 Sept. 1793, Charles City County Deeds, 4 (1789–1802); Samuel Holmes deed, 10 Oct. 1803, Mecklenburg County Deeds, 11 (1801–4). Holmes, probably Samuel Holmes Jr., specified that if Lucy or Rachel had any children, which was likely, the children would be free upon birth. Samuel Holmes Jr. also freed his slave Wat in 1796, with Wat's freedom delayed until 1809. Holmes's father, Samuel Holmes Sr., probably a Methodist, freed one of his slaves in 1785.

One result was that shortly after purchasing new slaves a number of Methodist slaveowners in Accomack County filed deeds of emancipation with dates of freedom set some years into the future. In effect they chose to purchase term slaves rather than slaves for life or rather than pay free workers. They must have calculated that this form of term slavery would still be profitable. When they, along with prominent Methodists such as the preacher Griffin Callahan, submitted copies of the emancipating documents to the congregation, they could simultaneously remain in good standing with the local church and continue to benefit from their enslaved workers' labor for several years until the emancipations took effect. Callahan, for example, drafted a deed of manumission freeing his slave Barshaba in 1805 but retained the right to her "services" until 1816.[49]

Given this logic, it is surprising that delayed emancipation was even more common for slaves emancipated by will than for those emancipated by deed since a deceased emancipator himself gained no additional benefit by keeping slaves in bondage. But it seems that many manumitters weighed very carefully their obligations to their heirs against their desire to free certain slaves. Frequently, the slaves' freedom was put off until the death or marriage of the emancipators' children. When the manumitter instead specified the length of the delay, it ranged from one to thirty-three years, with an average (mean) of eleven and a half years. Swepson Jeffries, for example, laid out a complicated plan for freeing some of his slaves. He lent eleven slaves to his wife and directed that three of them be freed upon her death, "or if they Choose they may live with any of my Children they make Choice of." It seems that those three slaves, Wagnor, Cloe, and Juno, were favorites with ties of affection to the family. Other slaves were to be hired out, and the profits put toward schooling Jeffries' sons. Jeffries also gave his children young slaves, including one yet unborn slave, "the Child that Tiller is now pregnant with," who were to be freed after more than twenty years "if the said Negro[s] should live as long."[50] Jeffries probably set such long delays for the young slaves he freed in order to guarantee that his heirs would recoup the costs of raising them. A number of other manumitters similarly chose to free the youngest of their slaves, which may have been a way to divest slowly from slaveowning.

One question that arose in such situations was whether children born to

49. Mariner, *Revival's Children*, 96–97; Griffin Callahan deed, 30 Sept. 1805, Accomack County Deeds, 11 (1804–7).

50. Swepson Jeffries will, 27 Jan. 1803, Mecklenburg County Wills, 5 (1802–7).

slaves who had been promised freedom by a deed or will became free when their mothers did or whether they were slaves for life. Nathaniel Graves addressed the issue in his 1801 deed of manumission to Sarah when he promised that she should "commence free the last day of December, [1811]," nearly eleven years hence. He detailed that "if she Should have Children hereafter while She remains in bondage, the male Children shall go free" at the age of twenty-four and the females at twenty-one. Under those terms, Graves could conceivably still own one of Sarah's children more than thirty years later, and that child, if male, would not be able to join his mother as a free person until as late as 1835. If Sarah cared to stay near her family, she would have to live near Graves, her former owner, for most or even all of her life. Perhaps he thought this equitable, ensuring that he would be repaid for the costs of raising Sarah's children in their infancy. Or perhaps he decided that it was only worth having slaves if one could be certain that they would not run away and that promising them freedom was a way to ensure their good behavior. For Sarah, the provisions of the deed were a reminder of how much power her former owner retained even after he emancipated her and of how difficult it was for a person of color to be truly free in Virginia. Other enslaved women simply assumed that any children they had after a deed of emancipation was written would be free when they were, and since unlike Graves most manumitters did not clarify the matter, it was left to the courts to settle a generation later (discussed in chapter 4).[51]

Delayed manumission shows again how slaveholders used emancipation or its promise as a way to control slaves and strengthen the system of slavery. Graves's manumission of Sarah hints that he, like other slaveowners, hoped his slaves' expectation of freedom would make them more loyal and dutiful. Although no direct evidence exists, it is likely that owners' hopes were fulfilled and that slaves who knew deeds of manumission had been drafted on their behalf or who had been told they would be freed in their owners' wills would not risk certain but delayed freedom for the immediate but precarious freedom of running away. Slaves looking forward to the day of their emancipation also would not be likely to jeopardize their liberty by resisting their masters' orders. A few legal cases indicate that judges validated deeds of emancipation

51. Nathaniel Graves deed, 16 Jan. 1801, Fauquier County Deeds, 14 (1798–1801). In a similar case the descendants of Nan, who in 1805 was promised freedom after twelve years, with any children she had before that to serve until they were twenty-eight, did not attain their liberty until 1859. *Fulton's Ex'ors v. Gracey & als.*, 56 Va. 314 (1859).

that set the date of freedom in the future and granted that freedom if owners tried to deny it.[52] But enslaved Virginians probably could not trust such eventualities and would do everything they could to remain in their masters' good graces until freedom actually came. For owners, delayed emancipation could be quite useful since they suffered little or no financial loss when they freed slaves whose productive years were mostly past and they benefited from the expectation that their slaves would serve loyally and profitably until the date they became fully free.

In effect, delayed emancipation created a new category of labor somewhat akin to a contract in which owners promised freedom in exchange for service, and the practice indicates how slaveholders could reshape the institution through the sum of their individual decisions even in the absence of laws redefining slavery. Ann Muir, for example, freed her slaves in 1806 "for and in consideration of the tenderness which she bears toward her . . . negroes after they the said negroes do serve for the term of years respectively as hereafter specified." She promised them "[f]reedom from slavery *upon the express condition* that the said negroes herein named do first serve myself and my heirs . . . [for] that portion of their time respectively before which period they are hereby intended to be and go free." Muir then laid out a schedule of manumissions according to which some slaves might not be free until 1849. Until that time they would remain as slaves to Muir, and then after her death they would serve Muir's sister and nephews. In an even more explicit exchange of freedom for good service, Foxhall Sturman promised to free a slave he had inherited from his father in one year "if the said negro Cupid shall well and truly perform the duties & services of a Servant to the said Sturman for the full end and term of Twelve months." Cupid, who apparently did fulfill his obligation, was freed in 1805. But this new, quasi-contractual form of slave labor was problematic. Since it arose from the day-to-day experiences and goals of slaveholders rather than from a legislative act, it left several legal issues open, particularly the status of children born to women who were serving out the terms of a deed of manumission. And since it created a condition somewhat between slavery and freedom, it blurred the neat division that Virginians had established in the seventeenth century between those two legal states.[53]

52. See Nicholls, "Squint of freedom," 54; and Stevenson, *Life in Black and White,* 265–66.
53. Ann Muir deed, 29 Apr. 1806, Accomack County Deeds, 11 (1804–7), emphasis mine; Ann Muir will, 30 May 1806, Accomack County Wills, 1806–9; indenture between Sturman, Baker, and Roe, 17 May 1804, Fauquier County Deeds, 16 (1804–7).

Indeed, ordinary slaveholders seems to have been much more comfortable with the complexities, ambiguities, and contradictions of slavery than were the men who made Virginia's laws, which is not surprising given that one of the goals of lawmaking is to clarify civil abilities and categorize human behaviors rather than obscure them. Still, it is significant that Virginia's manumitters took advantage of the ability to manumit their slaves in such various ways, for it demonstrates the inherent flexibility of slavery and the difficulty of legislating what was not only an economic system but a set of human relationships.

CONCLUSION

The years in which manumission was feasible in Virginia, 1782–1806, caught different communities and religious organizations at various stages of their development. The Quakers at that time were small in number, but they vigorously supported emancipation, while the free black community was in its infancy, with limited resources to purchase and liberate fellows but great motivation to do so. Methodists in the early 1780s also opposed slavery, and though the rapidly expanding church abandoned its antislavery requirement in 1785 to make room for slaveholding converts, some individual Methodists and local churches continued to advocate in favor of emancipation. Many Tidewater counties in the late eighteenth century had a surplus of slaves, while those in the Southside and Piedmont regions demanded new workers. And counties west of the Blue Ridge had hardly any slaves at all. These factors greatly affected the regional and temporal variations in manumission, but they fail to account for all of them. Manumission in Virginia was as much a cultural event as anything else. In localities such as Accomack, where local elites freed slaves, manumission was accepted as reasonable, even righteous behavior. In other places, such as Lancaster, which experienced similar economic trends, the county's elite did not support manumission, and the practice was consequently rare. Because manumitters often acted in groups, a strong individual personality, a tightly knit religious community, or a few energetic free blacks could affect the patterns of manumission in a county.

Of particular importance in Virginia's experiment with manumission in the generation after 1782 was the way that Virginia's slaveowners learned to use emancipation as a way to control slaves. Such behavior was the rule rather than the exception in slave societies, but the behavior in Virginia appears bizarre because it was so much in contrast to the experience of the colonial period, to the commonwealth's long-standing commitment to a racialized social system that could not admit free blacks, and to the general experience of the antebellum South. The 1782 law thus had a profound impact because for a short time it made Virginia slavery much more ordinary—unpeculiar—in the global context. It is probable that were it not for the 1806 law that curtailed manumission, manumission as a way to help control slaves, especially delayed emancipation, would have increased. In parts of Virginia the system might have come to resemble slavery in early national Maryland. There, especially in Baltimore, owners engaged regularly in term slavery, buying slaves for specific periods of time rather than for life.[54]

But to many white Virginians the innovations brought by manumission were disquieting, since they challenged long-held understandings of the relationships between race, slavery, and liberty and raised difficult questions. If "society" were white, how were whites to incorporate freed blacks into their communities? Did not liberating some prove that Africans could, in fact, survive in freedom and undercut the justification for racial slavery? On the other hand, perhaps freeing only a small minority of slaves, especially those who had "earned" it through good behavior or through self-purchase, implicitly validated the continued enslavement of the rest.

One hint of how white Virginians began to respond to those issues lies in the actions of John Cropper Jr. Although he had freed all of his slaves in 1794, "being impressed with the belief that all men by Nature are equally free and independent and that the Holding of Man in a State of Slavery is unjust and oppressive," he owned twenty-seven slaves upon his death nearly thirty years later. He did not free them in his will. Instead, he ordered that after his wife's death his executors should sell "my plantation and tract of land called Bowman's Folly, and my slaves and every other article in this will." For a time, Cropper had seen enslaved people as equal to himself in their basic natural rights, but by the time he wrote his will in 1821 he seems to have rejected the possibility of a society in which whites and blacks could both live as free people. Rather than as potential members of society, he treated his slaves as simply one part of his substantial estate. Like the gold epaulets and sword he had earned fighting for the cause of liberty, the enslaved people he owned were only some of the many "articles" he left behind.[55]

54. Whitman, *Price of Freedom*, esp. chap. 3.

55. The profits were to be divided among his children. In addition to the slaves, Cropper also mentioned servants with time left to serve. John Cropper will, 4 Jan. 1821, Accomack County Wills, 1819–21; inventory of John Cropper's estate, Accomack County Wills, 1824–25, 72–73.

3

"Deep-rooted Prejudices"

RACE AND THE PROBLEM OF EMANCIPATION, 1782–1806

Why not retain and incorporate the blacks into the State [upon emancipation] . . . ? Deep-rooted prejudices entertained by the whites; ten thousand recollections by the blacks; . . . the real distinctions which nature has made; and many other circumstances, will divide us into parties, and produce convulsions, which will probably never end but in the extermination of the one or the other race.

THOMAS JEFFERSON, *Notes on the State of Virginia,* 1785

CHANGES IN HOW WHITE Virginians approached the subjects of slavery, liberty, and race in the generation after the Revolution largely coincided with transformations in the practice and meaning of manumission from 1782 to 1806. The antiemancipation and antimanumission sentiment that had existed in Virginia since the 1770s grew stronger at the same time that manumission became less a response to the antislavery ideology embedded in American Revolutionary rhetoric. But in one way ideas and practice diverged. In the early 1800s, when manumission operated for slaveholders as a regular and even advantageous, if rare, feature of the slave system in Virginia, the legislature, in response to citizens' petitions, began to move against it. Legislators considered banning all forms of private manumission and finally decided to curtail it by requiring those manumitted after May 1806 to leave Virginia. The conversations white Virginians had among themselves on the topics of slavery and freedom and the dynamic exchange between leaders and their constituents on those subjects help explain why Virginia rejected manumission even as individual slaveowners accepted its multiple forms and uses.

When we view the discussions of the period 1782–1806 as part of an internal Virginia debate that would continue into the antebellum era, several things become apparent.[1] First, denunciations of slavery continued to come from two groups that would *not* be at the center of the attack on slavery by the 1830s: radical religious groups, including Quakers and, for a time, Methodists and Baptists; and a small secular elite opposed to slavery but also opposed to the incorporation of free blacks into Virginia's society and polity, which they instinctively understood to be white. This may seem obvious, but it is worth pointing out as a contrast to the later era, when antislavery sentiment would spring primarily from the political and cultural interests of western farmers who opposed eastern slaveholders. In fact, the seeds of that later geographic division over slavery were sown in the post-Revolutionary years as two related issues emerged as potentially divisive matters: demographic change, particularly growth in the free black population and a westward shift in the white population, and state constitutional provisions that left western whites underrepresented in the state legislature.

Second, antiemancipation rhetoric increased over time less in response to antislavery rhetoric than from a concern that the racial order was breaking down, a concern that first developed during the topsy-turvy years of the War for Independence and that grew as acts of manumission added to Virginia's free black population. Pronouncements against slavery did occasionally spur slaveholders to defend the institution in the generation after the Revolution, but on the whole antislavery organizations in Virginia seem to have bothered slaveholders little because they sensed their weakness: Methodists and Baptists could not enforce an antislavery discipline in churches in which laypeople, who in Virginia usually opposed large-scale emancipation, shaped local policy; and the secular elite could not conceive of any practical plan for the abolition

---

1. Previous studies have not focused on how Virginians' internal discussions evolved over time and have consequently tended to overlook the changes I trace in this chapter. Robert McColley's insightful and persuasive book *Slavery and Jeffersonian Virginia* is arranged topically in a way that obscures both a sense of debate and change over time. Peter Albert's analysis in his unpublished dissertation, "Protean Institution," also proceeds thematically, obscuring the debate between pro- and antiemancipation advocates, and says little of race. William Freehling in *Road to Disunion* does focus on debate and exchange, but the parties he identifies are the upper South's "Conditional Terminators" and lower South extremists, hence his analysis does not examine Virginia as a place of debate in the Revolutionary era. Duncan Macleod's perceptive study *Slavery, Race, and the American Revolution* also takes a broader approach that obscures a sense of debate within Virginia, especially because it focuses on intellectual and political leaders in the national sphere.

of slavery since they always linked abolition to a quixotic scheme of deporting all freed slaves.

The problem of race was thus key both to the growing expression of antiemancipation opinions and to the ultimate failure of antislavery among evangelicals and secular elites, a third conclusion to emerge from the evidence. Those opposed to individual manumission, as well as those opposed to a general emancipation of slaves, made race central to their argument, while those in favor of freeing slaves had to confront race in a way that undermined their position. A debate between two Richmond Academy students over the future of slavery, published in a 1788 newspaper, illustrates the problem well. "Juveniles Vindex," arguing against slavery, emphasized that all people were created equal by God and that the Creator had "never designed that one part of his people should be so subject to the other, as [in] the state of abject servitude now legalised in Virginia." His rhetorical opponent, "Juveniles Vindicis," attacked Vindex's contention that "the Creator hath . . . formed mankind alike" by noting the existence of racial differences. Rather than elaborate on the nature and importance of these racial distinctions, however, Vindicis simply asserted their obvious existence, saying with adolescent flourish that "a fact which is comprehensible by intuition, cannot receive an additional perspicuity from ratiocination." This tactic was effective because even the antislavery Vindex viewed race as marking a natural division among dissimilar peoples and understood the fear that "manumission would mongrel the nation and destroy our celestial complexion." Since Vindex admitted his own "aversion to such a union," his claim that "swarthy liberty is more eligible than a compound of white dominion and black servitude" rang a false note.[2]

Because even most white opponents of slavery subscribed, as slavery's defenders did, to the belief that blacks were inherently different, they could not envision a biracial society of equals. That failure of imagination posed awkward and even grave limits on antislavery thought in Virginia. The inability of white Virginians to imagine a world in which free blacks lived peacefully alongside free whites caused lawmakers to suppress individual manumission in 1806 and to enact in the generation after the Revolution the largest group of new laws regarding African Americans since colonial Virginians had first codified slavery in the late seventeenth and early eighteenth centuries.

2. *Virginia Independent Chronicle*, 23 Jan., 27 Feb. 1788.

Yet as much as race shaped white Virginians' belief that liberty in Virginia should be reserved for white people, when they tried to explain what constituted race, they, like Juveniles Vindicis, often found themselves inarticulate. Certainly historians have recognized the growing significance of race in post-Revolutionary Virginia, but they have often taken negative assessments of Africans to be a consequence rather than a cause of the failure to end slavery in Virginia; they have not paid enough attention to how manumission altered traditional racial divisions and consequently affected the discussion of race; and they have tended to accept race as a natural category, clouding their ability to see how white Virginians who viewed racial differences as a permanent and insoluble problem also seem to have suspected that, after all, race might not have much intrinsic meaning and that the racialization of liberty and slavery might not provide a firm basis for the social order. It was precisely the anxiety underlying many white Virginians' understanding of race that forced them to cling ever more vigorously to a black-white model that was increasingly inconsistent with the actual makeup of Virginia society and propelled them in 1806 to restrict a practice that many slaveholders had found could be useful, manumission.[3]

THE METHODISTS' 1785 ANTISLAVERY CAMPAIGN AND THE CONSERVATIVE RESPONSE

One revealing exchange on the subjects of slavery and emancipation took place in the mid-1780s among Methodist preachers, potential converts, and Virginia

---

3. Duncan Macleod writes that in "seeking a remedy" to the "unfavourable" impact slavery had on white society, southerners "came face to face with a problem always implicit in their society and now made explicit—race." This echoes my own views substantially, but Macleod's argument tends to explain the explicit consideration of racial differences as a consequence of the failure to end slavery rather than as part of the reason slavery persisted. Phillip Hamilton similarly argues that the Tucker family's assessment of their slaves became negative *after* St. George Tucker's plan for emancipation was rejected by the legislature. For Robert McColley, race is a central theme, but as a constant rather than a changing phenomenon, not significantly altered by manumission. Winthrop Jordan, who discusses antislavery's "weaknesses and limitations," does not focus on race among them and sees the "resulting pattern of separation" of blacks and whites as a consequence of the Revolution's failures. Macleod, *Slavery, Race, and the American Revolution,* 82 and passim; Hamilton, "Revolutionary Principles"; McColley, *Slavery and Jeffersonian Virginia;* Jordan, *White over Black,* chaps. 9 and 11. See also Egerton, *Gabriel's Rebellion,* 17, and Sidbury, *Ploughshares into Swords,* chap. 5, for discussions of how free blacks in post-Revolutionary Virginia took a wider role in the economy, which destabilized the racial order.

slaveholders. In those years, after the Quakers had won the passage of the manumission law, Methodist leaders who had great sympathy with slaves and a strong commitment to helping the less fortunate took the lead in promoting emancipation in Virginia. The number of Methodists who freed slaves in Accomack County is some indication of their success. But the relative failure of Methodism to promote widespread manumission in other counties, such as Botetourt, where Edward Mitchell lived and preached, points to the limited appeal of their message and was more typical of the Virginia experience. In fact, the high-water mark of the Methodists' antislavery efforts came early, in 1785, the first year of their existence as a separate church. In the church's founding conference, the Baltimore Christmas Conference of 1784, American Methodists, led by the Englishmen Francis Asbury and Thomas Coke, both energetic and charismatic preachers who had brought with them to America "a zeal against slavery as one of the great evils of the age," agreed that they should try to "extirpate this abomination [slavery] from among us." As noted above in chapter 1, church rules reflected Asbury and Coke's sentiment by requiring church members to free their slaves. Soon, however, resistance to their proemancipation message forced Methodists to move away from the antislavery rules and largely to abandon antislavery efforts in Virginia. Though familiar to historians, the details of this transition are worth reexamining because they reveal much about Virginia's culture more generally. In particular, reaction in 1785 to Thomas Coke's antislavery preaching and to the Methodists' antislavery petition of the same year underscores how committed to slavery most Virginia slaveholders remained in the post-Revolutionary years, a commitment also suggested by the majority of manumitters, who freed only one or two of their larger number of slaves.[4]

During the spring of 1785, when Coke visited Halifax County in Virginia's tobacco-growing Southside region as part of his preaching tour of the southern United States, there were only a few thousand Methodists in all of Virginia, a tiny proportion of Virginia's total population of nearly three quarters of a million people.[5] Coke was keen to build the church and almost as devoted to

4. Bennett, *Memorials of Methodism*, 129–31. The plan was that all slaves over forty were to be freed by the age of forty-five; slaves between twenty-five and forty were to be freed within five years; those between twenty and twenty-five were to be freed by the age of thirty; children were to be freed by the age of twenty-five; and all subsequently born children were to be freed at birth.

5. In the spring of 1784 Virginia circuits reported 4,453 members; in 1786 ministers counted 3,965 white members and 379 colored members; by 1787, a couple of years after the suspension of

spreading the message that slavery was wrong and that slaveholders should free their slaves. It seemed to be a good time to speak of emancipation, since Virginia's manumission law was already in place and the legal barriers to emancipation were few. But Coke soon encountered deep-seated, violent resistance to his antislavery message. When he preached it to Halifax County residents, they subjected him to, as he put it with his characteristic understatement, "a very little persecution." Coke's status as an outsider—not a Virginian and not even an American—probably helped inflame the "unawakened" people who walked out of the barn in which he was orating rather than listen to him speak against slavery. It looked as if events would turn ugly when the crowd that gathered outside the barn "combine[d] together to flog me . . . as soon as I came out. . . . When I came out, they surrounded me, but had only power to talk." Coke's escape appeared only temporary when on the following day "a mob came to meet me with staves and clubs. Their plan, I believe, was to fall upon me as soon as I touched upon the subject of slavery." Coke escaped a brutal beating by avoiding any further discussion of slavery or emancipation. Nevertheless, the local grand jury indicted him as a seditious person, and one man even plotted to shoot him, facts Coke learned of several years later.[6]

In response to the threat of violence, Methodists began almost immediately to modify their antislavery message for the Virginia audience. Thomas Coke, for one, learned to speak about slavery in such a way that he might deliver his words "without much offence, or at least without causing a tumult." His new approach combined an endorsement of slave discipline with arguments that slavery was in theory wrong, a tactic that calmed the fears of whites who suspected that any discussion of emancipation might cause slaves to revolt. Coke found that if he first addressed "the Negroes in a very pathetic manner on the Duty of Servants to Masters; . . . then the Whites will receive quietly what I have to say to them." Here were the origins of the church's later

---

rules regarding slavery, the number had nearly doubled to 7,274 whites and 645 blacks, which still made them a fringe group. Ibid., 232, 239. For general accounts of the progress of evangelical religion in Revolutionary and early national Virginia, and of the transition evangelicals made from being outsiders to being in the mainstream, see Isaac, *Transformation of Virginia;* and Heyrman, *Southern Cross.*

6. Coke, *Extracts,* 35–36. See p. 69 for an indication that the location was Halifax County. In later memory the incident grew in Coke's mind. In 1788 he returned to Halifax, where, he noted, he had "met with a little persecution on my former visit," but in 1789 he recalled that he had "met with *much* persecution four years ago." See ibid., 69, 108, emphasis mine.

stance on slavery, encouraging proper behavior (according to the standards of a slave society) on the part of both slaves and masters rather than promoting emancipation or condemning slavery as immoral.[7]

The retreat from the 1784 antislavery rules was even more rapid than Coke's story suggests. On the eve of the Virginia conference of May 1785 Francis Asbury recorded that he had "found the minds of the people greatly agitated with our rules against slavery," while Coke noted that "a great many principal friends met us here to insist on a Repeal of the Slave-Rules." That summer the Baltimore Conference retracted the emancipation rules, having deemed them a failure after well less than a year.[8]

About the same time, another revealing exchange between antislavery Methodists and proslavery Virginia residents took place. Though this time the Methodists' opponents used words rather than clubs and staves, their effort to quash Methodists' antislavery talk was equally effective. Following, perhaps, the example of the Quakers, the Methodists in 1785 decided to submit a "petition to the general assembly for the emancipation of the blacks" even though the "minds of the people" were "greatly agitated with our rules against slavery" and experience had already shown antislavery appeals to be ineffective. The Methodists selected Harry Fry, a delegate from Culpeper County, to introduce their petition to the legislature, an act that might jeopardize Fry's safety since anger toward evangelical religion already ran high. As one member of the Culpeper gentry had grumbled fearfully when Fry was elected, "These Methodists and Baptists will never rest, till they get their knives into our bellies."[9]

During the summer of 1785 as itinerant Methodist preachers toured Virginia looking for people to sign their petition calling for emancipation, opponents of emancipation also drafted petitions and gathered signatories to what has become one of the best-known early defenses of slavery in Virginia. In the context of contemporaneous petitions and newspaper essays, the anti-Methodist, antiemancipation petitions appear less remarkable for their early defense of slavery than they have to many historians, but they are nonethe-

---

7. Ibid., 37.

8. *Journal of Rev. Francis Asbury*, 1:495; Coke, *Extracts*, 39.

9. *Journal of Rev. Francis Asbury*, 1:495; Coke, *Extracts*, 43. Virginians seemed to think that Coke had authored the petition. While he probably played the leading role in drafting it, it was the product of a committee of several people. See ibid., 70.

less important as part of the evolving debate in Virginia over slavery and emancipation.[10]

The Methodist petition, signed by several hundred people, began with the central theme of the Revolutionary era, that "Liberty is the Birthright of Mankind." Recalling the "glorious and ever-memorable Revolution," the petitioners implied that any American upholding slavery was a hypocrite, since "the oppression exercised over them [the slaves] exceeds the oppression formerly exercised over the United States by Great Britain." Because this was, by then, a familiar antislavery argument, the Methodists had to go further. The petition also addressed the claims they knew slavery's defenders would make, which demonstrates that proslavery defenses had been articulated often enough by 1785 to be attacked point by point. The proslavery argument that slaves had been "Prisoners of War, when they were originally purchased," and had thus been legitimately enslaved was, the Methodist petition declared, "utterly invalid, for no right of conquest can subject any man to perpetual Slavery, much less his Posterity." The Methodist petition also challenged the common fear that emancipation would lead to severe social disruption. The Methodists contended that gradual emancipation would in fact make society more secure by incorporating formerly enslaved people as members whose interests would be bound to the state rather than opposed to it. (This was the calculation made by some individual Virginia manumitters and many slaveholders outside the United States.) Finally, as an indication of their own religious concerns, the petitioners noted that "above all" slavery brought about a "deep Debasement of Spirit" that generally incapacitated slaves to receive the "noble and enlarged Principles of the Gospel."[11]

Significantly, Methodists attacked proslavery racial arguments that blacks were by nature excluded from the legacy of the Revolution in a tone similar to the one Juveniles Vindicis took to prove the opposite: "[T]he arguments drawn from the difference of Hair, Features and Colour, are so beneath the Man of Sense, much more the Christian, that we would not insult the Honourable the Assembly by enlarging upon them." It is revealing that those on

---

10. Published in Schmidt and Wilhelm, "Early Proslavery Petitions," the anti-Methodist petitions of 1785, along with petitions from Hanover and Henrico counties from the year before, have gained wide notice from historians.

11. Antislavery petition, 8 Nov. 1785, LP, Miscellaneous Legislative Petitions.

both sides of the argument declared the importance (or unimportance) of racial differences to be both obvious and unquestionable rather than interrogate what differences among people meant. Their failure to explore the issue that was at the heart of the problem of racial slavery in a society dedicated to liberty points to the irony that even such an operative concept as race—one that shaped thought on a number of questions—could not easily be grasped by the Americans of the early national era. Perhaps the meaning of race was so often beyond their reach precisely because the men and women of that time sensed that ultimately it did not make sense to divide people up according to appearance and that appearance did not always accurately indicate to what group one belonged.[12]

Indeed, rather than take issue with the Methodists' assertion that proslavery racial arguments were "beneath the Man of Sense," anti-Methodist petitioners ignored the problem of race and focused instead on other ways to defend slavery against the Methodists' arguments, particularly by asserting that the Revolution supported rather than challenged slaveholding. More than a thousand citizens, most of them from the tobacco-growing counties south of the James River, where Methodist ministers, including Coke, had been particularly active, signed petitions countering the Methodists' arguments, far outnumbering the several hundred people who affixed their names to the Methodist document. The petitions comprised four separate but similar texts, and according to Peter Albert's data from Brunswick County, the signers came disproportionately from the ranks of large slaveholders, though smaller slaveholders and nonslaveholders endorsed the petition as well. Slavery's defenders suggested a new proslavery interpretation of the American Revolutionary struggle. By the 1830s it would be commonplace in much of the South to assert, as the 1785 antiemancipation petition did, that it had been "in order therefore to fix a Tenure in our property" that "we dissolved our union with our Parent country." In 1785 it was still novel to argue that the Revolution had "sealed with our Blood, a Title to the full, free and absolute Enjoyment of every species of our Property," including property in slaves. In this context, British advocates of emancipation, as Asbury and Coke both were, could be seen as part of a plot to reduce American liberties by depriving Americans of their slaves; such men were "Tools of the British Administration" whose scheme

12. Ibid.

"consists very well with the principles and Designs of a *Bute*, or a *North*, [British ministers under George III] whose Finger is sufficiently visible in it."[13]

The antiemancipation petitions went further to make a case for the legitimacy of slavery, with the bulk of their reasoning resting on the Bible, apt grounds on which to attack those who were "pretending to be moved by Religious Principles." Slavery was permitted by God himself, they pointed out, citing passages from Leviticus ("thy Bond Men and Bond Maids . . . shall be of the Heathen") and Genesis ("And he said cursed be Canaan; a Servant of Servants shall he be unto his Brethren"). Moreover, Jesus and his apostles had not abridged the Old Testament right to own slaves.[14]

The response of the members of the House of Delegates to these competing petitions affirms that their support for the manumission law only three years earlier should not be read as support for general emancipation. When first presented with both the Methodists' proemancipation petition and the first counterpetition in the fall of 1785, the delegates simply laid them on the table. But they could not ignore the issue when the additional antiemancipation petitions were introduced two days later. At that time the House of Delegates rejected the Methodists' petition without a single vote in favor of it. As James Madison, then serving as a delegate, described the events to George Washington,

> The pulse of the H. of D. was felt on thursday with regard to a general manumission, by a petition presented on that subject. It was rejected without dissent, but not without an avowed patronage of its principle by sundry respectable members. A motion was made to throw it under

---

13. Lunenburg petition, 29 Nov. 1785, Brunswick petition, 10 Nov. 1785, and Halifax petition, 10 Nov. 1785, in Schmidt and Wilhelm, "Early Proslavery Petitions," 140–41, 143, 145. A fourth text was submitted in identical copies from Amelia, Mecklenberg, and Pittsylvania counties on 10, 8, and 10 November 1785, respectively. According to Schmidt and Wilhelm, the total number of signatures on the six petitions was 1,244. Peter Albert compared the holdings of the petitioners with the holdings of the entire population of householders in the county and found that 21 percent of all householders had ten or more slaves but that among the petitioners nearly twice that proportion, 39 percent, had that many slaves. Albert, "Protean Institution," 214.

14. Brunswick and Amelia petitions in Schmidt and Wilhelm, "Early Proslavery Petitions," 143, 139. Oddly, considering the biblical focus of the arguments, the petitions failed to cite the Hamitic myth that Africans were the descendants of Noah's son Ham and cursed by God with both blackness and slavery.

the table, which was treated with as much indignation on one side as the petition itself was on the other.

Certainly proposing to throw the petition *under* the table signaled a degree of hostility not much less than that of the Halifax men who intended to flog Thomas Coke. And "avowed patronage" of the abolition principle by "respectable members" of the House meant little in reality if the delegates rejected the petition unanimously. Perhaps beginning to question their passage of the manumission act of 1782, they referred the antiemancipation petitions, including one calling for the repeal of the 1782 act, to the Committee of the Whole House for consideration.[15]

The legislature's unanimous rejection of the Methodists' call for abolition reinforced the move already under way in the Methodist Church to discontinue formal antislavery activities. As an explanation of their rapid retreat from the front lines of the battle against slavery, Coke noted in his journal, "We thought it prudent . . . , our work being in too infantile a state to push things to extremity." Coke's observation that their work was "in too infantile a state" was on the mark. Unlike the Quakers, who were a small, exclusive, established group who could enforce norms within their community and who cherished their differences from the dominant society, Methodists were an immature and growing sect. While in the 1770s they had taken pride in their status as outsiders, Methodists in Virginia in the 1780s wished to be inclusive, to preach to blacks as well as whites, and to spread the Gospel as far as they could. (And after the passage of the Virginia Statute for Religious Freedom in January 1786, which fully disestablished the Episcopal Church and provided for freedom of religious conscience, Methodists and other evangelical groups could no longer be considered outsiders in any formal way.) The Methodists' expansionist goals operated against upholding an antislavery stance, which would have driven away the large portion of potential members who not only would have rejected the Methodist message if it included antislavery ideas

---

15. James Madison to George Washington, 11 Nov. 1785, in *Writings of James Madison*, 2:192. The House Minute Book incorrectly refers to a Presbyterian petition, suggesting that Methodists and Presbyterians were viewed similarly as dissenters from the Episcopal orthodoxy. The entry for 10 November 1785 reads in part, "Presbyterian peto.—(about Slaves)—to whole in Commonwealth. . . . Emancipation peto:=motion to consider it= previous question disag'd—peto: rejected." Minutes of the House of Delegates, 1784–87, LVA, Archives Division.

but would have barred their slaves, also potential converts, from attending Methodist gatherings. In 1788 Coke acknowledged that "however just my sentiments may be concerning Slavery, it was ill judged of me to deliver them from the pulpit."[16]

Because for Methodists evangelizing was more important than ending slavery and salvation was of greater value than righting earthly injustice, Methodist ministers in Virginia and the southern states generally began to accommodate themselves slowly to the institution of slavery, to preach on the proper behavior of slaves toward their masters, and to speak less and less of emancipation. Even so, some Methodists preachers continued through the early 1800s to declare that slavery was wrong, and as we have seen, manumission records show that Methodists formed a significant portion of those who freed slaves in Virginia, especially on the Eastern Shore, where Methodism had taken hold strongly. Asbury noted with pride in 1788 that while a Virginia minister of another denomination preached against freedom for slaves, "[o]ur brother Everett with no less zeal and boldness, cries aloud for liberty—emancipation."[17]

BAPTISTS AND THE QUESTION OF EMANCIPATION IN VIRGINIA

Manumission records suggest that Baptists were less likely than Methodists or Quakers to free slaves, that they were, in other words, more like Virginia slaveholders on the whole. In fact, recent scholarship demonstrates that Baptists were more representative of Virginians than previously thought, so it is useful to listen in, as Baptist records allow us to, on their discussions over slavery. Such spying is possible through records of their yearly regional meetings and of some local meetings in which Baptists chronicled their discussions about slavery and emancipation. What we hear underscores once again how strongly white Virginians remained committed to slavery even though a number of them also believed the institution to be immoral.[18]

---

16. Coke, *Extracts*, 46, 69.

17. Bennett, *Memorials of Methodism*, 446–47; Mariner, *Revival's Children*; Essig, *Bonds of Wickedness*, chap. 6; *Journal of Rev. Francis Asbury*, 2:41.

18. On Baptists' representativeness see Spangler, "Becoming Baptists"; for an analysis of Baptists' struggle with slavery that emphasizes continuing divisions see Najar, "Meddling with Emancipation"; and for a sensitive account of how Baptist churches in southwestern Virginia dealt with liberty and slavery see Scully, "Somewhat Liberated."

Motivated by a combination of religious and republican principles and animated by the strains of egalitarianism in their doctrine, the Virginia Baptist General Committee in 1785 (the same year of the Methodist antislavery campaign) declared "heredit[ar]y slavery to be contrary to the word of God" and recommended that its member congregations consider the matter and report back to the committee. Most congregations simply failed to respond to the General Committee's request. The Black Creek Baptist Church, in Southampton County, which was led by the antislavery preacher David Barrow, did consider in 1786 whether it was "a Ritious thing" to hold people in slavery, but upon deciding it unrighteous took no action to end slavery or expel slaveholders. In their local communities white Baptists were generally more concerned with day-to-day affairs and with their own spiritual development than with the problem of slavery; they were more interested in finding a Christian way to behave toward slaves than in changing the society around them. Nevertheless, the General Committee in 1790 issued another resolution decrying slavery as a "violent deprivation of the rights of nature, and inconsistent with a republican government." The committee suggested that Baptists "make use of every legal measure, to extirpate the horrid evil from the land and pray" for a legislative act for general emancipation.[19]

The language was vivid—slavery was a "horrid evil" to be rooted out—but again the response of the Virginia Baptist congregations lacked similar vigor. Those Baptists who discussed the 1790 resolution in their local meetings were unenthusiastic about emancipation. The Roanoke Association, made up of congregations in southwestern Virginia, which was not largely a slaveholding area, even doubted whether slavery was sinful, stating that "we are not unanimously clear in our minds whether the God of Nature maintained that one human should ever hold another in slavery." They also voiced reservations about whether emancipated slaves would be able to care for themselves and refrained from imposing any rules on the congregants, leaving the matter to be decided by individuals as they saw fit but recommending that slaveholders behave justly toward their slaves. The neighboring Strawberry District Association responded more succinctly, saying simply, "[W]e advise them [the

19. *Minutes of the Baptist General Committee . . . 1791* (Richmond, 1791), quoted in Daniel, "Virginia Baptists," 65; Black Creek Baptist Church minutes, 1786–87, quoted in Scully, "Somewhat Liberated," 347; *Minutes of the Baptist General Committee . . . 1790* (Richmond, n.d.), quoted in Daniel, "Virginia Baptists," 66.

General Committee] not to Interfere in it." When the General Committee discussed slavery again, and for the last time, in 1793, they decided that the issue was the province of the government, not the church, and therefore ought not be discussed further.[20]

In spite of the noninterference policy established by the Virginia General Committee, some Virginia Baptists revisited the issue in the late 1790s when the Dover Association, composed of churches from the northern Tidewater region, recommended that its members join forces with the Abolition Society and petition the legislature for a gradual emancipation plan and when the Ketocton Association, made up of churches in the northern Piedmont, also discussed emancipation. The discussion among members of the Ketocton Association reiterated the one held in the General Committee, demonstrating how difficult it was within the representative and congregational organization of the church to impose antislavery rules or even to consider fully the subject of slavery but also showing that a vocal minority of Baptists felt strongly that slavery was wrong.[21]

The debate over emancipation within the Ketocton Association began when the Happy Creek church submitted a query to the Association in 1796 asking whether "holding Negroes in slavery" was "supported by scripture and the true principles of a republican government." The association refused to take up the question, declaring, as was the policy established by the General Committee, that it was an "improper subject of investigation in a Baptist Association." The next year another church delegation submitted in cloaked form a query regarding slavery, asking how "the honor of the Gospel [is] to be supported . . . with those who live in the habitual practice of . . . transgression of Divine Law." This effort to introduce the subject of emancipation was more successful, since the association agreed that it was "repugnant" to have fellowship with those who lived in sin and that slavery was indeed a transgression of divine law. Rather than ban slaveholders from the church, which was the logical consequence of the position they had just agreed to, the association stated that slavery ought to be removed by degrees and assigned a committee to draw up a plan of gradual emancipation. The association submitted the plan, which

20. Strawberry Baptist Association, Minute Book, 1787–1822, May 1792, 45, LVA, Archives Division, negative photostat of original manuscript at VBHS; Minutes of the Roanoke Association, June 1790, quoted in Daniel, "Virginia Baptists," 66–67.
21. *Minutes of the Dover Baptist Association, held at Bestland Meeting House*, 5.

was similar to the one imposed by the Methodist Church in its short-lived 1785 emancipation rules, to the member churches for their consideration.[22]

The response of the Ketocton Association churches to the prospect of emancipation was clear: "[We] disapprove of said plan, and viewing the magnitude of the subject, and the consequences resulting from any attempt made by this Association thereon, have determined that it is a business that the Legislature alone is competent to, and that the Association, in her religious capacity, have nothing to do with it." Because all church issues were decided by the white male members' posing questions and debating answers, it was unlikely that the constituent churches would have responded differently. Each group of Baptists, both in the local congregations and in the associations and the General Committee, contained a significant number of slaveholders, who were understandably resistant to the destruction of the slave system. In addition, as Stephanie McCurry points out in her discussion of Baptists in antebellum South Carolina, while the "evangelical message was irreducibly one of spiritual equality . . . its relation to social equality or status in this world was, even in the early years, deeply contested." White Baptists worked as much as other southern whites to maintain, not to disrupt, "the observation of gender, racial, property, and other distinctions" among their number.[23]

Because slaveholders had power in the Baptist Church to quash talk of emancipation, some members were concerned that they might place a gag order on all discussion of slavery, an undemocratic and unchristian maneuver indeed. Several members of the Ketocton Association protested to this effect, and in 1801 the association resolved that it would in principle be open to further discussions of slavery and could reconsider the matter of emancipation at any time, though there seems to have been no further consideration of emancipation. Instead the Ketocton Association grew more conservative on issues regarding slaves, clarifying in 1809 that black members had no vote in the church (and were therefore not true members) and noting in 1810 that

---

22. *Minutes of the Ketocton Baptist Association. Thumb Run*, 4; *Minutes of the Ketockton Baptist Association, Held at Frying-Pan*, 4–6. The emancipation plan drawn up by the committee formed for that purpose was as follows: slaves 14 years or younger would be free at age 22; those 14–20, at 25; and those 20–25, at 28, with those over 25 to serve five years and slaves subsequently born to be free. And "[a]ll who have been purchased with money, shall serve ten years from the time of such purchase."

23. *Minutes of the Ketocton Baptist Association, Continued at Broad-Run Meeting-House*, 5; McCurry, *Masters of Small Worlds*, 141.

churches had been too "indulgent" in allowing some African American members to preach. The association's new policy required that slaves not be allowed to preach without permission from their masters, part of a trend within Virginia's Baptist churches toward tighter regulation of black members and especially of black preachers.[24]

Of the three major denominations that took an antislavery stance, the Baptists were the least effective in promoting emancipation among their ranks and bringing the issue to the public. Part of the reason is that Baptists lacked charismatic antislavery leaders like Thomas Coke and were, like the Methodists, an evangelical group constantly seeking new converts, who were oftentimes slaveholders. A more significant factor was the church's looser organization, which made enforcement of antislavery policies more difficult than among Methodists or Quakers. The Baptists strove for consensus among their membership, and regional and statewide bodies sought the opinions of their constituent congregations. As in Virginia as a whole, it seemed that any push toward emancipation was stopped by the collective voice of the white community, whose material interests and cultural values rested on slavery.

The very ambiguity of the Bible and Christian doctrine on the subject of slavery also limited the ability of evangelical religious organizations such as the Baptists to advance emancipation. As antiemancipation writers had pointed out, the Bible in some ways supported slavery. Operating on a more subtle level were Christian ideals of humility and subservience that sanctified hierarchy and service, including the service provided by slaves to their masters. The language found in one Baptist circular letter demonstrates this: "The Church is commanded to be subject to them [preachers], as those that watch for their souls; whom Christ has employed as Stewards in his House, and placed as Overseers, to deal out to his servants and hand-maidens their meat in due season." If the words and images of slavery could so easily be used to explain the relationship between preachers and their flock, so too could this beneficent image of Christian overseers tending to their servants be used to sanctify the relations between slaveowners and their slave property.[25]

In spite of their sincere and sometimes brave efforts to advocate abolition,

---

24. *Minutes of the Ketockton Baptist Association, Held at Happy Creek Meeting House*, 7; *Minutes of the Ketocton Baptist Association, Holden at New Valley*, 5; *Minutes of the Ketocton Baptist Association, Holden at Waterlick*, 4; Scully, "Somewhat Liberated," 350–71; Heyrman, *Southern Cross*, 223–25.

25. *Minutes of the Ketocton Baptist Association. Thumb Run*, 6.

religious groups failed to change the course of slavery in Virginia as much because of their internal limitations as because of the resistance they encountered in the legislature and in the society at large. While the Quakers were impaired by their relative disinterest in the world outside their society, the evangelical Methodists and Baptists suffered from their desire to be a church of the people, many of whom were slaveholders. Rather than remain part of a slave society, not a few religious men and women who opposed slavery simply left. The number of Quaker meetings declined precipitously in the early nineteenth century as Quakers relocated westward, and many antislavery Methodist and Baptist leaders also left Virginia for free states, especially Ohio. As Francis Asbury predicted in 1798, "[P]oor men and free men will not live among slaveholders, but will go to new lands" in order to escape slavery.[26]

ELITE PROPOSALS FOR GENERAL ABOLITION AND THE PROBLEM OF RACE

Most of Virginia's elite, like most white evangelicals, had little interest in ending slavery in the commonwealth, but a few prominent members of that class did seek to reconcile republican ideals with Virginia's social and economic realities. Their proposals for the gradual abolition of slavery in Virginia, particularly the ones included in Thomas Jefferson's *Notes on the State of Virginia* in 1785 and in St. George Tucker's *Dissertation on Slavery* about a decade later, are well known and have been much discussed by scholars, especially because they suggest that it might indeed have been possible to end slavery in the Old Dominion. If, however, Virginia's leaders paid attention to talk among members of their community, if they followed the fate of antislavery Methodists and Baptists, they would have been quite hesitant to act on any such plan. Indeed, they never put any abolition proposal before the voters. Perhaps more important, and often overlooked, were the intrinsic limitations to the schemes elite Virginians drafted, all of which required the removal of freed slaves beyond the commonwealth's borders in order to preserve liberty in Virginia as white, a requirement that made the plans unworkable. Although Virginians' abolition plans unquestioningly accepted the whiteness of liberty in Virginia, they simultaneously revealed the ambiguities that inhered in the concept of race.

26. Thomas, "Second Great Awakening in Virginia," 7; Schwarz, *Migrants against Slavery*, 6, 84; *Journal of Rev. Francis Asbury*, 2:367.

The earliest Virginian emancipation plan, mentioned briefly in chapter 1, was originally part of the revisal of Virginia laws undertaken by Thomas Jefferson, George Wythe, and Edmund Pendleton during the early years of the Revolution (1776–79).[27] It is not clear what role each of the three revisers played in drawing up the emancipation-colonization plan, but all three were theoretically opposed to slavery. Though it was never submitted to the legislature, Jefferson included the plan in his *Notes on the State of Virginia,* and he included a similar but much less detailed abolition plan in his 1783 draft for a new state constitution, but the legislature never considered that proposal either because no constitutional convention was called that year. The revisers' plan of the 1770s therefore remains the most specific account of how Jefferson, along with Wythe and Pendleton, thought Virginians might effect a general emancipation of their slaves.[28]

According to Jefferson, the projected emancipation amendment to Virginia's laws would have freed all slaves born after the passing of the act and would have educated them at public expense in "tillage, arts, or sciences, according to their geniuses." When they became adults the free blacks would "be colonized to such place as the circumstances of the time should render most proper" and provided with implements necessary to starting a colony. Then they would be declared "a free and independent people," a sort of black reenactment of the Revolution. The newly independent black nation would still, however, have the "alliance and protection" of Virginia until it could fend fully for itself. Back in Virginia, the lost population would be replaced by sending out vessels to other parts of the world to bring in "an equal number of white inhabitants."[29]

The main idea of the revisers' plan, and the portion that Jefferson most elaborately explained and defended, was that emancipation necessitated the colonization of the freed slaves beyond Virginia's borders and the replacement

---

27. The revised code was not actually passed until 1785, and indeed Jefferson says in *Notes on the State of Virginia* that the code "probably will not be taken up till a restoration of peace shall leave to the legislature to go through such a work" (131).

28. Ibid., app. 2, 197–98; Miller, *Wolf by the Ears,* 22. Jefferson's 1783 proposal included a total ban on slave imports and a provision to end slavery after "the generation which shall be living on the thirty-first day of December, one thousand eight hundred; all persons born after that day being hereby declared free." John Miller says that this plan included "the stipulation that these children, after being trained as apprentices, should be deported from the state upon reaching maturity" (22), but I find no mention of such details in Jefferson's proposed constitution as it appears in his *Notes on the State of Virginia.*

29. Jefferson, *Notes on the State of Virginia,* 132.

of them by white workers. Why not, Jefferson asked rhetorically, "retain and incorporate the blacks into the State?" Because, he answered himself, of the "[d]eep-rooted prejudices" of white people, the anger of the black people toward their former masters, and the "real distinctions which nature has made." The differences between blacks and whites would not merely create tension; the two opposed groups would likely enter into a battle "which will probably never end but in the extermination of the one or the other race." Thus, according to Thomas Jefferson, maintaining peace in Virginia and preserving the existence of the white race required the removal of free blacks.[30]

Jefferson supported his argument for racial separateness with several somewhat digressive pages of commentary on the significance and depth of racial distinctions. In contrast to many contemporaries who assumed that the nature of racial differences was apparent (or in the case of the Methodist antislavery petition that the differences were as meaningless as they were apparent), Jefferson explored those differences in detail, perhaps because he originally wrote the *Notes* in response to queries from a French correspondent, who would not have been familiar with how race operated in Virginia. He explained the many ways he had observed blacks to differ from whites—in "color, figure, and hair," in experiencing a "greater degree of transpiration," in "requir[ing] less sleep," in possessing a "want of forethought," and in being "more ardent after their female," more musically gifted than the whites in "tune and time," and "dull" in imagination, with "inferior" reason. In spite of this detailed account, Jefferson still at some level found race impenetrable. He did not know how the differences he perceived originated and whether they denoted blacks' inferiority, "advanc[ing] it . . . as a suspicion only, that the blacks, whether originally a distinct race, or made distinct by time and circumstances, are inferior to the whites in the endowments both of body and mind." Jefferson's substantive discussion of race is significant not only for its content, to which scholars have paid considerable attention, and for the way it simultaneously describes and casts doubt on the significance of racial distinctions but also for its position and function in *Notes* as a whole. The passage is out of place in a section on the law, interrupting the flow of logic in Jefferson's exposition of how republicanism shaped Virginia's legal institutions just as race disturbed the logic of republicanism generally.[31]

30. Ibid., 132–33.
31. Ibid., 133–35, 138. Other analyses of Jefferson's discussion in *Notes on the State of Virginia* can be found in Dain, *Hideous Monster of the Mind*, chap. 1; Jordan, *White over Black*, 436–40; and Macleod, *Slavery, Race, and the American Revolution*, 128–30.

The inability to conceive of integrating free blacks into Virginia society—the problem of race—also determined the details of St. George Tucker's abolition proposal, which drew heavily from Jefferson's plan, but Tucker did not investigate the matter of racial difference the way Jefferson did. Tucker, like Jefferson, had been a student of the liberal jurist George Wythe, who taught at the College of William and Mary. Wythe trained his students to value republican principles, so it was not surprising that the Bermuda-born Tucker became, like Jefferson and Wythe, an ardent supporter of the Revolution and its ideals. Tucker understood well slavery's "incompatibility with the principles of our government." In 1795, when he was himself a professor of law at the College of William and Mary, he submitted a list of questions to Jeremy Belknap inquiring how Belknap's home state of Massachusetts had managed to end slavery. Belknap in turn distributed the questions to a number of prominent Massachusetts men, and Tucker used the responses, along with his own knowledge of Virginia's laws and the history of slavery in America, to draw up his *Dissertation on Slavery: with a Proposal for the Gradual Abolition of it in the State of Virginia*. Tucker published the *Dissertation*, originally part of a lecture course on law and police, in 1796 and submitted it to the General Assembly in the hope that the legislature would act on his proposal, for as he said in his preface, he considered the abolition of slavery "an object of the first importance, not only to our moral character and domestic peace, but even to our political salvation."[32]

The very act of submitting an abolition plan to Virginia's legislature was bold in 1796 since antislavery sentiment had waned by then. The assembly tabled the proposal and never considered it or referred it to committee, thus preventing what probably would have been a heated, even violent debate. This was so even though Tucker had formulated his plan not to "affect the interest either of *creditors* or any other description of person of the *present generation*." Moreover, Tucker tried unsuccessfully to negotiate between his theoretical belief in the equality of all people and the deep racial prejudices of the society in which he lived. After a general discussion of slavery and its evils—that it was incompatible with the liberal ideals at the heart of Virginia's government and the American Revolution, that the selling of people was cruel and the slave trade wreaked havoc on African societies, and that the enslaved popula-

32. St. George Tucker, *Dissertation on Slavery*, preface, 9; St. George Tucker to Jeremy Belknap, 24 Jan. 1795, in "Queries Relating to Slavery in Massachusetts," 380. See also Hamilton, "Revolutionary Principles," 531–37.

tion formed a potentially dangerous and insurrectionary force—Tucker considered how to end slavery. He argued, in agreement with Jefferson and citing one of Belknap's correspondents, that since freed slaves and their former masters could not live together in the same country, the abolition of slavery through the gradual emancipation of slaves necessitated emigration of the free African Americans. And since black people made up most of the "cultivators of the earth," abolition (removal of slaves) had to take place over a long period of time so that white cultivators could replace black ones and prevent a general famine. Oddly, neither Tucker nor other commentators could envision what actually did happen when slavery ended, that blacks would remain among whites as dependent agricultural workers. Furthermore, Tucker noted that the sanctity of property rights and the legitimacy of slave property under the law required that owners be given just compensation for freeing their slaves. Such strictures might seem to make abolition impossible, but Tucker nevertheless had a solution: "[T]he abolition of slavery may be effected without the *emancipation* of a single slave; without depriving any man of the *property* which he *possesses*."[33]

Tucker's detailed scheme of gradual abolition borrowed from the proposal Jefferson had described in *Notes* and more generally from the gradual abolition plans of some northern states where slaves born after a certain date were declared free, but it treated men and women quite differently, apparently valuing the labor of men more highly. Under Tucker's scheme, female children born to slave mothers after the adoption of the plan would be emancipated, although they would be released from bondage only after twenty-eight years in order that their labor might compensate their masters for the loss. The first generation of male slaves born after the adoption of the plan would remain enslaved for life. The second generation born after the plan was adopted, the children of the freed females, would all be free, though they would be bound to serve as apprentices until the age of twenty-one.

Criticizing the wholesale colonization of blacks as unfeasible, while as-

---

33. St. George Tucker, *Dissertation on Slavery*, preface, 9, 24–28, 39, 75–80. Tucker cited Jefferson on two important points, first that, in Tucker's words, "[t]he early impressions of obedience and submission, which slaves have received among us, and the no less habitual arrogance and assumption of superiority, among the whites, contribute, equally, to unfit the former for *freedom*, and the latter for *equality*." Tucker quoted Jefferson's discussion of the same point in a long footnote. Second, Tucker's discussion of the impossibility of blacks and whites living together relied heavily on Jefferson's *Notes on the State of Virginia*, which he cited at length.

serting the difficulties of the two races' living together, Tucker suggested that freed slaves could be kept in a state of *"civil* slavery," that is to say, of legal inequality, an idea that did presage the disfranchisement of many free blacks a century later. In Tucker's scheme, freed slaves would be barred from "taking, holding, or exercising, any public office, freehold, franchise or privilege, or any estate . . . other than a lease not exceeding twenty-one years." Moreover, they would not be allowed to bear arms, marry whites, serve as attorneys or jurors, or act as witnesses except against other blacks. They would legally be the equivalent of minors rather than adults, incapable even of making or executing wills. Tucker's hope was that by "denying them the most valuable privileges which civil government affords," he could "render it their inclination and their interest to seek those privileges in some other climate." Those free blacks who remained in Virginia despite its hostile environment and did not colonize themselves to some other land (Tucker suggested Spanish Louisiana) would at least be rendered harmless by their civil inequality. Tucker also suggested that over time prejudice against them might eventually wane.[34]

Although St. George Tucker was a man with a fine legal mind and a deep commitment to the Enlightenment principles of liberty and natural rights, his abolition scheme made little sense because it could not fully reconcile love of liberty with antipathy toward the idea of a mixed-race free society. Tucker hoped blacks would emigrate even though the first generation of males would remain slaves their whole lives. Did he expect women to leave their husbands and strike out for Louisiana on their own? Tucker proposed civil slavery to replace domestic slavery even though he had criticized slavery in his *Dissertation* precisely because of the way it distorted the law in denying people equal rights. He suggested that by legally infantilizing blacks, whites might learn to overcome their fear and their prejudices, that by institutionalizing racism in the law he could set the stage for its disappearance. Further, he argued that since enslaved people desired freedom, liberating African Americans from slavery would prevent rebellion; conversely, keeping them in civil slavery would repress, rather than stimulate, their desire for further freedom, burying the seeds of their ambition "too deep, ever to germinate." The contradictions of Tucker's scheme and the logical quagmire into which he fell sprang inevitably from his divided strategy: trying to rid Virginia of the evil of slavery while embracing American slavery's twin thought, the profound and unyielding be-

34. Ibid., 82–92.

lief that blacks and whites could live together only if blacks remained firmly under white control.³⁵

The conflicting goals of ending slavery while preserving white dominance and black subservience shaped two other plans suggested by prominent Virginians that have been noted by historians as emancipation schemes but are more properly understood as proposals for colonization: the scheme suggested by St. George Tucker's cousin, George Tucker, in the wake of the scare brought about by Gabriel's thwarted rebellion of 1800 and the plan of the Virginia planter Ferdinando Fairfax, published in 1790 in Philadelphia. Unlike Jefferson's or St. George Tucker's scheme, neither George Tucker's *Letter . . . with a Proposal for their Colonization* nor Fairfax's "Plan for Liberating the Negroes within the United States" would have required owners to free their slaves. In fact, Tucker rejected an emancipation scheme because "Negroes, if once emancipated, would never rest satisfied with any thing short of perfect equality," and equality was not a viable goal because of the "impossibility of amalgamating such discordant materials" as black and white. Driven by the fear of slave revolt and certain that the removal of African Americans from Virginia was the only way to guarantee white safety, George Tucker suggested placing a poll tax on slaves that would fund their purchase by the state and their subsequent removal to western territories. Like his cousin's, his thoughts turned to the Spanish lands west of the Mississippi, which might be purchased for the project. Fairfax, writing to a national audience rather than to fellow Virginians, explained that the "general feelings" of Virginia whites toward the idea of "free intercourse" with blacks were "very repugnant," and therefore blacks ought to be colonized elsewhere. He suggested Africa. His plan depended on voluntary manumission and would therefore end slavery in America only if all slaveholders relinquished their slaves of their own accord.³⁶

35. Ibid., 16–20, 93. Phillip Hamilton sees the main tension in Tucker's scheme as between property rights and natural rights but does not identify race as an impediment to Tucker's thought in part because his argument rests on the idea that the Tucker family's degradation of Africans came only after they were forced to accept slavery's permanence. Hamilton, "Revolutionary Principles," 535–37, 550–51. According to Joanne Pope Melish, in *Disowning Slavery,* the belief that blacks ought to be subordinated to whites dominated in New England as well and persisted well after slavery there ended.

36. George Tucker, *Letter to a Member of the General Assembly,* 14, 16, 17–20; Ferdinando Fairfax, "Plan for Liberating the Negroes within the United States," *American Museum* (Philadelphia) 8 (Dec. 1790): 285–87, reprinted in Nash, *Race and Revolution,* 146–50. Nash accepts Fairfax's plan as an

At least one anonymous correspondent joined the prominent Jefferson, Fairfax, and Tuckers in attempting to draft a workable proposal to remove slaves and slavery from Virginia and was similarly caught among conflicting ideas and impulses. "A.C." wrote to the *Virginia Independent Chronicle and General Advertiser* in 1790 to decry the inflammatory rhetoric of antislavery radicals, those who "call themselves friends to liberty (who hold no slaves)" but whose antislavery words "lessen the value of that kind of property." A.C. also attacked the most extreme proslavery arguments, particularly those that compared slaves simply to any other kind of property, such as cattle. Cattle, A.C. pointed out, "being devoid of common understanding may be bought and sold without knowing any change in their situation," while slaves were cognizant beings for whom talk of emancipation might inspire hope. If that hope for freedom were not fulfilled, "it will cause them to devise other means"—violent revolution—to "hasten *that* which they have but in vain waited for."[37]

While A.C. recognized enslaved blacks' full humanity, he did not think slavery was immoral since God had approved it. A.C. knew from the Bible that "one people were to be in perpetual bondage to another," though he was not certain whether race had been a factor in the time of Moses: "I . . . know not what *colour* the people were of whom the Almighty called '*the Heathen*' in the 25th chapter of Exodus." In America, he knew, color was important, and his proposal, like others, sprang from the premise that blacks were inferior and unable to care for themselves, a notion at odds with his fear that they might have the motivation and wherewithal to plan an insurrection. Fittingly, then, his scheme embraced at its core a contradiction, ending slavery without actually ending slavery. He called for an act of assembly freeing all slaves but requiring them and their descendants to remain with their masters "under the character of servants for and during the term of ninety-nine years—that their said masters shall provide for them necessary clothes, meat, drink," and other provisions. Servants would be protected from "unmerciful abuse" by the provision that such mistreatment would guarantee their full emancipation. By changing the name of the institution, calling slaves "servants," and by separating service from property rights, A.C. thought he could satisfy everyone. "The master will not be deprived of his servant—the value of him will not

---

abolition plan, even though it would not have ended slavery, and criticizes northerners for failing to support what I argue are unworkable southern proposals. Nash, *Race and Revolution*, 42–50.

37. *Virginia Independent Chronicle and General Advertiser* (Richmond), 2 June 1790.

be lessened—the friends to liberty will sleep quiet on their downy pillows . . . and the poor negroes will be put on a better footing than if they were let to wander up and down the country . . . without [possessions]."[38]

Like George Tucker's and Ferdinando Fairfax's proposals, then, A.C.'s plan was not really an abolition plan. Indeed, it was the least sensible of the bunch. Perhaps because all these schemes were designed not to offend, they did not inspire the kind of defense the Methodist attack on slavery did. Perhaps, too, Virginians failed to denounce them in public because their authors were insiders, members of the Virginia elite, rather than outsiders (as were both Asbury and Coke) seeking to alter Virginia culture. Most important was that most slaveholding readers could see that all of these authors sympathized with them and took into account the common assumption that free blacks and whites could not live together, that black liberty would somehow threaten white freedom and security. If white Virginians such as the authors of these proposals had had confidence in black inferiority, they would have assumed that free blacks, like enslaved blacks, would naturally submit to white rule. But they assumed instead that blacks would either rebel or seek equality, or both. In spite of their racism, they recognized the common humanity of all Virginians, if not always as explicitly as A.C. did. Their plans to reduce or end slavery paid homage to and were limited by racial prejudice even as they betrayed the sense that racial distinctions might be specious.

GROWING OPPOSITION TO MANUMISSION AND FREE BLACKS

While the threat of violence spurred some, such as A.C. and George Tucker, to consider how to ameliorate slavery, it convinced a larger number of the dangers of emancipation, since like Jefferson they viewed free blacks with anxiety and suspicion. From the 1780s to the turn of the century, social disruption and fear of racial disorder prompted many white Virginians to protest against both manumission and the existence of free blacks. The tumult of the recent War for Independence, demographic shifts in Tidewater Virginia's population, and evangelizing by new religious groups created a sense of unease among white Virginians, especially those living in the eastern parts of the state. Even more disturbing was news in 1791 that slaves in Saint Domingue, the French portion of the Caribbean island of Hispaniola, had revolted and declared their freedom. Nine years later the discovery of Gabriel's plot, a conspiracy of

38. Ibid.

slaves in the Richmond area to rise against the upper classes of white society, threw many whites into a panic. Because free people of color embodied social disarray—they were neither fully free nor fully enslaved, not white but since blackness signified enslavement not quite black either—white Virginians turned their attention to that group even when disruptive events had little to do with free blacks directly. They also endorsed reforming the laws regarding free and enslaved African Americans and petitioned their legislators to restrict manumission. In the generation after the Revolution demographic and economic change, along with convulsive events both inside and outside the commonwealth and the mistaken notion that free blacks would lead slaves to rebellion, shaped the evolving discussion over manumission and emancipation more than the preaching of antislavery enthusiasts or the unfeasible emancipation-colonization schemes of the liberal elite.

Two related developments altered the demography of eastern Virginia in the last quarter of the eighteenth century, generating apprehension among many white Virginians. First, the Tidewater economy, which had given rise to many of the colonial elites, continued to see a significant decline in tobacco production due to soil exhaustion and decreasing profitability, a trend begun in the late colonial period. Thomas Tudor Tucker was not alone when he lamented in 1783 that economic conditions had reduced him to "the Condition of a Beggar." Looking to make new fortunes elsewhere, the children of many Tidewater planters moved westward into the northern Piedmont, Southside, and Valley regions. While both the slave and white populations in recently settled areas of western and southern Virginia increased rapidly at the end of the eighteenth century, in the Tidewater the white population decreased both in absolute numbers and in relation to the black population. African Americans made up more than 50 percent of the population in most of the Tidewater at the end of the century, and their numerical dominance grew noticeably between 1790 and 1810.[39]

The greater incidence of manumission in eastern Virginia, itself partly a function of the declining Tidewater tobacco economy, also caused a marked increase in the number of free blacks there, which was at least as disturbing to whites as the fact that slaves made up a majority of the population.[40] A small

39. Thomas Tudor Tucker to St. George Tucker, 9 Feb. 1783, quoted in Hamilton, "Revolutionary Principles," 538; *Return of the Whole Number of Persons* (1791), 48–50; *Return of the Whole Number of Persons* (1800), 2H–2I; *Aggregate amount of each description of Persons*, 54–56.

40. But as noted above in chapter 2, the number of manumissions in a county did not correlate precisely to the size of the free black population.

but significant portion of free blacks migrated to urban areas, and it was there especially that they seemed to many whites to be growing out of control. As early as 1790 free blacks made up 7 percent of the total population of Richmond, and nearly 20 percent of Richmond's black population. In Petersburg too the free black population formed a sizable portion of the town's population, 11 percent in 1790 and 12 percent in 1800. Perhaps more important, the number of free blacks in Petersburg grew in proportion to the slave population over the course of that decade, from 25 percent to 29 percent of the total black population. In Norfolk free blacks formed only 2 percent of the population in 1790, but that proportion had more than doubled by 1800, to 5 percent, or about one-tenth of the African American population in the port city. Between 1790 and 1800 the total free black population in Virginia grew by more than one-third, to nearly twenty thousand people. Though most communities had no more than a few free black families, whites worried that the relatively large urban free black population would provide a haven for escaped slaves and would be the crucible in which plans for insurrection might be forged. Their fears were not entirely unjustified since urban centers did function as good hiding places for runaway slaves, who could not easily be distinguished from free blacks, and Gabriel's plot was hatched among slaves who worked in Richmond and Petersburg, though free blacks were not among Gabriel's top lieutenants.[41]

To some, the post-Revolutionary changes—talk of emancipation; a few well-publicized acts of emancipation by such notables as Robert Carter, who famously freed about 450 slaves; the actual growth of the free black population; the decreasing importance of plantation slavery in eastern Virginia; and the decline in white population there—all seemed to have eroded the control of whites over blacks in the older parts of the state. The frequent practice of hiring skilled slaves out to work for other people or of allowing them to hire themselves out, which was illegal, also seemed to be undermining social stability. Self-hire, which occurred especially in urban areas such as Richmond, provided privileged slaves with a moderate degree of independence and even gave them the means to raise money to purchase their freedom. Disturbingly to white Virginians, it was precisely in the locales that had the largest African

---

41. *Return of the Whole Number of Persons* (1791); *Return of the Whole Number of Persons* (1800); Bogger, *Free Blacks in Norfolk*, 22–23; Sidbury, *Ploughshares into Swords*, chaps. 5–6. In Baltimore too a large population of free blacks provided a community into which an escaped slave could disappear. See Whitman, *Price of Freedom*, 69–76.

American populations and the largest number of free blacks that the slave system seemed the least secure.[42]

It was also from those regions that almost all the petitions to the legislature protesting the 1782 manumission law came, and for the same reason: uneasiness about the state of society and about the stability of slavery and race. Opposition to manumission began in the 1780s, even before the number of free blacks began to rise noticeably, and increased over time. At first whites' fears of manumission were tied to the turmoil of the war years. Accomack County citizens' 1782 petition, which they hoped would prevent the passage of the manumission law but which arrived in the House of Delegates after the law had already passed, argued that individual manumission ought not to be allowed in part because freed slaves would provide shelter to runaways, who had already done "great damage" in "this place under sanction of [the] British Government." There were several other practical reasons not to allow manumission: to protect the tax base (slaves) in order not to "greatly lessen the Revenue"; to avoid having to support freed slaves, who would "likely become chargeable" to the county as indigents; and more generally to prevent the creation of a people whose "liberty would greatly endanger our own." Reflecting that paradox so common in American slave societies, public opinion as expressed in the petition stood squarely against actual behavior, since Accomack residents freed large numbers of slaves between 1782 and 1806.[43]

Petitioners from Hanover and Henrico counties also referred to the disruptions of the war years and expressed fears that free blacks would cause further social disorder. In their 1784 petitions (which were identical in their text) they complained that "slaves taken by the British Army are now passing in this Country as free men." In addition, "free Negroes" were operating as "agents, factors, and carriers" for slaves, transporting property stolen from their masters. Among the "many Evils" created by manumission was that it became

---

42. The *Virginia Gazette and General Advertiser* (Richmond) reported on 28 September 1791, "*We are informed, that Mr. Robert Carter, of Nominy, has emancipated* FOUR HUNDRED *and* FORTY TWO SLAVES." Placing the number of emancipated slaves in capital letters was the extent of the newspaper's comment. The argument in this paragraph follows that of Douglas Egerton and James Sidbury in their respective studies of Gabriel's Richmond, although I find Egerton's assertion that "slavery was in a dangerous state of chaos by the end of the eighteenth century" to be an overstatement. Egerton, *Gabriel's Rebellion*, 17–18; Sidbury, *Ploughshares into Swords*, 184–201. See also Frey, *Water from the Rock*, 222–27.

43. Accomack County petition, 3 June 1782, LP, Accomack County.

difficult to tell who was enslaved and who was free, a problem of particular relevance in Henrico's city of Richmond, where slave self-hire was as common as it was illegal. The petitioners feared that slaves would pass as free people and that owners who relied on their wealth in slaves to cover their debts might consequently be left bankrupt. To remedy the "Evils" they had described, the petitioners requested that the 1782 act authorizing individual manumission be repealed, that black people claiming to be free be forced to carry identification papers, and that free blacks not be allowed to trade with slaves. Only the last two provisions would have been necessary to address their concerns, and the 1782 law had indeed stipulated that free people of color who traveled out of their home counties carry copies of their manumission papers. The petitioners asked for repeal of the manumission law, which was not necessary to correct the injuries they enumerated, because they viewed the emancipation of even a few slaves as a threat to Virginia's social order.[44]

The 1785 anti-Methodist petitions calling for repeal of the manumission law can also be seen as a response to social disorder—the disruptive evangelizing of preachers who called for emancipation. That petition, unlike the previous ones, prompted the legislature to respond. Just three years after the passage of the manumission law, Speaker of the House Benjamin Harrison, whom the Quaker activist Robert Pleasants identified as an enemy to the antislavery cause, cast the deciding vote in favor of a resolution (not an actual bill) to repeal it. James Madison commented, "I hope the bill which must follow [the resolution] on the subject may be less successful. Many who concurred in the Resolution will probably be content finally with some amendment of the law in favor of creditors." Madison's hopes were fulfilled, as the bill to repeal the 1782 act failed by a vote of fifty-two to thirty-five, and the delegates decided instead to consider amendments to the manumission law, which they finally did two years later. The 1787 amendments, probably addressing the rights of creditors who had an interest in slaves who might be manumitted, included a provision that would have forced emancipated slaves to depart the state within twelve months of obtaining their freedom or else be taken up by the overseers of the poor and sold back into slavery, with the profits from the sales benefiting the poor of the county. This proposal, very similar to the law eventually passed in 1806, was soundly defeated by a vote of fifty-six to thirty-two, with more

---

44. Petitions of 16 Nov. 1784, LP, Hanover and Henrico counties, transcribed in Schmidt and Wilhelm, "Early Proslavery Petitions," 138.

than twenty members abstaining. George Mason, who had called for an antiimportation act and decried the existence of slavery in Virginia, was among those favoring the expulsion of freed slaves, highlighting again that antislavery sentiments could easily coexist with antiblack sentiments. The other amendments, of which there is no record, also failed.[45]

Peter Albert's examination of the voting patterns on both the 1785 bill to repeal the manumission law and the 1787 move to expel freed slaves shows that there was a nascent but still indefinite sectionalism in Virginia in the 1780s. Delegates from eastern counties that had a large population of blacks (enslaved and free) were more likely to support both measures, indicating their greater sensitivity to social change and their greater fear of free blacks. But the geographic distribution of the votes showed no clear lines, and in many counties delegates took opposing views. Ambivalence still marked many leaders' views toward manumission.[46]

Perhaps it was that ambivalence that kept lawmakers in the 1780s from heeding the calls of those who wished to end private manumission. In fact, the legislature served as a brake to slow the antiemancipation impulse. Along with the abolition schemes drafted by members of the Virginia elite, legislative records suggest that the leaders of the state were more liberal on the subject than many of their constituents. In the 1787 session, for instance, they confirmed two acts of manumission that predated the 1782 law. In one, the legislature rejected pleas from the descendants of Joseph Mayo, who had asked the legislature to void Mayo's pre-1782 (illegal) emancipation of his slaves and instead devise the slaves to them, Mayo's heirs. A year later, the legislature failed to act on a petition from citizens of Henrico County complaining that the manumission law was "imperfect and unjust" since certificates of manumission were "liable to forgery" and insufficient provision was made in them to "guard the

---

45. *JHD* (begun Oct. 1785), 91–92, 110; James Madison to Ambrose Madison, 15 Dec. 1785, in *Writings of James Madison*, 2:203–4; *JHD* (begun Oct. 1787), 35, 45, 48, 57, 126, 128–29. Albert notes that the delegates who asked leave to introduce the 1787 amendments all came from counties with a high proportion of African Americans—Charles City, Greensville, Halifax, King William, and Richmond counties. Albert, "Protean Institution," 227. Since no roll call was requested, the vote by which the bill "to amend the act, to authorise the manumission of slaves" was defeated is unknown. The expulsion provision had been voted on separately.

46. Albert, "Protean Institution," 227–32. Delegates who came from counties where the free black population was more than 1.1 percent were more likely to support expulsion.

rights of creditors." In 1791 the legislature again blocked a move to amend the manumission law.[47]

News of the revolution in Saint Domingue altered the mood in the legislature, as well as in the populace, white and black, at large. The revolution, in which free mulattoes and slaves battled whites in a long and bloody war that ended slavery and eventually released Saint Domingue from French colonial control, began with agitation among whites and mulattoes from 1789 to 1791 and developed into a full-scale war after the slaves revolted in August 1791. After that, the battles took place largely along racial lines, which in the context of the French Caribbean meant that free mulattoes and the darker-skinned rebel slaves fought against each other as well as sometimes in concert. The year before, a newspaper writer (commenting on A.C.'s observation that slaves were not like cattle) had warned, "Slaves have understanding enough to know, when so much noise is made by a part of the community about their emancipation, that the time perhaps may come when they shall be free—and that the time being spun out longer than they have patience to wait for, will be the cause of much bloodshed, by insurrections or other means equally as unlawful and unnatural!" Actual violence in Saint Domingue signaled that "bloodshed" and "insurrections" by impatient slaves might be at hand in Virginia. Of particular concern were reports of how the news of Saint Domingue had affected slaves. One was heard to say, "You see how the blacks has killed the whites in the French Island and took it a little while ago," and others apparently plotted rebellions, found out by whites in several locations in Virginia in 1792 and 1793.[48]

A few white Virginians saw the abolition of slavery as the only way to obviate a vengeful war prosecuted by enslaved rebels against their masters, but the majority disagreed and thought that emancipation, both individual, private manumission and any plan for general emancipation, would hasten rather than prevent insurrection. As individual manumission came under suspicion after 1791, white manumitters found themselves vulnerable to attack as enemies to their own people. The Accomack County delegate Thomas Evans, who freed three of his slaves that year, wrote later that other members of the Virginia legislature thought of him as "one who has set all his negroes free,"

---

47. *JHD* (begun Oct. 1787), 25, 75, 79; Hening, *Statutes*, 12:611, 613 (1787); *JHD* (begun Oct. 1788), 45; Albert, "Protean Institution," 230.

48. *Virginia Independent Chronicle and General Advertiser*, 2 June 1790; Ott, *Haitian Revolution*, 61–62; Jordan, *White over Black*, 381; Albert, "Protean Institution," 237–38.

when in fact he had liberated only some of his slaves, and as someone who "wishes by a law to affect a general emancipation, to cause to be reacted all the horrors of the West Indies," which was equally untrue, since he was "adverse [*sic*] to an indiscriminate and general emancipation, tho' I have lamented the evil of slavery in our Country." An anonymous writer explained the antimanumission logic in the pages of the *Virginia Gazette and General Advertiser*, arguing that even "a partial, though continued emancipation" would have many deleterious effects. Continuing to allow individual manumission would induce "those who remain slaves to become more restless and disobedient at seeing free negroes multiplied" and would provide free blacks with "great opportunities" to "form plans and make combinations with slaves for insurrection and all its horrors." By this reasoning, Evans's act of manumission, once judged perhaps as a noble deed in the spirit of the American Revolution, was dangerous. It was also politically damaging.[49]

Increasingly restrictive laws regarding manumission and free blacks reflected the new attitude of many legislators. The timing in and of itself does not prove that news of the bloodshed on Saint Domingue altered lawmakers' opinions, but at least one statute made specific reference to the West Indies. A 1793 law (mentioned in chapter 1) stated that slaves illegally brought into Virginia from Africa or the West Indies would not go free as the 1778 anti-importation law had provided but would instead be exported. White Virginians wanted to keep their commonwealth sealed off from foreign blacks, who might have dreams or experience of revolution. In 1792 the legislature modified the manumission law to favor the creditors and heirs of the emancipator by allowing emancipated slaves to be confiscated to satisfy debts their former masters had contracted before the act of emancipation had taken place, a provision probably similar to one in the rejected 1787 bill. This new provision threatened the security of emancipation and recognized property rights to be superior to the rights of "freed" slaves. A similar provision in a 1795 law allowed a widow to choose one-third of her husband's estate instead of what was provided to her in his will, including one-third of the slaves even if they had been emancipated by the will. Though not frequently enforced, the passage

---

49. Thomas Evans to John Cropper, 6 Dec. 1796, John Cropper Papers; *Virginia Gazette and General Advertiser*, 30 Oct. 1793. Also, the *Norfolk Gazette and Public Ledger*, 22 Sept. 1804, for example, reprinted an antislavery pamphlet that cited the Haitian Revolution as evidence of the kind of revenge slaves could take.

of these laws nevertheless signified an important change in values in Virginia and coincided with the changing practice of manumission as slaveholders began to free slaves more as a reward for good behavior than as a reflection of antislavery beliefs.[50]

While narrowing, though subtly, the ability of owners to free their slaves, the legislature also began to address the effects of manumission—the rapidly growing number of free blacks. In 1793 the legislators passed two important laws, one designed to slow the growth of the free black population by banning "the migration of free negroes and mulattoes into this commonwealth" and another that required free blacks to register with local officials, the first in a series of similar laws. The registration laws were designed to prevent the "great inconveniences" that arose from hiring out "negroes and mulattoes, who pretend to be free, but are in fact slaves." The 1793 registration law applied to free black laborers in Virginia's towns and rural areas, who according to the terms of the law had to register with the local town or county clerk and obtain at a cost of twenty-three cents certificates confirming their status. As with many of today's laws regarding illegal aliens, the law's burdens fell on employers; anyone who hired an African American who did not have a certificate would be subject to a fine and liable to a lawsuit. Registration laws, enforced sporadically, led to the creation of free negro registers, ledgers kept by clerks in which they recorded free blacks' names and vital characteristics.[51]

Forcing free black workers to register with local officials was only one way of defining society's rights in terms of race rather than in terms of free or slave status in the postmanumission era, and the effort to reinforce Virginia's racial divisions was made necessary precisely because the racial system seemed unstable. The 1792 slave code dictated that no African American, enslaved or free, could serve as a witness against white people, and a law setting out harsh punishment for striking or using abusive language toward a white person applied equally to free and enslaved people of color. Demonstrating their fear that free blacks would conspire with slaves, the legislature enacted a statute

50. Shepherd, *Statutes at large of Virginia*, 1:239 (1793), 1:128 (1792), 1:363–65 (1795). Traditionally a woman could choose her widow's share, one-third of the estate, instead of what was provided by her husband's will. The 1795 act, designed to prevent men from impoverishing their widows, said that if a widow could be provided her portion without including slaves, then the slaves could indeed be emancipated. For a case in which a creditor tried to claim emancipated slaves to satisfy a debt, see *Woodley and Wife and Others, v. Abby and Other Paupers*, 9 Va. 336.

51. Ibid., 1:238 (1793).

in 1797 stating that all free persons who "advise or conspire with a slave, to rebel or make insurrection, . . . shall suffer death without benefit of clergy, by hanging by the neck."[52]

In the same spirit of maintaining racial order legislators tried to shore up solidarity among Virginia whites. Laws prohibiting free people, including whites, from attending any illegal meeting of slaves were on the books from 1792 and provided that offending persons could be struck with up to twenty lashes. Since this type of corporal punishment was usually reserved for slaves and free blacks, it was particularly demeaning when applied to whites. White abolitionists were viewed with especial suspicion by legislators, who in a 1795 act referred to "great and alarming mischiefs" that had arisen in other states where abolition groups tried to help slaves obtain their freedom. In doing so, white advocates for emancipation acted against the proper "sovereignty and duty of society." Lawmakers laid out procedures by which slaves who felt they were due freedom might sue for it without the aid of abolitionists—*in forma pauperis,* as paupers represented by counsel who would serve without fee and would consequently have little financial incentive to act vigorously on behalf of their enslaved clients. The law also tried to limit the number of freedom suits by levying a steep fine against anyone who aided a slave in bringing a suit that proved unsuccessful. A few years later lawmakers reiterated their suspicion of white abolitionists, barring any person "proved to be a member of any society instituted for the purpose of emancipating negroes from the possession of their masters" from serving as a juror in a suit for freedom.[53]

Gabriel's plot, in 1800, further eroded support for emancipation in Virginia and increased suspicion of free blacks. Gabriel, an enslaved blacksmith, planned to exploit the division he perceived between two classes of whites: oppressive Federalist merchants and an alliance of Frenchmen, Republicans, Quakers, and Methodists who were on the side of liberty. Gabriel hoped that by storming Richmond in the late summer of 1800 with a force of about one thousand soldiers, he could convince the white elite to extend the rights of free people to him and his kind. As Douglas Egerton explains, Gabriel "dreamed of overturning the central class relationship in his society, but not that society itself. He was too much a part of it." To Gabriel, the issue was class more than

52. Ibid., 1:122–30 (1792), 2:77 (1797). The 1792 code also redefined a mulatto as anyone with a black grandparent; the 1705 code had included those with an African great-grandparent in the definition as well.

53. Ibid., 1:363–65 (1795), 2:77 (1798); Nicholls, "Squint of freedom," 55–57.

race. But most white Virginians did not look closely enough to see Gabriel's plot as anything other than a narrowly averted race war. When they got word of the plot from the slave Pharaoh, who told his master of it just before the rebellion was to commence, they reacted quickly. Officials sent out slave patrols and the state militia to enforce the peace and gather up the participants. They established courts of oyer and terminer to try the slave conspirators, and those courts sentenced twenty-seven men to death and decided to transport several others out of Virginia. Whites soon discovered another plot, one involving mostly slaves who worked along Virginia's waterways, in early 1802.[54]

Several details of the events surrounding Gabriel's plot show that Gabriel was right: the alliances in Virginia society did *not* divide precisely or consistently along racial lines. Gabriel had escaped immediate capture because a white Methodist boat captain named Richardson Taylor, who had himself freed his only slave, helped Gabriel make his escape. Eventually it was a fellow slave, a worker on Taylor's ship named Billy, who betrayed Gabriel to authorities, probably hoping that by offering up Gabriel he would receive a monetary award sufficient to purchase his own freedom. In another way too the line between white and black failed to hold. Substantial evidence offered at the trials of the would-be rebels of 1800 pointed to the participation of two white men, at least one of whom was French, in the plot. Governor Monroe apparently suppressed information regarding the collusion of Frenchmen in the plan, probably to protect his Republican Party's political interest (they took a pro-French stance) but probably also to maintain the image of a united white Virginia. Occasional friendships across racial lines appeared to whites to be particularly subversive, for the majority believed that peace, meaning white dominance, could only be maintained if whites stood together to keep the dark-skinned enemy that lived among them in its place, separate, inferior, and enslaved.[55]

To keep racial lines as clear as possible, even if they could not eliminate free blacks, even if experience showed the lines were never clear, the legislature in the wake of Gabriel's conspiracy passed a series of new laws that focused as much on free African Americans as on enslaved ones. They began by extending the free-black registration provisions. The new law required each county commissioner to post a list of the county's free blacks on the courthouse door

54. Egerton, *Gabriel's Rebellion*, 30, 38–51, and passim.
55. Ibid.; Sidbury, *Ploughshares into Swords*, 120–31.

so that all citizens would know who were the free blacks among them. Free people of color who subsequently entered the county would have to prove they had a means of employment, or else they would be treated as legal vagrants. No such provisions existed for whites, and white Virginians who roamed about did not come under the same level of suspicion. In 1802 the legislature required that all free blacks in Virginia's counties, not just laborers, register with the county clerks. A few years later, in early 1805, lawmakers tried to make sure free blacks would remain uneducated and therefore weak by making it illegal for the overseers of the poor to require that free black orphans learn "reading, writing, or arithmetic," as white orphans did. If literacy implied power, owning a gun did so even more. In 1806 the legislature passed a provision further restricting the right of "free negroes and mulattoes" to bear arms (it had been limited in 1723 and 1792 to householders or licensed residents of frontier areas) by prohibiting them from carrying any "fire-lock of any kind, any military weapon, or any powder or lead, without first obtaining a license from the court." In addition, legislators in the first decade of the nineteenth century tightened controls on slave meetings, restricted the movements of black watermen, and made it more difficult for slaves to travel to attend religious meetings. Finally, they tightened the law regarding slave self-hire, now punishing owners who allowed the practice by fining them ten to twenty dollars or by selling the enslaved person, the proceeds to benefit the poor of the county.[56]

The laws concerning emancipation and free blacks that were passed after the Haitian Revolution and the discovery of Gabriel's plot indicate that white Virginians' primary fear regarding emancipation was not so much that the slave system might be subverted by it but that the race system might be undone, both by collusion between free and enslaved blacks to overturn white society and by collusion between blacks and sympathetic whites. Faced with a rapidly growing free black population, legislators had to choose, as they first had had to do during the colonial period, whether to treat free blacks under the law more like free white people or like slaves. Privileging race over freedom, or more precisely, privileging racialized (white) freedom, they reenacted their earlier choice by treating them more like slaves, barring them, like slaves, from freely carrying guns, forcing them to register with local officials and carry certificates of identification, and denying free black orphans the right

56. Shepherd, *Statutes at large of Virginia*, 2:301 (1801), 3:124 (1805), 3:274 (1806), 3:372 (1808); *Revised Code of the Law of Virginia*, chap. III, sec. 67 (1819); Egerton, *Gabriel's Rebellion*, 164–65.

that white orphans had to a basic education. Such laws served as a message both to blacks and to whites that in spite of the manumission law of 1782, which allowed some slaves to be freed, and in spite of the interest some whites had in helping blacks obtain their liberty, the old order represented the ideal: Virginia ought to be two societies, with whites united above and against slaves and any free people who had at least one "negro" grandparent.[57]

RESTRICTION OF MANUMISSION

Eventually the impulse to maintain a clear racial order propelled lawmakers to restrict significantly the manumission of slaves. Just months after Gabriel's plot was uncovered citizens began to call again for an end to voluntary manumission. A group from the Tidewater county of King and Queen sent a petition to the House of Delegates asserting that it was "notorious that the Law for Freeing Negroes hath tended to bring upon us our Disturbed & Distressed Situation." Since the "Soil is our own & self preservation is the first Law in Nature and must be secured at all events," and since a "General Emancipation in their present condition is impossible with our safety," no slaves ought to be freed in the future "except for Meritorious Services." The petitioners asked for a repeal of the 1782 law, aware that banning manumission restricted the rights of slaveowners to do as they pleased with their slave property, including freeing that property, but convinced that the larger interest of society demanded the restriction. Once again racial fear was at the heart of the petitioners' concern: freedom for blacks seemed to open the door to racial mixture, and "commixture to our minds is abhorrent."[58]

---

57. Shepherd, *Statutes at large of Virginia*, 1:122–30 (1792), 3:123 (1805); *Supplement, containing the Acts of the General Assembly*, 93 (1811). Similar though not so extensive restrictions against free blacks had been put in place in the colonial period. See Brown, *Good Wives*, chap. 7. Duncan Macleod, in *Slavery, Race, and the American Revolution*, also notes that the treatment of free blacks demonstrated that "whites saw the basic division in society as lying not between slave and free but between black and white" (165). John Taylor, of Caroline, was an exception. His *Arator* letters, which focused on agricultural improvement, took note of free blacks as a force that weakened agriculture by making slaves "intractable" and by "entic[ing] them into a multitude of crimes and irregularities." His focus seems not to have been racial separateness so much as agricultural efficiency, which demanded a tractable, servile class. Taylor, *Arator*, 115–29.

58. Petition of 2 Dec. 1800, LP, King and Queen County. For a similar discussion of "attempts" to "repair the order" of society, see Macleod, *Slavery, Race, and the American Revolution*, 162–67, quotations from 162.

Though the legislature did not act on this petition, the push to limit manumission or ban it altogether continued. In 1803 the legislature took up a bill that required all slaves subsequently freed to leave the state or else forfeit their freedom. The text of the bill did not reveal its true intent so well as its title, "A Bill to prevent the partial emancipation of Slaves except in certain cases and under certain restrictions." The legislators hoped that by making emancipation difficult and inconvenient, by forcing owners to choose on their slaves' behalf between banishment and bondage, they would discourage manumission. Even if slaveowners did choose to free some slaves, the emancipated slaves would not join the growing population of free blacks that so many white Virginians feared. Legislators were not yet willing to take the retrogressive step of restricting manumission, however, and voted it down by ninety to sixty-one.[59]

Two years later the legislators considered an even more restrictive measure, a bill "to prevent the emancipation of slaves within this Commonwealth," which would have made it unlawful to free any slaves by deed or by will. One legislator commented that "this appears to be a most cruel Law which neither the Safety nor the policy of the state will warrant." While acknowledging that Virginia's stated commitments to "Liberty and the rights of man" were "theoretical principles [that] ought in certain cases to give way for the sake of practical advantages," he did not find in this case that the practical advantages outweighed the value of liberty. Even in 1805 legislators still saw manumission as evidence of Virginia's commitment to Revolutionary ideals—"Liberty and the rights of man"—and saw at the same time that those rights were limited by societal constraints. Apparently other legislators agreed that the bill went too far; it was modified to allow emancipations by deed if the freed slaves left Virginia within six months. The bill still banned emancipation by last will and testament, however, and perhaps for that reason was rejected by the House, but by a narrower margin than the previous bill, eighty-one to seventy-two.[60]

---

59. "A Bill to prevent the partial emancipation of Slaves except in certain cases and under certain restrictions," 28 Dec. 1803, Rough Bills, House of Delegates, LVA, Archives Division. The bill was introduced on 28 December 1803 and sent to the Committee of the Whole House. Then it was ordered to lie on the table. The bill was considered on 24 January 1804, then postponed until 31 March. No further action on the bill was noted.

60. Richard Drummond Bayly to John Cropper, 6 Jan. 1805; "A Bill to prevent the emancipation of slaves within this Commonwealth," 8 Jan. 1805, Rough Bills, House of Delegates, LVA, Archives Division.

By 1806, after several failed attempts to ban manumission, antiemancipation forces had gained strength. During January of that year the House of Delegates again discussed modifications to the manumission law. The original bill considered by the legislature prohibited "by any means whatsoever" the emancipation of slaves. Such a rigid law still did not sit well with the delegates. John Love, from Fauquier County, offered a substitute bill that like the bill of the previous year would have banned emancipations by will. It also would have prohibited delayed emancipations but still allowed emancipation by deed. Love's bill did not state the justification for banning delayed manumission and manumission by will, but the apparent goal was to make manumission less attractive to slaveholders, who would not be able to delay it until some future date or until their death. Love's proposal launched a contentious debate.[61]

The January 1806 debate over how and whether to modify Virginia's manumission law reiterated the essential problem of emancipation, slavery, and race after the American Revolution, namely, the inability to reconcile the basic principles and rights at the core of American political philosophy with one another and with the reality of racial slavery. The rights to property, to liberty, and to safety competed for precedence, and arguments both for and against emancipation could be made by invoking any of these three values. To some extent this discourse revealed how flexible the language of "rights" could be and how "rights" could serve a number of different interests.

John Love, who had offered the substitute bill, began the debate by implicating property rights. He explained that he "conceived the right to emancipate ought not to be taken away" because among the property rights of slaveowners was the right to free slaves. Thomas Robertson, a delegate from Dinwiddie County, countered by invoking society's right to peace and safety, asserting that emancipation "might have a tendency to produce those very evils we would avoid," insurrection. It was by 1806 a familiar cry, but Robertson painted the situation with vivid and horrible strokes. Though, according to Robertson, the numbers of blacks and whites were about equal in Virginia, if it came to race war white women would not fight, while "the females of the blacks would be as ferocious and formidable as the males. Thus the force of the blacks is to the whites as 2 to 1." By portraying black women as fierce warriors, Robertson played on racist notions of Africans that were rooted in

61. *Virginia Argus*, 17 Jan. 1806.

gender, in the idea that Africans were particularly savage because not only their men but also their women were brutal. In contrast, the white women, who would not fight, embodied the gentility of Virginia culture, a gentility that lay vulnerable to depredation. The clear implication of his terrifying prediction was that the necessity of preventing the slaughter of white women and children trumped abstract political rights. Since emancipation only encouraged insurrection—because slaves who see "others like themselves free . . . will repine," because free blacks "obtain some education . . . [and] can thus organize insurrection," and because free blacks "will, no doubt, unite with the slaves"—slaveowners' right to emancipate should be curtailed. "Tell us not of principles," Robertson declared. "Those principles have been annihilated by the existence of slavery among us."[62]

With this pronouncement the level of debate rose to consider the basic values Virginians claimed. Love reiterated that "the right to dispose of property freely should be preserved." But Robertson restated that it was not a question of rights or principle but of policy. If Love were so interested in principle, he ought to recognize that slavery "violates *principle*." Another delegate replied in favor of principle, begging his fellow delegates to remember their political heritage. "In past days these walls have rung with eulogies on liberty. A comparison between those times and the present is degrading to us. We may be equal in intelligence and virtue, but not in the love of liberty." Robertson said again that his concern was "public happiness," a utilitarian rather than an Enlightenment morality. After some further discussion the Speaker of the House, Peter Johnston, put the question succinctly: "Is emancipation an evil or not?" He thought it was, but anyone who did not "might give his slaves a pass to go in the state of Ohio, where he would be free." In other words, Virginia was a land of slavery and could become nothing else. In essence Johnston and Robertson had conceded that although the slave system distorted and violated basic American ideals, the exigencies of the system took precedence over those ideals and could even be used to reshape them.[63]

Legislators as a body were not quite willing, however, to acknowledge that theirs was a society implicitly antagonistic to the principles of the Revolution. They rejected Love's compromise bill that would have banned emancipation

---

62. Ibid. For the ways race and gender shaped each other in the colonial period see Brown, *Good Wives*, passim.

63. *Virginia Argus*, 17 Jan. 1806.

by will and also rejected, but just barely, the original bill banning emancipation altogether by seventy-five to seventy-three. Instead the House adopted a provision forcing slaves freed after 1 May 1806 to leave Virginia within twelve months. Those who did not would "forfeit all such right [to freedom], and may be apprehended and sold by the overseers of the poor of any county or corporation in which he or she shall be found, for the benefit of the poor of such county or corporation." Because legislators had not actually outlawed manumission but only ensured that future emancipations would not add to the free black population, they could feel that they had successfully mediated between important rights and the practical imperative to provide for public safety. But the intent of the law was to curtail manumission, and that was its effect: the number of manumissions in Virginia dropped drastically, and the growth of the free black population slowed markedly after 1806.[64]

Of course there was a flaw in the logic that impelled Virginians to reject emancipation and cast out free blacks. At least one Virginia delegate recognized it. John Minor, from Spotsylvania County, had pointed out during the debate over manumission that free blacks did *not* tend to ally with slaves and that it was not in their interest to foment race war. Minor suggested that public safety would be better served by allowing some slaves to be freed and splitting the black population into two classes. "'Divide and conquer' is as true in policy as it is as a military maxim. The free blacks are sureties for the slaves. It will be their interest to give information of insurrection." Minor pointed out that Gabriel and his followers had been slaves, noting that "in the late insurrection one free black only was accused and he was acquitted." Indeed, in most slave societies it was the case that freed slaves allied with the master class rather than with the slaves; that was, for the masters, a great benefit of manumission.[65]

Unrestricted private manumission had another benefit that had eluded those opposed to it but had been understood by so many of Virginia's manumitters in the years before 1806. As Minor put it, "What will be the situation

64. Shepherd, *Statutes at large of Virginia*, 3:252; *Virginia Argus*, 22 Apr. 1806. See chapter 4, below, for more on the effect of the 1806 law. Iaccarino notes a party split in the final vote on the 1806 law, with most Federalist delegates opposed to the restriction and the majority of Republicans, who outnumbered the Federalists, in support of it. Iaccarino, "Virginia and the National Contest over Slavery," 108–10.

65. *Virginia Argus*, 17 Jan. 1806.

of the blacks if you shut this only door through which they can enter the sacred ground of liberty? They will be fixed in the deepest state of damnation, despair without hope. In such a situation they will prefer death to existence." Rather than take their freedom through violence, slaves who expected emancipation would "wait patiently in hopes of relief." Clearly the majority felt otherwise, that manumission was like a crack in the dam, a dangerous break in the integrity of the race-slave system that might precipitate a deluge of violence. Given the opportunity in the years after the Revolution to redefine race in Virginia so that free people of African descent could be incorporated into society, white Virginians refused, preferring instead to return to the colonial settlement of white over black. The problem with this choice was that it required a constant battle against the reality of change. White Virginians would fight that battle for many years.[66]

In addition to the amended manumission law, the year 1806 brought two other events that helped mark the end of the Revolutionary era. First, the legislature further modified the 1778 law banning the importation of slaves into Virginia, which had already undergone several changes in favor of those who wished to bring slaves with them when they immigrated to Virginia. Now, illegally imported slaves would be "sold for cash" by the overseers of the poor, rather than liberated as the 1778 law had originally provided. No longer would the anti-importation law serve as a vehicle to freedom.[67]

Also, Virginia leaders began to speak in self-consciously racial terms about the meaning of liberty. Significantly, the new language came out of the sectional struggle among whites for power in the state. In the same months that Virginians were debating manumission, some also were attempting to alter their 1776 state constitution. That constitution, which had not provided for amendment and could therefore be changed only through a constitutional convention, had preserved the suffrage requirements and representative scheme of the colonial era. The House of Delegates, like the House of Burgesses, contained two representatives from each county, which gave citizens of small Tidewater counties proportionally more power than those in larger and more populated counties farther west. Voting was reserved for white males with a freehold estate, which the laws at the time of the Revolution defined as either one hundred acres of uncultivated land, twenty-five acres with a house, or a

66. Ibid.
67. Shepherd, *Statutes at large of Virginia*, 3:251 (1806).

house and lot in town and which a 1785 law modified to be fifty acres or, for town-dwellers, an estate worth more than fifty pounds. Thomas Jefferson had long advocated broad suffrage and proportional representation, and western Virginians, who were at a disadvantage under the 1776 arrangement, took up the call for change after the turn of the century. In an 1806 speech in favor of broader suffrage and a more equitable representation scheme, John Burwell, from the southwestern Virginia county of Henry, still used the metaphor of slavery, as so many had during the Revolution, to describe political disfranchisement. Burwell declared disfranchised white men to be "as much *enslaved* as those unfortunate beings who inhabit the Turkish empire." But no longer were *slavery* and *liberty* universal terms. Rather, Burwell had chosen an example that would call up an image of *white* slavery only, and not slavery in general or slavery in Virginia. Similarly, Burwell viewed suffrage as a right not for all free Virginians but only for free whites. Indeed, the idea that freedom for blacks might enfranchise them seemed preposterous, "[f]or in what situation should we be placed, were we to see the sable race crowding round our polls and controuling our elections?" Through such language the sectional quest for greater power took on racial meaning: westerners demanded rights they ought to have not merely as free people but specifically as free white people, the beginning of an argument that would find greater articulation in the state constitutional convention of 1829–30.[68]

CONCLUSION

A number of conditions shaped the changes that occurred in Virginia from the 1780s to the early 1800s, but two stand out. First, Virginians lived in a slave society in which 40 percent of the population was held in bondage, which made white Virginia an implicitly proslavery community, a fact that had been masked briefly by the fervor of the Revolution and the theoretical commitment to universal liberty on the part of so many of Virginia's Revolutionary leaders. Those who promoted emancipation in the Methodist and Baptist

---

68. *Virginia Argus*, 31 Jan. 1806, emphasis mine; Bruce, *Rhetoric of Conservatism*, 2–3; Shade, *Democratizing the Old Dominion*, 53; Curtis, "Jefferson's Chosen People," 66–67 and, for discussion of the political significance of a freehold, chap. 2. Interestingly, Burwell was less opposed to suffrage for women: "For the same reason perhaps, minors and females should be excluded from the right of suffrage, though for my own part . . . I have no very strong objection to the latter." The push for a convention to amend the state constitution continued until one was finally convened in 1829. See chapter 5, below.

churches or proposed schemes for gradual abolition quickly learned that they had little support. They could not advance their antislavery plans in the face of an almost universally shared commitment among whites to a society of white and free people over black and enslaved ones, a commitment that sprang superficially from a belief in black inferiority but deeper down grew out of an anxiety that blacks might, in fact, be whites' equals. Recognizing black equality would, however, have required white Virginians to reconceptualize what it meant to be white or abandon their commitment to whiteness altogether, which would have been too profound a change for most white Virginians of the era to begin to contemplate. Even the small group who proposed a general emancipation of slaves believed that free blacks ought to be expelled in order to preserve the meaning of white freedom in Virginia. Those outside Virginia agreed too. James Sullivan, of Massachusetts, commented, "We have in history but one picture of a similar enterprise [emancipation of a whole race of people], and there we see it was necessary not only to open the sea by a miracle, for them to pass, but more necessary to close it again to prevent their return." Defeated by both external opposition and internal limitations, advocacy for general emancipation in Virginia waned along with Revolutionary sentiments and with ideologically motivated acts of manumission.[69]

The practice of individual manumission persisted, nonetheless, in part because slaveholders had come to understand that manumission could support slave discipline and also because slaveholders viewed their own slaves differently than they did others' slaves. While the enslaved people they owned and knew well were clearly human beings who might sometimes deserve reward, the general population of Virginia's slaves appeared to be a potentially insurrectionary mass. The disjunction between slaveholders' views of their own slaves and their views of slaves in general explains the disjunction between the behavior of manumitters in their local communities and the decisions made in the state legislature. It was in fact typical of Virginia and other slave states that laws and policy, which often represented slaveholders' worst fears, were far more restrictive than the day-to-day behavior of slaveholders. Such was the case with the 1782 law banning slave self-hire, which slaveowners regularly vio-

---

69. James Sullivan to Jeremy Belknap, quoted in St. George Tucker, *Dissertation on Slavery*, 77. Scholars have recently begun to examine the historical development of "whiteness" as a privileged racial construction. The starting place for these works is Roediger, *Wages of Whiteness*.

lated, just as they and their slaves ignored laws elsewhere barring slaves from selling produce at markets or from keeping their own garden plots.[70]

The growth of a larger and more visible free black population, a consequence of the hundreds of acts of manumission that took place in the years 1782–1806, was a second factor affecting the hardening of public attitudes toward private manumission, general emancipation, and free people of color. Free blacks became the scapegoat for white Virginians' anxieties over the social and economic changes of the post-Revolutionary years, and whites channeled their urge to reestablish order into a program for controlling free blacks and limiting manumission. In the process, logic forced them to become more explicit about the limits of liberty in post-Revolutionary Virginia. The convulsions of the Saint Domingue revolution in the 1790s and Gabriel's plot in 1800 provided additional impetus to curtail emancipation, since so many white Virginians believed, despite the evidence and sometimes in spite of their own desire to free one or more favorite slaves, that emancipation promoted insurrection and race war.

Many advocates of emancipation, realizing by the end of the eighteenth century that they had little hope of effecting abolition, accommodated themselves to the shift in temperament and values. Francis Asbury, for example, wrote in 1798, "I am brought to conclude slavery will exist in Virginia perhaps for ages; there is not a sufficient sense of religion nor of liberty to destroy it." By 1809, perhaps to ease his mind or to lessen his sense of failure, he had turned his attention to the condition of slaves instead of the possibility of abolition, asking, "Would not an *amelioration* in the condition and treatment of slaves have produced more practical good to the poor Africans, than any attempt at their *emancipation?*"[71]

---

70. On ignoring laws regarding slave self-hire see Egerton, *Gabriel's Rebellion*, 25–26; and Sidbury, *Ploughshares into Swords*, 192–93 (Sidbury mistakenly dates the law to 1781).

71. *Journal of Rev. Francis Asbury*, 2:367, 3:298.

4

"White negroes" and "inchoate freedom"

LIFE AFTER MANUMISSION

> She is a woman of the most unexceptionable character and uncommon respectability of her colour, ... an usefull and excellent citizen, ... [W]e should regrett the losing her notwithstanding her colour.
>
> TESTIMONIAL OF WHITE CITIZENS ACCOMPANYING THE PETITION OF JANE BELL, 1827

EVEN AFTER THE 1806 amendment barring subsequently freed slaves from Virginia took effect, whites' attitudes toward emancipation and the position of free blacks in Virginia remained complex and sometimes contradictory. Though the first decades of the nineteenth century were a time when official policies toward enslaved and free blacks became harsher, judges in suits of freedom less lenient, and race even more salient, most white Virginians did not claim slavery was desirable. They did, however, continue to try to re-establish the racial order of the pre-Revolutionary period, in which white and black had coincided more neatly with free and slave, even as they acknowledged the problems of the post-Revolutionary age, in which free blacks existed in substantial numbers, in which many white Virginians remained ambivalent about slavery's morality, and in which personal relationships between blacks and whites often undermined the ideal of racial separateness. These ambiguities had a deep impact on African Americans in the Old Dominion, typified by the life of Samuel Johnson, who was born a slave in 1775 and grew up to represent all the tensions of a society caught between race and liberty. After purchasing his freedom in 1811, Johnson petitioned the Virginia legislature for permission to remain in the state as an exception to the 1806 law. Thirty-eight of the county's white citizens endorsed his petition, stating that "he wishes to remain amongst us, we wish it also," and the legislature approved too. In subsequent petitions, in which Johnson appealed to the legislature to allow him to free his wife and children, whom he had purchased, many more of the white citizens of Fauquier County, hundreds of them, endorsed Johnson's requests. Johnson, free but colored, worked nearly his whole adult life to attain what almost all white men could count on: living in the place of his choice with family members who were free. He was by all accounts a model citizen, a hard worker, a responsible adult. But he was denied the fulfillment of his dream by the ever-stronger conviction of white Virginia over the first three decades of the nineteenth century that if dark-skinned people were to be on American soil, they ought to be so only as slaves.[1]

THE QUEST FOR FREEDOM AFTER 1806

Freedom for African Americans became more difficult to attain and more precarious after 1806, with the major exception that during the War of 1812 enslaved Virginians once again gained an opportunity to run toward the British and freedom. One measure of the general difficulty slaves had in becoming free after 1806 was the precipitous drop in the number of manumissions effected after that date. In Chesterfield County, for example, no one freed slaves by deed of manumission from 1807 to 1818, and from then to 1860 only seven parties manumitted slaves, compared with the twenty-nine people who had liberated 119 slaves from 1782 to 1806. In the town of Petersburg, where 173 slaves had gained their freedom from 1782 to 1806, not a single slave was emancipated in the five years following the passage of the 1806 law, and from 1810 to 1820 the free black population there grew only minimally. In Loudoun County only nine manumission documents appeared in the records from 1806 to 1818, while sixty-three were filed from 1790 to 1806. In Accomack County too the number of deeds of manumission dropped quickly after 1806, although county residents continued to manumit slaves regularly in their wills until about 1808.[2]

1. Sam's petition, 1811, LP, Fauquier County. Evidence of Johnson's age comes from the free black register. See *Fauquier County, Virginia Register of Free Negroes*. Johnson registered in 1817 and was listed as aged about forty-two or forty-three.

2. General Index to Deeds, 1749–1913, Chesterfield County Deeds; Lebsock, *Free Women of Petersburg*, 92, 94; Stevenson, *Life in Black and White*, 264; Accomack County Wills (1806–9). See also tables in Berlin, *Slaves without Masters*, 46, 136. As John Russell puts it in *The Free Negro in Virginia*, "The adoption in 1806 of a new policy respecting manumitted slaves should be considered as the point of division between two stages in the progress of manumission in Virginia" (74–75).

John Heveningham, of Chesterfield County, stated the major reason for the decline in manumissions. In his will of 1809 he wrote, "My intent and design was to have made those slaves absolutely free and my wish is that they shall be so, if ever the existing law providing that emancipated slaves shall remove themselves out of this Commonwealth shall be repealed." Zorobabel Ames, of Accomack County, also wished to free his slaves but did not want to force them to leave Virginia. Therefore, he offered his adult slaves (those over twenty-five years) the option of remaining in service to his wife "untill it should be so that they could be freed without leaving the State, at which time if they choose it my desire is they should be free." Heveningham, Ames, and others weighed the cruelty of slavery against the cruelty of exile and decided that the latter was worse. Especially if would-be freedpeople had family members in Virginia who were still enslaved, forcing them to leave for unknown territory would have been callous and cold. Other, less-informed citizens interpreted the 1806 statute as a "law prohibiting emancipation," which it was not. Nevertheless, that perception also accounted for the decline in the incidence of manumission after 1806.[3]

When whites did manumit slaves after 1806 they followed the pattern established in the mid-1790s: they generally freed slaves in exchange for special service or sentiment, not as a response to natural-rights philosophy. For example, Thomas Higginbotham was "induced" to free his slave Archy Cary in 1827 because Archy had "behaved himself with much propriety" and was "an honest, and faithful servant." Dick Skurrey was emancipated as a reward for serving his mistress well as the foreman of her plantations, and Jane Bell was "left free by the bill of Abraham Waters . . . in consequence of her good Conduct."[4]

The character of manumission as a whole did shift, however, as the proportion of African American manumitters grew significantly after 1806. Fully one-third of Petersburg manumitters between 1806 and 1860 were black, for example. Not surprisingly, free blacks often freed family members, such as "Robin Justice (free negroe)," of Accomack County, who by his deed did

---

3. John Heveningham will, 18 Dec. 1809, Chesterfield County Wills, 7 (1808–13); Zorobabel Ames will, 3 Dec. 1809, Accomack County Wills (1809–12); Old & others petition, 1809, LP, Amelia County.

4. Thomas Higginbotham to Richard Harrison, 17 Dec. 1833, attached to Archey Cary petition, 27 Dec. 1833, LP, Amherst County; Dick Skurrey petition, 1834, LP, Amelia County; Jane Bell petition, 1827, LP, Fauquier County.

"emancipate and set free from slavery... my wife Eve (whom I formerly purchased of Henry Parker of the aforesaid County,) and her two children Bowman and Peggy." Justice, who had been allowed to hire himself out and had earned the money necessary to purchase his own freedom in 1803, gained permission from the legislature in 1811 for his family, if freed, to remain in Virginia with him, and he manumitted them the following year. He marked the deed emancipating his wife and children with a crude and unsteady but clear *X,* suggesting simultaneously the paucity of his experience with pen and paper and the significance with which he held the act that put the pen in his hand.[5]

The year 1812 brought freedom for Robin Justice's family because he had successfully appealed to white leaders, but many more enslaved Virginians would find freedom in the next few years through a more direct means made possible by the military conflict between America and Great Britain. In a reprise of Revolutionary events British commanders during the War of 1812 discovered that American slaves could be effective allies against American whites, and slaves themselves, most likely carrying memories of the earlier era, saw the British as benefactors who would grant them liberty. As described by Frank Cassell, enslaved Virginians began to seek the protection of British forces starting in May 1813, when British warships were raiding along the coast. A year later, in April 1814, British Vice-Admiral Sir Alexander Cochrane, commander of the British forces in American waters, issued a proclamation making the informal policy official (again recapitulating events of the Revolutionary era, when official policy had lagged behind practice). Cochrane's proclamation stated that those "disposed to emigrate" from the United States "will have their choice of either entering into his Majesty's sea or land forces, or of being sent as FREE settlers to the British possessions in North America

5. Lebsock, *Free Women of Petersburg,* 96; Robin Justice deed, 28 Apr. 1812, Accomack County Free Negro and Slave Records, Manumissions, 1783–1812; William Justice bond and William Justice deed, 8 Jan. 1803, Accomack County Deeds, 10 (1800–1804); Robin Justice petition, 1811, LP, Accomack County. According to his petition to the legislature, Robin Justice had purchased his wife in 1804 but had not finished paying the sixty-eight pounds he owed and therefore was not entitled to emancipate her until 1811. Between 1804 and 1811 Eve had two children. Justice was "informed that a Law had been passed... subjecting all slaves emancipated after that time to a sale by the overseers of the Poor if they remain in this Commonwealth one year after their emancipation." The legislature probably granted his request because Justice had purchased Eve with the intention of freeing her before the 1806 law took effect. See below in the chapter, under "Petitioning to Remain in Virginia."

or the West Indies." The slaves who left for the coast in response frequently found that they could board British ships. In later years John Quincy Adams, acting in his capacity as secretary of state, "reported that 2,435 slaves had 'been carried off' from Virginia and Maryland during the war," but according to Cassell, the actual numbers may have been considerably higher, between three thousand and five thousand. Two hundred of the men were even formed by Admiral Sir Richard Cockburn and Sergeant William Hammond into a fighting unit that helped secure British victories in the summer of 1814.[6]

The sight of black troops attacking American positions at Pungoteague, on the Eastern Shore, that summer must have horrified white Virginians and may have helped reshape laws regarding manumission and freed slaves, just as earlier disruptions had spurred amendments to the manumission law. Legislators considered several new bills restricting the movements of free blacks and slaves in 1814, and while they did not pass those, in 1815 they did pass a law rationalizing the process by which slaves freed after 1806 might apply for permission to remain in Virginia. Before that period slaves wishing to stay in the commonwealth as an exemption to the 1806 law petitioned the legislature on an individual basis. The 1815 statute transferred to county courts the burden of deciding whether a particular freed slave might remain and stated that such permission could only be granted if the freed person had been emancipated for "extraordinary merit," a stipulation designed to restrict the number of free blacks in Virginia. The law did, however, allow for the "court to extend the like permission" to remain to the "emancipated wife or husband" of the original petitioner "or to his or her emancipated children." Freed families of "extraordinary merit" could thus stay in Virginia legally. Apparently because these provisions were considered too lax, an 1819 amendment further restricted permission to remain to those who had performed specific acts of meritorious service, not merely those who had "proof of good general character and conduct alone however excellent such general character and conduct may be." Emancipated slaves also had to gain the unanimous support of the county magistrates; the commonwealth attorney had to defend the application; and notice of the freed slave's intention to remain had to be posted at the courthouse for five weeks before the hearing. If permission were granted the freed

6. Cassell, "Slaves of the Chesapeake"; Cochrane Proclamation, 2 Apr. 1814, PRO, Adm. t/508, p. 579, quoted in ibid., 150; John Adams, *American State Papers: Foreign Relations*, 4:802–18, quoted in ibid., 154n. See also Iaccarino, "Virginia and the National Contest over Slavery," 140–51.

slave could remain only in his or her home county. If the application were rejected, the decision was final and there was no appeals process.[7]

While probably inspiring legislators to address the circumstances of freed slaves in 1815, blacks' flight to freedom during the War of 1812 appears to have had minimal impact on discussions of emancipation more generally, stirring less debate than Gabriel's plot of 1800 had or than Turner's rebellion in 1831 would, even though those events involved fewer slaves. One reason for the muted white response might be that the form of resistance the slaves chose— running away—could be seen merely as an extension of normal activity, less cause for alarm than an outright rebellion would be. Recent scholarship has demonstrated that slaves frequently used short-term flight as a negotiating tool with masters, so whites might not have read slaves' running away during the War of 1812 as a noteworthy challenge to slavery. If mass flight did indicate that slavery in Virginia might be unstable or that slaves desired freedom, whites' main response late in the second decade of the nineteenth century and in the third decade as well was to focus as they had in earlier years not on slavery but on free blacks.[8]

Indeed, the free black population remained the object of white concern after 1806, particularly when it became apparent that a significant number of free blacks were residing in Virginia in violation of the 1806 statute. While some of the manumitters who emancipated slaves after 1806 had provided for their transportation out of the state, and some recently freed slaves had obtained official permission to remain in Virginia from the legislature or local county court, it appears that most white and black Virginians simply ignored the provisions of the 1806 law. One historian estimates that by 1860 between one-quarter and one-third of Virginia's free blacks lived there illegally, and while that number may be high, certainly hundreds of freed slaves and thousands of their descendants lived in the commonwealth without permission.[9]

Occasionally, white Virginians' anxieties about the free black population built to a critical point and spurred attempts to remove free people of color by enforcing the terms of the 1806 statute. Brenda Stevenson describes how

7. Cassell, "Slaves of the Chesapeake," 150; *Revised Code of the Law of Virginia*, chap. III, sec. 62 (1819).

8. On running away as a form of resistance see Morgan, *Slave Counterpoint*, 151–54 and passim; Whitman, *Price of Freedom*, 69–78; Michael Mullin, *Africa in America*, 231–32; and Gerald Mullin, *Flight and Rebellion*, 106–9.

9. Russell, *Free Negro*, 156.

in the 1830s the commonwealth attorney Richard Henderson tried to expel free blacks who resided in Loudoun County illegally but was frustrated by the large number of illegal residents and by his low success rate in prosecuting them. Accomack County officials in the 1820s had similarly mixed results in their campaign to enforce the 1806 law. Significantly, what appears to have been the most vigorous effort to remove free blacks occurred in that part of the commonwealth where slave-based agriculture had long been in decline, where the number of manumissions had been high, and where both white and black residents had felt the effects of British raids during the War of 1812. The changes of the previous generation had unsettled relations between blacks and whites in Accomack, and on the Eastern Shore generally, more than elsewhere in the state. In June 1825 the overseers of the poor of Accomack County, who were by law the body in charge of enforcing the 1806 statute, decided to reimpose the order they felt had been lost. As they explained, "[T]he whole number of free negroes in the whole state of Va. did not exceed Forty thousand, of whom *at least* two thousand three hundred were in the said county of Accomack; and in this state of things the said overseers of the poor felt it incumbent upon them no longer to delay the discharge of the duty imposed upon them by law of selling the free negroes within their county of the description abovementioned."[10]

Since the main goal of the 1806 statute and of the Accomack overseers of the poor was "to rid this Commonwealth of its free black population and *not* again to subject to slavery those who had been once emancipated except as a means of accomplishing the chief design," the overseers thought they would make an example out of a few free African Americans in the hope that they could then incite other illegal residents to leave on their own. Accordingly, they arrested Jack Bagwell, a free black man, and put him in jail in preparation for selling him back into slavery. Bagwell escaped that fate because a friend paid his jail fee and financed his transportation out of the state. The incident had its desired effect: many others, "perhaps several hundred in number, who were similarly situated were induced by the influence of this example to leave the county of Accomack and emegrate to the Northern states."[11]

Many illegal residents remained even after hundreds had left, and so in

---

10. Stevenson, *Life in Black and White,* 269; John G. Joynes petition, 1834, LP, Accomack County.

11. John G. Joynes petition, 1834, LP, Accomack County.

September 1825 the Accomack overseers of the poor posted notice that they would arrest all the remaining illegal free black residents the following January. January came and went without action on the part of the overseers, who were probably reluctant to take such a draconian step. Again white residents demonstrated their ambivalence toward free blacks, their failure to act on stated principles. Perhaps the county's free blacks relaxed, thinking the threat only that. But in March the overseers posted another notice, saying that they would arrest and sell one free person of color each month in every district in the county. This time action followed their words, and they arrested a total of eight free people of color and sold them as slaves at auction, depositing the money into the public treasury to the credit of the Literary Fund. Presumably these formerly free people remained slaves for life, except for Jim Outten, who was purchased by Littleton Henderson for fifty dollars. But Henderson never received the "slave" he had bought, since Outten had been in Baltimore at the time of the sale and had never, in fact, been in the custody of the overseers. Henderson sued John Joynes, one of the overseers, and obtained a judgment of ninety-eight dollars, as well as reimbursement from the legislature for the fifty dollars he had paid for Outten. Joynes also requested reimbursement from the legislature for the money he had to pay Henderson and for the court costs of the suit. He was due this reimbursement, he said, since he had acted in good faith and had only made errors of judgment. Surprisingly, considering that he had sold a man not actually in his custody, the legislature agreed to Joynes's request.[12]

The events that took place on the Eastern Shore in 1825–26 show that whites in the mid-1820s did not necessarily think slavery was good; they wished, after all, not to *"subject* to slavery those who had been once emancipated except as a means of accomplishing the chief design" of ridding Virginia of free blacks.[13] Rather white Virginians of that era generally thought the existence of free blacks was worse than the existence of slavery, and they were occasionally willing to go to great lengths to rid themselves of the perceived free black menace. The overseers' actions also underscore white Accomack citizens' mixed response to the law of 1806. On the one hand, they continued

12. Ibid.; L. P. Henderson petition, 1827, LP, Accomack County. Although he had had to pay court costs, Henderson in the end made more than twenty dollars from his attempt to purchase Outten.

13. John G. Joynes petition, 1834, LP, Accomack County, emphasis mine.

to free slaves, though in much smaller numbers than before, which created more free blacks; on the other, they increasingly found the free black population frightening and threatening and began to focus attention on reducing the number of free African Americans in Virginia. Finally, it is worth noting that their efforts did not permanently reduce the free African American population in the county; Accomack continued to have a high proportion of free blacks, one of the highest in the state throughout the antebellum era.[14]

The ambivalence of Accomack's white citizens reflected the attitude of Virginia's whites more generally. Like so many other laws regarding "slaves, free negroes and mulattoes," the provision requiring blacks freed after 1806 to leave the state was, judging from available evidence, more often ignored than enforced. Part of the problem was the difficulty of legislating complicated human relationships. As in their view of slaves, a disjunction existed between white Virginians' view of free blacks generally, a view that held them as threatening and violent, and their ideas about the individual free black people whom they knew as members of their communities and whom they sometimes counted as friends.

PETITIONING TO REMAIN IN VIRGINIA

Samuel Johnson was one of those free blacks with many white friends. Yet, like others who had gained their freedom after 1806, he was also subject to the unpredictable whims of the whites among whom he lived. Apparently sensitive to their vulnerable position, Samuel Johnson and a number of other black Virginians sought assurance that they would not be forced to leave, sending numerous petitions to the legislature in the years after 1806. The petitions requesting special permission to remain in the state, which continued even after the 1815 law transferred the responsibility of deciding such cases to the county courts, illuminate some of the details of the petitioners' otherwise obscure lives and demonstrate the intensity of many enslaved Virginians' desire to be free. Samuel Johnson's case in particular shows the doggedness with which some pursued liberty. The legislature's response to the petitions confirmed the master class's commitment to keeping the growth of the free black community

14. The Accomack incident may also have influenced the passage of an 1827 law that altered the method by which blacks residing illegally in Virginia would be dealt with. The 1827 statute removed the overseers of the poor from the process, providing instead that a grand jury be called to present possible violations of the 1806 statue as misdemeanors. *Supplement to the Revised Code of the Laws of Virginia*, 241.

small, since it denied many of the requests it received, especially those from women who might have children who would add to the free black population. But again the behavior of whites betrayed mixed feelings; many of the petitions were endorsed by tens or hundreds of white citizens who put aside racial fears to help out a black neighbor.[15]

The petitions of free or would-be free African Americans who wished to remain in Virginia became a literary genre, with shared ideas and phrases that emphasized the petitioners' obedience, humbleness, and worth to the community. Most were probably written with the help of educated white people, and the handwriting on many indicates that they were transcribed by professional clerks. Jane Bell attempted to prove her worth to the community by asserting that she was a "discreet and good Citizen" and by including testimony from white members of the county who did not wish her to leave. Sterling, a carpenter from Chesterfield County who had been promised his freedom in the 1790s but whose owner died before the emancipation could be effected, emphasized that he was "always attentive and obedient to his Superiors" and that he adhered to "the principles of honesty and fidelity in the service of his imployers, and . . . acquired the confidence and esteem of his master and mistress and also the notice and confidence of many of the good inhabitants of Chesterfield." Sterling also had the support of neighbors, about fifty subscribers who affirmed his "good moral character" and his "well known honesty and veracity." Other petitioners emphasized their ties to the community with dramatic declarations of their love for Virginia, hoping that such declarations

15. A historian who uses legislative petitions extensively to explore the lives of free blacks is John Russell, in *Free Negro*. It can be difficult by examining the petitions to determine their final fate, since some of those found reasonable by the committee to which they referred never became law. I examined thirty-two petitions dating from 1811–39 requesting permission to remain in Virginia from Accomack, Albemarle, Amelia, Amherst, Bedford, Charles City, Chesterfield, Fauquier, and Powhatan counties. Of those, five were granted, with bills passed in accord; two were found reasonable, but with restrictions (in one case the petitioner was allowed to stay for three years only, and in the other the wife but not the children of Frank Gowen, a free black man who had purchased them, was allowed to remain); seven were found reasonable, but there is no indication on the petitions whether a bill was drawn up; five were found reasonable, but no law was passed in accord; one contains no notation; and twelve, eight of which regarded women, were rejected outright. Even if the seven found reasonable whose final fate I am uncertain of did become law, the majority, seventeen of thirty-two, did not. Stevenson states that many Loudoun petitioners whose petitions were accompanied by support from their communities were successful. Stevenson, *Life in Black and White*, 271.

of affection would sway the legislators. The petition of Steven Bias described his emigration to Ohio in accordance with the 1806 law after he had, at about age sixty, been freed by his owner. But after a lifetime in Virginia, he could not adjust to "the manners and habits of the people of Ohio when contrasted with those amongst whom he had been raised," and he returned to his home county of Albemarle. Begging for permission to remain, he said that his love for his homeland was so great that "he would prefer being sold into slavery in Virginia to being again compelled to emigrate to & reside in the state of Ohio."[16]

Samuel Johnson's 1811 petition similarly emphasized that he belonged in his local Virginia community rather than elsewhere. The testimony of thirty-eight subscribers accompanied Johnson's request. The subscribers, all white men, called him "uniformly Diligent sober accommodating, faithful and honest," assuring the legislature that Johnson was a man unlikely to make trouble. In fact, he was, they said, "possess'd of those qualities essential to form a valuable citizen." The subscribers expected that Johnson, once free, would enter the community as a citizen and member of the social body even if he would never have all the legal rights white citizens held. He "wishes to remain amongst us, we wish it also, and it is for this reason as well as because he is a meritorious man, and therefore entitled to our good offices that we recommend him to the general assembly." One more argument supported Johnson's request: his example might prove to be a "wise encouragement to others to behave as he has behav'd, and by a like fidelity and honesty to deserve as he deserves." Especially after 1806, whites saw manumission as a reward for and encouragement of faithful service as a slave.[17]

Johnson's petition and accompanying documents persuaded the legislature to act on his behalf, probably in large part because the agreement by which he was to receive his freedom predated the 1806 law. It was possible to argue that his emancipation actually dated from 1802, when he and his then owner, Edward Digges, had agreed that he should pay five hundred dollars for his liberty, even though it took Johnson an additional nine years to raise the money and complete the terms of the contract. A certificate from Digges accompanying the petition emphasized that "he had agreed to emancipate the said Sam"

16. Jane Bell petition, 1827, LP, Fauquier County; Sterling petition, 1814, LP, Chesterfield County; Steven Bias (also Bears) petition, 1839, LP, Albemarle County. See also Stevenson, *Life in Black and White*, 270–71.

17. Sam's petition, 1811, LP, Fauquier County.

before 1806 and that the agreement would have "been carried into full effect had the money been paid before the passage of the said [1806] Act." The legislators, reflecting the same mixed feelings regarding emancipation held by many less well placed Virginians, ignored the fact that slaves could not legally enter into contracts, which they could have used as a reason to deny Johnson's request, and passed an act in 1812 that gave Samuel Johnson permission to remain in Virginia. The legislature acted similarly in other cases in which the slave's claim to freedom predated the 1806 law.[18]

Samuel Johnson's petition and the legislature's response revealed a significant contrast between Johnson's self-perception and the way the white men with whom he dealt viewed him. To Richard Brent, to whom he had been transferred in 1802 (it was not uncommon for slaves who bought their freedom to be transferred to a third party as part of the exchange) and the person who actually manumitted him, he was "my Slave Sam." To the legislature, he was Digges' Sam, referring to the name of his original owner, and the bill was enrolled under that name. But on his own terms he was Samuel Johnson, sometimes Johnston, "free mulatto," even before he was technically emancipated. To the white men who acted on his behalf, Sam was a subordinate defined primarily by his relationship to his owner: he was a man with no last name and a diminutive proper name. In his own eyes, Samuel Johnson was a member of the community who happened to have been born a slave. His self-identification as mulatto emphasized white ancestry; his self-appellation as Samuel Johnson invoked a sense of dignity; and even before he was legally manumitted, he felt that his hard work had earned him the right to refer to himself as "free."

Indeed, acquiring freedom for himself and his family, including the freedom to remain in his home state of Virginia, was Samuel Johnson's main goal in life, "the end to which all the anxious labour and privations of your petitioner have been directed," as he noted in an 1815 petition.[19] As a black Virgin-

---

18. Ibid. Examples of others with a claim to freedom from before 1806 include Sterling, mentioned above, who had been promised freedom by his owner, who died in 1798 before effecting the emancipation. Similarly, Jingo's owner had allowed him to act as a free man since 1798, but no deed of manumission was actually drafted until 1810. Robin Justice's family, also mentioned above, also had a claim to freedom from before 1806. All were allowed to remain. Sterling petition, 1814, LP, Chesterfield County; Jingo petition, 1810, LP, Accomack County; Robin Justice petition, 1811, LP, Accomack County.

19. Samuel Johnson petition, 1815, LP, Fauquier County.

ian in the 1810s, he would have to make an extraordinary effort to achieve this apparently simple aim. First, he had to purchase his wife and children, which he did within just a few years after earning his own liberty, apparently by saving the money he made working in the tavern at the county seat of Warrenton. Once he had bought his family, he began a campaign to obtain their liberty, petitioning the legislature for permission for his family to remain in Virginia if he emancipated them. The legislature ignored his first request in 1815, allowing it to lie on the table.

Even if Johnson could not immediately free his family because he could not be assured they could stay in Virginia legally, he could work to build a life for them in Warrenton as integral members of the town. The financial and social success he achieved testifies to the possibility for free people of color to become part of a mixed-race community in spite of objections to their presence that were codified in law and reflected in the legislature's tacit denial of his 1815 petition. By 1820, when at forty-five years of age he petitioned the legislature regarding his family for a second time, Johnson's household included several other people in addition to his wife and children, and he owned a house and some land. Johnson's 1820 petition emphasized his financial ability to part with his slave property (he would not need them, his wife and children, for credit or collateral) and to support them once they were free. His claim that he had "accumulated a tolerable estate, consisting of real, and personal property" was backed up by an assessment of Johnson's property that put its worth at more than three thousand dollars. Johnson also emphasized that the residents of Warrenton looked upon his family favorably, stating that "the conduct of said slaves, and the management of your petitioner, towards them, has merited and met with the approbation of all the most sober and proudest part of the Community," a claim supported by the fact that some of the most prominent members of the county endorsed his petition.[20]

20. Samuel Johnston [sic] petition, 1820, ibid. According to the 1820 census, he owned one male slave who was more than forty-five years old and had in his household three free black men in addition to himself and his son. Neither of his children appeared in the census; they were probably working as apprentices to other Warrenton citizens. There was only a small free black community in Warrenton, and so Johnson had to have close relations with whites as well. In 1820 Warrenton had 629 residents, of whom 23, or just under 4 percent, were free blacks. Fourth Census of the United States, 1820 (Washington, DC: National Archives Microfilm Publications, 1959), reel 134. For the house and land see bill of sale, John Love to Samuel Johnson, 24 Nov. 1818, Fauquier County Deeds, 23 (1818–19). Also, in 1822 Johnson paid $175 for a half-acre parcel of land

Samuel Johnson was more prosperous than most of the free African Americans in Virginia, who were usually among the poorest in the state, but even these poorer free people of color played important roles in their communities. Most lived in the eastern half of the state, and compared with whites, a disproportionate number of them lived in urban areas. In the cities free black women usually found employment doing housework such as laundry, domestic service, and sewing. After about 1820 they also worked in tobacco factories, and although there is little direct evidence for it, a number of urban free black women probably worked as prostitutes. Free black men had a wider range of occupations. In Norfolk many were draymen who transported merchandise from the docks and through the city. Free black men there and elsewhere also worked as barbers, coopers, carpenters, mechanics, or in other similar occupations. Some free people of color, both men and women, were even shopkeepers or like Samuel Johnson worked in local taverns or retail establishments. While it is clear that a number of free blacks migrated to urban areas after they had been emancipated, most, like Samuel Johnson, stayed in the neighborhood where they had lived while enslaved. Extant free negro registers show that most rural free blacks, at least those who registered with the county clerk, had been born in the county they resided in as adults. Altogether, four-fifths of Virginia's free blacks remained in rural areas, where they often worked as tenant farmers or as farm laborers, though a few owned their own land. Many of the property holders had bought their farms, but some had received land from those who had emancipated them. Others continued to work for their former owners in various occupations, including as carpenters, sawyers, or coopers, and Johnson also continued to work in the tavern where he had been employed while enslaved.[21]

---

adjoining Warrenton, near the well square. Indenture between John A. W. Smith and Maria L. Smith and Samuel Johnston [*sic*], Nov. 1822, Fauquier County Deeds, 26 (1821–23).

21. Russell, *Free Negro*, 15, 150; Lebsock, *Free Women of Petersburg*, 97–99; Bogger, *Free Blacks in Norfolk*, 61–80; Jackson, *Free Negro Labor*, 102; Sidbury, *Ploughshares into Swords*, chap. 5; Stevenson, *Life in Black and White*, chap. 10. For evidence of emancipated slaves who continued to work for their former owners see, e.g., the deed of manumission from Frank Jenkins to his wife Betty, in which Frank identifies himself as "a black man paid by Mary Ann Jenkins," who was his former owner. Frank Jenkins deed, 26 Apr. 1803, Accomack County Deeds, 10 (1800–1804). The examples of occupations come from "A list of free negroes," 1804, Accomack County Free Negro and Slave Records, Lists of Free Negroes, LVA, Archives Division. For evidence that most rural free blacks remained in the county in which they had been born see, e.g., the Accomack list of free

Knowing as he did from his day-to-day life in Warrenton and his success in accumulating a "tolerable estate" that he was indeed a member of a community who shared with his white neighbors many of the same hopes, successes, and challenges, Johnson must have assumed that the legislators too would recognize him as a fellow Virginian and grant him permission to remain there with his wife and family. The 1820 petition pointed out all he shared with the legislators themselves, a common human concern for one's family, "feelings incidental to all men." That appeal, the evidence of his financial success, and the endorsement of thirty-nine of the county's white citizens persuaded some of the legislators to grant him at least part of his wish. The committee of the Courts of Justice, to which such petitions were referred, found his request for his wife to stay reasonable, though they rejected the additional requests that his children be allowed to remain. The legislators probably thought their decision a judicious compromise between allowing Johnson some reward for his labors by permitting his wife to remain and keeping the growth of the free black community to a minimum by denying similar dispensation to Johnson's progeny. They drew up a bill on behalf of Samuel's wife, Patty Johnson, but for unknown reasons the bill never became law.[22]

Two failed attempts to gain permission for Johnson's wife and children to remain in Virginia did not deter him from petitioning again, for he knew that his family, as slaves, would be in a precarious legal position if he died, and he was anxious to obtain legislative sanction to free them and allow them to remain in the state. Johnson petitioned the legislature in 1822, 1823, 1824, 1826, 1828, 1835, and 1837. It appears that his son died sometime between 1820 and 1822, for there was no further reference to him, and from then on Johnson's main concern was that his daughter, Lucy, be allowed to remain in Virginia. Perhaps he decided that gaining his wife's legal freedom was less important than gaining his daughter's since Lucy was more likely to outlive him, and her descendants would not be free unless she was. Although the legislature sometimes assented to his requests and sometimes drew up a bill, none of these bills made it through the required three readings to become enacted as law.

The semifreedom in which Johnson's family lived as a result affected the most basic aspects of their lives, and he was tempted occasionally to try to lib-

---

Negroes and *Fauquier County, Virginia Register of Free Negroes*. For an overview of the antebellum free black community's experience see Berlin, *Slaves without Masters;* and for a portrait of a free black Virginia community that had numerous ties with whites see Ely, *Israel on the Appomattox.*

22. Samuel Johnston [*sic*] petition, 1820, LP, Fauquier County.

erate them even without legislative approval. When in 1827 Lucy, then twenty-two years old, married a twenty-three-year-old free mulatto man named Spencer Malvin, Johnson had to manumit her or the marriage would not be legal, since the law did not recognize slave marriages.[23] In spite of the deed of manumission that he drafted the same day that Lucy and Malvin filed their marriage bond, neither Johnson nor Lucy asserted her status as a free woman, and his subsequent requests that she be allowed to remain in the state continued to identify her as his slave. To do otherwise would be to draw attention to her tenuous legal position, and she, in theory, could be indicted by a grand jury and sold by the county sheriff. Johnson drafted another deed of manumission in 1837, freeing Lucy and the three children she then had, Sam, Rebecca, and Thomas T. Withers Malvin, even though the legislature had not acted on the petition he had sent earlier in the year requesting permission for Lucy and her children to remain in Virginia if emancipated. His final petition to the legislature spelled out the probable reason he manumitted his family that year. He was "getting old," he said, and desired to "liberate his said daughter and her children before his death."[24]

When Samuel Johnson died five years later, an old man at sixty-seven, he still held his family as his legal slaves. His will took no notice of the two previous deeds of manumission that freed Lucy and her children, and so the first item in it was to emancipate them and his wife. He gave his property in trust to three friends, including the town's white doctor, Thomas Thornton Withers, after whom one of Lucy's children was named. He asked that the trustees "endeavour to obtain permission for my wife, Daughter and grandchildren abovenamed and emancipated, to remain in the Commonwealth of Virginia." If they were allowed to remain, his property was to be transferred to them. But if not, the trustees were to sell his estate—there was not much of it left—and use the money to provide for the removal of his family "to such non-slaveholding state" as they should choose.[25]

23. Samuel Johnson deed, 27 Sept. 1826, Fauquier County Deeds, 29 (1826–28); Gott, *Fauquier County, Virginia Marriage Bonds*, 129. Lucy Johnson and Spencer Malvin had a marriage bond dated Sept. 27, 1826 and were married by Richard H. Barnes in 1827. In *Fauquier County, Virginia Register of Free Negroes*, Spencer Malvin is listed as a mulatto man with short bushy hair, born free on Feb. 12, 1804, and registered June 28, 1825.

24. Samuel Johnson deed, 18 July 1837, Fauquier County Deeds, 37 (1836–38); Sam Johnson petition, 1837, LP, Fauquier County.

25. Samuel Johnson will, 11 Mar. 1836, and codicil, 10 Aug. 1842, recorded 22 Aug. 1842, Fauquier County Wills, 17 (1840–42).

In one sense, Samuel Johnson's story can be read as a failure. The main object of his life was to gain the legal right for his family to remain in Virginia as free people, which he was not able to do. And yet Johnson carved out a life for himself and his family that was rich with community ties and, relative to most free blacks and even many whites, financially stable. After his death his family did in fact stay in Fauquier County, illegally but apparently unmolested. The surviving documents attest to the many affectionate links Johnson had with other residents of Warrenton, white and black. They included Doctor Thomas Thornton Withers, Doctor James Wallace, who attested to Johnson's "very superior character," and all the people who signed Johnson's many petitions to the legislature, 85 of them in 1823 and 229 in 1826. Johnson had close ties with other free blacks as well. His own household included several free blacks outside his immediate family, and his daughter's marriage linked him with the Malvins, another free black family of Warrenton.[26]

Johnson's story demonstrates particularly clearly the divided response white Virginians had to emancipation and the consequences their behavior had for Virginia's free blacks. Whites endorsed emancipation for some individuals after 1806, especially those such as Samuel Johnson, whose freedom might be "a wise encouragement to others to behave as he has behav'd." They supported Johnson's efforts to obtain liberty for his family and acknowledged him as "a valuable member of the community." But the author of those words still feared and distrusted the free black population as a whole. Judge Jonathan Scott, who was a member of the legislature when Johnson obtained his freedom and who endorsed Johnson's effort to obtain a similar concession for Lucy, said that Johnson was "most exemplary in his conduct" but also declared that "the white negroes (if you will allow the term) which you have at Warrenton, are a great deal worse than the black bond or free." Scott was willing to help Samuel and Lucy Johnson because he saw them as individuals of worth, in part because they had adopted values and norms of behavior so like his own. They were honest, upright citizens. But when black people started acting like white people—free, dignified, and ambitious—they became "white negroes,"

---

26. Samuel Johnson petitions, 1823, 1824, 1826, LP, Fauquier County. Evidence of Lucy's persistence in Fauquier comes from court records from 1847 showing that she was sued for debts owed out of her father's estate and from a record that her second husband, Sandy Elkins, performed work for the county in 1852. *Fant v. Elkins,* Ended Causes, Fauquier County Chancery 1847–052, and Sandy Elkins account, Ended Causes, FN/S 1852-013, Fauquier County Circuit Court Clerk's Office, Warrenton, VA.

an oxymoronic term that captured perfectly the anomalous position free blacks held in Virginia society.[27]

RACE AND FREEDOM IN COURT CASES

If the manumission of about ten thousand slaves in the generation after the Revolution upset the relatively neat division that had existed between enslaved blacks and free whites, creating "white negroes," and if the behavior of Virginians toward free blacks was marked by deep ambivalence, judges and juries were left to clarify the resulting ambiguities. Suits for freedom that rested primarily on the race of the plaintiffs show how Virginians sought to define more clearly the racial identity of slaves and to reestablish a sense of racial order in the first decades of the nineteenth century. Importantly, the decisions of courts and juries rested on the *appearance* of the plaintiffs more than on their genealogies, establishing legally that race was based on how a person looked even more than who his ancestors were. This was true in spite of the 1792 law defining a mulatto as anyone with a "one fourth part or more of Negro blood."[28] The court decisions of the postmanumission era demonstrate how Virginians continued to create and recreate race and its meanings and how they attempted to clarify in law distinctions that they found to be blurry in practice.

The well-known, precedent-setting case of *Hudgins v. Wrights* (1806) provides the best example of how Virginia's judicial leaders perceived race, freedom, and slavery to be related in the early nineteenth century. The descendants of the "Indian called Butterwood Nan" claimed to be free because their ancestor Nan had been an Indian woman enslaved illegally. There were two main problems with the claimants' case. First, they could not prove that Nan's mother had been an Indian, though her father had been. If, as the defense argued was possible, Nan's mother had been an enslaved "negro woman," Nan and all her progeny were also legally slaves. Second, it seemed that Nan had been brought into Virginia between 1679 and 1705, the period during which Virginians could legally enslave American natives.[29]

---

27. Sam's petition, 1812, and Jonathan Scott to D. C. Brigg, 9 Jan. 1834, included with Samuel Johnson petition, 1835, both in LP, Fauquier County. For another sort of "white negro" see the story of Christopher McPherson in Sidbury, *Ploughshares into Swords*, 214–16.

28. Shepherd, *Statutes at large of Virginia*, 1:123 (1792).

29. *Hudgins v. Wrights*, in Hening and Munford, *Reports of cases*, 1:134–44 (Nov. 1806). For another account of this case see Cover, *Justice Accused*, 51–55.

Much of the important evidence of the case had to do with the first point rather than the second and focused on the appearance of Nan's descendants as proof of their race. Nan's descendants were found to have the "characteristic features, the complexion, the hair and the eyes... the same with those of whites." Other witnesses testified that Nan's daughter "had long black hair [and] was of the right Indian copper color." These were significant facts of the case when it reached Virginia's High Court of Chancery, the court that decided matters of equity. George Wythe, the chancellor who heard the case, looked at the plaintiffs himself in order to decide whether they were slaves. He perceived "from his own view, that the youngest of the appellees was perfectly white, and that there were gradual shades of difference in colour between the grand-mother, mother, and grand-daughter (all of whom were before the Court;) and considering the evidence in the cause, determined that the appellees were entitled to their freedom." The other evidence of the case had been only equivocally in favor of Nan's descendants; the non-African appearance of the plaintiffs—their color, hair, and facial features—was at the heart of Wythe's decision to find them free.[30]

George Wythe, one of the most liberal judges in Virginia, went further in *Hudgins v. Wrights*, putting the issues of liberty and race directly on the table by asserting the natural rights of both blacks and whites. Wythe argued that "freedom is the birth-right of every human being, which sentiment is strongly inculcated by the first article of our 'political catechism,' the bill of rights." As a consequence of that principle, "whenever one person claims to hold another in slavery, the *onus probandi* [burden of proof] lies on the claimant." This was a radical claim in a society that held approximately 40 percent of its population as slaves, for it suggested that all of those slaves, regardless of appearance, had a basic claim to freedom. Wythe's argument and the fact that he had decided the case "upon his own view" incited the defendants' counsel, who appealed the decision.[31]

When the case reached the Supreme Court of Appeals, the issue of race and the appearance of the plaintiffs remained at the center. Edmund Randolph, who argued for the defendants, objected to this, saying that the "circumstance of the appellees being *white*, has been mentioned, more to excite the feelings of the court as *men*, than to address them as *judges*." The proper focus of the case, he stated, should be the property rights of those who claimed Nan's

30. *Hudgins v. Wrights*, in Hening and Munford, *Reports of cases*, 1:134–35.
31. Ibid., 1:134, 137.

descendants as slaves, rights and rules that should "not be departed from, because *freedom* is in question." He attempted to fix the judges' attention on the questions regarding Nan's parentage and her date of entry into Virginia and to place the burden of proof back on Nan's descendants. Randolph's objection to the racial focus of the case underscored the extent to which race—appearance and color—still lay at the heart of how Virginians understood both freedom and slavery, even as race was increasingly important apart from slavery and even though the *Hudgins* case demonstrated how uncertain race could be. White Virginians were "excited," as Randolph had put it, to find whites enslaved, just as they were disturbed by the presence of free blacks, because both circumstances overturned what most Virginians still felt at a preconscious level to be the natural order of things.[32]

As judges, and not only as white men of Virginia, the members of the Court of Appeals had to address the relationship between race and liberty in their decision on *Hudgins v. Wrights*. First, Judge Tucker concluded that "all American Indians are *prima facie* free," having found that the 1705 law outlawing Indian slavery actually dated to 1691 and therefore that only between 1679 and 1691 could Indians be brought into Virginia as legal slaves. If Indians were held as slaves in early-nineteenth-century Virginia, the burden of proof lay on "the party claiming to hold them as slaves." Similarly Tucker asserted, "All *white persons* are and ever have been free in this county. If one [is] *evidently white* . . . the proof lies on the party claiming to make the other his slave." Tucker took pains to point out that Wythe, his former teacher, had made an error when he implied that black Virginians too had a basic claim to freedom. Tucker explained, quite correctly, that the Bill of Rights "was notoriously framed with a cautious eye to this subject, and was meant to embrace the case of free citizens, or aliens only; and not . . . to overturn the rights of property," or give freedom to those people who had been slaves (property) at the time of the Revolution. St. George Tucker, who usually wrote with great precision, did not make clear what "this subject" was around which the Bill of Rights had been cautiously framed. Did he mean blacks? Did he mean a right to liberty? Did he mean property rights? Or did he mean all of them, the equal claim of all people to certain basic liberties, including the liberty to own other people as property, a liberty so problematic that Tucker could not write about it clearly?[33]

32. Ibid., 1:136.
33. Ibid., 1:140–41.

Tucker's decision in *Hudgins v. Wrights* established as a legal principle that physical appearance determined who bore the burden of proof in suits for freedom, confirming ideas Virginians had long held regarding race and slavery but that needed to be reiterated after the Revolutionary age and after Virginia's experiment with manumission. Judge Roane agreed: "*[A]ppearance* ... will suffice for the claim of her [Nan's daughter Hannah's] posterity [to freedom], unless it is opposed by counter-evidence." Ordinary white men who served on juries agreed too. The jurors who were asked to judge in *Hook v. Nanny Pagee and her children* (1811) whether Nanny Pagee was due her freedom were not trained legal scholars. Nevertheless, they had an intuitive sense that if a person appeared white, the burden of proof that she or he was a slave lay with the "owner." Nanny Pagee had been brought into Virginia from North Carolina by Thomas Jones in apparent violation of the anti-importation law of 1778. While the jury found that Jones had indeed complied with the law, they also found "from inspection, that ... Nanny Pagee is a white woman." This was "*prima facie* evidence, from complexion, that this woman was free," sufficient to grant her liberty (because her owner could not offer definitive proof that her maternal ancestors had been slaves). The appeals court judges affirmed the jury's verdict, citing *Hudgins:* "[W]here *white* persons are claimed as slaves, the *onus probandi* lies on the claimant." Therefore, "the finding of the jury that, from inspection, ... Nanny Pagee, is a *white* woman ... was quite sufficient." Since the seventeenth century, when color had become essential in determining slave status, enough racial mixing had occurred to confuse the racial basis of slavery. The ease of manumission in the period 1782–1806 had eroded further the concomitance of skin color and slave status. In the early nineteenth century Virginians responded to the relative disorder by reaffirming the colonial settlement: people who looked white should be free, and darker people ought to be slaves.[34]

The *Hudgins* and *Hook* cases demonstrated that Virginians defined race

---

34. Ibid., 1:141–42; *Hook v. Nanny Pagee and her children*, 2 Munford 379 (1811), in Catterall, *Judicial Cases*, 121. To be precise, the fact that Nanny Pagee appeared white placed the burden of proof on her owner, who could offer no definitive evidence that she was a slave. It would have been hard to do, since Pagee was originally from North Carolina and her supposed owner would have had to bring witnesses from there to testify to her background. It is quite possible that she was legally a slave, since she did not sue on the grounds of illegal enslavement; but because she appeared white and circumstances made it difficult to prove the legality of her enslavement, she was set free.

primarily by color but that other factors also helped Virginians determine racial differences.[35] Since the Virginians of the early national era were reticent about what constituted race and how they read other people's bodies to determine which race they belonged to—even Thomas Jefferson focused on the qualities of the races rather than on what defined them—Tucker's discourse on "the natural history of the human species," which he included in his decision on *Hudgins*, is especially illuminating. He began with the assertion that "[n]ature has stampt upon the African and his descendants two characteristic marks, besides the difference of complexion, which often remain visible long after the characteristic distinction of color either disappears, or becomes doubtful; a flat nose and woolly head of hair." The distinctively kinky hair of Africans was the last characteristic to disappear, so that if a person descended "in equal degree" from Africans and Indians, his hair would have "a degree of flexure, which never fails to betray" his African heritage. Revealing his mental association of both Indians and Africans with animals, Tucker noted that the difference between Africans and Indians was so strong "that a man might as easily mistake the glossy, jetty cloathing of an American bear for the wool of a black sheep, as the hair of an American Indian for that of an African, or the descendants of an African." The fact that witnesses described Nan's daughter's hair as "long, straight, black hair" was therefore crucial; she could not have had African ancestry or be descended from a black slave. According to Tucker, a judge presented with a suit for freedom had to take factors other than color into account in order to determine who should hold the burden of proof. If three people came before him, one with "a flat nose and woolly head," another who was "copper-colored" with "long jetty black, straight hair," and a third with a "fair complexion, brown hair, not woolly nor inclining thereto, with a prominent Roman nose," the judge "must judge from his own view" of the plaintiff's appearance, holding the woolly-headed individual as a slave unless he could definitively prove his freedom, while discharging the straight-haired and Roman-nosed plaintiffs unless their "owners" could definitively prove their enslavement.[36]

Tucker's arguments in *Hudgins* marked a shift in his consideration of race that mirrored the shift in Virginia as a whole. Ten years earlier, in 1796, he

35. In chapter 14 of *White over Black* Jordan argues differently, focusing on Americans' obsession with color in particular, including their interest in what made a person's skin dark and whether environmental conditions could cause it to lighten and eventually eliminate racial distinctions.

36. *Hudgins v. Wrights*, in Hening and Munford, 1:139–40.

had argued in his *Dissertation on Slavery* that slavery was "perfectly irreconcilable . . . to the principles of democracy which form the *basis* and *foundation* of our government" and that blacks ought be treated as "fellow men, and equals." This idealistic declaration had accompanied an emancipation plan that was, nevertheless, implicitly racist in its assumption that blacks could not live freely side by side with whites. By the time of the 1806 *Hudgins* case Tucker had developed his ideas about race further and made them more explicit. He asserted that racial differences not only determined who held the burden of proof in suits for freedom but established who was entitled to basic civil rights. In the first decades of the nineteenth century Virginians repeated more vigorously a process they had begun in the colonial period as they asserted that appearance did and should determine who should be free and who should be a slave.[37]

QUESTIONS OF FREEDOM

The racial identity of a supposed slave was only one basis on which a suit for freedom might be decided. Other cases rested on ambiguities or irregularities found in original instruments of emancipation. Many of the deeds and wills of manumission written in the years 1782–1806 left a legacy of litigation in cases where a manumitter's relatives claimed as slaves individuals who believed themselves to have been freed. Often the court had to weigh legal technicalities against the broad value the law and society placed on liberty. Reflecting broader changes in Virginia, the courts' decisions had become more rigid, less favorable to liberty, and more hostile to manumission by the early 1830s, so it was unfortunate for many African Americans that the era in which their cases were decided was one more antagonistic to them than the era in which the original instruments of manumission had been drawn up.[38]

One important legal question regarded delayed emancipation, which had been common from 1782 to 1806. When an owner wrote a deed or will of manumission but set the actual date of freedom at some point in the future, was the object of the deed of manumission a free person from the date of the deed, still legally a slave, or did the act of delayed emancipation create a new legal category? More important, were children born to women between the date a deed of manumission was written and the date freedom was to

37. St. George Tucker, *Dissertation on Slavery*, 49–51, 57, 66. See also Hamilton, "Revolutionary Principles," for an analysis of Tucker's changing attitudes.

38. For similar discussions of changing standards regarding hearsay evidence in freedom suits see Macleod, *Slavery, Race, and the American Revolution*, 109–26; and Nicholls, "Squint of freedom."

take effect enslaved or free people? Since manumitters rarely considered these complications and did not often specify the answer in their deeds and wills of emancipation, a number of lawsuits arose out of these questions.

The first case in which the general court considered the issue of delayed emancipation was the famous case of *Pleasants v. Pleasants*, in which the Quaker activist Robert Pleasants sued family members who refused to free their slaves as had been directed by the wills of John and Jonathan Pleasants, Robert's father and brother. John Pleasants had died in 1771, before individual manumission was legalized in 1782, and had directed that his slaves be free "when they arrive to the age of thirty years and the law of the land will admit them to be set free." Jonathan Pleasants died in 1776 and made a similar provision in his will. The Court of Appeals decided in favor of the slaves' freedom in 1799, but because both John and Jonathan had stipulated that their slaves be freed after they reached thirty years, it was not clear whether children born to women under thirty were free upon birth, free when they themselves reached thirty, or slaves for life. The majority decision of the court held that the slaves in each generation would have to serve until they were thirty years old, which they did until the time of the Civil War. In their decision the members of the court effectively created a new species of property: slaves who awaited liberty until a specific date and were in the interim neither fully enslaved nor fully free and whose children would inherit the same liminal status.[39]

Because the circumstances of the *Pleasants* case were unique, the case was not generally used as a precedent, and through the first two decades of the nineteenth century lower courts had to determine for themselves the status of children born to women who had been promised but had not yet attained their full liberty. Their decisions varied. Some lower-court judges and juries held that such children were slaves, ruling that a woman whose freedom was promised to her at some date in the future was still a slave, and so children born while she was still a slave were also slaves.[40] Benjamin Watkins Leigh, who in later years would be one of the Virginia's great conservative leaders, held a relatively liberal position toward manumission in 1808 and ruled differently in the case of Tom Abba. Abba's freedom was in question because it was not clear that his mother, Hannah, had been free when Tom was born. Hannah had been emancipated in a deed dated 11 February 1790 but was not to be at

39. Kettner, "Persons or Property?" 136–55; Judge Green's decision in *Maria v. Surbaugh*, 2 Randolph 228 (1824), in Catterall, *Judicial Cases*, 138.

40. The lower court in *Maria v. Surbaugh*, discussed below, decided this way, for example.

liberty until 10 February 1802. Leigh decided that if, as Hannah claimed, Tom had been born in October 1802, his freedom was unquestionable. But even if he "was born in the interval between the date of Henry Featherstone's deed of manumission of Hannah his mother & others, and the 10th February 1802, when she was to come to the enjoyment of her freedom . . . still I hold that [he] is entitled to his freedom." He explained that "the deed of manumission most explicitly acknowledges his mother's natural right to Liberty, and only postpones the enjoyment of it to a convenient given period." Since her children would, under the law, follow in her condition, they too were only "bound to serve as long as she was so bound & no longer." Leigh implied that from 1790 to 1802 Hannah had been living in a state of "inchoate freedom" rather than slavery, and so any children born in that interval would not be slaves.[41]

Did a deed or will of delayed emancipation in fact create a condition of semifreedom entitling the children of such semifree women to liberty? If so, was their liberty to be delayed, as was held for the Pleasantses' slaves, or immediate, as Leigh decided in the case of Tom Abba? The answers remained legally vague until the Virginia Court of Appeals ruled on *Maria v. Surbaugh* in 1824. In that case a woman held as a slave, Mary, sued on behalf of herself and her four children *in forma pauperis,* and they were appointed counsel by the court. The case was based on the will of William Holliday, who in 1790 had bequeathed "his [infant] slave Mary to his son William, with a declaration, that she shall be free as soon as she arrives at the age of thirty-one years," in 1818. Before she turned thirty-one Mary had four children, Maria, Nancy, Solomon, and Samuel, and was sold several times to different owners. After her thirty-first birthday Mary's owner refused to free her and her children, and so she filed suit. Mary won her freedom, but the status of her children remained in question. It was not clear whether the will that had emancipated Mary and given her a right to future freedom had made her still a slave or rather a free woman with "an obligation to serve as a servant." Chancellor Wythe and Judge Roane had argued in the minority in the *Pleasants* case that the latter interpretation was correct, suggesting that children of slave women to whom freedom had been promised should be free. The judges in 1824 were more rigid. One took direct issue with Wythe and Roane's interpretation, saying that it "would directly counteract the policy of the law of 1782, in regard

41. Benjamin Watkins Leigh decision, Chesterfield County Court Records, Dead Papers, 1808, LVA, Archives Division. It is interesting that like Tucker, Leigh altered his views over time. See discussion in chapter 5, below.

to emancipation," because that law stated that owners could not free minors unless they bound themselves to support the minors until they were adults. Therefore, Mary, a minor when the will was written, remained a slave. She was still a slave when her children were born (although she was, presumably, no longer a minor when she had at least some of her children), and consequently "the children of Mary were born slaves, without any right to future liberty."[42]

The principles established in *Maria v. Surbaugh*, which did not conform with manumitters' apparent intention to free their slaves, were confirmed in most subsequent cases. In general, children born to women who had been promised freedom but who were not yet free remained enslaved for life. In one case, however, the judges decided differently. In *Isaac v. West* (1828) the particular language of the instrument of manumission operated to gain Isaac his liberty. Abel West, of Accomack County, had emancipated his slaves by a deed in April 1806. He wrote, "I, Abel West, . . . set free the following negroes at my death; they shall serve me as long as I live, and at my death shall go free from all persons." The judges decided that in this case the deed could be "construed to give immediate freedom, to all intents and purposes, except to hold them bound to serve West himself, personally, during his life." That is to say, the deed had in fact freed the slaves but kept them bound as servants, not slaves, until West's death. Isaac's mother, Hannah, mentioned in West's deed, was therefore free when Isaac was born in 1813, and thus Isaac was free as well. Isaac was lucky; West, knowingly or not, had drafted his deed of manumission in such a way as to grant liberty to the unborn children of his female slaves. The cases of *Isaac v. West* and *Maria v. Surbaugh* show how precarious was the fate of African Americans in Virginia who sued for their freedom or the freedom of family members in the years after 1806. Liberty could rest on small technicalities, turns of phrase, and points of law that would-be emancipators probably never considered or anticipated.[43]

Certainly the manumitters of the late eighteenth and early nineteenth centuries could not have predicted how attitudes toward African Americans and

---

42. *Maria v. Surbaugh*, 2 Randolph 228 (1824), in Catterall, *Judicial Cases*, 138.

43. *Isaac v. West*, 6 Randolph 652 (1828), in ibid., 157. *Maria v. Surbaugh* was confirmed in *Crawford v. Moses*, 10 Leigh 277 (1839); *Henry v. Bradford*, 1 Rob. Va. 57 (1842); and *Ellis v. Jenny*, 2 Rob 597 (1844), all noted in [Benjamin Watkins Leigh?], "Principles in Questions of Freedom," n.d., Chesterfield County Free Negro and Slave Records, Registrations and Papers, LVA, Archives Division. See also Catterall, *Judicial Cases*, 194, 202, 204.

judicial decisions regarding liberty would change. In cases in the first generation after the Revolution, judges often presumed "in favor of liberty." Even the compromise *Pleasants* decision acknowledged the eventual right to liberty of the Pleasants slaves in each generation. The judges in 1804 also upheld the pre-1782 will of manumission enacted by the Quaker Gloister Hunnicutt in *Charles v. Hunnicutt,* reasoning that because Hunnicutt was a Quaker, he was aware of efforts to obtain a manumission law and intended his slaves to be freed only after a law permitting manumission had been passed. This reasoning was somewhat of a stretch, since Hunnicutt's will said no such thing, but the judges' decision respected both Hunnicutt's intention to free his slaves and the value of liberty. As Judge Fleming put it, "Devises in favour . . . of liberty, ought to be liberally expounded." The judges were often willing to give secondary importance to technicalities and to rule *in favorem libertatis.*[44]

After about 1820 the intent of the manumitter was clearly less important to Virginia's high judges than whether the would-be manumitter had complied with the letter of the law. The judges began consistently to treat suits for freedom like other questions of property. In an 1831 decision regarding the admissibility of hearsay evidence to prove a plaintiff's freedom, Judge Carr noted that his generation of judges had more exacting standards: previous "judges (from the purest motives, I am sure) did, *in favorem libertatis,* sometimes relax, rather too much, the rules of law, and particularly the law of evidence. Of this, the court in later times, has been so sensible, that it has felt the propriety of gradually returning to the legal standard, and of treating these precisely like any other questions of property."[45]

Suits for freedom were not, however, like other questions of property. Treating them as such had tragic consequences for many individuals. In one case, the court had to determine the validity of a Mr. Schwartz's deathbed emancipation of his slaves Bob, Frank, Letty, and Polly, and Letty's and Polly's children. Schwartz had been told by his doctor that he would die soon, and the doctor suggested that Schwartz make his will. The doctor handed pen and paper to a third party, Morgan, so that Morgan could record Schwartz's deathbed declarations. With his slaves gathered around him, Schwartz spoke some of his last words. He asked his slave Bob whether he wished to be freed.

---

44. *Coleman v. Dick and Pat,* 1 Wash. Virginia 223 (1793), in Catterall, *Judicial Cases,* 102; *Charles v. Hunnicutt,* 5 Call 311 (1804), in ibid., 109.

45. *Gregory v. Baugh,* 2 Leigh 665 (1831), in ibid., 163.

Bob answered diplomatically that "he was very willing to serve *him*, but he had rather be freed than have another master." Schwartz responded, "He should be freed." Schwartz also asked Frank whether he wished to be freed, and Frank said yes. Then Polly asked for her and her children's freedom, and Bob asked whether Schwartz would also free his wife Letty and their children. Schwartz assented to those requests, declaring that both Polly and Letty, along with their children, should also be freed. The attending physician reported these words to Morgan, who wrote them down. Bob, Frank, Letty, Polly, and Letty's and Polly's children consequently thought themselves emancipated. But after Schwartz died, his descendants ignored his deathbed wishes and claimed Bob and the others as slaves. The (freed?) slaves sued for their liberty. The case rested on the question of whether what Morgan had written down was a valid nuncupative will. The lower courts disagreed, and so the Court of Appeals put the case to rest, finding that there was "no expression, indeed, or act of the sick man, to shew that he thought himself making his will . . . or that he wished any person to bear testimony to what was doing." Because the court decided that Schwartz's words had not counted as a valid will, Bob, Frank, Letty, Polly, and their children were condemned to lives as slaves. The court also questioned whether a nuncupative will could count as an instrument of emancipation but left that issue for a future case. By the time Schwartz died in the late 1820s, a Virginian who wished to free his slaves had to be very attentive to the legalities of doing so. Had Schwartz known he had to state more clearly that he was making a will, he probably would have. But common ignorance such as his and the court's attention to narrow points of law over principles of liberty made freedom increasingly difficult for slaves to attain after 1820.[46]

PEOPLE OF COLOR

The ambiguities about liberty and race that judges, juries, and county officials tried to clarify in the early nineteenth century remained, however, and found their way into the very language Virginians used to identify people of African descent. In the colonial era Africans had been described first as servants and then increasingly as slaves, until finally the word *negro* and the word *slave* became almost synonymous. The usage reflected the social reality, since most

---

46. *Winn v. Bob and others*, 3 Leigh 140 (1831). The court left alone the issue of whether a nuncupative will was a valid instrument of emancipation, deciding to wait for a case in which that was the operative issue.

African Americans in that era were slaves. In more popular use—in letters, diaries, newspapers, and court papers—Virginians consistently described their slaves as "my negroes." Samuel Johnson used a term unfamiliar to that earlier era when he identified himself in his petition of 1820 and in subsequent petitions as a "free man of color," a shift even from 1812, when he had called himself a "free mulatto." In the era after the Revolution the term *person of color* came into use to describe African Americans both enslaved and free, and it became a common phrase after about 1815. The first time the phrase *man of colour* was used in the court proceedings collected by Helen Catterall, for example, was in 1819. The phrase captured the fact that with manumission, racial mixing, and the establishment of a small but noticeable free black community (less than 5 percent of the total population), color and other racial markers became decreasingly accurate as indications of enslavement. In spite of some Virginians' best efforts to move the hands of time back to an earlier era, Virginians understood that the language colonials had used to describe the two basic categories of Virginians, free and negro, no longer sufficed. Moreover, the new phrase emphasized that the main social division in Virginia was no longer between a negro/slave and a white/freeperson but between all people of color and whites. Race, not slave status, was the dividing line, and race remained a dualistic concept even though a number of Virginians in the early nineteenth century had both European and African ancestors.[47]

The subtle distinction between the phrase *person of color* and the words *negro* and *mulatto* was suggested by context. In an 1828 affidavit regarding the arrest of William Albert on suspicion of being a runaway slave, Samuel Binford "affirmed that he has this day examined a *negro* man who has been committed to the Jail of this county as a runaway, by the name of William Albert, and knows the said William Albert to be a *free man of color.*" The word *negro*, unlike *man of color*, still implied slave status. A negro man committed to jail was assumed to be a runaway slave. Upon identification as William Albert, a free person, the negro man became a man of color. In addition, the word *negro* had a more pejorative connotation than did *person of color*. When Fauquier County citizens protested the amount of work they were required to do on the county roads, they complained that they had to work like "a herd of

---

47. Jordan, *White over Black*, 53–63, 71–82, 95; Handlin and Handlin, "Origins of the Southern Labor System"; Catterall, *Judicial Cases*, 131. While several historians have argued that Americans became more attentive to race after the Revolution, none, so far as I am aware, has noted the introduction of the term *person of color*.

negroes," an image that called up animalistic exertions and was meant to incite sympathy for their suffering. The distinction persisted through the antebellum period. One old man remembered in a 1910 interview that there had been two classes of free blacks. Those who were respectable, prosperous, and law-abiding were known by "the respectful name of 'men of color;' individuals of the latter class [the lower element seen as evil associates of slaves] were called 'free niggers.'"[48]

Not only was the term *person of color* more dignified than *negro*, and certainly more respectful than *nigger*, but it obscured the slave or free status of the individual it described, both for contemporaries and for historians. This ambiguity was useful when the status of the person of color was in question. African Americans who petitioned the legislature, for example, often referred to themselves as people of color. Sometimes they were free people who had already stayed in Virginia past the legal deadline, and sometimes they were still enslaved people who hoped to obtain legislative permission to remain in Virginia if they were freed. Henry Carter, a "free man of color" who petitioned the legislature in 1815 to allow his wife, Priscilla, whom he had purchased, to remain in Virginia, included an endorsement of her character that stated that she, "(a woman of colour)," is "a person of good character and as far as I know her conduct generally has been correct." Describing Priscilla as a "woman of colour" left unclear whether she had already been emancipated by her husband; if she had, and if a year had elapsed since the act of manumission, she could be forced to leave Virginia. If she had not been emancipated, the phrase *woman of colour* was preferable to *slave*, since the former imparted personhood to an individual who could be part of the community, while the dehumanizing word *slave* denoted a state of being outside the social body. Similarly, Roderick and Sterling, both still enslaved, described themselves as men of color in their respective petitions of 1814 and 1815. For those like Priscilla, Roderick, and Sterling, whose situation was tenuous, who stood between slavery and freedom, and who wanted to share in the rights and privileges of free people, the less definitive term *person of color* was both appropriate and useful.[49]

48. Chesterfield County Free Negro and Slave Records, Registrations and Papers, emphasis mine; petition of 23 Jan. 1830, LP, Fauquier County; Russell, *Free Negro*, 159.

49. Henry Carter petition, 1815, LP, Charles City County; Sterling petition, 1814, LP, Chesterfield County; Roderick petition, 1815, ibid. Carter's petition was laid on the table, and it appears that Priscilla was not given permission to remain. Although the examples cited here involved people still enslaved, a "person of color" could just as easily be free: John Charleston and Davy

Because the term *person of color* was much more ambiguous and fluid than *negro* or *mulatto*, it also made sense when context rendered enslaved status temporarily unimportant. In an early usage of the term, Chesterfield County's Tomahawk Baptist Church appointed Edward Friend in 1793 "to write a letter of Dismission for Sister Sue (a woman of colour) the property of Richard Elam." Only by including the fact that Sue was the property of Elam did the church's secretary make clear she was enslaved, since the parenthetical "woman of colour" described only skin tone and did not connote slave status. Use of the phrase arose in this instance from the context of a church community in which Sue was "Sister Sue" regardless of whether she was enslaved or free, black or white, and was appropriate to a situation in which Sue's Christian fellowship figured larger than her status as an enslaved woman. Identifying Sue as a woman of color imparted a slightly greater degree of equality than identifying her as "negro Sue" would have done.[50]

The new language underscored how race, which had always been intimately tied to ideas about and definitions of slavery and freedom, became by the early nineteenth century an important concept to Virginians *apart* from their ideas about slavery. This development occurred because white Virginians had to decide whether the new group of "free negroes," as they were first called, that arose from the manumissions of the post-Revolutionary era were more free or more negro. In the end, racial categorization as nonwhite trumped free status. Virginians divided themselves by race rather than by enslaved or free status in almost every arena possible. In Baptist church membership lists, for example, African Americans were usually described as "persons of color" and listed separately from white members, with little or no distinction made between the black members who were slaves and those who were free. In addition, some churches for the purpose of membership lists divided whites into male and female but listed black men and women together. Sometimes even gender was subsumed by race. The growing importance of race accompanied growing hostility to liberty in Virginia, as seen in the legal decisions of the 1820s. Both developments made African Americans' lives more difficult,

---

were both free when they, as men of color, applied for permission to remain in Virginia in 1814 and 1830, respectively. John Charleston petition, 1814, LP, Amherst County; Davy petition, 1830, LP, Bedford County.

50. Tomahawk Baptist Church, Records, 1787–1856, VBHS.

but it was not yet clear what effect the changes would have on whites. Might the assault on liberty affect disfranchised whites, too?[51]

51. For example, Emmaus Baptist Church, Pleasant Vale Baptist Church, and Mill Creek Baptist Church listed black and white members separately, while Carter's Run Baptist Church and Broad Run Baptist Church listed white men and women separately but all "coloured male & female" members together (quotation from Broad Run records). Emmaus Baptist Church, Minutes, 1792–1841, VBHS; Pleasant Vale Baptist Church, Fauquier County, Minute Book, 1799–1851, LVA, Archives Division, photostat; Mill Creek Baptist Church, Botetourt County, Minute Book, 1804–42, LVA, Archives Division, photocopy; Carter's Run Baptist Church, Fauquier County, Minute Book, 1816–50, LVA, Microfilm Collections, misc. reel 436; Broad Run Baptist Church, Fauquier County, Minute Book, 1762–1873, LVA, Microfilm Collections, misc. reel 472.

5

A "contest for power"

SLAVERY AND EMANCIPATION BECOME
POLITICAL ISSUES IN THE 1820S

> We are engaged ... in a contest for power—. ... [A]ll our metaphysical reasoning and our practical rules, all our scholastic learning and political wisdom, are but the arms employed.
>
> CHAPMAN JOHNSON, 1829

SAMUEL JOHNSON SURELY NOTICED several changes in Virginia in the 1820s, particularly the ways in which liberty became constricted and harder for African Americans to attain. But from his vantage point Johnson probably could not see how developments in Virginia reflected and were tied to national trends in that decade, a decade that marked an important transition in Virginia's and the nation's history. The main concern of Americans in that era, one that both shaped and was shaped by discussions of slavery and race, was defining the form and limits of the body politic: Who made up the citizenry? How should government mediate among groups with different interests and with claims to competing liberties? What role, if any, should wealth, including wealth in slaves, play in determining representation in state legislatures? How far did the Revolutionary language of rights go in defining the actual powers and privileges of Americans? Nationally, these questions came to the fore during the Missouri Crisis of 1819–21, an affair that soon affected Virginians' understanding of their rights and of their role in the Union. Within Virginia, important questions about the form of the state's government and the relationship between slaveholding and nonslaveholding Virginians percolated throughout the decade and finally rose to the surface in the 1829–30 Virginia Constitutional Convention.

Revealing parallels existed between the two events, and both sparked discussions about the role of slavery in a society dedicated to liberty. The Missouri Crisis occurred in the context of a rising political antislavery movement that grew in large measure out of the question of whether the lands of the American West would be slave or free. Northerners feared that if slavery expanded into new, western states slaveholders would gain disproportionate power in the national government (as a result of the three-fifths rule), and they also objected to slavery because they were beginning to believe that the existence of slavery debased white freedom, part of an incipient free-labor philosophy. The Virginia Constitutional Convention also took place in the context of political and demographic change. By 1830 almost half of all white Virginians lived west of the Blue Ridge, and a sizable majority of them did not hold slaves, while eastern Virginia's white population continued to decline in both number and proportion compared with that section's black population, both enslaved and free. The demographic division between western and eastern Virginia took on a political character when western Virginians demanded political power equal to that of the easterners, who had traditionally controlled the state government. Like many Americans in the northern and western states, western Virginians opposed the disproportionate power of slaveholders and were dedicated to the progressive political ideas of the Jacksonian age, including equal representation and universal white manhood suffrage. Conservative slaveholders, on the other hand, argued that the peculiar nature of slave property deserved special protection in the form of more votes for slaveholders, achieved through disproportionate representation and property requirements for voting.[1]

Changes in antislavery ideas and behavior in Virginia were closely tied to the discussions of the 1820s about the structure of the polity and the role of slavery in it. In that transitional period after the fading of Revolutionary-era antislavery activity, proemancipation sentiment found expression in a new organization that attracted a relatively large number of adherents, the American Colonization Society (ACS). In addition to the antislavery strain in the colonization movement, which survived in Virginia into the early 1830s, a new political form of antislavery advocacy arose in Virginia in the 1820s. Signifi-

---

1. For an overview of the rise of Jacksonian politics see Watson, *Liberty and Power*, chaps. 2 and 3; for an interpretation of the period focusing on the relationship between democracy and capitalism see Sellers, *Market Revolution;* and for an essay exploring the interrelated changes of the 1820s, presaged by events of the year 1819, see Davis, *Challenging the Boundaries of Slavery*, chap. 2.

cantly, political antislavery sentiment was closely linked with political opposition to Virginia slaveholders, whose behavior and changing ideas inspired the antislavery response. In the Revolutionary era slaveholding leaders had celebrated universal liberty, by which they implicitly meant white liberty. Of course, universal white liberty had not actually existed at the time of the Revolution, but few had then defended political inequalities among white citizens. Two generations later, in the 1829–30 Virginia Constitutional Convention, some conservative slaveholders championed a more limited form of liberty that excluded some whites, and when they defended white inequality, they spurred their opponents to develop an antislavery argument that focused more on white than on black freedom. Although antislavery ideas in antebellum Virginia differed significantly from those of the Revolutionary period, and antislavery advocates came from a different segment of society, white Virginians' concern for their own liberty and security remained central to their thought about slavery and black people.

THE COLONIZATION MOVEMENT AND EMANCIPATION IN VIRGINIA

From late in the second decade of the nineteenth century to the early 1830s, Virginians who, in the tradition of Jefferson and St. George Tucker, still hoped that slavery might be ended peaceably channeled their energies into the ACS because they believed, as one former Virginian explained in her memoirs, that "[i]f my negroes are ever free, it cannot be here" but must instead be across the "mighty ocean" in Africa. Others found colonization appealing for a very different reason, seeing it as a way to remove free blacks and thereby reduce or even eliminate a population they thought threatened both white safety and slave discipline. The decidedly ambivalent ACS gained popularity in Virginia in the 1820s precisely because it spoke to these conflicting goals, but as ambivalence itself became less useful in the 1820s, as individual Virginians and institutions like the ACS had to decide whether to side with or against slavery and slaveholders, and as the colonizationists became divided over issues of "State Rights" and federal power in the decade after the Missouri Crisis, the ACS in Virginia declined in popularity and importance. The history of the ACS in Virginia from its formation to the early 1830s reveals much about how ideas about slavery, liberty, and race evolved in that era.[2]

2. [Hall], "Imaginationist," 94, VHS. The most comprehensive study of the ACS in Virginia, emphasizing the antislavery component of the ACS in the 1820s, is McGraw, "American Colonization Society in Virginia." *State Rights* was the contemporary term. Although modern historians

Though most widely endorsed in Virginia in the 1820s, the idea of colonization had a long history and had been part of white Virginian thought about the problem of slavery and freed slaves since the Revolutionary era. Thomas Jefferson's and St. George Tucker's gradual abolition plans had both included the deportation of freed slaves (though not necessarily to Africa) as key elements, and George Tucker's and Ferdinando Fairfax's schemes to reduce the African population in Virginia also rested on the colonization of slaves and free blacks beyond the commonwealth. In 1801, just after the discovery of Gabriel's plot, when fear of free blacks ran particularly high, the Virginia legislature passed a secret resolution instructing Governor James Monroe (a supporter of colonization and in later years president of the ACS) to request that President Jefferson seek out lands beyond the United States to which insurgent slaves and free people of color could be sent. The legislators' concern with both rebellious slaves and free blacks indicated that their primary wish was to remove what they saw as noxious persons, but the 1801 resolution and the Monroe-Jefferson correspondence were later interpreted by antislavery colonizationists and by some historians as a sign of Virginia's long-standing commitment to ending slavery.[3]

When in 1816 the Loudoun County delegate Charles Fenton Mercer learned of the secret Monroe-Jefferson letters of 1801, he disclosed them and pushed for similar action in support of colonization. The House of Delegates followed Mercer's lead, in December 1816 passing his resolution asking for federal aid in locating a colony. The resolution stated that the General Assembly had "repeatedly sought to obtain an asylum . . . for such persons of colour as had been, or might be emancipated" and instructed the governor to write to President Madison "for the purpose of obtaining a territory on the coast of Africa, or at some other place . . . to serve as an asylum" for free blacks and subsequently emancipated slaves.[4]

---

often refer to *states' rights,* I find it useful when trying to recapture nineteenth-century Virginians' thoughts to use the language they did.

3. Carey, *Letters on the Colonization Society,* 5–6; Staudenraus, *African Colonization Movement,* vii. Carey wrote that before 1801 the Virginia legislature twice debated colonization in secret session, but I have not yet found independent confirmation of this. Staudenraus interprets colonization generally as an antislavery movement, stating, "Colonizationists, like most Americans of the early nineteenth century, were troubled by slavery and wished an end to it."

4. Staudenraus, *African Colonization Movement,* 31; Carey, *Letters on the Colonization Society,* 7; Egerton, *Charles Fenton Mercer,* 105–7, 110–11.

The Virginia House of Delegates' official endorsement of colonization in 1816 coincided with the founding of the ACS in Washington, DC, that December, which had also resulted, though indirectly, from Charles Fenton Mercer's efforts. Like other benevolent societies of the period, the ACS combined the energy of the Second Great Awakening—evangelical zeal and belief in moral uplift—with the enterprising spirit of the modernizing young nation. Colonizationists in Virginia and other states thought that removing free blacks to Africa would benefit all involved: America would be rid of an unwanted population and the threat of race war; blacks would be released from the prejudices of American society; Africa would acquire, in the persons of African American immigrants, a civilizing and Christianizing influence; and slaveholders who wanted to manumit some slaves could do so without worrying that they would increase the menacing free black population. Removing the whole of America's free colored population seemed entirely possible to the enthusiastic leaders of the ACS. Indeed, they accomplished the unlikely, creating the colony of Liberia on Africa's western coast and transporting several thousand African Americans back to the continent of their ancestors by the end of the 1830s.[5]

The growth of the colonization movement after 1816 resulted also from changes in the international order. As the Virginia resolution explained, previous colonization efforts had been frustrated in part "by the disturbed state of other nations," which made negotiations for a colony difficult. Such had been the case in 1802, when the Sierra Leone Company rebuffed President Jefferson's efforts to send Virginia's rebellious slaves there because allowing slaves in Sierra Leone would violate the colony's prohibition on slavery (Jefferson was not interested in freeing the rebels). When Jefferson considered other destinations for Virginia's unwanted blacks, he found, as he wrote to Monroe, that the "convulsions prevailing in the French West India islands" precluded innovations, such as colonization of American blacks to Haiti, "which at other times would be admissible." The turmoil of the Napoleonic

---

5. For the annual number of colonists sent, a total of 3,709 through 1839, see the appendix to Staudenraus, *African Colonization Movement;* for a typical summary of the ACS's goals see Carey, *Letters on the Colonization Society;* for Mercer's influence on the founding of the ACS see Egerton, *Charles Fenton Mercer,* 108–11; and for discussions of the religious motivation of colonizers see Varon, *We Mean to Be Counted,* 43–47, and van Riemsdijk, "Time and Property from Heaven," chap. 5.

years and the War of 1812 also made unlikely the international cooperation that was necessary for colonization, even as that turmoil reminded Virginia slaveholders of the potential instability of slavery since thousands of slaves had fled Chesapeake plantations during that war. By 1816 "peace" had "healed the wounds of humanity." In addition, the European nations had generally united against the Atlantic slave trade, and the international antislavery movement was on the rise. In that context the Virginia dream of colonization seemed newly feasible.[6]

Virginians took the lead in the ACS during the organization's early years because the impulses of white Virginians, especially their fear of free blacks, matched up so well with the mixed agenda of the ACS. Charles Fenton Mercer continued to support colonization in his capacity as a congressman, introducing and promoting bills favorable to colonization in the national legislature; Chief Justice John Marshall headed the Virginia branch of the organization; and Bushrod Washington, an associate Supreme Court justice and nephew of George Washington, was one of the national society's first board members. None of these men, however, was primarily an antislavery advocate. Mercer's goal was more to "drain . . . pauperism" (free blacks) from Virginia than to act against slavery. John Marshall's support for colonization stemmed, according to a recent biographer, from his doubt that "whites and blacks could live peaceably in the same society" and from his conviction that the removal of free blacks would strengthen the Union and relieve it "from a danger whose extent can scarcely be estimated." Bushrod Washington's antislavery commitment came under suspicion in 1821, when a newspaper reported that he had sold more than fifty slaves to the South. If these three prominent members of the ACS seemed more interested in removing free African Americans than ending slavery, others, such as the Reverend William Meade, later Virginia's Episcopal bishop, did hope to see slavery's demise. Meade was an early agent of the society and continued to support colonization throughout his career.[7]

The membership of the most important and powerful Virginia ACS auxil-

6. Virginia Resolution of 1816, quoted in Carey, *Letters on the Colonization Society*, 7; Thomas Jefferson to James Monroe, 24 Nov. 1802, printed in *JHD* (begun Dec. 1831), doc. no. 10.

7. Charles Fenton Mercer, *An Exposition on the Weakness and Inefficiency of the Government of the United States of North America* (n.p.: privately printed, 1845), 169–70, quoted in Egerton, *Charles Fenton Mercer*, 107; Robarge, *A Chief Justice's Progress*, 276; John Marshall, quoted in ibid., 277; Stevenson, *Life in Black and White*, 280–81 (on Washington selling slaves).

iary, the Richmond and Manchester Society, was similarly divided in its goals. Founded in 1823 and headed from that time until 1827 by John Marshall, the Richmond branch became the head of the new state organization, the Colonization Society of Virginia (CSV), in 1828. Some members, such as John Taliaferro, for example, thought of colonization as "opening a door I hope not only for the free people of culler to injoy the comforts & priviledges of a free government, but more especially paving a way as I earnestly hope at some future day, for us to get clear of our slave population." But the declared goal of the CSV was to remove free blacks. As their constitution stated, "The object of this Society shall be to aid the American Colonization Society in its efforts to colonize the free people of colour of the United States on the coast of Africa"; no mention was made of promoting emancipation. In order to effect its stated goal, the society collected money from subscribers, which it forwarded to the national organization; lobbied the Virginia legislature for state support; and asked clergymen to take up collections in their churches to fund colonization. Donors to the CSV and other Virginia colonization societies, many of whom were women, generally were Presbyterians, Methodists, and especially Episcopalians.[8]

The participation of women in the colonization movement highlighted how antislavery action in Virginia had evolved since the 1780s, when it had been mostly the province of men. Women formed several female colonization societies in the state and made up a significant, visible part of the movement in Virginia, an interesting contrast to the mostly male personnel of ACS auxiliaries in the North. The male-dominated Richmond society thought female auxiliaries boded well for the "future hopes and prospects of the Society" because of women's special role as moral guardians and also because the Richmond and Manchester Female Society had collected and forwarded $170 to the ACS. Prominent female colonizationists in Virginia were generally well-to-do Episcopalian ladies who were closely related to leading male members of the ACS. Ann Page, sister of the Reverend William Meade, typified the

---

8. American Colonization Society, Virginia Branch, Records, 1823–59, 1, 54–56, VHS; John Taliaferro to Benjamin Brand, 31 May 1825, Benjamin Brand Papers, VHS; McGraw, "American Colonization Society in Virginia," 56–58. McGraw says that the formation of the CSV was part of a move toward state control of colonization (80), though Staudenraus's book dates this trend to the 1830s. The Richmond branch included other prominent members, such as Beverly Randolph, William W. Hening, and Carter J. Nicholas, all of whom joined as lifetime members at a fee of ten dollars. Benjamin Brand Papers, items 179–95.

earnest, religiously inspired colonizationist in her wish that "Western Africa be seasoned with divine salt, from American Christians!" For Page and others, colonization appealed because it could simultaneously encourage manumission and discourage rebelliousness among slaves. She hoped, for example, "to persuade my dear sisters people [slaves] so clever and good as they are, to go [to Africa]—in stead of taking up . . . with American emancipation, which is but a *sorry state full of evil*."[9]

Nancy Turner Hall was similarly inspired by a mix of Christian faith, antislavery feeling, and the belief that it was "a natural impossibility that they [colored people] could ever enjoy the privileges of free citizens among the whites in this country." Though she was not an activist, she shared the hope that colonization might ease the burden of American slavery, which she thought was a "sin calculated to call down the vengeance of Heaven." Convinced that "[t]he colored man must cross the mighty ocean, ere his foot can rest on a land of freedom to him!" Hall determined to free the slaves she had inherited from her father and to send to Africa those who wished to go through the aegis of the ACS. She had particular hopes for "Uncle Jack," who wished to "preach the Gospel in Africa." But when Jack died shortly after his arrival in Liberia, she questioned her actions and her motives. Was colonization—transportation over a vast distance to a strange and dangerous land—really the best way? With no other suitable options apparent, the answer was yes: "I could not blame myself. . . . I wished to make the slaves free, . . . & I knew of no better way to do it." Because for Virginians such as Nancy Hall, Ann Page, and John Taliaferro colonization made emancipation feasible, it was not without cause that opponents suspected it of being a covert form of antislavery activity. One critic blasted the ACS and its auxiliaries for being "so many *hotbeds* for the nurture and propagation of principles unfriendly to the tenure of Southern slavery."[10]

---

9. Dorsey, *Reforming Men and Women*, 138–49; American Colonization Society, Virginia branch, 1828 newspaper clipping attached to p. 53; Ann Randolph Page to Mary Lee Custis, n.d., Mary Lee Custis Papers, VHS. For accounts of women's importance to the ACS in Virginia see Varon, *We Mean to Be Counted*, chap. 2; and van Riemsdijk, "Time and Property from Heaven," chap. 5. Dorsey notes the overwhelming (20 to 1) dominance of male to female ACS branches in the ACS auxiliaries in the North and argues that the members of the ACS "actively promot[ed] their reform movement as a vehicle for masculine identity for black colonists and white reformers alike" (139).

10. [Hall], "Imaginationist," 35, 94, 165–67; *Controversy between Caius Gracchus and Opimius*, 74.

After slavery became an issue of public debate during the Virginia Constitutional Convention of 1829–30, eastern slaveholders became particularly suspicious of the colonization movement, and partly as a result the movement began to decline. As one Richmond colonizationist wrote to a friend in 1830, "[T]he cause of African Colonization is almost dead in this region . . . because our friends in the Convention Judge Marshall & Messr's Mercer Fitzhugh &c, deemed it most prudent to pass it over, fearing that a determined and bitter opposition to us would have resulted from it." Moving away from any appearance of being an antislavery society, the CSV in January 1832 renewed its pledge "to adhere to that original feature in its constitution which confines its operations, to the removal of the free people of color, only with their own consent." Indeed, by the mid-1830s colonization in Virginia was largely the province of conservative politicians who thought exporting free blacks could strengthen slavery in the state.[11]

The dream of colonization encapsulated all of white Virginians' ambivalence about slavery and emancipation. It could legitimately be viewed *both* as a form of antislavery and as a form of proslavery activity even though by 1835 its antislavery purpose had been subsumed in Virginia by the goal of removing free blacks. While the antislavery element had obtained, however, it said something important about the evolution of proemancipation sentiment in Virginia. By the 1820s the radical antislavery tradition in the state, never a broad or dominant movement, had disappeared. Most supporters of emancipation now came from an essentially cautious class, women and men who were well established among Virginia's elite, insiders who stood in marked contrast to the outsiders—evangelicals and Quakers—who had agitated for emancipation in the 1780s. Whereas some members of the Revolutionary-era elite, such as Thomas Jefferson and St. George Tucker, had envisioned emancipation as a way to end slavery, proemancipation colonizationists were mostly religious individuals who endorsed *voluntary* emancipation only, since their primary concern was removing slaves rather than removing slavery.[12]

11. William Crane to Mary Blackford, 8 Oct. 1830, Blackford Family Papers, Southern Historical Collection, University of North Carolina, Chapel Hill; American Colonization Society, Virginia branch, 60; McGraw, "American Colonization Society in Virginia," 18, 223–24; Varon, *We Mean to Be Counted*, 59–61. For an extended treatment of how colonization was transformed in Virginia through the late 1820s and early 1830s see also Iaccarino, "Virginia and the National Contest over Slavery," 206–30.

12. For colonizationists as cautious and well established among the elite see McGraw, "American Colonization Society in Virginia," 229–30.

The chimerical nature of the ACS's goal—to resolve the problem of race by creating a homogeneous free white society either with or without an accompanying enslaved black population, depending on one's stance on slavery—underscores how intractable the interrelated problems of liberty, race, and the American character remained for the white Virginians of the early national era. While mass emigration legitimately seemed more feasible to them than it might to us, since America was in the process of enforcing the mass emigration of Native Americans to western lands, and since the memory of America's own growth from a collection of struggling colonies to an independent republic was so recent, colonization failed several logical and practical tests. First, most free African Americans did not wish to go to Africa, which by the 1820s was to them a foreign place and not "home." In addition, promoters of colonization never resolved the problem of how to fund such a massive venture. Unlike the removal of American Indians further westward, colonization required a huge outlay of capital, and unlike the slave trade it was meant to reverse or the European colonization of America it was meant to mimic, there was no lure of profit that could tempt investors to finance it. Finally, the natural growth of the free black population in the United States was so vigorous that only an effort of unprecedented and almost unimaginable scale could have removed free blacks faster than they reproduced. Colonizationists clung to their hopes, however, because like so many other white Americans, they could not conceive of a future in which black people and white people lived together as American citizens, and thus the antislavery members among them had no way to dream of emancipation without removal of the freed slaves. Colonizationists even failed to acknowledge that, in fact, free blacks and whites and people of mixed ancestry actually *did* live together in America, sometimes quite peaceably, if not as equals. For the ACS, creating an idealized white nation, rather than effecting universal liberty, was the main impetus toward action.[13]

EXTERNAL POLITICS: THE MISSOURI CRISIS, THE STATE RIGHTS ARGUMENT, AND THE QUESTION OF EMANCIPATION

If the popularity of the ACS in Virginia and in America more generally ultimately reflected a commitment to a white polity, Virginians' response to the Missouri Crisis demonstrated the extent to which their ideas about the

---

13. Varon, *We Mean to Be Counted*, 57; Nash, *Forging Freedom*, 237–38. I am indebted to David Brion Davis for the point that colonization legitimately appeared possible.

structure of that polity, particularly ideas about federal-state relations and how to balance the interests of slaveholding versus nonslaveholding regions, were in flux in the 1820s. The Missouri Crisis of 1819–21, along with other developments, including Supreme Court decisions favoring the federal over state governments and the passage of tariff laws unfavorable to southern farmers, helped persuade Virginia leaders early in the decade that their interests, particularly in slave property, could only be safeguarded by a narrow construction of the federal Constitution and an assertion of State Rights. The emergence of the State Rights argument also contributed to the demise of the colonization movement in Virginia, since so many agreed that federal power, including the power to colonize free blacks, ought to be strictly limited and to yield to the rights of the individual state governments. At the same time, growing sectional antipathy in the nation—the Northeast battling the South for power in the West—began to push Virginia leaders to choose between North and South, between the theoretical hope still voiced by some leaders that slavery might one day be ended and Virginians' practical, material, and political interest in defending what was an increasingly peculiar institution against attack.[14]

The 1819 congressional debates over the admission of Missouri to the Union were important partly because they established the State Rights position as particularly southern, in opposition to northerners' nationalist perspective. Before that time, antifederal arguments had found just as welcome a home in the northern states as in the southern ones. The Virginia and Kentucky Resolutions (1798), arguing that states could declare void any federal laws they believed unconstitutional, found their northern echo in Massachusetts citizens' 1809 protests against Jefferson's Enforcement Act, which allowed warrantless searches of ships to enforce the embargo then in place on American shipping. Northerners also adopted an antinational stance in the Hartford Convention of 1814, when northern Federalists, angry at the Republican (and Virginian) administrations, which seemed to disregard their interests and well-being, suggested several ways to strengthen the power of the local over the national government and to restructure the national compact to lessen the power of southerners.[15]

14. For a good general discussion of Missouri and the rise of State Rights arguments, see Fehrenbacher, *Constitutions and Constitutionalism*, chap. 2.

15. See Banner, *To the Hartford Convention*. The convention proposed granting to the states powers of military self-defense and repealing the three-fifths rule. The full text of the proposals may be found at The Avalon Project website, at http://www.yale.edu/lawweb/avalon/amerdoc/hartconv.htm.

Befitting their long tradition of formulating influential political ideas, Virginians led the South in fighting for the admission of Missouri as a slave state, and more particularly in developing an articulate and comprehensive argument that emphasized that slavery should be firmly under state and not national control and that further justified slavery as both constitutional and republican. When in February 1819 New York Congressman James Tallmadge Jr. proposed an amendment to the Missouri admission bill outlawing the future importation of slaves into Missouri and freeing all slave children born after Missouri became a state, Virginia Congressman Philip P. Barbour helped shape the southern response. The Tallmadge amendment, Barbour argued, violated Missouri's right to an equal standing with the other states, all of which had sovereignty over slavery within their borders. Slavery, he said, had been and ought to be a matter of state and not federal jurisdiction. Arguments proffered on the pages of Virginia's premier political organ, the *Richmond Enquirer*, largely reiterated Barbour's point—that Congress did not have the power to impose conditions on the admission of a state to the Union except that the new state's constitution be republican in form. When northern antislavery agitators and northern congressmen suggested that slavery violated republican values, Virginians asserted that slavery *was* compatible with republican government and thus the Congress had no power to prohibit it in any state. Slavery was even sanctioned in the federal Constitution, with its fugitive slave provision and three-fifths clause. As a "Southron" (probably George Tucker) emphasized, "So far from contemplating the general emancipation of our slaves, the federal constitution not only recognizes our rights as masters, but secures to us their enjoyment. It provides for their recovery within other jurisdictions, and graduates our representation upon principles, pre-supposing their continuance in bondage." Through such arguments southerners began to stake out a State Rights position that always implicitly concerned a state's right to protect slavery within its borders and that would remain central to their political thought up to the Civil War.[16]

The Missouri Crisis also forced Virginians to revisit ideas about the spread of slavery. Did allowing slaves into areas where they had not previously been constitute the diffusion of a poison that rendered it less toxic, or did the spread of slavery infect virgin lands with a horrible new pestilence? During the Revolutionary era Jefferson, for one, had thought restricting slavery to the southern

---

16. Moore, *Missouri Controversy*, 45–46; Fehrenbacher, *Slaveholding Republic*, 263–66; *Richmond Enquirer*, 29 Dec. 1819, 1, 6 Jan. 1820.

states would be the best way to end it, and for that reason he had pushed for the ban on slavery in the Northwest Territory. Jefferson and other Virginians now took the opposite position. Restriction of slavery from Missouri, they argued, would not benefit a single slave but would instead make it more difficult for the southern states ever to enact emancipation schemes, since the concentration of black people in the South was an impediment to freeing them. If slavery were spread throughout the country, emancipation would be feasible, and "we confidently believe that in half a century, there would not be a slave in the United States." It was a convenient but not particularly sincere argument, as their heated reaction to the Tallmadge amendment's provision for enforced emancipation suggested.[17]

Although Virginia whites said that the dispersal of slavery into Missouri would benefit America generally because it would help pave the way for emancipation, they were agitated by the possibility that northern leaders held abolition as their ultimate goal. One warned that when "they shall have succeeded in excluding from the western settlements every southern man . . . an universal emancipation may be the next scheme suggested by visionary philanthropists or promoted by designing politicians." Simultaneously reading the northern position as a cynical bid for political power spurred by "jealousy of the influence of the southern states" and as a misguided effort by antislavery radicals, many Virginia commentators became nervous and defensive. They threatened disunion if northern antislavery forces persisted. "An American" predicted correctly that "in less than half a century . . . the Southern people will be reduced to the necessity of abandoning the Union, or submitting to the unnumbered evils of some system of emancipation."[18]

If the nation's unity seemed threatened, Virginia's did not: *all* of the Old Dominion's congressmen voted against both the anti-importation and *post nati* emancipation provisions of the Tallmadge amendment in 1819. Most—eighteen of twenty-two—also voted against the portion of the compromise reached in 1820 that barred slavery in the territories north of latitude 36°30'. Indeed, Virginians were more united in their opposition to that compromise than members of other southern states. In the state legislature delegates drafted and passed a strongly worded resolution against the restriction of slavery in Missouri, arguing that restrictions on slavery "violate and degrade the sovereign footing" of Missouri and that "an attack upon the sovereignty of

---

17. *Richmond Enquirer,* 8 Feb. 1820; McColley, *Slavery and Jeffersonian Virginia,* 173–75.
18. *Richmond Enquirer,* 23 Dec. 1819, 1 Jan. 1820.

one [state] must be considered an attack upon the sovereignty of all." Virginia therefore stood "in common cause" with the people of Missouri and would "cooperate with them in resisting with manly fortitude, any attempt which Congress may make to impose restraints" not authorized by the Constitution. Framing the issue as one of manhood, as the debates in 1829–30 would as well, revealed how much Virginians of the era understood political participation in gendered and not only racial terms.[19]

A lone antislavery voice stood against the majority in the Virginia Senate and refused to endorse the Virginia resolution on the Missouri question. Presaging Virginia's own sectional strife, it was a westerner, state senator Daniel Bryan, of the Valley county of Rockingham, who ignored the constitutional arguments and attacked slavery on the basis of the American "political creed." Bryan reverted to the rhetoric of an earlier era. He quoted the Declaration of Independence and proclaimed that the "law of nature gives no right to one man to sell another." If the Constitution admitted slavery, it was only because the task of trying to forge a union in the wake of a destructive war had created an "unconquerable *necessity* . . . [that] *compelled* the Convention of 1787 to incorporate with the constitution those articles which pertain to slavery." Bryan ended with a flourish, trying to sway his fellow Virginians by reminding them of their Revolutionary heritage. If Virginia were to endorse the extension of human bondage, "then let her drag from this magnificent dome—and conceal in its darkest vault—secure from contempt and mockery—the forgotten statue of her Washington! and then let her pile the vacant enclosure with manacles, scourges, and all the implements of torture—the appropriate badges of slavery!" It was an extraordinary speech, remarkable because Virginia leaders rarely denounced slavery in such strong words even if some of them disliked the institution. Perhaps eager to forget the incident, Virginians seem to have ignored Bryan's remarks and offered no rejoinder on the pages of the *Richmond Enquirer*, where his words had been printed.[20]

The excitement over the Missouri issue evident in Virginia newspaper essays and in the General Assembly subsided quickly after the Congress reached a compromise in February 1820, but the crisis permanently affected Virginians' thought about the possibility of emancipation in several ways. Most immedi-

19. Moore, *Missouri Controversy*, 53, 55, 111; Virginia Resolution, *Richmond Enquirer*, 13 Jan. 1820. For a discussion of how women challenged the notion that only men could participate in the political process see Isenberg, *Sex and Citizenship*.

20. *Richmond Enquirer*, 15, 17 Feb. 1820.

ately, the new attention to State Rights altered the course of the colonization movement in the commonwealth. As one critic of colonization pointed out in an 1825 essay that appeared in the *Richmond Enquirer,* the ACS hoped to combine its own efforts with those of the national government, the only body that could coordinate and fund large-scale colonization. The writer objected that the federal government did not have the constitutional powers to take such action. Even some supporters of colonization agreed and worried that the federal support sought by colonizationists might repel potential donors. Future president John Tyler was among them, writing in 1828, "I deprecate every such interference" of the national government in colonization, "not only because its first effect would be justly to excite the alarms of the slaveholders throughout the Union, but secondarily to break down the efforts of those friendly to the original objects of the [American Colonization] Society in the different States." Tyler worried with reason, since colonization in Virginia had withered by the mid-1830s partly because Virginians rejected a cause that required for its success the broad powers of the national government.[21]

In addition, the Missouri Crisis showed Virginians that there were at least two ways to understand American liberty: either as liberty to own slave property, which most Virginia leaders had argued was the true meaning of constitutional liberty, or as liberty from slavery, which Tallmadge, Bryan, and others argued was the case. These issues were just coming to the fore in the 1820s, however, and would remain vague for several more years.

The Missouri Crisis also spurred Virginians to explain why the abolition of slavery was unfeasible, though they did so without advancing a strident proslavery argument. Partly because the crisis was relatively short lived, Virginia's spokesmen in the years 1819–21 were able to respond effectively to northern criticism with arguments that focused on federal-state relations, the role of slavery in the Constitution, and the rights and liberties of slaveholders rather than on the morality of slavery itself. When other Virginians, particularly anonymous newspaper essayists, did take up the issue of slavery's morality, they defended the institution in traditional terms, reviving the claim made

21. *Controversy between Caius Gracchus and Opimius,* 10–11; John Tyler to John W. Nash, 6 May 1828, Nash Family Papers, VHS; McGraw, "American Colonization Society in Virginia," 17–18, 164. The compromise combined the admission of Missouri as a slave state and Maine as a free state with a restriction against slavery in the territory north of Missouri's southern border. The parts of the compromise were ushered through by Henry Clay in separate bills, and Virginia did not support the restriction on slavery.

in response to the Methodist petitions of 1785 that slavery was compatible with the Bible. "An American" asked rhetorically, "Will any Christian say that slavery must necessarily be excluded from our territory, when it was *expressly* sanctioned by the old, and recognized without censure by the new, testament?" A detailed essay in three parts by "An Inquisitive Slave-holder" laid out its thesis in its lengthy title, "Scriptural Researches *Concerning tenures of Involuntary Service, which result in demonstration that slaveholding never was prohibited by the* Word of God—*but that from the earliest ages the purchase of servants and the usage of rendering their service an inheritance, was sanctioned*—I. Under the *Primal Theocracy;* II. Under the *Mosaic Law;* and III. Under the *Gospel Dispensation.*" The argument failed to capture the imagination of many Virginians who, along with the publishers of the essay, insisted instead that they did "not vindicate servitude; we wish no slave had touched our soil; we wish it could be terminated."[22]

Indeed, slaveholders in the 1820s and early 1830s found that they could deflect the harshest criticism their northern counterparts expressed by agreeing with rather than denying the premise from which antislavery advocates reasoned. The fictional Tidewater planter Frank Meriwether spoke for real planters in John Pendleton Kennedy's novel *Swallow Barn* (1832) when he acknowledged that slavery was "theoretically and morally wrong; and, of course, it may be made to appear wrong in all of its modifications." But Meriwether went on to defend Virginia planters to Mark Littleton, the novel's main character, a visitor to Virginia from the North. Since slavery had been introduced "without our agency," Meriwether explained, Virginia slaveholders could do little but to "administer wholesome laws for their government, and to make their servitude as tolerable to them as we can." He continued, arguing that Virginia's slaves did "less work than any other labourers in society," lived relatively comfortably, and received compassionate treatment from their masters. Most slaveholders, in fact, were "men of kind and humane tempers, as pliant to the touch of pity and compassion as any class in any country; and as little likely to inflict sufferings upon their dependants." Similarly, a newspaper essayist in 1820 asserted that slaveholders were "high-minded humane people" and that their slaves were as "well fed, as well clothed, and as happy, as any class of whites of the same grade in society."[23]

22. *Richmond Enquirer,* 1 Jan., 10 Feb. 1820.

23. Littleton, *Swallow Barn* (1832), 1: 227–28; *Richmond Enquirer,* 20 Jan. 1820. According to Lucinda MacKethan, Kennedy began the novel in 1825, and the sentiments voiced through

Focusing on slaveholders' kindness to their slaves romanticized the institution in a new way and presaged proslavery arguments of the early 1830s, but the cry that slavery was not the fault of well-intentioned Virginians was an old one, and particularly after northern congressmen began to attack slavery on the floor of the national legislature it functioned to fend off condemnation for the sin of slavery. Since the Revolutionary era at least, Virginians, including St. George Tucker and Thomas Jefferson, had portrayed themselves as victims of English greed upon whom slavery had been foisted against their will. Especially when speaking to northerners, Virginians pointed out their objection to the slave trade and their interdiction of it in 1778 (even if, in fact, Virginia had banned slave importation in 1778 for pecuniary and self-interested more than ideological reasons). In 1820 the editor of the *Richmond Enquirer*, who fiercely supported the right of Missouri to allow slavery, still described slavery as a curse not chosen by Virginia's forefathers but "imposed upon them, and curtailed upon ourselves." These arguments allowed Virginians to grant themselves a measure of moral absolution for the crime of slavery, the psychological benefit of which was to relieve slaveholders, particularly those who admitted that slavery was in theory wrong, of the immense guilt they might otherwise feel for continuing to hold other people in bondage. Asserting blamelessness for the existence of slavery in Virginia also had an important tactical benefit by putting slaveowners on common ground with opponents of slavery and softening attacks from outsiders. If northern leaders believed that southerners wished to see an end to slavery, and their rhetoric during the Missouri Crisis indicates that some of them did believe that, they would be less likely to take a hard line against the slaveholding states.[24]

The crisis over Missouri's admission to the Union had awakened Virginians to the dangers the issue of slavery might pose to the nation, had helped them develop a State Rights view of politics that weakened the colonization movement in the commonwealth, and had spurred renewed but not particu-

---

Meriwether, who was "very clearly modeled on Kennedy's uncle Philip Clayton Pendleton," probably reflect those of planters in the late 1820s. In a reprint of the novel Kennedy claimed that he had striven for accuracy, that the work was "a faithful picture of the people . . . exhibiting the lights and shades of its society with the truthfulness of a painter who has studied his subject on the spot." Lucinda H. MacKethan, introduction to Kennedy, *Swallow Barn* (1986), xx, 10.

24. Jefferson, *Summary View of the Rights of British America*, 16–17; St. George Tucker, *Dissertation on Slavery*, 45–46; McColley, *Slavery and Jeffersonian Virginia*, 115–16; *Richmond Enquirer*, 10 Feb. 1820.

larly strident defenses of slavery. It had also indicated white Virginia's unity on the slave issue. It must have been surprising to Virginians, therefore, to find that less than a decade later they were embroiled in a debate that pitted slaveholding and nonslaveholding regions against each other, as the Missouri Crisis had done, but this time in a divided Virginia.

INTERNAL POLITICS: POWER, ECONOMY, AND SLAVEHOLDING IN VIRGINIA

Profound economic and demographic changes altered the internal politics of the commonwealth between the time of the Revolution and the Jacksonian era, pitting Virginians against one another in the state constitutional convention of 1829–30 and inserting the issue of slavery into discussions about the form and purpose of government and the definition of citizenship. During the Revolutionary era Virginia's white population had been a relatively homogeneous English community dependent on tobacco farming, and almost the entire (non-Indian) population of Virginia had been located in the eastern portion of the state. Even if, as Woody Holton has recently argued, the gentry were insecure in their dominance and influenced by pressures from below, it is still true that the planter elite peopled the halls of government and made decisions for the commonwealth, demanding deference from social subordinates. By 1830 Virginia's society had grown more complex and pluralistic, and its economy had diversified. Whites of English, German, and Scots-Irish backgrounds lived in a state that, in addition to areas dominated by plantations, contained bustling cities, large tracts of land cultivated without the use of slaves, and several important mining and manufacturing facilities. If gentry dominance had been insecure in the Revolutionary period, now there were outright challenges to it, buttressed by the ideology of that revolution. Despite the complexity of Virginia's geography in 1830, the state was basically divided into two sections by the imaginary line marking the crest of the Blue Ridge Mountains. It was, as William Shade has recently described it, "actually two slave states," one in which slavery formed the basis of the economy and culture and one in which slavery existed but did not play a crucial role.[25]

The changes that underlay this transition had begun in the years after the Revolution and continued through the first decades of the nineteenth century.

---

25. Holton, *Forced Founders*, xvii–xx; Isaac, *Transformation of Virginia*, 110–14; Shade, *Democratizing the Old Dominion*, 20.

By 1830 some parts of the Piedmont were seeing transformations similar to those experienced in the late-eighteenth-century Tidewater as white Virginians continued to move westward away from the declining tobacco economy and toward new opportunities. Charles Fenton Mercer described conditions in his Piedmont home of Loudoun County, noting that "where there were formerly tobacco fields and wheat-patches, there are now wheat-fields and tobacco patches." Although eastern Virginians often lamented the development, the mixed economy of wheat, other grains, and livestock to which they had turned was in fact strong, and in some areas, such as the Southside, tobacco still dominated. But the changes experienced from the 1770s to the 1830s came at the expense of the traditional heart of Virginia's economy and culture. Of particular concern to the whites of eastern Virginia, the Tidewater region continued to lose white population between 1800 and 1830, while the white population of the east as a whole (Tidewater and Piedmont) grew only about 10 percent in that period, from about 336,000 inhabitants to nearly 376,000. The black population east of the Blue Ridge grew much more rapidly, increasing by nearly 35 percent in the same era, and outnumbered the white population by a margin of almost three to two in 1830. Most of those African Americans were enslaved, but the free black population, always worrisome to Virginians, had also grown significantly. Statewide it had more than doubled between 1800 and 1830, to more than 40,000.[26]

In contrast, the population of the region to the west of the Blue Ridge crest more than tripled, from about 120,000 in 1790 to nearly 380,000 in 1830, growing from 16 percent of the entire Virginia population to 31 percent. Most of the western population was white and by 1830 composed 46 percent of Virginia's white population. There were important cultural differences between whites in the west and those in the east, since so many westerners descended from German and Scots-Irish migrants who had come south to Virginia's Great Valley from Pennsylvania and other northern agricultural regions beginning

---

26. *Proceedings and Debates,* 336; Beeman, *Evolution of the Southern Backcountry,* 11, 16, 167; Shade, *Democratizing the Old Dominion,* 32–34; *Return of the Whole Number of Persons* (1800); Freehling, *Drift toward Dissolution,* appendix. Shade notes, "The tendency of historians to emphasize the Old Dominion's leading staple crop has led to an obsession with the problems of these declining planters.... In fact, antebellum Virginia had a balanced and thriving agricultural economy." John Majewski describes how the decline of tobacco led to calls for agricultural reform in Albemarle County (Piedmont) in *House Dividing,* 21–25. For changes in the black population see also Dunn, "Black Society in the Chesapeake," esp. maps on pp. 54, 57, 60.

in the latter half of the eighteenth century, as the names in Botetourt County records, for example, indicate. The Brughs, McDowells, and others of that county established small farms on which they grew hemp, wheat, corn, and flax and raised cattle, hogs, and horses for market. They also operated small manufacturing businesses, such as weaving, milling, or metalworking. Settlers in other Valley and Trans-Allegheny counties, including foreign-born immigrants from a host of European countries, followed similar pursuits, and also mined the coal located beneath the surface of the western mountains and valleys.[27]

As we have seen, there were hints even in the 1780s that these demographic shifts might yield a distinct sectionalism. Over the next few years a more decisive east-west split emerged in Virginia politics. In Norman Risjord's words, "Fundamental political issues, based on social and economic differences, tended to divide Virginians into fairly well-defined geographical sections" from the late 1780s through to 1829. By 1806, after decades of white settlement west of the Appalachians, westerners' sense of themselves as a distinct group vying for power with easterners was apparent in John Burwell's speech in favor of a state constitutional convention. But wishing to play down tensions, Burwell called the division "produced by the Blue Ridge" an "artificial" one because it arose from an unrepublican distribution of state power rather than from natural or geographic differences between the "two great districts" of Virginia. (As mentioned earlier, the 1776 constitution had preserved the political power of the colonial era's slaveholding Tidewater aristocracy through a representation scheme in which each county sent two delegates, giving smaller eastern counties proportionally more representation.)[28]

Significantly, sectional divisions in the early nineteenth century did not align with pro- and antislavery views the way they would by 1830 since westerners from the turn of the century through the early 1820s did not actively oppose slavery or the growth of slavery. In 1806 western delegates voted in favor

27. *Return of the Whole Number of Persons* (1791); *Aggregate amount of each description of Persons;* Freehling, *Drift toward Dissolution,* appendix; Stoner, *Seed-Bed of the Republic,* 22–46; Shade, *Democratizing the Old Dominion,* 22. Coal was also mined in Chesterfield County, in the east.

28. Risjord, "Virginia Federalists," 492–96, quotation on 496; *Virginia Argus,* 1 Feb. 1806. For hints of sectionalism in the 1780s see the section "Growing Opposition to Manumission and Free Blacks" in chapter 3, above. Also, according to Norman Risjord, in debates over the ratification of the constitution in 1788 Federalists came largely from the western areas of the state, as well as from the Tidewater, while most counties in the Piedmont opposed ratification.

of the bill that relaxed restrictions on slave importation, and in 1819 they again supported the further importation of slaves by voting for the bill that, for most purposes, rescinded the domestic provisions of the 1778 anti-importation act. Such behavior had been presaged in the Revolutionary era, when easterners, not westerners, had pushed to end the slave trade. At the turn of the century slavery was surprisingly strong even in the mountainous northern portion of the state, where Frederick County's five thousand slaves, for example, made up nearly one-quarter of its population. At that time many westerners, probably those who had migrated from eastern Virginia rather than from Pennsylvania, wanted to imitate the eastern model by buying slaves to work on their farms. Twenty years later westerners still appeared more to support slavery than to oppose it when they voted as a bloc with other Virginia congressmen to defeat Tallmadge's amendment. Daniel Bryan's speech to the Virginia Senate hinted that perhaps Revolutionary antislavery rhetoric was better preserved to the west, but the absence of any recorded reply to his words suggests that slaveholders did not perceive him to be part of a coherent western antislavery movement that ought to be confronted. It was not at all obvious or predictable that western Virginians would adopt an antislavery attitude a decade later.[29]

It was the push by westerners for greater power within the state that led them to oppose eastern slaveholders by 1829. In concrete terms, westerners wanted more votes in the legislature so that they could pass laws for building canals and roads and for creating banks to finance new ventures, internal improvements less needed by residents of the settled eastern areas, especially the Tidewater region with its many navigable rivers and long-established plantations. With their disproportionately small share of delegates in the Virginia General Assembly, westerners found themselves unable to push legislation for internal improvements through the House of Delegates. It was galling to westerners that the Tidewater county of Charles City, for example, with fewer than twenty-five hundred whites and more than three thousand slaves in 1810, had the same number of representatives as Rockingham County in the Shenandoah Valley, which had about eleven thousand whites and fewer than fifteen hundred slaves. The suffrage provisions of the 1776 constitution, which limited voting to men with an "interest" and "attachment" to the community, also focused westerners' attention on the power of slaveholders; more of that

29. Albert, "Protean Institution," 126–29; Alexander Knox speech of 17 Jan. 1832, *Richmond Enquirer*, 11 Feb. 1832; *Return of the Whole Number of Persons* (1800).

wealthy class possessed the amount of land needed to cast a ballot. While about one-quarter of the white men in the Tidewater were disfranchised in the 1820s, nearly half of the white men of the Trans-Allegheny region could not vote, according to one study. Especially in the context of changes in other states where suffrage had been extended in the period from the 1810s to 1820s, Virginians' disabilities were maddening.[30]

In the late 1820s westerners focused their complaints on the disproportionate power of the east, not on slavery itself, and if easterners had yielded more readily to western demands for broader suffrage and proportional representation, sectionalism would have been substantially muted and the issue of slavery might never have become the subject of intense debate within Virginia. It was easterners' refusal to share power more equitably that drove westerners to oppose the basis of slaveholders' power—slavery—by 1832. To some extent, easterners' refusal to give up power can be explained as the natural inclination of any group that has ruled by tradition. But the contrast between Virginia and slaveholding states whose leaders did broaden suffrage and reapportion representation in the first decades of the nineteenth century suggests that Virginia's ruling class felt particularly insecure in comparison with elites elsewhere, perhaps because of the increasingly sectional nature of slavery in the state. In South Carolina, by contrast, a "small and fabulously wealthy planter elite" maintained their hold on the state's politics even as they incorporated all "Free Men" into the polity. Two decades before Virginia reconsidered its representative scheme, South Carolinians had amended their 1790 constitution to reapportion representation in the lower house "according to a formula that weighed white population and taxable property equally" and passed a law (the nation's first) eliminating property requirements for voting. Although South Carolina, like Virginia, was divided geographically and economically between east and west, the divisions there were less stark than in Virginia since even in South Carolina's western regions staple-crop agriculture dominated and slaveholding was relatively widespread.[31]

30. Ambler, *Sectionalism in Virginia*, 118; Sutton, *Revolution to Secession*, 59; Bruce, *Rhetoric of Conservatism*, 2–3; *Aggregate amount of each description of Persons*; Shade, *Democratizing the Old Dominion*, 53; Watson, *Liberty and Power*, 50. Some Piedmont counties, however, were also interested in internal improvements, as documented in Majewski, *House Dividing*, chap. 1.

31. McCurry, *Masters of Small Worlds*, 239–41, quotation on 139; Ford, *Origins of Southern Radicalism*, 106–8, quotation on 106, and, for an overview of the upcountry economy, chap. 2.

In Virginia the eastern slaveholding elite, apparently fearing that westerners would attack their interests, refused to compromise as planters in South Carolina had done and continually rebuffed western demands for a convention to revise the state constitution and reform suffrage and representation. (Earlier calls for reform in the 1780s and 1790s, some from the likes of Jefferson and Madison, had also failed.) In 1803 a bill to reapportion the state Senate districts, which had been drawn to favor the east, failed by seventy-two to fifty-two in a party vote led by Jeffersonian Republicans. Western Republicans who voted with the majority were subsequently turned out of office. Two years later petitions sent from Patrick and Henry counties, both located in the western Piedmont bordering the Valley, sparked some debate, but the legislature voted them down by ninety-eight to fifty-eight. From 1807 to 1815 the legislature habitually rejected citizens' petitions for a constitutional convention, as well as proposals that the people be allowed to vote on whether *they* desired a constitutional convention. Generally, delegates cast votes along sectional lines, with westerners supporting a convention and easterners opposing one. After the failure of an 1816 bill calling for a convention, frustrated westerners met in local and regional meetings over the summer to protest the legislature's recalcitrance. In many western counties citizens drafted resolutions asking that representation in the House of Delegates be based on the white population and that suffrage be extended to all white males. At Staunton that August sixty-five delegates from thirty-five counties passed a resolution asking that Virginians be allowed to vote for or against a convention. The Staunton Convention had the endorsement of Thomas Jefferson, who wrote a letter outlining his views in favor of free white suffrage, equal representation based on the white population, and the election (rather than appointment) of the governor, judges, and sheriffs.[32]

Although the 1816 Staunton Convention moved easterners to action, the compromise they allowed proved too grudging to stave off a constitutional convention for long. In the 1816–17 session of the General Assembly easterners agreed to a measure that changed the basis of representation in the state Senate, but not in the House of Delegates, to the white population as described in the 1810 census. There was no provision, however, for future modification

32. Bruce, *Rhetoric of Conservatism*, 16–19; *Virginia Argus*, 31 Jan., 22 Apr. 1806; Sutton, *Revolution to Secession*, 59–71; *Proceedings and Debates*, 81; Ambler, *Sectionalism in Virginia*, 94; Risjord, "Virginia Federalists," 507–8, 515.

to keep pace with population changes, so by the 1820s westerners again found themselves underrepresented in the Virginia Senate. In addition, eastern delegates promised to fund internal improvements and to establish branch banks in western counties, but after the financial panic of 1819 easterners concerned about Virginia's financial security were less willing to act on their promise. Unhappy with the extent of the changes, which by the late 1820s seemed paltry compared with the proportional representation and white manhood suffrage other states had by then adopted, westerners again called for reform. Through the decade of the 1820s the struggle between conservatives and reformers intensified, marked by a second convention at Staunton in 1825, by extensive newspaper essays both for and against a convention, and by contentious discussions in the legislature. Finally, conservatives yielded, passing a law that allowed the people to vote for or against a convention. In a largely sectional vote in the spring of 1828 Virginians chose to hold a constitutional convention in order to replace the antiquated 1776 constitution with one that would better reflect the values of the Jacksonian democratic age. The next session of the legislature decided on parameters for the convention, which gathered in the autumn of 1829.[33]

THE VIRGINIA CONSTITUTIONAL CONVENTION OF 1829–30

The debates of the Virginia Constitutional Convention of 1829–30 highlighted not only that eastern and western Virginians had opposing interests but that by 1829 those interests had led them to different understandings of the meaning of the American Revolution and its promise of liberty. The issue of slavery was central to the discussion partly because the struggle was one for power between slaveholders and nonslaveholders but also because the debate focused on the basic means and ends of republican government and thus put into question ideas about liberty, equality, and hence slavery. Importantly, conservative Virginians expressed views that laid the groundwork for a coherent and elaborate proslavery argument, even if they did not make that argument for another several years. The reformers, on the other hand, outlined an argument that had much in common with the free-soil ideas northerners es-

---

33. Sutton, *Revolution to Secession*, 64–71; Freehling, *Drift toward Dissolution*, 40–42; Shade, *Democratizing the Old Dominion*, 63. After the 1817 law, the western portion gained five senators, and the eastern portion lost five, so that the ratio of western to eastern senators was nine to fifteen instead of four to twenty.

poused in the antebellum era, one that focused on a particular vision of white liberty, but they held back from attacking slavery directly since they wanted slaveholders to agree to their demands.[34]

The delegates met in Richmond in the first week of October 1829. Among them were some of the most respected and prominent Virginia leaders, including several from the Revolutionary generation—James Monroe, James Madison, and John Marshall—as well as younger men like John Tyler, Hugh Blair Grigsby, Benjamin Watkins Leigh, and Philip Barbour. But such an esteemed group could not guarantee unanimity of mind or of purpose. With four delegates chosen from each state senatorial district, the convention had disproportionately more members from eastern Virginia, though the imbalance was less than it would have been if the convention had mirrored the House of Delegates. The events of the first days of the convention presaged the rancor with which easterners and westerners would later debate the central issues of representation and suffrage. It took the members of the convention nearly a week to decide not only how to organize their work but how to organize the organizing committee. They finally distributed the tasks of the convention to four large committees—on the legislature, the judiciary, the executive, and the Virginia Bill of Rights and remaining issues—that would report on suggested amendments to the 1776 constitution. In contrast to the Revolutionary-era meeting, in which delegates had deferred to the judgments of their superiors and voted unanimously to accept the constitution, the 1829–30 convention was from the beginning a contest of competing interests; division, not accord, was its hallmark. That in itself marked the political distance traveled over the previous two generations.[35]

The report of the Committee on the Legislature sparked the most, and the most important, debate. In part because the committee was chaired by the elderly James Madison, who like Thomas Jefferson favored liberal suffrage requirements and equal representation, the committee report resolved that representation in the House of Delegates be apportioned according to the

---

34. For extensive discussion and explication of the conservative position see Bruce, *Rhetoric of Conservatism*. Other discussions of the convention can be found in Shade, *Democratizing the Old Dominion*, 59–77; Freehling, *Drift toward Dissolution*, chap. 3; and Curtis, "Jefferson's Chosen People," chap. 3. All of these accounts are useful, but none focuses squarely on how issues regarding white liberty and black slavery were related or on the racial definition of liberty.

35. *Proceedings and Debates*, 1–22.

white population and that suffrage be extended to leaseholders and to white male heads of household regardless of whether they held a freehold estate. Delegates representing both reform and conservative interests immediately offered several other plans, and after some confusion about how the debate would proceed, the convention turned to the question of representation. At issue was whether to accept the committee's report on white-basis representation or to vote for an amendment offered by Judge John W. Green that, as in South Carolina, the number of representatives in the House of Delegates be proportional both to the white population and to the amount of taxes paid from each county, allowing areas with more wealth (slaves) greater voice in the legislature.[36]

Because the issue of representation was a question of the relative power of slaveholders and nonslaveholders in the General Assembly, and because slaveholders were concentrated geographically east of the Blue Ridge, the debate pitted easterners against westerners from the beginning. The crux of the reformers' argument was, as James Monroe (siding here with westerners) summarized it, that "putting the citizens in an equal condition" by apportioning legislative representation according to the white population "is just" because it "is founded on the natural rights of man" and because "the revolution was conducted on that principle [of equal rights]." Benjamin Watkins Leigh, speaking for the conservative slaveholding class, reviled the white-basis representation Monroe supported as a "cruel, palpable and crying injustice" because it would "put the power of controlling the wealth of the State, into hands different from those which hold that wealth." Leigh and others feared that if the House of Delegates reflected the population of Virginia, it would be dominated by those who did not hold slaves, and the slaveholding minority would suffer the tyranny of the majority.[37]

The slaveholders' fear of the majority, expressed earlier in the Missouri Crisis, now had meaning within Virginia as well as in the national context. As a result, it was slaveholders, and not their opponents, who injected into the discussion the issue of slavery and what was to them the horrifying possibility of emancipation. John Green warned that "the people in the lowlands will never feel secure: the jealousies and an interminable hostility will be generated, and perpetuate feuds and heart-burnings between different sections

36. Ibid., 39–53; Sutton, *Revolution to Secession*, 79.
37. *Proceedings and Debates*, 149, 53.

of the state." At stake was the power slaveholders had traditionally held in Virginia politics and, more crucially some of them thought, the security of the slave system itself because there "exists in a great portion of the west, a rooted antipathy to this species of population." The warning that if given proportional representation, westerners might deprive owners of their slaves made for effective rhetoric. It also reflected slaveholders' genuine anxiety that in a sectional battle they might lose control over the basis of their wealth and power. Since there existed no political organization in western Virginia to end slavery in the state, it was with little reason that the Hanover delegate Richard Morris shrieked, "I care not, whether this agency be manifested by the passage of a law of emancipation, or a tax-law depriving the master of the power of holding his slave: and soon a sword will be unsheathed, that will be red with the best blood, of this country, before it finds the scabbard." Nevertheless, his words resonated with those slaveholders who because of their day-to-day struggles to keep slaves under control understood power in absolutes and therefore viewed any incursion into their realm of power as an entering wedge by which they might be destroyed.[38]

Morris's prediction of a violent and bloody confrontation between the slaveholding and nonslaveholding sections typified easterners' focus on the sectional and antagonistic nature of the debate. Reformers, who lacked sufficient power to effect changes without some support from eastern politicians, generally played down the division and tried to argue that all Virginians had a common interest. Coaxing eastern slaveholders toward the reformers' position was exceedingly difficult, however, because slaveholders balked at any interference in their affairs and so easily bristled against perceived insults. As Morris said next, "This thing between master and slave, is one, which *cannot* be left to be regulated by the Government." Morris's cry—leave us, and our slaves, alone!—was what slaveholders had been saying since at least 1820, but now it was directed at fellow Virginians rather than at northerners.[39]

The issue of suffrage, closely related to the question of representation, sparked more theoretical debates regarding slavery and emancipation, expos-

---

38. Ibid., 64, 116. There is a vast literature on the mind of slaveholders. The studies include Genovese, *Political Economy of Slavery;* Faust, *James Henry Hammond;* and Oakes, *Ruling Race.* The all-or-nothing view adopted by slaveholders also had its roots in an American political tradition that viewed liberty as the fragile prey of despotic power. For an explication of that view in the eighteenth century see Bailyn, *Ideological Origins,* chap. 3.

39. *Proceedings and Debates,* 116.

ing growing divisions in Virginians' understanding of basic American values. Reformers argued quite sensibly that the Virginia Declaration of Rights and the principles upon which the state and federal governments were founded granted to all members of society equal political power, which ought to be effectuated through the franchise. Suffrage was an inherent social right, said one delegate, citing John Locke's writings on civil society, because in making the social compact men had exercised the right of consent. Consent, or suffrage, "was the cause of the compact, not the effect of it; it was, therefore, original and inherent." To deny citizens suffrage was therefore to deprive them of one of their most important original rights.[40]

Reformers' arguments for broad suffrage based on natural-rights philosophy had radical implications, as they and their opponents soon noticed. If suffrage were a right that devolved to all members of the society, should not women and free blacks also have the franchise? Conservative members said that it was obvious that women and black people ought not vote, and so the very premise from which reformers operated must be wrong. Proponents of white male suffrage had to tread carefully, explaining why equal political rights applied to white men but not to women (who were under men's protection), to children (who were minors), or to free blacks (who were outside society). They thus revealed that the terms of debate involved gender as well as race. To them, political liberty connoted manhood, and to be denied suffrage was to be emasculated, reduced to the level of women, children, or blacks, who, even if male, were not seen as *men*. In addition, these arguments demonstrated how simultaneously powerful and dangerous appeals to first principles could be and how ambivalent white male Virginians were toward a political philosophy that bolstered their claims to political equality while at the same time undermining their claims to special privilege as whites and as men. These issues marked the debate as a nineteenth-century rather than an eighteenth-century discussion because changes elsewhere in the first four decades of the nineteenth century were helping redefine manhood as being part of the body politic.[41]

While reformers explained that natural rights were limited by race and sex, some conservative members were inclined to reject altogether the political

40. William Naylor speech, in ibid., 130.

41. *Proceedings and Debates*, 68, 83, 100–101, 226–27. Advocates of broad suffrage disagreed on whether paupers ought to have the right to vote and whether extreme poverty placed one outside society. On gender and politics see McCurry, *Masters of Small Worlds*, 259–61; and Isenberg, *Sex and Citizenship*.

philosophy of the Revolution in order to protect slavery. When John Rogers Cooke pleaded with conservative members not to abandon the principles of the Revolution, Abel Upshur responded with a declaration that would have shocked America's Revolutionary leaders. "[T]here are no original principles of Government at all," he emphasized. Government, Upshur argued, was a practical exercise, and principles ought to follow from rather than precede its formation. In the Revolutionary era, leading Virginians had found a way to champion egalitarian principles without endorsing social change, particularly emancipation. Some newspaper essayists had employed racial arguments, casting Africans as lesser beings who did not deserve liberty. And as a group Virginia's leaders had constructed the Virginia Declaration of Rights to exclude those outside "society." They had also approved a state constitution that distributed political power in a decidedly undemocratic way, which had been acceptable in 1776, before the full implications of the Revolution were felt. Now, in the 1829–30 constitutional convention, with their interests threatened by the literal meaning of Revolutionary-era documents and, more importantly, by an opposing group that argued from those documents, Virginia's conservative leaders had to state it baldly: slavery was not compatible with a philosophy that celebrated liberty, and so (reasoning backwards) that philosophy (and not slavery) must be suspect. As Philip Barbour, who had expounded the position of the southern states during the Missouri debates, explained his opposition to white-basis representation, "[I]f you give to the language [of the Virginia Declaration of Rights], all the force which the words literally import (and they are, I believe, but an echo of those in the Declaration of Independence,) what will they amount to, but a declaration of universal emancipation, to a class of our population, not far short of a moiety of our entire number, now in a state of slavery?"[42]

Many of the older generation had paid at least rhetorical homage to the idea that slavery ought to yield eventually to liberty, but to Virginia's new generation of conservative leaders such thoughts were irresponsible. During the convention James Monroe repeated the old trope that Virginia "has always declared herself in favour of the equal rights of man," would abolish slavery if it were practicable, and "did all that was in her power to do, to prevent the extension of slavery, and to mitigate its evils." The younger Benjamin Watkins Leigh focused instead on social stability, warning that equal representa-

---

42. *Proceedings and Debates,* 59, 69, 90.

tion and general suffrage would usher in a type of anarchy—"the liberty of Virginia expiring with excess"—similar to that in France during the French Revolution.[43]

James Monroe and Benjamin Watkins Leigh embodied the tension between past and present, between the Revolution itself and the memory of the Revolution. For Monroe, the question of emancipation entered immediately into the discussion. Within the first few minutes after he rose to speak Monroe had turned to the equal rights of man and the problem of slavery. He recalled the dilemma of the leaders of the Revolutionary generation, whose philosophy had urged them toward emancipation but who had faced practical constraints and racial concerns that made emancipation nearly impossible. Black people, he said, "are separated from the rest of society, by a different color; there can be no intercourse or equality between them; nor can you remove them" using state resources. The only solution, as Monroe saw it, was federal aid in deporting freed slaves. "If emancipation be possible," Monroe continued, "I look to the Union to aid in effecting it." The problem of slavery should be viewed as a national concern, he said, and the states should help one another. If slavery still proved impossible to remove, then at least the northern states would realize it, and the effect would be "to abate the great number of petitions and memorials, which are continually pouring in upon the Government."[44]

For Leigh, in contrast, emancipation was *not* a question raised by the discussion at hand nor by any other discussion he thought good or reasonable. He saw great evil in Monroe's position, asking "how large a dose of French rights of man it [Virginia] can bear, without fever, frenzy, madness and death." Furthermore, Leigh emphasized that slavery was a state issue, not a national one. State Rights, not federal aid, ought to be Virginia's object. And echoing Upshur's pronouncement, he indicated that the purpose of government was to manage affairs in a practical manner, not to effect a philosophical principle. While Monroe seemed compelled to return to the subject of slavery and emancipation, since it was to him "one of the most important that can come before this body," Leigh inveighed, "*Liberty* is only a *mean:* the *end* is *happiness.*"[45]

Monroe and Leigh thus laid out the contours of a significant shift in Vir-

43. Ibid., 149, 173.
44. Ibid., 149.
45. Ibid., 151, 172–73. Leigh was born in 1781.

ginian and American thought. The earlier generation had invoked racial arguments to resolve the tension between the ideals of the Declaration of Independence and slaveholding; Leigh and his generation instead rejected idealism and universal liberty generally even as they moved toward a stronger pro-slavery stance. This seems to have been a shift that occurred during Leigh's adult life, for as a young judge he had ruled in favor of liberty in the case of Tom Abba.[46] Perhaps it was his own inner conflict over the value of liberty that pushed him to argue from practicality and not philosophy and thus to avoid the question whether slavery was good and instead to defend slavery on the basis of property rights, State Rights, and the practical purposes of government. Significantly, the context in which Leigh and others proffered these arguments was a political one, a struggle over power among whites. Perhaps in the absence of challenges to their traditional power, Leigh and others might have retained some of the liberality of their younger days.

While turning away from the value placed on liberty and from the ideals of the Revolutionary leaders, conservative eastern politicians nevertheless claimed the Revolution as their own and found a way to attach their cause to the great struggle of the founding generation. As they read it, the conflict with England had been about who would control the colonists' property, which echoed arguments from the 1785 anti-Methodist petitions. Defenders of slavery claimed that relations between the colonists and the mother country had been satisfactory until Parliament decided unfairly to tax the Americans, who could control neither the amount of the tax nor the way the monies were spent. Similarly, western Virginians, if given control over the legislature, would be able to dictate to easterners how to dispense with their property. "The Commons of Great Britain claimed power over our property, and we insisted that the control over it belonged, of right and exclusively, to us the owners; so our fellow-citizens of the west ask us to give them the absolute power of taxation over us, and we insist on retaining that power in our hands." The parallel was imperfect, surely, since easterners would still have a voice in the legislature proportionate to their numbers if not their wealth. But it seemed to Benjamin Watkins Leigh and others a good argument to state that American political representation ought to be a manifestation of property interests (in this case slavery) since property rights were the cause for which independence from Britain had been fought. In reality, the conservative slaveholders of eastern

---

46. For the Abba case, see discussion in chap. 4, above, under "Questions of Freedom."

Virginia were not demanding equal representation but special privileges to protect the power they had traditionally held.[47]

The competing ways in which both sides claimed the Revolutionary tradition—seen by all to be at the center of American political life—revealed that the political and philosophical contest in which Virginia was engaged in its constitutional convention was a battle over the meaning of the Revolution and thus of America itself. Debates over representation, the purpose of government, federal-state relations, and even internal improvements all came back to the subject of slavery because the existence of slavery in a polity dedicated to liberty was the great problem at the core of the American system, one that could not be separated from the most basic questions of governance. And while all participants in the struggle waved the flag of Revolutionary tradition, the shrillness of the conservative argument indicated that slaveholders sensed themselves on the losing side, forced to emphasize pecuniary interest and political power over natural rights and liberty.

The conservative argument, with its focus on material interest, highlighted how the alignments of interests and ideas had changed over the previous two generations. In Virginia during the colonial and Revolutionary periods (and in other southern states in the early nineteenth century) black slavery and white liberty had been compatible because of a consonance of interests among whites. The existence of racial slavery had allowed them to band together, to share the fruits of freedom, to mute the animosities of social class by highlighting division between the races. White solidarity achieved at the expense of black degradation may not have come about through conscious design, but at least one Virginian argued that the arrangement should be preserved. William Gordon, of Albemarle County, contended that white manhood suffrage would bind white Virginians together in the face of blacks. "I am for extending the right of suffrage," he declared, "not merely because I think it proper in itself, but because it is the only way to counteract the effects of the increase of the black population in Virginia." Gordon's statement failed to resonate among his fellow delegates, however, because by the late 1820s slavery

---

47. Speech of Benjamin Watkins Leigh, in *Proceedings and Debates*, 156. Leigh's concern here was similar to Patrick Henry's in his objection to the U.S. Constitution. According to Robin Einhorn's analysis, Henry's main fear was that the Constitution would allow nonslaveholding regions to pass tax laws that would make slavery untenable. Einhorn, "Patrick Henry's Case against the Constitution."

divided rather than united white Virginians. A new philosophy was emerging among westerners that slavery threatened rather than supported white liberty; and in the Jacksonian age it was more difficult than before for poor white men to accept lesser status and political power in exchange for the freedom of whiteness.[48]

The outcome of the constitutional convention boded ill for the unity of white Virginia and for the peaceful emancipation of enslaved black Virginians. Nearly deadlocked, the convention finally approved by a vote of fifty-five to forty a constitution that was meant as a compromise between eastern and western Virginia. In reality, those in the east had won, granting only minor concessions to reformers. The new constitution extended suffrage to some white male Virginians—leaseholders and heads of households—and changed the basis of property requirements from acreage to dollar value, but many, probably between one-third and one-half of all white men, remained disfranchised. Representation would not be based on the white population alone but would reflect the white population of 1820 plus a portion of the slave population. Nor would representation change over time to reflect alterations in Virginia's population; the formulation was to be permanent.[49]

The problem Virginia faced, of a slaveholding minority who feared loss of their power and whose position hardened over time, heightening sectional discord, was analogous to the problem confronting the nation as a whole. In both Virginia and the nation there had in the past been a greater alignment of interests. At the beginning of the Revolution slavery had been legal in all the colonies, and in Virginia slaveholders had formed about half the white population. As the northern states outlawed slavery, as the settlement of Virginia's western regions added many nonslaveholders to the state's population, as the domestic and international antislavery movements gained strength, and as nonslaveholders began to criticize the disproportionate political power held by those with slave property, slaveholders in the South and in Virginia's eastern section had cause to feel threatened. Only a few years earlier a number of Vir-

---

48. *Proceedings and Debates*, 145. For the classic articulation of connections between white unity and black enslavement see Morgan, *American Slavery, American Freedom*, which focuses on the seventeenth century. For a similar argument for a Virginia county in the nineteenth century see Beeman, *Evolution of the Southern Backcountry*.

49. Bruce, *Rhetoric of Conservatism*, 66–67; *Proceedings and Debates*, 897–99. The 1830 constitution is poorly worded and confusing, reflecting the difficulty of arriving at a compromise.

ginia leaders could endorse the ACS as a means of encouraging emancipation. But by the end of the 1820s slavery had become a political issue, and there was less room for the kind of ambivalence inherent in the colonization movement. The weapons the conservatives wielded to defend themselves were stronger than the job necessitated, however. Their intransigence and unwillingness to distribute political power fairly among white men only increased the level of tension and primed their opponents for the next confrontation. Although western Virginians in 1820 had stood together with easterners on the subject of slavery, their experience in the succeeding decade pushed them to contemplate an antislavery stance. Moreover, the debate in the Virginia Constitutional Convention revealed two distinct and equally American ideas about the relationship between racial slavery and liberty. Conservatives assumed that slavery ensured their own freedoms but also that liberty itself was not a universal or original right, while reformers began to argue, though tentatively, that the existence of black slavery and of a minority slaveholding class threatened liberty generally. The two sides would face off again in 1831 and 1832 in the wake of Nat Turner's rebellion, when Virginians paused to consider the future of slavery in their state and the possibility of emancipation.

6

The "most momentous subject of public interest"

THE PUBLIC DEBATE OVER SLAVERY AND EMANCIPATION, 1831–1832

> Having arrived at the conclusion that emancipation is impracticable, it would seem superfluous to pursue the subject further. . . . Of what avail is it to demonstrate that slavery is an evil, unless it can be shown that it is possible to get rid of it?
>
> JOHN THOMPSON BROWN, 1832

WHEN NAT TURNER LED a group of fellow slaves on a murderous rampage through Southampton County in late August 1831 the specter of slave insurrection that so haunted white Virginians, and that had presented itself ominously in 1800 with Gabriel's plot, instantiated itself in particularly gruesome form. Turner, a religious exhorter and mystic who had been inspired by signs from the heavens, spurred a small band of men to go from house to house killing the white inhabitants with axes and swords, gaining followers as they proceeded. Lubricated with alcohol, the growing number of rebels, just over sixty at their maximum, continued their slaughter over the course of a day. They killed approximately sixty white men, women, and children before they were themselves killed or captured. The white response, equally brutal, included the torture, shooting, and decapitation of probably one hundred or more innocent blacks along the Virginia–North Carolina border.[1]

The response of white Virginians continued well beyond their initial fit of violence and included the most public, focused, and sustained discussion of slavery and emancipation that ever occurred in the commonwealth or in any other southern state. As one contemporary explained it, "The tragical issue of the insurrection in Southampton, in which above sixty whites fell a sacrifice

---

1. Oates, *Fires of Jubilee*; Aptheker, *Nat Turner's Slave Rebellion*.

to the vengeance of their slaves, . . . has awakened the slave states out of their slumbers, and excited considerable attention towards our coloured population." The issues white Virginians discussed over the next several months, particularly the threat they felt from a growing free and enslaved black population, were not in themselves new, only newly salient. Citizens gathered in their county courthouses to consider the insurrection and draft petitions to their legislators; the press "broke the silence of fifty years" by publishing copious editorials on the future of slavery; and then in January 1832, "what is *more remarkable* in the History of our Legislature, we now see the whole subject ripped up and discussed, with open doors, and in the presence of a crowded gallery and lobby."[2]

The debate over slavery arose, too, from the many political, economic, and social changes that had occurred in Virginia and the nation over the previous generation. The Virginia Constitutional Convention of 1829–30 had only heightened the tensions between the eastern, slaveholding section and the western, mostly nonslaveholding section of Virginia. On the national scene the early 1830s saw the rise of zealous abolitionists in the North, including those led by William Lloyd Garrison, who declared war on slavery in the first issue of his newspaper the *Liberator* in January 1831. The abolitionist literature, combined with David Walker's 1829 *Appeal*, a militant condemnation of slavery addressed to African Americans and smuggled into the South, where slaves might read it, announced a new era in the national struggle over the slavery question. Indeed, Governor Floyd referred to abolitionists as part of the cause of Nat Turner's rebellion in his speech to the General Assembly. Blaming abolitionists for unrest in Virginia conveniently located the source of slaves' dissatisfaction outside the slave system itself, which served to ease slaveholders' consciences. But drawing attention to the rising abolitionist movement made Virginia slaveholders, who already felt vulnerable as a result of the Missouri Crisis and the Virginia Constitutional Convention, even more sensitive to any threat to their power or property. When they defended slavery in response, nonslaveholding whites perceived in their defenses an attack on the universality of white liberty and on the basic values nonslaveholders held, values they saw as distinct from and superior to those of the slaveholders.[3]

2. Carey, *Letters on the Colonization Society*, 5; *Richmond Enquirer*, 12 Jan. 1832.

3. For Governor Floyd's speech, see *JHD* (begun Dec. 1831), 10–11; for discussion of the changing nature and tactics of northern antislavery movements, see Newman, *Transformation of American Abolitionism*, chaps. 4–6.

The 1831–32 Virginia debate over slavery was consequently a heated contest. The meaning of liberty was itself in question. It also marked a turning point in Virginia's history since it seemed to settle the question of emancipation, to end finally the utility of ambivalent statements and behavior regarding slavery, and therefore to put Revolutionary-era dreams of a free Virginia firmly in the past. The debate prompted slaveholders to develop more comprehensive defenses of slavery and spurred the publication of the first pamphlets justifying what had by then become a peculiar institution, and it presaged the events that would eventually break the state apart during the Civil War.[4]

CITIZENS' PETITIONS TO THE LEGISLATURE

Even after the militia had crushed Turner's rebellion, white Virginians remained wary and frightened. Several wrote letters to the state's newspapers, urging the legislature to make changes that might prevent future insurrections, including silencing black preachers like Turner, enhancing white security forces, and reducing the number of free and enslaved African Americans in the state. Many more signed petitions urging various forms of action regarding the state's black population. The citizens' petitions, which have received less attention than the debates that followed, revealed the spectrum of views held by Virginia whites and helped spur the legislative debate over emancipation. Democracy as it existed in antebellum Virginia meant that lawmakers took seriously the concerns and suggestions of their constituents. In the absence of petitions, one Virginian said, "it is not to be presumed that your representatives . . . would take one step in a matter of such magnitude."[5]

Approximately forty petitions expressing apprehension about Virginia's African American population reached the House during the 1831–32 session,

---

4. For other treatments of the debate see Robert, *Road from Monticello*, which focuses on sectionalism and views the debate as a turning point in Virginia history; Freehling, *Drift toward Dissolution*, which argues by contrast that the debate was part of "an ongoing contest" among members of the white community that demonstrated "the inability of either abolitionists or conservatives to win this battle" (xi–xii); and Shade, *Democratizing the Old Dominion*, 191–213, which revives the view of the debate as a sectional contest as part of Shade's analysis of the political developments of that period.

5. *Richmond Enquirer*, 13, 20 Sept., 15 Nov. 1831. The letters to the editors of Virginia's main newspapers, along with the editorials written by the publishers, reiterated all the main points expressed in the petitions and in the legislative debate. Because they add little to the discussion here, I have largely neglected them in this chapter.

mainly in December and early January. More than two thousand Virginians, mostly men, signed them (see appendix B). The common themes were the fear of future insurrections, the increasing danger posed by a growing black population, and the need to act without delay. Some of the petitions recommended gradual emancipation and removal of the freed slaves, but most emphasized instead the need to deport free blacks. Of course, Virginians who were satisfied with the status quo were unlikely to draft pleas to their representatives, so the petitions may not represent the full range of white Virginians' views. They do, however, betray their anxieties.

Two of the petitions stood out from the rest because they called for the total and gradual abolition of slavery in Virginia and proffered specific plans for emancipation. The first came from the Quaker Yearly Meeting held in Charles City County, the sole petition to echo the tone of Revolutionary-era antislavery rhetoric. Arguing from the "belief in the interposition of God in human affairs," the Quakers interpreted the "present important crisis" as a sign of God's judgment against Virginia for supporting the "evil" of slavery. Slavery violated not only God's law but also the "first principles of our republican institution and the immutable laws of Justice and Humanity." For the Friends, "the abolition of Slavery in this Commonwealth and the restoration of the African race to the inalienable rights of man, is imperiously demanded by the laws of God; and inseparably connected with the best interests of the Commonwealth at large." Specifically, the Quaker meeting recommended passing an act that would emancipate all persons born after a certain date. In addition, they suggested that the state, perhaps with help from the federal government, "provide some territory, . . . for the formation of a colony for people of Colour, and also to aid in removing such free persons as may be disposed [to] emigrate, and such slaves as may be given up for that purpose." In the two generations since the Revolution the Friends' focus on the immorality of slavery had not shifted. But in another way the Quaker petition did reflect the changes that had taken place by 1831 because it embraced the colonization of freed slaves, which earlier Quaker antislavery advocates had not done. When it came to the subject of slavery, this generation of Quakers was less idealistic, more practical, and more in tune with their contemporaries than their parents and grandparents had been.[6]

A petition submitted from the Piedmont county of Buckingham similarly

---

6. Quaker petition, 14 Dec. 1831, LP, Charles City County.

recommended a plan of general emancipation and colonization. In contrast to the Quakers but consistent with the dominant white sentiment, the Buckingham petitioners were concerned with the "rapid increase of the colored population" and with the projected numerical dominance of blacks over whites in the coming decades rather than with the immorality of slavery. The petitioners believed that Virginia would slowly become depopulated of whites as wealthy slaveholders bought up the lands of nonslaveholders in order to have occupations for their slaves, forcing the nonslaveholding whites to move west. As the number and proportion of whites decreased, they would have diminished ability to repress slave rebellions like the one that occurred in Southampton. The petitioners recommended the plan of Thomas Jefferson, who had lived in neighboring Albemarle County, and quoted from him regarding the "blessed effects" of gradual abolition. As the petitioners summarized it, Jefferson's proposal called for the liberation of children born to enslaved mothers after a certain date. Those children, though declared free, would work for their masters until adulthood and be trained in "industrious occupations" until they were deported beyond Virginia. Though the petition focused on the safety of whites, something all white Virginians could agree was a vital consideration, the radical proposal to eliminate slavery altogether gained only seventeen supporters, one of whom changed his mind after signing the petition and asked that his name be removed.[7]

Other petitions also looked toward the end of slavery and the establishment of a racially homogeneous state. Consequently, they too linked abolition with colonization, but they did not submit any specific plan of action. Citizens from the northern Piedmont county of Loudoun had convened in a public meeting and resolved that "the only adequate remedy for the evil . . . is the gradual emancipation of the slaves of the Commonwealth, and the removal of the entire colored population." The Loudoun petitioners, led by some of the county's most prominent slaveholding citizens, believed that ending slavery was indeed "practicable" and that "upon this assumption, the continuation of slavery is forbidden by the true policy of Virginia, repugnant to her political theory and christian profession, and an opprobrium to our . . . dominion." While this language condemned slavery in terms reminiscent of the Quakers,

7. Buckingham petition, 16 Dec. 1831, LP, Buckingham County. One of the signatures is scratched out, and the notation "taken off by request" appears by it. At least two of the other signers were members of the local chapter of the ACS.

with their moral and Godly concerns, the three reasons the Loudoun petitioners gave for their opposition to slavery were more worldly. First, they said, slave labor was, "in a community like ours, the most expensive that can be used." Second, slavery "tends to lay waste to the region in which it subsists." Finally, "it fills with apprehension and inquietude the bosoms of those who employ it."[8]

Similarly, the 215 "females of the county of Augusta" who called for the "extinction of slavery, from amongst us" yearned to be free from the black people who threatened them. Remarkable because it was brought by women, who usually stood outside the political process, the Augusta petition emphasized "the fears which agitate our bosoms, and the dangers which await us, as revealed by recent tragical deeds." Indeed, it had been particularly disturbing to Virginians that so many of the victims of Nat Turner's rebellion were women and children. In order to feel safe, these women of Virginia's Valley region begged for the removal of "the bloody monster which threatens us," arguing that the "labors & hardships" of parting with their slaves would be less than the terror of keeping them. "The bloody monster" was not slavery as an institution but slaves as persons, especially menacing because of their proximity, because they were "warmed & cherished on our own hearths." The object the women sought was not to liberate slaves—to grant them their natural rights—but to get rid of them. As they put it, they wished to be like those people who had left Virginia for free lands, to "exult in their deliverance from their quondam slaves," an ironic turn of phrase that highlighted the ways in which the institution of slavery also bound whites.[9]

Though the petitions asking the delegates to end slavery can be read as progressive, liberal pleas because their object was state-enforced abolition, it is clear from their content that they were complicated documents reflecting a variety of motives and interests that differed significantly from the moral imperatives at the heart of both the antebellum radical abolition movement and the Revolutionary-era antislavery movement. The Virginians calling for emancipation in 1831–32, with the exception of the Quakers, acted out

---

8. "Petition of sundry citizens of Loudoun concerning Slaves," 23 Dec. 1831, LP, Loudoun County.

9. "The Memorial of the Ladies of Augusta" (submitted in three identical copies), 19 Jan. 1832, LP, Augusta County. See Varon, *We Mean to Be Counted*, 49–53, for a discussion of women's participation in the debate.

of self-interest more than because of religious or philosophical ideals. That the antislavery petitioners represented a broad spectrum of society—men and women, slaveholders and nonslaveholders, and eastern and western Virginians—pointed less toward a growth in moral antipathy toward slavery in Virginia than toward the increasing proportion of Virginians who did not depend on plantation agriculture (farmers in Loudoun County, for instance, had generally turned from tobacco to grains) and who saw African Americans more as a threat than as a necessity.[10]

Closer to the center of the plantation economy, white Virginians concerned themselves more with the removal of free blacks and the reduction of the slave population through voluntary emancipation and state-supported colonization. Citizens from the contiguous Tidewater counties of Caroline, King William, and Hanover, along with men from the Valley county of Rockbridge, submitted identical petitions that described slavery as a "curse" and called for the removal of "this heavy and alarming evil." Using data from the federal censuses, the petition demonstrated the numerical and proportional growth of the black population east of the Blue Ridge over the previous forty years and argued that the black majority would only continue to grow in subsequent decades. The petitioners proposed a specific plan for preventing further increase in black dominance: a tax on enslaved and free blacks that would defray the cost of colonizing slaves voluntarily surrendered to the state by their owners or purchased by the state for that purpose, a plan similar to George Tucker's 1801 proposal. In addition, the petitioners recommended that no future emancipations be allowed unless the freed slaves were removed from Virginia and that free blacks be forced to leave with the help of the state if they lacked the funds to emigrate. The several hundred petitioners, who declared themselves slaveholders, said they hoped that by these means the number of blacks would be diminished considerably, leading eventually to "the total eradication of the evil," meaning both slavery and black people, that hindered the "peace and happiness, quiet and prosperity" of white Virginians.[11]

10. On the Loudoun County economy see Stevenson, *Life in Black and White*, 175–76; and *Proceedings and Debates*, 336.

11. Hanover petition, 14 Dec. 1831, LP, Hanover County; Rockbridge petition, 16 Jan. 1832, LP, Rockbridge County; King William petition, 18 Jan. 1832, LP, King William County; Caroline petition, 20 Jan. 1832, LP, Caroline County. A notice appeared in the *Richmond Enquirer* on 15 November 1831 from a "native of eastern Virginia" stating that a "memorial is circulating among you, the object of which is to call the attention of the ensuing Legislature to the subject of the

While most of the petitions received by the legislature expressed white Virginians' desire to shrink the number of slaves in the state in order to lessen the threat they felt blacks posed to whites, a significant minority of petitions received by the legislature, more than one-third of the total, focused instead on removing free blacks in order to strengthen and preserve slavery, and the people who signed these petitions outnumbered those who wished to see fewer slaves in Virginia.[12] The proslavery petitions came mostly from Tidewater residents, who clung to a romanticized past when the line between slave and free and the line between black and white had nearly coincided. The tone and content of the petitions recalled a slave society that had been, and could again become, productive, ordered, and secure. If Turner's rebellion had revealed faults in the system, the petitioners implied, they were not faults in the slave system but rather faults in the social and legal system that allowed the existence of free people of color.

The citizens of the Eastern Shore county of Northampton, for example, had gathered together in public meetings in response to Turner's insurrection to discuss the increasing proportion of "free persons of colour" among Northampton's population. The chief outcome of those meetings was the Northampton citizens' recommendation that the problematic group be removed to Liberia. Like its neighbor, Accomack County, Northampton had one of the largest free black populations in the state, a fact that inspired anxiety similar to that which had led to the expulsion of some free blacks and the reenslavement of others in Accomack in 1826. The Northampton petition explained the roots of that anxiety: free blacks were an "anomalous population" that stood "in a middle position between the two extremes of our society." They were a discontented class because they were "[i]nferior to the whites in intelligence & information; degraded by the stain which attached to their colour; excluded from many civil privileges which the humblest white man enjoys, and denied all participation in the government." Lacking "sympathy with

---

bond and free coloured population of the state," and urging that "meetings of the qualified voters be held in all the counties in this State, on their respective Court days in December to deliberate upon this momentous subject and to urge upon them the necessity of devising some means by which the blacks may be removed beyond our borders, and by which too the number of slaves may be gradually diminished." It is likely that the memorial to which the article referred was that submitted from these four counties.

12. Fourteen petitions focused exclusively on the problem of free blacks. See appendix B.

our people" and sharing with slaves familial ties and a "common complexion," free blacks would combine with slaves and gain "confidence in their physical power, . . . enlarge their means of information, . . . and thus add to their means of mischief." The events of the summer had served as proof to Northampton's white leaders that such mischief, particularly insurrection, could and would take place. This logic was as faulty when voiced by Northampton's citizens in 1831 as it had been when articulated by Virginians earlier in the century, for most slave rebellions in the United States, including Turner's rebellion and Gabriel's plot, were instigated, led, and dominated by enslaved and not free African Americans. Nevertheless, the claim rang true for contemporaries who saw all black people as potential enemies, who especially feared blacks who lived outside slavery's controls, and who likely recalled Denmark Vesey's foiled insurrection in South Carolina in 1822, one of the few revolutionary schemes led by a free African American. Additionally, Northampton citizens' focus on free blacks allowed a neat solution to the problems before them: "getting rid of our free negroes, whom we regard as a most prolific source of evil to our community." They were even willing to pay for it, proposing special county taxes to finance the "removal to Liberia of such of them as are willing to go there." The petitioners also asked the legislature for laws that might "rid us promptly, effectually & entirely of our free coloured population," and the legislature complied by passing a statute that allowed Northampton County to borrow money and to levy taxes as requested.[13]

Other petitions echoed Northampton's claim that free blacks were the root

13. Colonization petition, 16 Dec. 1831, LP, Northampton County; Egerton, *He Shall Go Out Free*. The Northampton petitioners additionally pledged not to deal with any free blacks after arrangements for their removal had been made and as a matter of general policy to refuse to rent any house or land to any free black person in order to make Northampton an inhospitable place for them. The statute, found in the *Supplement to the Revised Code of the Laws of Virginia*, 248, included no guidelines as to how colonization ought to be effected, except that the removal of the "free people of colour" should be prompt and "in a manner as humane and as little oppressive as possible." The preamble to the law also made clear the link between colonization and the protection of slavery: "[I]t is absolutely necessary, not only to correct the government of their slaves, but also to the peace and safety of their society, that the free people of colour should be promptly removed from that county." Only rarely did white Virginians question whether free blacks did indeed threaten slavery and the security of whites, as did "P.Q.O." in a letter in the *Richmond Enquirer* on 18 November 1831. "P.Q.O." asserted that free blacks had not been involved in Southampton, except for two whose wives were slaves, and that though they were a nuisance, their presence tended toward security, not against it.

of the problem, including a group of identical appeals that arrived from the citizens of eleven counties and that represented the sentiments of close to half of all the people who signed petitions regarding the Southampton rebellion. A total of about a thousand men, most of them living in the Tidewater and eastern Piedmont, endorsed the notion that because free blacks were "neither free men nor slaves," they posed a danger to white Virginia society. Without actually using the word *colonization* the petitions reiterated the main argument of the ACS, that free people of color, so indolent in Virginia, might become "industrious" and "moral" if they lived instead in "other lands." In their absence, Virginia's enslaved blacks and free whites would both be safer. Similarly, Northumberland petitioners decried free blacks as a "species of population . . . highly dangerous to the safety & permanent tranquility of the community" because they "would ever in the event of any insurrectionary movement among our slaves be master spirits [and] the most active promoters of & inciters to rebellion." Northumberland's petitioners reiterated the logic that appealed to so many of the Virginians supporting colonization in the early 1830s, namely, that the existence of free blacks could cause slaves to yearn for similar freedom and become more likely to rebel, so it was imperative to remove them.[14]

The large number of petitions recommending the deportation of Virginia's free blacks is significant for three reasons. First, the transference to free blacks of white Virginians' anxieties about slavery was made both possible and necessary by their inability to conceive of a society in which skin color and other racial markers did not coincide with social status. In other slave societies race

14. The text for the identical petitions from the eleven eastern counties first appeared in the *Richmond Enquirer* on 18 October 1831, having previously been published in the *Petersburg Intelligencer*. Its publication aided the transmission of the text among the counties. The Westmoreland petitioners, for example, simply clipped the text from one of the papers and attached it to a sheet with 189 signatures, representing about 20 percent of the white male population of the county. The other petitions were from Surry, Isle of Wight, and Nansemond counties, all of which bordered Southampton in the southern Tidewater region; James City and York counties, just north of these three across the James River; Fairfax, which, like Westmoreland, lay in the northern Tidewater; Goochland, Powhatan, and Amelia, three contiguous counties in the easternmost area of the central Piedmont; and Frederick County, in the northern Valley region. The first of these identical petitions to be introduced were those from Isle of Wight and Amelia on 7 December, and the last, from nearby Surry County, was introduced on 11 January. As far as I could tell, all the signers were men. For the petitions see the respective county collections of legislative petitions for December–January 1831–32. For the Northumberland petition see Northumberland petition, 23 Jan. 1832, LP, Northumberland County.

and class existed in degrees. From the 1780s onward white Virginians consistently resisted that development and tried repeatedly and without success to divide their world into black and white, slave and free. When they perceived a problem in their society—Turner's rebellion, like Gabriel's plot before it, was evidence of something gone wrong—they identified that problem as the anomalous group of free blacks that stood between slaves and free people and saw the remedy as removal of that group. Second, the focus on free blacks obscured the fact that enslaved Virginians had risen up because they desired to be free, not because they had been duped or led by self-interested agitators. The free black population became a scapegoat, allowing whites to avoid confronting the fact that those they held as slaves were fully human and desired liberty and thus to avoid admitting their own complicity in an unjust system. Third, the petitions underscore the meaning of colonization to Virginia's white citizens by 1832. At that time most procolonization sentiment in Virginia was not, as both contemporaries and later historians sometimes thought, concomitant with antislavery leanings or proemancipation ideas, though it often had been ten years before. Some petitions did still pay homage to the idea of abolition, and some Virginians sincerely hated slavery and wished to see it end. But generally, support for colonization indicated antipathy toward black people above and beyond antipathy toward slavery and was sometimes combined with explicitly proslavery sentiment. Since the 1780s, Virginians concerns about free blacks had changed little in content but had increased in intensity.

TOWARD OPEN DEBATE OVER SLAVERY

If in the wake of Nat Turner's rebellion the intellectual and moral problems white Virginians confronted regarding slavery were not so different from those of the post-Revolutionary years, and if their focus remained on free blacks as the evil disrupting society, the scope of the debate in 1831–32 differed dramatically from the occasional debates that had taken place over the previous generations. But holding a broad and far-reaching public debate on the issues of slavery, emancipation, and colonization had not been part of the design when the House of Delegates began its session. The governor had urged the legislature to respond to the "grave and distressing" occurrences of the summer by punishing "disturbers of our peace," meaning antislavery activists and northern abolitionists; by outlawing African American preachers; and by revising the slave laws in order to strengthen the control of whites over their darker bondspeople. Governor Floyd had also suggested that free people of color might "convey all the incendiary [abolitionist] pamphlets and papers with which we are sought to be inundated" and that it might therefore be wise to "appropriate annually a sum of money to aid in their removal from this Commonwealth." As the legislature began to take up these issues, conflicts over the citizens' petitions, aided by the governor's behind-the-scenes actions, pushed the legislature toward open debate, a remarkable event in Virginia and national history.[15]

As a first step in confronting the issues raised by Turner's rebellion the House of Delegates created a select committee to consider that part of the governor's message relating to the insurrection and the removal of free people of color. The many citizens' petitions regarding those subjects were also referred to the select committee, whose responsibility it was to draft resolutions in response and to report back to the full House. In addition, the House of Delegates on 12 December explicitly ordered the select committee to address the possibility of state-supported funding for the colonization of free blacks. The committee, variously referred to as the "select committee on the subject of the Southampton insurrection," the "committee on the subject of slaves, free negroes and mulattoes," or the "committee on the subject of the coloured population of the state," among other appellations, was composed originally of thirteen delegates, most from eastern counties with black majorities. Later the committee was enlarged by a special vote, but it was still dominated by easterners.[16]

The many names by which the select committee was known reflected its confused purpose. Should the committee consider issues of security, armaments, and the militia? Should it draft laws to ensure the subordination of

---

15. *JHD* (begun Dec. 1831), 10–11.

16. Ibid., 15, 25–26. The members of the select committee were William Brodnax, of Dinwiddie, who had helped put down the insurrection; Jeremiah Cobb, of Southampton; Willoughby Newton, of Westmoreland; William Roane, of Hanover; Miers Fisher, of Northampton; George Stillman, of Fluvanna; Hezekiah Anderson, of Nottoway; John T. Brown, of Petersburg; James Gholson, of Brunswick; Rice Wood, of Albemarle; John Campbell, of Brooke; John B. D. Smith, of Frederick; and Samuel Moore, of Rockbridge. The majority of these men represented the Tidewater and Piedmont regions, with only Campbell, Smith, and Moore hailing from west of the Blue Ridge. See Leonard, *General Assembly of Virginia*, 359–61. Brodnax asked for the appointment of eight additional members on 31 December 1831, including two more easterners, giving a total of twenty-one members, sixteen of whom were from the east. For the addition of the new members see Robert, *Road from Monticello*, 17; and Bryce speech of 11 Jan. 1832, *Richmond Enquirer*, 19 Jan. 1832.

slaves? Or was its primary purpose to address the more general problem of Virginia's colored population? Was it to draw up plans for the expulsion of free blacks? Or ought it consider the abolition of slavery? The committee was eventually saddled with the burden of deliberating upon all of these options. Responding to the Southampton rebellion was to many delegates, as it had been to the public, tied intimately to and even conflated with the problem of "the coloured population" generally. This is somewhat curious; it was not necessary for white Virginians in the wake of Turner's rebellion to call into question the role of African Americans in their state. They did so because their concerns about slavery, race, and their own liberty remained entwined and because the recent changes in Virginia and the nation had heightened their sensitivity to the problems posed by racial slavery. As William Brodnax explained, "The spark was indeed communicated to the tinder, by the tragical events which occurred in Southampton; but the elements for ignition, had been much longer in existence."[17]

One of the elements igniting the debate on slavery was the wide range of views held by the delegates, which was evident in the legislature's response to the citizens' petitions. While some delegates, most but not all from western counties, wanted to address the question of emancipation, stridently conservative eastern members did not. The contest between those who wished to encourage discussion and those who wished to quash it first arose in mid-December, when William Roane, of Hanover County (in the western Tidewater), introduced two petitions, one from his own county advocating state-supported removal of free blacks and voluntarily emancipated slaves and the Quaker petition from Charles City County recommending the gradual abolition of slavery. Roane suggested that rather than simply referring the petitions to the select committee, they be read to the whole House first, "in order that members might catch the ideas and views of the citizens of various sections of the state" on a subject of "such absorbing interest." This move raised the hackles of some eastern slaveholders. After the first petition was read, Vincent Witcher, of Pittsylvania (in the Southside region), rose to protest. These petitions were not about free blacks, he said. They seemed instead "related to the emancipation of slaves, a subject utterly irrelevant to that which the Committee was appointed to consider," and he "understood that the second [Quaker] petition was still more objectionable than the first." The legislature's action,

---

17. *Speech of William H. Brodnax*, 10.

Witcher emphasized, was "to be confined to free negroes and mulattoes," and not to address emancipation.[18]

The skirmish over the Quaker petition foreshadowed what was to come a month later. After the Quaker petition was read in spite of Witcher's initial objections to it, William Goode moved that the House reject the petition, an unusual act because petitions were normally referred to committee as a matter of course. Goode, of the Southside county of Mecklenburg and a leader of the conservative members, justified his motion by announcing that his object was "to prevent the unnecessary consideration of a subject which must be agitated in vain." Stating that nothing could be done to remove slavery and so any discussion of the institution was pointless avoided confronting the issue of slavery's morality, a common technique among conservative slaveholders. But not to receive a citizens' petition violated the democratic spirit and provoked other delegates to speak in favor of considering the petitions, including Samuel Moore, from the Valley county of Rockbridge, and William Brodnax, from Dinwiddie, in the Southside, who said that the legislature ought to confront the issue of slavery in an open manner. Brodnax also introduced some of the arguments that would animate the great debate over slavery a month later, asking whether "there is a man who considers the decay of our prosperity, and the retrograde movement of this once flourishing Commonwealth, who does not attribute them to the pregnant cause of slavery?" Brodnax's question echoed the lamentation of George Mason and others two generations earlier that slavery retarded economic development. Not all slaveholders saw the institution as a winning business proposition, and as businessmen they looked to its end. Though Brodnax's diagnosis of the state's ills may have reflected the sentiments of only a minority of Virginia slaveholders, most of the delegates agreed with him that they should show their good faith and consider all petitions. The House of Delegates voted overwhelmingly, ninety-three to twenty-seven, to refer the Quaker petition to the select committee, thwarting conservatives' early attempt to obviate a discussion of slavery's place in Virginia.[19]

Throughout December and early January the select committee considered the many petitions before it, reporting on some of the less controversial ones in the first week of the new year. For example, the committee rejected a petition asking that all black Virginians, enslaved and free, be barred from ap-

18. Legislative proceedings from 14 Dec. 1831, *Richmond Enquirer*, 15 Dec. 1831.
19. *JHD* (begun Dec. 1831), 29; *Richmond Enquirer*, 17 Dec. 1831.

prenticeships in the mechanical trades, as well as a petition requesting that all blacks be prohibited from working as millers. Restrictions that so severely curtailed free blacks' economic activities and slaveholders' abilities to put their slaves to work however they liked went too far for the legislators. They further rejected many of the petitions from individuals who had suffered losses during the insurrection and were asking the legislature for compensation.[20]

In the meantime, Governor Floyd, a western Virginian who privately wished for a debate on slavery, seems to have used his influence to stir up enthusiasm among the delegates, apparently to some effect. In its 20 December edition the *Enquirer* had commented on the important issues before the legislature without mentioning anything to do with the Southampton rebellion. A few days later Floyd wrote in his diary that the "question of the gradual abolition of slavery begins to be mooted. The eastern members, meaning those east of the Blue Ridge Mountains, wish to avoid discussion, but it must come if I can influence my friends in the Assembly to bring it on." Just a few weeks later, perhaps because of his "influence," Richmond's newspaper editors began to view slavery and emancipation as important questions of public consideration. The *Enquirer*'s editors even advocated some "gradual, systematic" plan for reducing, if not necessarily eliminating, "the mass of evil, which is pressing upon the South, and will still more press upon her, the longer it is put off."[21]

With slavery and emancipation becoming increasingly salient public issues, with the select committee yet to make its report on those subjects, and in the midst of informal discussions among some of the delegates, who, according to Governor Floyd, were "begin[ning] to talk of debating the question of gradually emancipating the Slaves of Virginia," some conservative members began to feel nervous. William Goode, who had led the effort to reject the Quaker petition, again attempted to quash any discussion of emancipation when he proposed on 11 January a resolution that the select committee be discharged from consideration of all petitions that had the manumission of slaves as their object. The result was exactly the opposite of what Goode had

20. *JHD* (begun Dec. 1831), 84.

21. Ambler, *Life and Diary of John Floyd*, 172; *Richmond Enquirer*, 20 Dec. 1831, 7 Jan. 1832; Freehling, *Drift toward Dissolution*, 135–36. The diary entry, for 26 December 1831, also stated, "I will not rest until slavery is abolished in Virginia." This was a bit of hyperbole, since Floyd did not actually put much direct effort into the cause of abolition. Floyd intended the diary to be read and used by succeeding generations of leaders, and this statement may reflect in part his care for his legacy.

intended. Since on the previous day he had announced his design to "put the question of emancipation to rest," delegates who favored consideration of emancipation came prepared with a response. After Goode made his motion, Thomas Jefferson Randolph, named after his esteemed grandfather, rose to offer an alternate resolution. Randolph proposed that the committee be instructed to discuss the expediency of submitting a gradual emancipation plan to the qualified voters of the state. Randolph's plan was not, as some have interpreted it, an abolition plan the legislature might have approved and enacted. It was instead a proposal for a popular vote on abolition, a tactic that Edward Coles, in a recent letter to Randolph, had suggested might yield more success.[22]

Even though Randolph's resolution called for submitting an emancipation scheme to the voters and Goode's resolution proposed terminating consideration of certain petitions, two technically different subjects, it was obvious that discussion of the competing resolutions would, in effect, constitute an open debate over the role and future of slavery in the commonwealth. Several delegates spoke that day, some to express their desire to let the committee do its work and to avoid a general discussion. But the vote the following afternoon indicated that the delegates were overwhelming interested in a debate, some because they supported abolition and others because they thought discussing the subject would "settle and sink it forever." By a margin of 116 to 7 the legislators decided to take up the Goode and Randolph resolutions, which had been laid on the table. Governor Floyd commented with some apparent satisfaction that "the slave party have produced the very debate they wished to avoid, and too, have entered upon it with open doors."[23]

At first the Goode and Randolph resolutions provided the structure of the debate, but after several days of argument among the House members the select committee on Monday, 16 January, finally submitted its report on the "memorials praying the passage of some law providing for the gradual abolition of slavery in this commonwealth," effectively making moot Goode's proposal that the committee not further consider those memorials. The committee's report stated "that it is inexpedient for the present to make any legislative enactments for the abolition of slavery." At that point the House could have voted whether

---

22. Ambler, *Life and Diary of John Floyd*, 173; *Richmond Enquirer*, 12 Jan. 1832; Edward Coles to Thomas Jefferson Randolph, 29 Dec. 1831, in "Letters of Edward Coles," 107.

23. *Speech of John Thompson Brown*, 4; *JHD* (begun Dec. 1831), 93–95; Ambler, *Life and Diary of John Floyd*, 173–74.

to accept or reject the committee's report. Instead, William Preston, a nephew of Governor Floyd's, moved to amend the report by changing "inexpedient" to "expedient." The Preston amendment, if approved, would have stated the House's intention to enact laws toward the abolition of slavery, though it offered no particular proposal nor any timeline for the enactment of an abolition measure. Even though the debate in the first few days over the Goode and Randolph resolutions was, strictly speaking, distinct from the debate over the committee's report and the Preston amendment, the two weeks of legislative speechmaking on slavery and abolition may be considered as a whole and was viewed as such by contemporaries.[24]

The significance of the debate lay not only in the uniqueness of a legislative discussion regarding emancipation in Virginia but also in the fact that it was held with "open doors," observed intently by a full gallery of men and women who by their presence became participants, and published in the newspapers, where thousands more could observe the debate indirectly. The debate was consequently an important public event, at once political and symbolic. Through their speeches delegates could situate themselves in relation to Virginia politics and the national party structure, and they could air the anxieties piqued by Turner's rebellion. The act of speaking had meaning in itself, since it allowed delegates to establish their moral credibility as either opponents or supporters of slavery without obligating them to a specific course of action. William Roane revealed that he, at least, was aware of the ways his speech might reverberate. Though he denied slavery to be a fit subject for discussion by the House of Delegates, he nevertheless rose to speak "in order that on that great day of trial, which will most certainly come, when posterity will arraign the present generation . . . at the bar of patriotism, I may by sustained by the irrefragable testimony of what I may this day utter."[25]

DEBATE OVER EMANCIPATION SCHEMES

The utterances of the delegates in the Virginia slavery debate largely reiterated the themes central to the citizens' petitions: fear of the increasing black population, both slave and free; fear of insurrection; and concerns for Virginia's

---

24. *JHD* (begun Dec. 1831), 95–99.

25. William Roane speech of 16 Jan. 1832, *Richmond Enquirer*, 4 Feb. 1832. The evidence that women as well as men were in attendance in the hall of the House of Delegates is from a speech by John Chandler in which he noted "the females who grace this auditory." *Speech of John A. Chandler*, 4.

future. Several other important issues, touching on the deepest legal, cultural, political, and moral values white Virginians held, emerged from the debate. Discussions of property rights, alternate emancipation schemes, and the morality of slavery put in question Virginians' basic beliefs. The debate revealed a wide spectrum of views that generally coincided with geography. The divisions did not bode well for the unity of the commonwealth, and because so many of the views expressed were shared by Americans in other states, did not bode well for the unity of the nation either.[26]

One of the great issues of the debate was the conflict between any gradual emancipation scheme and the property rights of slaveholders, an issue raised first by the plan that Randolph proposed the electorate vote on. Apparently inspired by his grandfather and urged on by Edward Coles, Thomas Jefferson Randolph suggested that "the children of all female slaves who may be born in this state on or after the fourth day of July, 1840, shall become the property of the commonwealth, . . . if detained by their owners within the limits of Virginia, . . . to be hired out until the nett sum arising therefrom shall be sufficient to defray the expense of their removal beyond the limits of the United States." Under Randolph's scheme slaveowners would retain title to the after-born slaves until the slaves reached adulthood. If they wished to, owners could sell their slaves beyond Virginia, reaping the profit rather than forfeiting the slaves to the state. Randolph's scheme sought not to guarantee freedom for African Americans so much as to rid Virginia of slaves, and to do so very slowly, with the first slaves not to be liberated until 1858. Nevertheless,

26. Joseph Robert, Alison Freehling, and William Shade divide legislators into groups based on voting patterns. Robert and Freehling both describe three groups. Robert calls them "the emancipators," "the slavery party," and "the compromisers" and notes that the "votes showed characteristic sectional alignments." Freehling describes the three groups as "abolitionist," "conservative," and "moderate" and deemphasizes correspondences between these groups and particular geographic regions, though the maps in her book indicate distinct regional patterns in the voting. William Shade analyzes the votes as defining five groups—"progressive antislavery," "backcountry antislavery," "radical proslavery," "conservative proslavery," and "the moderates." He sees these groups as tied to specific regions, as the appellation "backcountry antislavery" suggests, but the map in his book depicts three groups, not five. My analysis focuses more on language and discourse than on these voting blocs. For my discussion of the votes, which describes antislavery, antiemancipation, and moderate members, see below in this chapter, under "The Outcome of the Debate." Robert, *Road from Monticello*, 31–33; Freehling, *Drift toward Dissolution*, 136, 163; Shade, *Democratizing the Old Dominion*, 199–203, 297–98.

the date he chose for the implementation of his scheme unmistakably recalled Virginians' attachment to the ideal of universal liberty and the glowing words of Jefferson in the Declaration of Independence.[27]

Though Randolph attempted to resolve the tension between emancipation and property rights by reserving emancipation to those born after a future date so that no slave alive in 1832 would be freed (similar to the schemes suggested in a couple of the petitions, proposed in Revolutionary-era Virginia, and enacted in states such as Pennsylvania and New York), conservative members did not accept Randolph's assumption that unborn slaves were not property and that a *post nati* scheme did not violate property rights. Thomas Marshall, who was Chief Justice John Marshall's son and represented the Piedmont county of Fauquier, asserted that slaveowners held property rights in unborn slaves because the potential of increase inherent in female slaves was part of their present value. When supporters of *post nati* abolition iterated their belief that unborn slaves were not property to which slaveholders could claim title, James Bruce, of Halifax County, in the conservative Southside region, protested that such a notion was "the most extraordinary doctrine that was ever broached in this Hall. If we have no property in the future increase of our slaves, we certainly have none to those now in being, for the property in both must necessarily be derived in the same way." The same argument was implicit in James Gholson's protest against the Randolph plan, which he called "*monstrous and unconstitutional*" because it "proposes the confiscation of property, without crime—the appropriation of private property to public uses, *without just compensation.*" Here, then, was the necessary corollary to the argument for property rights in unborn slaves: the right to hold slaves was as "perfect and inviolable as that to any other property we possess."[28]

Hence, supporters of abolition had to do more than assert that unborn slaves were not property; they were impelled by the course of the debate to challenge the inviolability of property rights in general. The western delegate

---

27. *JHD* (begun Dec. 1831), 93. Though Thomas Jefferson had been dead only a few years, he had already achieved immense symbolic importance to Virginians. Delegates on all sides of the debate used his words and actions to lend legitimacy to their own positions. This was possible because Thomas Jefferson had been so equivocal on the subject of emancipation and because his words and deeds tended to contradict each other.

28. *Speech of Thomas Marshall*, 3; James Bruce speech of 19 Jan. 1832, *Richmond Enquirer*, 26 Jan. 1832; James Gholson speech of 12 Jan. 1832, ibid., 21 Jan. 1832; *Speech of William H. Brodnax*, 10.

William Preston, for one, acknowledged that if the right to slave property were "a right both to those now in existence and to those hereafter to be born, which is *superior to all law and above all necessity,*" then no emancipation scheme could ever be effected. But property rights, Preston and others countered, did not take the form that conservative antiabolition men had described. First, property rights were not absolute, especially when weighed against "the supreme law of the land—the safety of the people; a law superior to the right of property." The limits of property rights could be best explained by analogy, comparing slavery to other threats the government regularly acted against. One speaker asked his audience to imagine a house teetering on a precipice and endangering those who might pass below. Did not the local government have the power to tear down the house if the owner would not? Could not a merchant who kept a large quantity of gunpowder in his store be forced to remove it? Similarly, the government of Virginia had the power to control the dangerous form of property known as slaves, "a species of property truly described as a curse to the land." Another delegate, making the same point, vented his frustration with the antiemancipation position, declaring, "I am sick with the clamor in this debate, about this property, this wealth. I consider it all as mere trash, when weighed against the public safety."[29]

In addition to pointing out the limits on property rights, some pro-emancipation advocates attacked the sanctity of the positive law that allowed slavery. They argued that the statutory foundation for slavery in Virginia could rightfully be altered, just as any other statute could be amended. As Charles Faulkner said, "Property is the creature of civil society." Slaveowners "hold their slaves—not by any law of nature—not by any patent from God, . . . but solely by virtue of the acquiescence and consent of the society in which they live. So long as that property is not dangerous to the good order of society, it may and will be tolerated. But sir, so soon as it does become pernicious . . . the right by which they hold their property is gone."[30]

In response to these two points, John Thompson Brown, of Petersburg, countered that the statutory origin of property rights in slaves made those rights no less sacrosanct. It was not necessary, he said, "to show that the right of property in slaves, is founded in nature," in order to prove its validity. And

29. William Preston speech of 16 Jan. 1832, *Richmond Enquirer,* 9 Feb. 1832; *Speech of John A. Chandler,* 6–7; *Speech of Henry Berry,* 4.
30. *Speech of John A. Chandler,* 7–8; *Speech of Charles Jas. Faulkner,* 14.

while he acknowledged the right to safety as an important concern, he questioned the idea of declaring a whole population a "nuisance" (a term with legal import since the examples offered by supporters of emancipation related to property defined as a nuisance) and argued that the degree of danger that could impede property rights had to be urgent and inevitable rather than doubtful, as he thought the danger of insurrection was. James Gholson, one of the most ardent supporters of slavery, agreed. He indicated that he might be convinced of the need for emancipation and removal if it could be proved that "the horrors of insurrection are gathering round us, and this is our only refuge." But he was not convinced: "I reject the evidences offered here. . . . The dangers they imagine, do not exist." Opponents of slavery could only restate their fears and warn that if private property rights in slaves were inviolable, then "slavery is held to be extinguishable but no otherwise than by insurrection and blood."[31]

These arguments pointed to the main question of how to weigh the competing rights of white and black Virginians. As the westerner George Summers put it, "Here, then, are two conflicting rights to the same thing. The master asserts an absolute, unqualified right to the slave, and authority to direct and controul his every motion. The slave, at the same time, has a right to direct and controul his own actions . . . a right paramount to all conventional guarantees or civil compacts." While he had isolated the truth at the heart of the debate, it was one not acknowledged by the most reactionary delegates, who denied that African Americans had any rights that ought to be considered and noted that the Virginia Declaration of Rights did not apply to slaves. To them, the question was one of social order, maintaining the "sacred principle of 'meum et tuum,'" which arose from the "principles of justice" and by which society was bound.[32]

But it would be a mistake to assume that attacking slavery required viewing slaves as persons with rights and that defending slavery necessitated viewing them only as objects. Delegates on all sides of the debate considered slaves as both people and property. When the issue was whether they were a harmful form of property that ought to be removed, conservatives like John Thompson Brown could counter that they were people, "an organic part of the frame

---

31. *Speech of John Thompson Brown*, 11–12; Gholson speech of 12 Jan. 1832, *Richmond Enquirer*, 21 Jan. 1832; *Speech of James M'Dowell, Jr.*, 17.

32. George Summers speech of 17 Jan. 1832, *Richmond Enquirer*, 16 Feb. 1832; *Richmond Enquirer*, 21 Jan. 1832.

and character of the body politic." But when the question was emancipation, Brown spoke of slaves primarily as valuable property that formed about one-third of the wealth of the state. Similarly, opponents of slavery such as John Chandler focused on slaves as people when speaking of natural rights but as noxious property when arguing that they were dangerous. The dual identity of slaves proved useful to delegates, allowing them great flexibility in their arguments but tempting speakers on all sides to expound beyond the constraints of logic.[33]

In addition to sharing the understanding that slaves were both people *and* property, the delegates, in spite of their conflicting views on the benefits of slavery, shared an understanding of their goal; they sought to preserve white society, white liberty, white values, and white safety. That was obvious in the conservative argument, but proponents of emancipation-colonization schemes were also animated more by the desire to safeguard white society than by a desire to improve the welfare of blacks. Their collective desire to protect white Virginians' lives and liberties was as important a part of the debate as the delegates' diverging views on how to meet such ends.

The common concern for the safety of white society emerged especially in discussions over several abolition plans proposed in addition to Randolph's plan. In true Virginia style, all the plans included the deportation of freed slaves as a central feature. The most prominent came from the self-styled moderate William Brodnax, a slaveholder from the Southside region, where Turner's revolt had taken place. Brodnax had helped put down the insurrection and felt acutely that "something must be done" about the status of black people in the commonwealth. The stated goal of his plan was "the gradual diminution, or ultimate extermination of the black population of Virginia," not the ending of slavery per se. Several principles guided his scheme: first, that "no emancipation of slaves should ever be tolerated, unaccompanied by their immediate removal from among us"; second, that private property should not be interfered with; and finally, that no slave should be taken from his owner without the owner's consent or ample compensation for the value of the slave. Brodnax thought that these terms could be met and that six thousand free blacks could be removed from Virginia each year if a tax of about thirty cents were levied on every white person in the state. Free blacks would be transported first, and after that the state could purchase slaves from their owners

---

33. *Speech of John Thompson Brown*, 12.

and transport them as well. Brodnax believed there would be little need for the state to purchase slaves for deportation, however, since many owners would voluntarily surrender their slaves if they knew they would be colonized beyond Virginia's borders. According to his calculations, "in less than 80 years there would not be left a single slave or free negro in all Virginia," though no owner would ever have been forced to give up any slaves. By 1910, Brodnax thought, Virginia could achieve its goal of an all-white society, notwithstanding whatever might occur in neighboring states, which seemed to be of little concern to Virginians.[34]

Fanciful as it might sound to modern ears, the compromise scheme Brodnax proposed made sense in the context of its own time, when colonization received support from many of the nation's most esteemed leaders. In his speech Brodnax cited Henry Clay, for example, and Virginians had only to open the newspapers to learn of ships setting out for Liberia and to read positive reports from the ACS. Some delegates nevertheless saw serious flaws in Brodnax's proposal. Henry Berry objected that Brodnax "seems to flatter himself that his number [of slaves] will be given up annually by their owners, to be colonized." Charles Faulkner similarly criticized Brodnax's plan, saying that since its object was compromise, "it deals too much in contradictions, and seeks too fancifully to reconcile impossibilities. It is a scheme which proposes to remove property, and yet respect, in its operations the most Quixotic notions of the right of property. It is to revolutionize this commonwealth; and, yet, to carry on that revolution so quietly, that none can perceive the change."[35]

Faulkner and Berry attacked Brodnax's plan in part to advance their own *post nati* emancipation schemes. Berry suggested that slave children born after some future date be declared free but be obligated to act as servants until their labor had reimbursed their masters for the cost of raising them. The free blacks would then be hired out to raise the money requisite to transport and settle them beyond Virginia. Berry's plan differed from Randolph's in that after-born children would be free from birth and could not, as under Randolph's scheme, be sold. Berry argued that his plan "would give stability and security to this property; it would tranquilize the public mind; even the colored classes, seeing that a settled policy was adopted towards them, would become more quiet and reconciled, and would abandon all vain hopes and imagination of any general or immediate emancipation." Faulkner's proposal

---

34. *Speech of William H. Brodnax*, 26–35.
35. *Speech of Henry Berry*, 6; *Speech of Charles Jas. Faulkner*, 13.

was almost identical. He shared with Berry the sense that a gradual, delayed scheme of emancipation and colonization was in fact a compromise that ought to satisfy slaveowners, nonslaveholders, and enslaved people alike.[36]

Randolph, Brodnax, Berry, and Faulkner offered their emancipation-colonization proposals with the sincere hope that they might resolve Virginia's troubles, but all four schemes so strained under the necessary burden of removing freed slaves as to make them unworkable in practice. All except Brodnax's plan sought to translate the labor of enslaved Virginians into funds sufficient to remove them, a system hard to imagine in operation since earning wages high enough to cover the costs of food, lodging, clothing, *and* transportation out of Virginia would probably have required higher labor rates than white Virginians were willing to pay and was only possible in a cash-based economy, an economy in which many slaveholding and rural Virginians still did not participate. Brodnax's idea of taxing white Virginians in order to fund removal of slaves depended on, as Faulkner put it, the quixotic idea that owners would voluntarily give their slaves up and estimated the cost of removal at what seems to be an unreasonably low rate (thirty cents per white Virginian per year). Furthermore, all four plans required the involvement of the state on a scale unprecedented in American history—keeping track of, hiring out, maintaining, and removing thousands upon thousands of people. But because white Virginians universally agreed that "free white people, free blacks, and slave blacks cannot and ought not to constitute one and the same society," by the 1830s even Virginia's Quakers could not conceive of emancipation without colonization.[37]

DEBATE OVER THE PLACE OF SLAVERY IN VIRGINIA

Rather than focus on the practical issues the emancipation-colonization schemes raised, which would have indicated serious consideration of the plans, delegates instead turned to a discussion of slavery's place in Virginia. A few people weighed in on slavery's morality, but in general delegates focused on slavery's practical benefits or ills. The legislators' discussion of slavery in Virginia revealed their evolving attitudes, especially changes in the proslavery argument. In a romantic reinterpretation of slavery, some of its defenders now asserted that it sheltered slaves from the storms of the world as it held them in its protective grasp, though they stopped short of asserting that slavery was in

---

36. *Speech of Henry Berry,* 5–6; *Speech of Charles Jas. Faulkner,* 17–19.
37. William Roane speech of 16 Jan. 1832, *Richmond Enquirer,* 4 Feb. 1832.

the abstract morally right. Following from their recent arguments in the Virginia Constitutional Convention, slavery's defenders also began to reinterpret the value Virginians ought to place on liberty.

Slavery's defenders were moved to reinterpret the value of liberty because some delegates invoked traditional natural-rights arguments in their attack on slavery in Virginia. Samuel Moore, of the Valley county of Rockbridge, reminded his audience that the principle that "'all men are by nature free and equal' is a truth held sacred by every American and by every Republican." Even the mildest form of slavery, he insisted, was wrong because it was wrong to hold people against their consent. George Summers went so far as to say that the right to liberty gave slaves the right to rebel, that a slave could "assert and regain his liberty, if he can." The abstract right of all men to liberty had been on William Preston's mind as well when he moved that the select committee's report be amended to say that efforts for abolition were "expedient." Preston explained that his amendment in favor of considering an abolition scheme "was the twin thought of the Declaration of Independence."[38]

But even the most vocal and radical proponents of abolition denied that the natural-rights argument was the *impetus* for their attack on slavery. They emphasized instead the inconvenience and negative economic and political effects slavery produced, and in this way their arguments differed importantly from those of the Revolutionary era. As Preston proclaimed in the final words of his speech, "We attack that property, because it is dangerous—we attack it because it is subversive of the well being of society—we attack it on principles of necessity and policy—we wish to remove the danger from the East, and to prevent its existence in the West." Thomas Jefferson Randolph explained that slavery reduced the "free population of a country," which led to decreased economic opportunities for whites and the dissolution of social ties. Poor whites suffered especially under slavery because the "wealthy are not dependent upon the poor for those aids and those services, compensation for which enables the poor man to give bread to his family. The ordinary mechanic arts are all practised by slaves."[39]

Other supporters of emancipation did not refer to natural-rights ideas at

---

38. Samuel Moore speech of 11 Jan. 1832, ibid., 19 Jan. 1832; Summers speech of 17 Jan. 1832, ibid., 14 Feb. 1832; Preston speech of 16 Jan. 1832, ibid., 9 Feb. 1832.

39. *Speech of Thomas J. Randolph*, 14; Preston speech of 16 Jan. 1832, *Richmond Enquirer*, 9 Feb. 1832.

all. Thomas Marshall "objected to slavery, not because it implies moral turpitude, or because it is a sin to be the owner of a slave." Nor was it, he said, "because of its demoralizing tendency that slavery should be abolished." Instead, he denounced slavery as a *practical* evil, particularly in that part of the country with which he was best acquainted [the northern Piedmont]—exclusively a grain-growing region." James M'Dowell argued in the same vein, asserting that it was not necessary to consider whether the existence of slavery in Virginia comported either with the abstract principles of their government—"that principle of absolute freedom on which they erected their own independence"—or with basic morality. M'Dowell based his opposition to slavery on its effect upon Virginia. As a result of slavery, he said, Virginia was "meagre, haggard and enfeebled—with decrepitude stealing upon her limbs—as given over to leanness and impotency, and as wasting away under the improvidence and the inactivity which eternally accompany the fatal institution that she cherishes."[40]

Perhaps Marshall, M'Dowell, and others refrained from attacking slavery in theoretical terms simply because it was politic not to impugn the moral integrity of slaveholders, whom they wished to enlist in their cause. But the general emphasis in the debate on the practical rather than the abstract evils of slavery also represented a genuine concern that slavery hindered Virginia's social and economic development. It was significant that slavery became the object of relatively widespread condemnation only when it seemed to threaten the economic interest of a sizable portion of Virginia's white population. Furthermore, their discussion clarified what most delegates meant when they described slavery as an "evil": not that slavery was a sin but that like the Bank of the United States or the tariff, also described as evils, slavery had ill effects on white society.

Not surprisingly, opponents of emancipation also focused more on practical than on moral questions, reiterating many of the arguments against emancipation that they had made over the previous two generations. One anti-emancipation delegate believed that no one "has had the hardihood to assert, that one man had a right to enslave another. The discussion of the abstract question of slavery has nothing in the world to do with the subject now in debate." Indeed, slavery had few champions. William Patteson, for instance, one of the few to vote against referring the Quaker petition to committee,

---

40. *Speech of Thomas Marshall*, 5; *Speech of James M'Dowell, Jr.*, 5, 9.

nevertheless said that he did not stand "as the advocate for slavery as an abstract proposition."[41]

But as one western delegate noted, slavery did have "its *apologists*," who suggested that slavery benefited white society, protected republican institutions, and even bettered the fortunes of African Americans. Alexander Knox claimed that slavery was the cause of the "high and elevated character which she [Virginia] has heretofore sustained." Slavery was necessary as well, since "its existence is indispensably requisite in order to preserve the forms of a Republican Government." Knox did not explicate *how* slavery preserved republican government nor how the northern states managed to retain their republican character without it, but he did assert that slavery's benefits devolved to African Americans as well because slavery imparted to them the "moral principle" they would not have access to in their ancestral "land of darkness." A related argument, one that grew in popularity in subsequent years, was to defend the condition of slaves as better than that of the poor in other countries. William Daniel claimed that "the lower orders of almost every nation in Europe, would benefit by the exchange of their condition for that of our slaves." William Brodnax, while not defending slavery in the abstract, agreed with Daniel "that in point of fact, their [slaves'] condition is superior to that of the peasantry of any other country, in possessing the ordinary comforts of life." Besides material comforts, slavery's apologists pointed to the psychological benefits of slavery. Brodnax thought that slaves who had "good masters" were "in a happy condition," since "they have no care on their minds to provide a subsistence." Rice Wood, of Albemarle, conceived of slavery as a set of mutual obligations that created an affectionate bond. He noted that slaves and their owners "had reciprocal duties to discharge, and the debt of gratitude was mutual. The master loved the faithful slave, and in turn the faithful slave loved the master." If it seemed occasionally that slaves were unhappy, that was because of the meddlesome influence of abolitionists ("philanthropists"). Slaves, said Daniel, "would continue to be happy and to love us, if modern philanthropy did not use so many arguments to convince them that they are miserable, and ought to hate us as their oppressors." Moreover, "[w]e too, Sir, are comparatively happy in the possession of them."[42]

41. William Daniel speech of 20 Jan. 1832, *Richmond Enquirer,* 31 Jan. 1832; William Patteson speech of 15 Jan. 1832, ibid., 3 Apr. 1832.

42. *Speech of Charles Jas. Faulkner,* 20; Knox speech of 17 Jan. 1832, *Richmond Enquirer,* 11 Feb. 1832; Daniel speech of 20 Jan. 1832, ibid., 31 Jan. 1832; *Speech of William H. Brodnax,* 23; Rice Wood speech of 16 Jan. 1832, *Richmond Enquirer,* 7 Feb. 1832.

Earlier defenses of slavery dating back to the 1780s had suggested that slavery might support republican institutions and had described masters as kind and slaves as generally happy, but the arguments proffered in January 1832 signified a shift in the proslavery defense toward a greater concern with the condition of slaves. It was innovative to argue that slaves were actually *better* off than whites elsewhere and relatively new to imply that ties between masters and slaves were affectionate. These claims fit with the general intellectual and cultural shift from Enlightenment ideas to romanticism and were part of what several historians, following Willie Lee Rose, have described as the domestication of slavery.[43]

Another fairly new defense of slavery was to argue, as had been recently voiced in the Virginia Constitutional Convention, that liberty itself was limited, a creature of civil society and not an abstract right, so slavery did not violate any basic principles. William Roane suggested how new that argument still seemed when he stated that if he were to discuss the "metaphysical doctrines of the natural equality of man, or the abstract moral right of slavery," he might "shock the tender nerves of many good people" because he was "not one of those who have ever revolted at the idea or practice of slavery, as many do." Roane continued that slavery was an inevitable feature of human societies and therefore dwelled beyond the reach of moral arguments. The institution, he said, "has existed, and ever will exist, in all ages, in some form, and to some degree. I think slavery as much a correllative of liberty as cold is of heat." James Gholson also resigned himself to the eternal fact of slavery: "It is here; and no reproaches on the one hand, or regrets on the other, can avoid it." Gholson consequently denied that antislavery philosophy was one of the great moral developments of the era. With great rhetorical flourish, he expounded,

> The gentleman from Rockbridge [James M'Dowell] has admonished us that we cannot resist the lights of the age. . . . I have heard of these lights before, but I have looked for them in vain—I have never seen them. The wretched and misguided fanatic [Nat Turner], who excited the horrors of the late Southampton massacre, thought *he* saw them. It proved, however, a delusive meteor, and conducted him to his death. . . . Northern lights have appeared. Incendiary publications have scattered their illuminating rays among us, to conduct the slaves to massacre and blood-shed. But these are not lights of the age, or

---

43. See, e.g., Hamilton, "Revolutionary Principles," 545; Lewis, "Problem of Slavery in Southern Political Discourse," 284–90; and Rose, "Domestication of Domestic Slavery."

lights from heaven.—It is the "glare of Avernus—a darkness visible" in the light of which, demons and devils alone, delight to dwell.

While defenders of slavery asserted that slavery improved the fortunes of both whites and blacks and denied the abstract value of liberty, they did not go as far as the proslavery ideologues of the 1840s and 1850s in asserting slavery's benefits. Yet the words of the delegates in 1832, like the arguments advanced in defense of slavery in the 1780s, did presage those later proslavery polemics.[44]

Significantly, arguments on both sides continued to focus on race. Proslavery ideas rested on the conviction that racial inequality marked by facial features as well as color justified enslavement. As William Roane said, "I no more believe that the flat-nosed, wooly-headed black native of the deserts of *Africa* is equal to the straight-haired white man of Europe, than I believe the stupid scentless greyhound is equal to the noble, generous dog of *Newfoundland*." Antislavery thought sometimes arose out of the contrary belief that people of all races were essentially the same, especially in their love of liberty, that a slave, though "soiled in his character and degraded in his fortunes, indeed, [is] yet still a member of a common race." But racial antipathy was also important to the antislavery position, since the fear of race war, which had such a long history in Virginia, motivated most of the delegates who spoke in favor of emancipation and removal. The position of these delegates would therefore more accurately be described as antislave than antislavery.[45]

Perhaps most important was that for the first time Virginia's leaders spoke their views aloud in a public forum, even if many of the ideas they gave voice to had been found earlier in newspaper columns, citizens' petitions, occasional pamphlets, and legal judgments. The exercise revealed the wide variety of beliefs Virginians held on slaves, slavery, and race, which surprised some contemporaries. The western delegate Henry Berry did not expect anyone to deny slavery to be a "grinding curse on this state." He could only explain the defense of slavery as a result of "pecuniary interest." Berry's analysis was trenchant but ignored the fact that attacks *against* slavery also sprang from interest and that

---

44. Roane speech of 16 Jan. 1832, *Richmond Enquirer*, 4 Feb. 1832; Gholson speech of 12 Jan. 1832, ibid., 21 Jan. 1832. William Jenkins in his examination of the South as a whole argues, by contrast, that the "positive good theory" of slavery arose in the 1820s. Jenkins, *Pro-Slavery Thought*, 77.

45. Roane speech of 16 Jan. 1832, *Richmond Enquirer*, 4 Feb. 1832; *Speech of James M'Dowell, Jr.*, 19.

on both sides interest was bound up with culture and morality in a way that made those elements difficult to separate.[46]

RACE, LIBERTY, AND SECTIONALISM IN VIRGINIA

At the root of the arguments over property rights, emancipation-colonization schemes, and the place of slavery in Virginia was the essential conflict between two competing visions of Virginia society—a conservative vision of a plantation economy in which whites could attain a level of equality and gentility possible only with black slaves and a view in which free white farmers and mechanics would make Virginia prosperous through their industry. Two notions of the relationship between race and liberty accompanied these visions. In one, with its roots in the seventeenth century, black slavery guaranteed white liberty; as Knox claimed, it was "requisite" to preserve republican government. With all blacks enslaved, all whites could share equally in liberty in spite of class differences among them, even though in reality eastern slaveholders denied equal rights to whites through the representation and suffrage provisions of the recent state constitution. In the other view, which had its roots in the Revolutionary era, liberty as a universal value could not be said to exist if slavery existed as well. Therefore, black slavery was antithetical to liberty, including white liberty. And since most white Americans conflated slavery with black people, blacks were also antithetical to white liberty. Neither of these conceptions was limited to Virginia. The former was shared by many of the slaveholders of the South and became central to the proslavery arguments of the 1840s and 1850s, and the latter was shared by many of the inhabitants of the North as part of the free labor ideology of that same era. The Virginia slavery debate, in which these ideas competed, was therefore an American debate. It was a battle over which group of whites would dominate the culture and politics of the society and which values would guide the community. In Virginia, as in the nation, it took on a sectional character, since the opposing ideas were tied to material, social, and cultural interests that corresponded to geography.[47]

The incipient free-labor ideology of the western Virginians found expression in the words of James M'Dowell, who explained that by "general deduction

---

46. *Speech of Henry Berry*, 2.

47. Eric Foner discusses northern political ideology in the antebellum era in *Free Soil, Free Labor, Free Men*.

from the principles of human nature, and by observed facts, . . . the labor of a free white man, in the temperate latitude of Virginia, is more productive than that of a slave—yielding a larger aggregate for public and for private wealth." Even some residents of the slaveholding east thought Virginia's economy might be stronger without slaves. If there were no slave population, "would not these very wastes [in the eastern lowlands] have now been thickly studded with the smiling cottage of the freeman—the abode of peace, of happiness, of virtue, intelligence, and patriotism?" Free labor was also seen as morally advantageous, promoting greater happiness, virtue, intelligence, and patriotism than slave labor. When slaves performed much of the agricultural labor, labor became "very generally regarded as a mark of servitude, and consequently degrading and disreputable," leading to an "almost universal indisposition of the free population, to engage in the cultivation of the soil." The result was that free whites of moderate means were "too proud to till the earth with their own hands" and were "wasting away their small patrimonial estates, and raising their families in habits of idleness and extravagance." Moreover, independent farmers who viewed their hard work with pride were "not prepared to render labour dishonorable, by associating it with involuntary servitude."[48]

Free white labor, on the other hand, made farming noble, and white yeoman farmers were thought to be morally superior to both planters and slaves. The choice between free and slave labor was one between "the hardy, independent tenantry of our country" and "those who have no other rule than to work as little and waste as much as they can," an epithet that could apply as easily to slaveowners as to their chattels. The yeomanry of Virginia were its greatest wealth; they "constitute our pride, efficiency and strength; they are our defence in war, our ornaments in peace; and no population . . . upon the face of the globe, is more distinguished for an elevated love of freedom—for morality, virtue, frugality and independence, than the Virginia peasantry west of the Blue Ridge." Choosing a future of slavery over a future of freedom would therefore be ruinous. Thomas Marshall outlined the alternatives when he denounced slavery and promoted free labor. Slavery, he said,

> retards improvement—roots out an industrious population—banishes the yeomanry of the country—deprives the spinner, the weaver, the

---

48. *Speech of James M'Dowell, Jr.*, 4; Robert Powell speech of 14 Jan. 1832, *Richmond Enquirer*, 31 Jan. 1832; Moore speech of 11 Jan. 1832, ibid., 19 Jan. 1832; Summers speech of 17 Jan. 1832, ibid., 14 Feb. 1832.

smith, the shoemaker, the carpenter, of employment and support. The evil admits of no remedy. It is increasing, and will continue to increase, until the whole country will be inundated by one black wave, covering its whole extent, with a few white faces here and there floating on the surface.... If cultivated by free labor, the soil of Virginia is capable of sustaining a dense population, among whom labor would be honorable, where "the busy hum of men" would tell that all were happy, and that all were free.[49]

In contrast to western delegates' glowing vision of a prosperous, free, white Virginia, eastern planters offered their ideal of a genteel life achieved through the use of slaves. Employing a vivid metaphor that made slavery the fertilizer nourishing the plant of white freedom, William Roane said that history had taught him that "the torch of liberty has ever burnt brightest when surrounded by the dark and filthy, yet nutritious atmosphere of slavery." Slavery also fostered cultural achievements. According to Rice Wood, Virginians, in contrast to the Puritans of the northern regions, had been devoted to "social intercourse, to the cultivation of elegant literature and fine oratory. In these, they excelled not only any race of men in this Union, but perhaps in the world." The vision of refined plantation society was implicit in one delegate's fear that if an emancipation scheme were implemented, the "hospitable mansion that was animated with the voice of mirth, and its halls quickened into gaiety by the festive dance, will be closed, with the shadow of ruin fixed upon its portals."[50]

Because proponents of both free-labor ideology and the plantation ideal shared the Anglo-American belief that liberty was fragile and could be preserved only under carefully guarded conditions, each side saw great danger in the other's vision—liberty would be annihilated either by the spread of inefficient and demoralizing slave labor or by the removal of the economic institution that had supported Virginia's great cultural and historical achievements. Trying to explain how Virginians could hold such divergent views on a value—liberty—that lay at the core of American politics and society, Alexander Knox pointed to differences in economic interest. The rift, he said

49. Summers speech of 17 Jan. 1832, *Richmond Enquirer*, 14 Feb. 1832; *Speech of Charles Jas. Faulkner*, 9; *Speech of Thomas Marshall*, 6.
50. Roane speech of 16 Jan. 1832, *Richmond Enquirer*, 4 Feb. 1832; Wood speech of 16 Jan. 1832, ibid., 7 Feb. 1832; Knox speech of 17 Jan. 1832, ibid., 11 Feb. 1832.

caustically, did not result from the "more elevated sense of liberty" to the west than "that which animates the bosom of Eastern Virginia." In fact, Knox reminded his audience, western Virginians had originally desired slaves and had voted to lift restrictions on their importation. But the number of slaves had never grown large in western Virginia because "the climate, [and] the soil" predicated against the production of staple crops associated with plantation agriculture.[51]

Knox had a point, but by 1832 economic differences between eastern and western Virginia were not easily separable from cultural ones. The westerner James M'Dowell played on the cultural stereotypes of the inhabitants of the two regions when he imagined what would happen if a genteel woman from the eastern lowlands fell in love with a strapping man from west of the Blue Ridge:

> It is true that the West is occasionally considered a *terra incognita* of refinement and its young men are apt to be rated as contraband articles in treaties of marriage. But it does not all do: they will sometimes succeed. Father and mother may sneer or may scold but love will do what it lists and despite of their frostiness, despite of their lowering, the daughter, in the innocence of her hopes will sometimes—she cannot help it—look with an eye of more favor upon the Buckskin of the Mountain than on the Crab of the Lowlands. But the "beauty and the booty" are won together: the lover gets the bride, and the West gets the slave.

M'Dowell's concern was that the west could not protect itself against growth in the slave population because, as part of Virginia, it could not bar the entrance of slaves. (Virginians could, by contrast, keep out slaves from other states, as the 1778 anti-importation law had done.) Apparently he did not think, as Knox did, that the climate and soil of western Virginia would prevent the growth of slavery there. Recognizing and even poking fun at the social distance between the eastern "daughter" and the "Buckskin of the Mountains" made manifest the fear that if the west were unprotected, it might develop an economy, and consequently a culture, like that of the east, dependent on slavery and subject to all its attached ills.[52]

The depth of the differences between east and west and the desire to pre-

---

51. Knox speech of 17 Jan. 1832, ibid., 11 Feb. 1832.
52. *Speech of James M'Dowell, Jr.*, 21, 32.

serve them prompted a few western Virginians to consider dividing the state. Talk of division had begun as early as November, when an anonymous writer published an article in a western newspaper, the *Rockbridge Intelligencer,* calling for separation from the east. The article's author had cited the political disadvantages westerners held, the differences in "manners, habits, and customs" between the regions, and his "dread that the aristocracy of Eastern Virginia will not permit the introduction of republican principles into the Constitution." But newspaper editors from across the state denounced the proposed division for both political and emotional reasons. The *Warrenton Gazette,* in the Piedmont county of Fauquier, "deprecate[d] the idea of a division of this ancient commonwealth," and most delegates abhorred the idea of division. They pleaded alternately that its possibility was cause for immediate action against slavery or a reason to cease the discussion.[53]

Finally, as in the national struggle over slavery, the question turned to minority rights since according to Knox fewer than one-third of Virginia voters were directly interested in slavery in the early 1830s. Slaveholders' plea for minority rights and their demand that those most interested (financially) in slavery be the ones to address it echoed arguments from two years earlier in the constitutional convention and foreshadowed one of the great themes of the national sectional controversy. And just as slavery was the issue that threatened the Union and eventually wrenched it apart, so too did slavery threaten and eventually break apart Virginia. The delegates who pointed out the destructiveness of the slavery question were prescient; they saw that there was no likely peaceful resolution to the conflict between the two groups of people, one of whom was dedicated to achieving a society without slavery, while the other was committed to slavery's preservation.[54]

THE OUTCOME OF THE DEBATE

The Virginia legislative debate over slavery came to an end two weeks after it began when the House of Delegates finally voted on the select committee's report. After rejecting the Preston amendment, which called legislation against slavery "expedient," the House decided in favor of a preamble authored by Archibald Bryce Jr. The final version of the report (preamble and resolution) as approved by the House of Delegates read,

53. *Richmond Enquirer,* 22 Nov. 1831.
54. Knox speech of 17 Jan. 1832, ibid., 11 Feb. 1832.

> Profoundly sensible of the great evils arising from the condition of the coloured population of this commonwealth: induced by humanity, as well as policy, to an immediate effort for the removal in the first place, as well of those who are now free, as of such as may hereafter become free: believing that this effort, while it is in just accordance with the sentiment of the community on the subject, will absorb all our present means; and that a further action for the removal of the slaves should await a more definite development of public opinion:—*Resolved as the opinion of this committee,* That it is inexpedient for the present, to make any legislative enactments for the abolition of slavery.

In sum, the resolution stated that the delegates favored the removal of free blacks and any subsequently freed slaves but thought that since effecting their removal would use up all available funds, and since the people of Virginia were not definitively in favor of removing slaves, no action toward the "removal of slaves" should be taken. The resolution was carefully worded to avoid the terms *abolition, emancipation,* and *colonization,* and its approval prevented the legislature from finding out what the voters of Virginia actually did want and whether, as Randolph had hoped, they might approve an abolition scheme.[55]

The meaning of the resolution voted on by the House, and thus the outcome of the debate, is not easily apparent, since the resolution's words support several interpretations. One historian calls the Bryce preamble moderately antislavery because of "its expectation of gradual, peaceful abolition," while another student of Virginia politics labels it moderately proslavery, since it "favored colonization of free blacks but postponed indefinitely consideration of the 'removal of slaves.'"[56] Examination of the roll-call votes shows that the Bryce preamble was approved by moderates and by those in favor of emancipation, suggesting that the delegates thought it was a statement against slavery. On the other hand, calling any legislative action on emancipation "expedient"—calling for some kind of plan to rid Virginia of its slaves—was rejected both by moderates and, of course, by conservatives. A relatively small number of moderate members who aligned with antislavery forces in sentiment (feeling slavery to be an evil that ought to be eventually, if not imme-

---

55. *JHD* (begun Dec. 1831), 109–10.

56. Freehling, *Drift toward Dissolution,* 149, 163; Shade, *Democratizing the Old Dominion,* 199.

diately, eliminated) but with conservatives in action (refusing any possibility of legislative action against slavery) thus held the balance between the almost evenly matched number of antislavery and antiemancipation delegates. The vote of moderates explains why the final resolution married a preamble favored mostly by westerners to a statement against emancipation supported largely by easterners. The amended resolution, a compromise measure, was approved without the support of antiemancipation easterners, however, because they so disliked the sentiment of the Bryce preamble that they voted against the resolution that included it. The voting patterns and the words of the final resolution together point to the same conclusion: there was in Virginia in 1832 significant interest in antislave and even antislavery policies and a broad consensus that the free black population ought to be reduced, but the debate ended in victory for conservatives who opposed emancipation, since the legislature decided not to consider any abolition scheme and never broached the subject again.[57]

The issue of colonizing free blacks, however, remained on the table. At the end of January the select committee submitted a bill "for the removal of free persons of colour from the commonwealth," as well as a report that declared it "expedient to apply to the general government to procure a territory" to which to send free blacks. The bill would have required the removal of all free people of color under age forty-five if male and under forty if female. Those who did

57. Especially helpful in analyzing the votes is Robert, *Road from Monticello*, which includes detailed tables. The vote to reject the Preston amendment, which stated that action on abolition was "expedient," was most decisive. The proemancipation amendment was defeated by a vote of 73–58. The other two important votes, in favor of the preamble and final report, were closer. The preamble was approved by a relatively narrow margin of 67–60, and the amended committee report (preamble plus resolution) was adopted by a vote of 65–58. Joseph Robert calculates that if representation had been based on free white population, "the majority against the Preston amendment would have been reduced from fifteen to approximately eight." As part of her argument that the House debate "dramatized slavery's tenuous status" in Virginia, Alison Freehling asserts that if the representation in the legislature had been proportional to population, "legislators would have come within one vote of declaring emancipation 'expedient.'" It is equally likely, however, that some delegates who voted for the Preston amendment did so as a symbolic gesture, knowing that the amendment would be defeated, and might have voted differently if it had seemed that the amendment might pass. Robert, *Road from Monticello*, 33n; Freehling, *Drift toward Dissolution*, 162–64. For additional analysis see Shade, *Democratizing the Old Dominion*, 199–203; and for the roll-call votes see *JHD* (begun Dec. 1831), 109–10.

not depart voluntarily would be forcibly expelled. Many delegates found the idea of rounding up tens of thousands of free blacks and forcing them onto ships offensive, and some of them offered a substitute bill. The alternate bill, which required involuntary deportation only for those who had no legal claim to remain in Virginia (because they or their ancestors had been emancipated since 1806), passed by a comfortable margin of seventy-nine to forty-one. The bill for the removal of free blacks found support among delegates who had favored legislation against slavery, including Thomas Jefferson Randolph, but also among those who argued against emancipation. In spite of broad support in the House, the bill met a cooler reception in the Senate, where after several weeks of consideration the senators voted to postpone it indefinitely. The Senate vote of seventeen to fourteen came after the senators had made several modifications that would have decreased the bill's effectiveness, including reducing the appropriation for 1833 from ninety thousand dollars to fifty thousand.[58]

Since the bill for removing free blacks has been characterized mistakenly as a step toward abolition, and since the Virginia Senate vote to kill the bill has been viewed erroneously as a close and therefore bitter defeat for antislavery forces in Virginia, it is worth some added comment. While it is true that antislavery goals and colonization were sometimes linked, and that support for the bill came from all regions of the state and both from delegates who had supported measures against slavery and those who had opposed them, the chain of events leading to the eventual defeat of the colonization bill and the votes as they were finally cast demonstrate that the bill was not intended as an abolition measure. Rather, the strongest and most consistent support for the bill came from the region most committed to slavery, the Tidewater. Even if the bill had passed and the government of Virginia had funded the deportation of free African Americans to Liberia, it is unlikely that the institution of slavery in Virginia would have been weakened as a result or that the number of manumissions would have increased significantly. The 1832 law allowing Northampton County to borrow up to fifteen thousand dollars to remove the free people of color of that county did not substantially decrease the free

---

58. *JHD* (begun Dec. 1831), 112, 120, 148, 158; *A bill, Providing for the removal of free persons of colour*, [1832], and *Substitute for a bill "providing for the removal of free persons of colour,"* Feb. 1832, both in Rough Bills, House of Delegates, 1832, LVA, Archives Division; *Richmond Enquirer*, 13 Mar. 1832.

black population there and certainly did not encourage emancipation. When the Virginia Assembly did pass a colonization law in 1833 funding removal for those who agreed to go voluntarily, the provision had almost no effect, since so few free black Virginians chose to leave the state for Africa.[59]

The legislature's final act regarding Virginia's African American population in 1832—in fact the only legislation actually passed—was to amend the black code in order (whites hoped) to make future insurrections less likely. The new law barred black Virginians from preaching, placed tighter restrictions on the movements and assembly of slaves, and prescribed harsh punishments for anyone who promoted slave rebellion. The law also further reduced free blacks toward the status of slaves by requiring that they be tried in the slave courts (courts of oyer and terminer) in cases of larceny or felony instead of before a regular judge and jury and by barring them from owning guns (earlier laws allowed free people of color to own guns if they had a license, which was not required for whites). Important for the future of manumission in Virginia, the law also made it illegal for free people of color to purchase slaves except immediate family members, thus reducing the ability of the free black community to help enslaved fellow African Americans attain liberty. Surely this provision underscores the legislature's interest in preventing rather than encouraging emancipation.[60]

Since the time of the Revolution the problematic and interconnected issues of slavery, liberty, emancipation, and race had been played out in the realm of abstract discussion as well as on the ground where slaveholders and free people of color manumitted slaves and where a growing number of free black Virginians challenged the two-race system of the pre-Revolutionary era. In the Virginia Constitutional Convention of 1829–30 and in the legislative de-

---

59. Freehling, *Drift toward Dissolution*, 215–21. Freehling reads the colonization measure as emancipationist, arguing that if apportionment in the Senate had reflected the 1830 white population, "a republican senate . . . could then have endorsed state colonization of manumitted slaves and thereby have committed Virginia to the voluntary emancipation policy already sanctioned by the house" (192). There is significant confusion on the colonization measure. For example, in *Democratizing the Old Dominion* William Shade incorrectly assumed that the 1832 bill became law (212). The 1833 law appropriated less money than the 1832 bill, eighteen thousand dollars per year for five years.

60. *Supplement to the Revised Code of the Laws of Virginia*, 246–48; *Revised Code of the Law of Virginia* (1819), 423.

bates of 1831–32 those long-standing issues became topics of political as well as ideological and practical import. When they did—and not during the Revolutionary era—antislavery sentiment in Virginia reached its maximum. But political antislavery sentiment in Virginia was not strong enough to effect change, for in the political arena the victory went to the group that in Virginia consistently held the most political power, the eastern elite, who carried on the traditions and values of their seventeenth- and eighteenth-century ancestors.

Epilogue

VIRGINIA AND THE NATION

VIRGINIA'S STORY RESONATED BEYOND the commonwealth in the years after the debate of 1831–32. Of particular significance, the debate spurred Virginia slaveholders to articulate a clearer and more formal defense of slavery, which greatly influenced proslavery writers throughout the South in the antebellum era. William and Mary professor Thomas Dew's "Review of the Debate in the Virginia Legislature" became one of the most important proslavery essays in U.S. history, cited consistently by subsequent writers. The essay, published shortly after the end of the debate, recapitulated in greater detail many of the points made by antiemancipation delegates, isolating the problem of race as the main question and denouncing colonization as unfeasible. Dew asked whether "these two distinct races of people, now living together as master and servant, [can] be ever separated?" Dew's answer was no, since emancipation and colonization schemes were "*totally* impracticable." Furthermore, no two races of people could ever live together "on a footing of equality." Slavery, then, would persist, but Dew found that perfectly acceptable. Dew, like William Roane, said that slavery was a natural feature of human societies, that it benefited blacks and whites, and that emancipation would engender more evils than slavery. But in denouncing colonization and arguing that Virginians must accept the inevitability of slavery, Dew moved away from the position still voiced by some in the Tidewater that reducing the number of free blacks and slaves was both desirable and possible. Other writers articulated arguments similar to Dew's in extensive newspaper essays, including those written by "Appomatox" (Benjamin Watkins Leigh), who also denounced colonization, and "Locke," who denied that the legislature had the power to end slavery without "just compensation" to the owners.[1]

American politics and culture would also take note of the ideas and values with which Virginians had struggled in the generations after the Revolution. Thomas Marshall's image of free white Virginia—"labor would be honorable, . . . 'the busy hum of men' would tell that all were happy, and that all were free"—was part and parcel of the free-labor ideology of the North, which, as Eric Foner puts it, "involved not merely an attitude toward work, but a justification of ante-bellum northern society, and it led northern Republicans to an extensive critique of southern society." Though the fiery words of the radical abolitionists stand out today as the voice of the antebellum antislavery movement, it was the broad northern consensus on the value of free labor over slave labor, pithily reduced to the Republican political slogan "Free Soil, Free Labor, Free Men," that bound the North to the antislavery cause and helped bring on the Civil War. Similarly, Virginians' State Rights ideas, in place by the 1820s, were shared by other southerners and became the main political argument the South invoked in the sectional struggle.[2]

The sectionalism that had come into place by 1832 and that presaged West Virginia's secession from Virginia during the Civil War did not, however, persist unchanged or unabated. And in important ways Virginia's history again reflected the nation's. Starting in the late 1830s the second party system largely muted sectional disagreements in Virginia and replaced them with partisan ones over such issues as banking, tariffs, internal improvements, and the distribution of money from sales of western lands. In most counties the competition between Whigs and Democrats was very close, and in some years, particularly after the Panic of 1837, Whigs even won a majority in the state legislature. Even so, sectionalism stood waiting at the wings of the political stage, making an appearance whenever the distribution of political power among whites arose as

---

1. Dew, "Review of the Debate," 287; Shade, *Democratizing the Old Dominion*, 203–5; "Appomatox" essays in *Richmond Enquirer*, 4, 28 Feb. 1832; "Locke" essays in ibid., 15, 20, 27 March, 3, 17 Apr. 1832, quotation from 17 April installment. Alison Freehling in *Drift toward Dissolution* acknowledges that Dew's essay "did indeed represent a departure from Virginia's revolutionary heritage" but asserts that "Dew did not present a consistent proslavery ideology" (203).

2. *Speech of Thomas Marshall*, 6; Foner, *Free Soil, Free Labor, Free Men*, 9.

an issue. In 1850–51, just as the nation was confronting its own sectional divisions over the future of the newly acquired lands of the West, another Virginia state constitutional convention met to reconsider the structure of Virginia's government and to reform it according to mid-nineteenth-century American values. In the Virginia Constitution of 1851 reformers achieved a fairer (though still not white-basis) representation in the state legislature, along with universal white manhood suffrage. But the convention was divided, as the earlier one had been, along sectional lines on the key issue of representation and, to a slightly lesser extent, on a provision to lower taxes on slaves. Again mirroring national developments, sectionalism flared following the election of Abraham Lincoln. Just before the February 1861 election of delegates to a state convention to consider secession, an electoral realignment took place in Virginia that brought sectional difference rather than partisan disagreement to the fore. Easterners were much more likely to vote in favor of secession than delegates from the counties that would soon form West Virginia.[3]

As in the nation as a whole, western expansion meant that sectionalism in Virginia in 1861 conformed to a different geography than it had in 1832. Slaveholding interests had moved into counties that in the 1832 slavery debate had been home to strong free-labor, antiplanter sentiment, just as James M'Dowell had feared they would, and several of those counties decided in 1861 to remain part of a commonwealth committed to slavery and State Rights. Symbolic of the shift was that among those who voted for secession in 1861 were two men whose participation in the 1832 debate had predicted otherwise, William Preston and Thomas Jefferson Randolph, both of whom had stood on the floor of the House of Delegates and made clear their interest in considering an emancipation scheme. Preston, who had aligned himself with the Whig Party but could not in 1861 remain in a Union he viewed as inimical to state sovereignty, was the one to introduce the ordinance of secession on 16 April, and Thomas Jefferson Randolph, along with his younger brother George Wythe Randolph, voted for it the next day. The original George Wythe, one of the Revolutionary generation's most uncompromising haters of slavery, would surely have found George Wythe Randolph's vote to be a rejection of Revolutionary ideals that Wythe had held so dear.[4]

If the move away from certain Revolutionary principles marked how much had changed in the preceding three generations, an abiding interest in colo-

3. Shade, *Democratizing the Old Dominion*, 169, 278–83, 287–91.
4. Ibid., 288–90.

nization as a solution to the problems posed by emancipation underscored that white Americans' assumptions about racial separateness remained central to their thought. Abraham Lincoln during the war suggested that America's blacks might find refuge in Central America, since "this physical difference [between black and white] is a great disadvantage" and it is "better for us both, therefore, to be separated." African Americans, however, rejected the plan as well as the underlying notion of racial distinction, just as Virginia's black residents had so often chosen to remain in their homes in Virginia rather than strike out for foreign lands and had striven while in Virginia to prove their worth as people, not only as people of color. After the war, Americans in North and South struggled with how to integrate black people into society as citizens, just as Virginians had earlier had to wrestle with the place of free blacks in their commonwealth. Unfortunately, the postwar American solution mirrored the antebellum Virginian solution by making free blacks second-class citizens in most places in the Union and by denying them the most basic rights of citizenship in many southern states until the 1960s.[5]

Virginia's story is thus America's: slavery promoted white liberty in the colonial period; slavery helped define liberty during the Revolution; and because slaves in America were never white, liberty itself became a racial concept. Proponents and opponents of abolition both shared this intellectual and cultural heritage. Consequently, from the Revolutionary era onward defenders of slavery turned almost immediately to racial explanations for why slaves did not deserve freedom and by 1832 began to describe slavery in terms of an affectionate bond between master and slave. They also began to redefine liberty, to limit white liberty in order to protect their interest in slavery. Both cause and effect of that shift, arguments against slavery moved away from those of the Revolutionary period, based on universal liberty and common humanity, to those of the antebellum period, based largely on ideas about white freedom, including freedom from the presence of blacks and slavery. The problems of race and liberty have persisted, from the separate-but-equal doctrine of the 1890s to the 1950s pronouncement that separate was inherently unequal to today's debates over affirmative action, racial preferences, and reparations for slavery. There is hope that just as previous generations forged the link between race and liberty, we might melt it down and end, as well, our obsession with race as we build a new America, more diverse than ever before.

5. McPherson, *Negro's Civil War*, 93–99.

Appendix A

RELIGION OF MANUMITTERS IN DEEDS OF MANUMISSION WHOSE RELIGIOUS AFFILIATION COULD BE IDENTIFIED

Religion	Year of deed	County	Name	Occupation	Freed all slaves?
Quaker	1775	Accomack	Daniel Mifflin		yes
Quaker	1782	Accomack	Thomas Crippen		yes
Quaker	1782, 1792	Mecklenburg	Thomas Madkins		yes
Quaker	1783	Mecklenburg	James Williams		?
Quaker	1791	Botetourt	James Wright		yes
Quaker	1791, 1795, 1796	Charles City	Samuel Hargrave		yes
Quaker	1796	Charles City	Mary Leadbetter		yes
Quaker	1798	Charles City	John Crew		yes
Quaker	1799	Charles City	Martha Charles		?
Quaker	1806	Charles City	Robert Evans		yes?
former Quaker (dismissed 1788)	1803	Chesterfield	Cornelius Buck	Businessman; justice of the peace	no
Baptist	1782	Accomack	William White		yes
Baptist	1790	Accomack	Levin Dix	Minister	yes
Baptist	1790	Accomack	George Layfield	Preacher	yes
Baptist	1793	Chesterfield	Reubin Winfree	Deacon	?
Baptist	1796	Charles City	James Bradley		no
Baptist?	1806	Fauquier	Alexander and Mary Loggie		?
Methodist	1783, 1802, 1805	Accomack	William Downing	Reverend	yes
Methodist	1785	Mecklenburg	James O'Kelly	Itinerant Preacher	?

APPENDIX A

Religion	Year of deed	County	Name	Occupation	Freed all slaves?
Methodist	1785, 1803	Mecklenburg	Samuel Holmes		no
Methodist	1789	Accomack	William Onions		yes
Methodist	1789, 1806	Accomack	James Melvin	Preacher	yes
Methodist	1790	Accomack	Elias Broadwater		yes
Methodist	1790	Lancaster	John Dogget	Reverend	no
Methodist	1790	Accomack	Benjamon Floyd		yes
Methodist	1790	Botetourt	Edward Mitchell	Preacher	yes
Methodist	1790, 1806	Accomack	Thomas Bagwell		no
Methodist	1791	Accomack	Henry Custis Jr. (Bayside)		no
Methodist	1791	Accomack	Thomas Evans	Surveyor; member, House of Delegates	no
Methodist	1791	Accomack	Isaiah Garrison		yes
Methodist	1792	Accomack	Johannes Watson		no[1]
Methodist	1793	Charles City	Benjamin Dancy	Minister	yes
Methodist	1798	Accomack	William Elliot		yes
Methodist	1802	Accomack	James Ashby		?
Methodist	1802	Accomack	Stephen Drummond		yes
Methodist	1803	Accomack	Richard Bloxum		?
Methodist	1804	Accomack	William Seymour		yes
Methodist	1805	Accomack	Levin Ames		yes?
Methodist	1805	Accomack	Zorobabel Ames		yes?
Methodist	1805	Accomack	Griffin Callahan	Preacher	?
Methodist	1805	Botetourt	Samuel Mitchell	Preacher?	yes
Methodist	1805	Accomack	James Poulson		yes
Methodist	1806	Accomack	Jesse Ames		yes
Methodist	1806	Accomack	Richard Ames		yes
Methodist (as of 1834)	1800	Accomack	John Edmunds		yes?
Methodist?	1793	Accomack	Thomas Ames		yes
Methodist?	1794	Charles City	John Bowry	Minister?	no
Methodist?	1802	Accomack	John Downing		?
Methodist?	1805	Accomack	Jonathan Garrison		no
Methodist?	1806	Charles City	John West		yes?

1. Freed all but one.

Religion	Year of deed	County	Name	Occupation	Freed all slaves?
Episcopal/ Methodist	1806	Accomack	Charles Snead	Ship captain	no
Episcopal	1787	Accomack	John Teackle	Merchant	yes
Episcopal	1793	Accomack	George Parker		no
Episcopal	1794	Accomack	John Cropper Jr.	Military; member, House of Delegates	yes
Episcopal	1803	Accomack	Zoro Killum		no
Episcopal	1804	Accomack	Henry Parker		no
Episcopal	1805	Accomack	Elizabeth, Ann, and Sarah Muir		no
Episcopal	1805, 1806	Accomack	John S. Ker	Merchant	no
Episcopal	1806	Accomack	Ann Muir		yes
Episcopal?	1789	Accomack	William Beavans		yes
Episcopal?	1792	Accomack	Thomas Cropper		yes
Episcopal?	1803	Accomack	William Justice		?

Appendix B

PETITIONS REGARDING SLAVERY, EMANCIPATION, AND COLONIZATION SENT TO THE HOUSE OF DELEGATES IN 1831–32

Date	Region	County	Content	Number of signers[1]
PETITIONS ASKING FOR AN END TO SLAVERY AND REMOVAL OF SLAVES AND FREE BLACKS					
12/14/31	Tidewater	Hanover	Asks for end to slavery by gradual removal of free and enslaved blacks, funded by a new tax (printed petition) Text A (see below)	9
12/14/31	Tidewater	Charles City	Society of Friends asks for gradual emancipation and removal of free blacks and slaves from Virginia	1 (secretary)
12/16/31	Tidewater	Henrico	Proposes a tax on slaves to support their removal from the state	?
12/23/31	Piedmont	Loudoun	County meeting petition asks for gradual emancipation and removal of entire colored population	9
1/16/32	Valley	Rockbridge	Asks for end to slavery by gradual removal of free and enslaved blacks, funded by a new tax (printed petition) Text A	68
1/18/32	Tidewater	King William	Asks for end to slavery by gradual removal of free and enslaved blacks, funded by a new tax (printed petition) Text A	102
1/19/32	Piedmont	Buckingham	Ladies' petition for end to slavery, asks owners to be responsible for slaves' actions	70–75
1/19/32	Valley	Augusta	Ladies' petition for speedy extirpation of slavery	215

1. In some cases the paper was torn or the signatures were faded and difficult to see, and I have marked the approximate number.

PETITIONS SENT TO HOUSE OF DELEGATES IN 1831–1832

Date	Region	County	Content	Number of signers[1]
1/20/32	Tidewater	Caroline	Asks for end to slavery by gradual removal of free and enslaved blacks, funded by a new tax (printed petition) Text A	78

PETITIONS ASKING FOR REMOVAL OF FREE PEOPLE OF COLOR

Date	Region	County	Content	Number of signers[1]
12/6/31	Tidewater	Northampton	County meeting petition asks for removal of free people of color	Ca. 200
12/7/31	Piedmont	Amelia	Asks for removal of free people of color Text B (see below)	62
12/7/31	Tidewater	Isle of Wight	Asks for removal of free people of color Text B	Ca. 61
12/8/31	Tidewater	Westmoreland	Asks for removal of free people of color (printed petition) Text B	189
12/12/31	Tidewater	York	Asks for removal of free people of color Text B	43
12/15/31	Piedmont	Goochland	Asks for removal of free people of color (printed petition) Text B	88
12/16/31	Piedmont	Buckingham	Asks for removal of free people of color, suggests plan of Thomas Jefferson be adopted	17
12/22/31	Tidewater	Nansemond	Asks for removal of free people of color Text B	33
12/23/31	Piedmont	Powhatan	Asks for removal of free people of color (newspaper clipping) Text B	93
12/27/31	Tidewater	James City	Asks for removal of free people of color (printed petition) Text B	97
12/28/31	Valley	Frederick	Asks for removal of free people of color Text B	Ca. 60
1/7/32	Tidewater	Fairfax	Asks for removal of free people of color Text B	Ca. 100
1/11/32	Tidewater	Surry	Asks for removal of free people of color (printed petition) Text B	
1/23/32	Tidewater	Northumberland	Asks for removal of free people of color who are "obnoxious to the community"	Ca. 35
2/20/32	Piedmont	Fauquier	Asks for law excluding free people of color from Virginia	119

Date	Region	County	Content	Number of signers[1]
		PETITIONS ASKING FOR REMOVAL OF FREE BLACKS AND SLAVES		
12/7/31	Piedmont	Fauquier	Asks for removal of free people of color, purchase and removal of slaves, and a constitutional amendment for federal funding to support same (printed petition) Text C (see below)	94[2]
12/8/31	Valley	Page	Asks for removal of free people of color, purchase and removal of slaves, and a constitutional amendment for federal funding to support same (printed petition) Text C	35
12/17/31	Piedmont	Nelson	Asks for removal of free people of color, purchase and removal of slaves, and a constitutional amendment for federal funding to support same (printed petition) Text C	81
12/17/31	Trans-Allegheny	Washington	Asks for removal of free people of color, and reduction of number of slaves by purchase and removal	17
12/20/31	Piedmont	Fauquier and Loudoun	Asks for removal of free people of color, purchase and removal of slaves, and a constitutional amendment for federal funding to support same (printed petition) Text C	39
12/28/31	Piedmont	Fauquier	Asks for removal of free people of color, purchase and removal of slaves, and a constitutional amendment for federal funding to support same (printed petition) Text C	16
12/30/31	Piedmont	Fauquier	Asks for removal of free people of color, purchase and removal of slaves, and a constitutional amendment for federal funding to support same (printed petition) Text C	60
1/4/32	Valley	Botetourt	Asks for removal of free people of color, purchase and removal of slaves, and a	41

2. Signers include Enock Foley, who freed his slave Fanny in 1800. See chapter 3.

PETITIONS SENT TO HOUSE OF DELEGATES IN 1831–1832   245

Date	Region	County	Content	Number of signers[1]
			constitutional amendment for federal funding to support same (printed petition) Text C	
1/23/32	Piedmont	Fauquier	Asks for amendment to U.S. Constitution to support colonization	17
PETITIONS ASKING FOR AID FOR COLONIZATION EFFORTS
12/20/31	Tidewater	Henrico ACS	Local colonization society asks for state aid	
12/21/31	Piedmont	Buckingham ACS	Local colonization society asks for state aid	4
1/3/32	Valley	Frederick ACS	Local colonization society asks for state aid	
PETITION DENOUNCING THE DEBATE
1/30/32	Tidewater	Hanover	Deprecates any action on the abolition of slavery	At least 35

TEXT A:

... [W]e now approach you, on a subject of the liveliest and deepest interest to the future happiness and quiet of this State, as well as one of the most delicate nature.

An evil has existed among us from almost the first settlement of the Commonwealth, of the heaviest and most serious character. It has grown with us, and in every moment of our advance, it has more than kept pace with us, until at last the alarming truth bursts from every lip; that if we wish peace and happiness, quiet and prosperity, the fatal, paralyzing, destroying mischief, must be removed. . . . Do not all know it is the existing curse of slavery to which we allude? . . .

For this object we approach you as the lawgivers of the land, with no moral or constitutional restrictions on your powers in the accomplishment of this great and holy purpose; a purpose which when attained will be a blessing of forever continuing effect on our own country and the unhappy and degraded race of Africans, whose presence deforms our land. . . .

Should the legislature require any facts or arguments to convince them of the imperious necessity for taking some decided measures on this subject, we most respectfully submit to them the following. . . . We affirm, that for the last forty years the black population . . . has been gradually but surely increasing in that part of the State east of the base of the Blue Ridge of mountains, in a greater ratio than the white population. . . . [The text continues with detailed explication of the demographic changes.]

. . . Let but the Commonwealth raise by a tax on the blacks, free as well as slave, a reasonable sum sufficient to defray the expense of the removal and maintenance for a time, of such as individuals may voluntarily surrender to the State, and for the purchase of a few hundred annually of the young and healthy of both sexes, and for their removal and maintenance in like manner. . . .

But these measures, your memorialists confidently believe should be accompanied by some others. The first should be, the total prohibition of emancipation by individuals, but upon the condition of removal out of the State.

The second should be, the immediate classification of the free blacks, and requiring at stated periods their removal. . . .

Your memorialists are slave-holders; this is the country of their birth. . . . Humanity must weep over a continuance of our present condition, while patriotism, self interest, and our own happiness and that of our offspring call equally strong for the application of some remedy to remove this appalling and increasing evil. . . .[3]

TEXT B:

The mistaken humanity of the people of Virginia, and of your predecessors, has permitted to remain in this Commonwealth a class of persons who are neither free men nor Slaves. The mark set on them by nature precludes their enjoyment, in this country, of the privileges of the former; and the laws of the land do not allow them to be reduced to the condition of the latter. Hence they are, of necessity, degraded, profligate, vicious, turbulent, and discontented.

More frequently than whites (probably in tenfold proportion) sustained by the charitable provisions of our poor laws, they are altogether a burden on the community. . . .

But their residence among us is yet more objectionable on other accounts. It is incompatible with the tranquility of society; their apparent exemption from want and care and servitude to business, excites impracticable hopes in

---

3. Hanover petition, 14 Dec. 1831, LP, Hanover County.

the minds of those who are even more ignorant and unreflecting and their locomotive habits fit them for a dangerous agency in Schemes Wild and visionary, but disquieting and annoying.

We would not be cruel or unchristian, but we must take care of the interest and morals of society, and of the peace of mind of the helpless in our families. It is indispensable to the happiness of the latter, that this cause of apprehension be removed. And efforts to this end are, we firmly believe, sanctioned by enlightened humanity towards the ill-fated class to whom we allude.... [I]n other lands they may become an orderly, sober, industrious, moral enlightened and christian community; and be the happy instruments of planting and diffusing those blessings over a barbarous and benighted Continent.

Your petitioners will not designate a plan of Legislative operation—they leave to the wisdom and provident forecast of the General Assembly, the conception, adoption and prosecution of the best-practicable scheme....[4]

TEXT C:

The undersigned inhabitants of the County of ... [left blank, to be filled in by respective counties] respectfully declare that they believe the time has arrived when it is highly expedient that the General Government should possess the power to raise and appropriate money to transport free persons of Colour to the coast of Africa, and also, the power to purchase slaves and transport them likewise. Therefore they petition the Legislature to take the earliest and most effectual means to procure an amendment to the Constitution of the United States, which will give the Congress of the Union, power to pass the necessary Laws to carry into effect the above stated objects.[5]

---

4. Isle of Wight petition, 7 Dec. 1831, LP, Isle of Wight County.
5. Fauquier petition, 30 Dec. 1831, LP, Fauquier County.

Bibliography

PRIMARY SOURCES

Public Records

Library of Virginia, Archives Division, Richmond
House of Delegates
    Legislative Petitions
        Accomack County
        Albemarle County
        Amelia County
        Amherst County
        Augusta County
        Bedford County
        Botetourt County
        Brunswick County
        Buckingham County
        Caroline County
        Charles City County
        Chesterfield County
        Fairfax County
        Fauquier County
        Frederick County
        Goochland County
        Halifax County
        Hanover County
        Henrico County
        Isle of Wight County
        James City County
        King and Queen County
        King William County
        Lancaster County

Loudoun County
Mecklenburg County
Miscellaneous Legislative Petitions
Nansemond County
Northampton County
Northumberland County
Powhatan County
Pittsylvania County
Rockbridge County
Surry County
Westmoreland County
York County
Minutes of the House of Delegates, 6 May 1782 to 2 July 1782
Minutes of the House of Delegates, 1784–87
Rough Bills
County Records. Free Negro and Slave Records.
Accomack County
Affidavits and Certificates about Slavery
Lists of Free Negroes
Manumissions, 1783–1814
Arlington County
Manumission Papers, 1794–1843
Botetourt County
Emancipation Papers
Charles City County
Papers and Registrations
Registers of Free Negroes
Special Court Papers, Patrols, and Guards
Chesterfield County
Registrations and Papers
Fluvanna County
Certificates of Emancipation, 1789–1802
Lancaster County
Emancipation Deeds
Free Negro Register
Middlesex County
Emancipations, 1806–10
Court Records
Dead Papers. Chesterfield County, 1808, 1810, 1814.
Chancery Papers. Chesterfield County, 1773–1821.

Library of Virginia, Microfilm Collections, Richmond
Court Order Books
    Botetourt County Circuit Superior Court of Law and Chancery. Common Law Orders, 1838–43.
    Chesterfield County Court
        Order Book 17 (1808–9)
        Order Book 18 (1810–11)
        Order Book 20 (1814–16)
Deed Books
    Accomack County
    Botetourt County
    Charles City County
    Chesterfield County
        General Index to Deeds, 1749–1913
    Fauquier County
    Lancaster County
    Mecklenburg County
    Tazewell County
    Wythe County
Registers of Free Negroes
    Chesterfield County Register of Free Negroes, No. 1, 1804–30
    Goochland County Register of Free Negroes, 1804–57
    Mecklenburg County Register of Free Negroes, No. 1, 1809–41
Personal Property Tax Records
    Accomack County
    Botetourt County
    Charles City County
    Chesterfield County
    Fauquier County
    Lancaster County
    Mecklenburg County
    Tazewell County
    Wythe County
Will Books
    Accomack County
    Botetourt County
    Charles City County
    Chesterfield County
    Fauquier County
    Lancaster County

Mecklenburg County
Tazewell County
Wythe County

Manuscripts Collections

Southern Historical Collection, University of North Carolina, Chapel Hill
Blackford Family Papers
McDowell, James, Papers
Ruffin and Meade Family Papers

University of Virginia, Charlottesville
Bonner, Mercer, and Pelham Family Papers, 1762–1888
Meade, William, to Mary Lee Custis, 1825 (from original at VHS)

Virginia Historical Society, Richmond
American Colonization Society. Virginia Branch. Records, 1823–59.
Bagby, George William, Papers
Brand, Benjamin, Papers
Burwell Family Papers
Carmichael, Mary Carter (Wellford), Papers
Carrington Family Papers
Carter, Robert, letter of 12, 14 October 1803, typescript
Cropper, John, Papers
Cropper, John, Papers, photocopies (from collection at Smith College)
Custis, Mary Lee, Papers
[Hall, Nancy Johns (Turner)]. "The Imaginationist, or Recollections of an old lady, a native of one of the Southern States, now a resident in the State of Ohio in the year 1844." Typescript by Robert C. Smythe.
Madison, Dolley (Payne) Todd, Papers
Mead, Stith, Letterbook
Nash Family Papers
Preston Family Papers
Randolph, Richard, will, typescript
Wickam, John, essay on slavery

Church Records

Eastern Shore Public Library, Accomac, Virginia
John Mason Kelso Papers
St. George's Parish, Accomack County. Records, 1793–1841.

Library of Virginia, Archives Division, Richmond

Black Creek Church, Southampton County. Minute Book, 1776–1818. [photostat of original at VBHS]
Fincastle Presbyterian Church, Botetourt County. List of Church Members, 1803.
Meherrin Baptist Association. Minute Book, 1804–25. [negative photostat of original at VBHS]
Mill Creek Baptist Church, Botetourt County. Minute Book, 1804–42.
Pleasant Vale Baptist Church, Fauquier County. Minute Book, 1799–1851. [photostat of original at VBHS]
St. George's Parish, Accomack County. Vestry Book, 1763–87.
Society of Friends. Virginia Yearly Meeting. Yearly Meeting Miscellaneous Records, 1749–1827. [photostat of originals at the Huntington Library]
Strawberry Baptist Association. Minute Book, 1787–1822. [negative photostat of original at VBHS]
Upperville Baptist Church, Fauquier County. Minute Book, 1802–1809. [photocopy of original at VBHS]

Library of Virginia, Microfilm Collections, Richmond

Accomack County. Parish Records, 1787–1819.
Broad Run Baptist Church, Fauquier County. Minute Book, 1762–1873.
Carter's Run Baptist Church, Fauquier County. Minute Book, 1816–50.
Morattico Baptist Church, Lancaster County. Minute Book, 1778–1844.
Thumb Run Primitive Baptist Church, Fauquier County. Minute Book, 1771–1890.
Westover Parish, Charles City County. Parish Register, 1833–88.

Virginia Baptist Historical Society, Richmond

Accomack Association. Minutes, 1815–24.
Bethel Baptist Church. Minutes, 1817–41.
Dover Baptist Association. Minutes, 1793–1813.
Emmaus Baptist Church. Minutes, 1792–1841.
Grove Baptist Church, Fauquier County. Minutes, 1811–52.
Ketocton Baptist Association. Minutes, 1792–1834.
Long Branch Baptist Church. Minutes, 1807–41.
Middle District Baptist Association. Annuals, 1791–1852.
North Fork Primitive Baptist Church. Minutes, 1784–1809, 1808–31.
Tomahawk Baptist Church. Records, 1787–1856.

Virginia Historical Society, Richmond

Society of Friends. Fairfax Monthly Meeting, Loudoun County.

Newspapers

Alexandria Daily Advertiser
Alexandria Expositor
Alexandria Expositor and Columbian Advertiser
Norfolk Gazette and Public Ledger
Petersburg Intelligencer / Virginia Gazette and Petersburg Intelligencer
Petersburg Republican
Richmond Enquirer
Richmond Examiner
Virginia Argus (Richmond)
Virginia Gazette and Weekly Advertiser (Richmond)
Virginia Gazette or the American Advertiser (Richmond)
Virginia Independent Chronicle (Richmond)
Virginia Independent Chronicle and General Advertiser (Richmond)
Virginia Gazette and Alexandria Advertiser (Alexandria)
Virginia Gazette (Williamsburg: Purdie & Dixon)
Virginia Gazette (Williamsburg: Rind)

Printed Laws, Legislative Materials, and Public Documents

A bill, Providing for the removal of free persons of colour from this commonwealth. [1832].
Acts passed at a General assembly of the Commonwealth of Virginia, begun . . . on Monday the fifth day of December, one thousand eight hundred and eight. . . . Washington, DC: Statute Law Book, 1832.
Aggregate amount of each description of Persons within the United States of America. Washington, DC, 1811. Reprint, New York: Norman Ross, 1990.
At a General Assembly, Begun and Held at the Capitol, in the City of Williamsburg on Monday the twentieth day of October in the year of our Lord one thousand seven hundred and seventy seven, and in the second year of the Commonwealth. Williamsburg: Alexander Purdie, 1777.
Catterall, Helen Tunnicliff, ed. *Judicial Cases concerning American Slavery and the Negro.* Vol. 1. Washington, DC: Carnegie Institution of Washington, 1926. Reprint, New York: Octagon Books, 1968.
The Code of Virginia. . . . Richmond: William F. Ritchie, 1849.
Hening, William Waller. *The Statutes at Large; Being a Collection of all the Laws of Virginia from the First Session of the Legislature, in the year 1619.* 13 vols. Richmond: Samuel Pleasants, 1809–23. Facsimile reprint, Charlottesville: University Press of Virginia, 1969.
Hening, William Waller, and William Munford. *Reports of cases argued and determined in the Supreme Court of Appeals of Virginia: with select cases relating chiefly to points*

of practice, decided by the Superior Court of chancery for the Richmond district. 4 vols. Philadelphia: Smith & Maxwell, 1808–11.

Index to Enrolled Bills of the General Assembly of Virginia, 1776–1910. Compiled by John W. Williams. Richmond: Davis Bottom, 1911.

Leonard, Cynthia Miller, comp. *The General Assembly of Virginia, July 30, 1619– January 11, 1978: A Bicentennial Register of Members.* Richmond: Virginia State Library, 1978.

Proceedings and Debates of the Virginia State Convention of 1829–30. To which are subjoined, the new constitution of Virginia, and the votes of the people. Richmond: Samuel Shepherd for Ritchie & Cook, 1830.

Return of the Whole Number of Persons within the Several Districts of the United States. Philadelphia, 1791. Reprint, New York: Norman Ross, 1990.

Return of the Whole Number of Persons within the Several Districts of the United States. Washington, DC, 1800. Reprint, New York: Norman Ross, 1990.

The Revised Code of the Law of Virginia: Being a Collection of all such acts of the General Assembly . . . as are now in force. Richmond: Thomas Ritchie, 1819.

Shepherd, Samuel. *The statutes at large of Virginia: from October session 1792, to December session 1806, inclusive, in three volumes (new series,) being a continuation of Hening.* 3 vols. Richmond: Samuel Shepherd, 1835–36. Reprint, New York: AMS Press, 1970.

Supplement, containing the Acts of the General Assembly of Virginia, . . . passed since the session of the Assembly which commenced in the year one thousand eight hundred and seven. Richmond: Samuel Pleasants, 1812.

Supplement to the Revised Code of the Laws of Virginia: being a collection of all the Acts of the General Assembly, . . . passed since the year 1819. . . . Richmond: Samuel Shepherd, 1833.

Tucker, St. George. *Blackstone's Commentaries, with notes of reference to the Constitution and laws of the federal government of the United States, and of the Commonwealth of Virginia. . . .* Philadelphia: William Young Birch & Abraham Small, 1803. http://www.lonang.com/exlibris/tucker/.

Legislative Journals (in chronological order)

Journal of the House of Delegates of Virginia. Williamsburg: Alexander Purdie, 1777.

Journal of the House of Delegates of the Commonwealth of Virginia; Begun and Held at the Capitol, in the City of Williamsburg, on Monday, the Twentieth Day of October, in the Year of Our Lord One Thousand Seven Hundred and Seventy-Seven. Richmond: Thomas W. White, 1827.

Journal of the House of Delegates of the Commonwealth of Virginia; Begun and Held at the Capitol, in the City of Williamsburg, on Monday, the Fourth Day of May, in the Year of

Our Lord One Thousand Seven Hundred and Seventy-Eight. Richmond: Thomas W. White, 1827.

Journal of the House of Delegates of the Commonwealth of Virginia; Begun and Held at the Capitol, in the City of Williamsburg, on Monday, the Fifth Day of October, in the Year of Our Lord One Thousand Seven Hundred and Seventy-Eight. Richmond: Thomas W. White, 1827.

Journal of the Senate of the Commonwealth of Virginia; begun and held in the City of Williamsburg, on Monday, the 5th day of October, in the year of our Lord 1778, and in the third year of the Commonwealth. Richmond: Thomas White, 1828.

Journal of the House of Delegates of the Commonwealth of Virginia; Begun and Held at the Capitol, in the City of Williamsburg, on Monday, the third day of May, in the year of our Lord one thousand seven hundred and seventy-nine. Richmond: Thomas W. White, 1827.

Journal of the House of Delegates of the Commonwealth of Virginia; Begun and Held in the Town of Richmond. In the County of Henrico, on Monday the First day of May, in the year of our Lord one thousand seven hundred and Eighty. Richmond: Thomas W. White, 1827.

Journal of the House of Delegates of the Commonwealth of Virginia; Begun and Held in the Town of Richmond. In the County of Henrico, on Monday the Seventh day of May, in the year of our Lord one thousand seven hundred and Eighty-one. Richmond: Thomas W. White, 1827.

Journal of the House of Delegates of the Commonwealth of Virginia; Begun and Held in the Town of Richmond. In the County of Henrico, on Monday the First day of October, in the year of our Lord one thousand seven hundred and Eighty-one. Richmond: Thomas W. White, 1828.

Journal of the House of Delegates of the Commonwealth of Virginia; Begun and Held in the Town of Richmond. In the County of Henrico, on Monday the Twenty-first day of October, in the year of our Lord one thousand seven hundred and Eighty-Two. Richmond: Thomas W. White, 1828.

Journal of the House of Delegates of the Commonwealth of Virginia; Begun and Held in the City of Richmond, in the County of Henrico, on Monday, the Eighteenth Day of October, in the Year of Our Lord One Thousand Seven Hundred and Eighty-Four. Richmond: Thomas W. White, 1827.

Journal of the House of Delegates of the Commonwealth of Virginia; Begun and Held in the City of Richmond, in the County of Henrico, on Monday, the Seventeenth Day of October, in the Year of Our Lord One Thousand Seven Hundred and Eighty-Five. Richmond: Thomas W. White, 1828.

Journal of the House of Delegates of the Commonwealth of Virginia; Begun and Holden in the City of Richmond, in the County of Henrico, on Monday, the Fifteenth Day of

October, in the Year of Our Lord One Thousand Seven Hundred and Eighty-Seven. Richmond: Thomas W. White, 1828.

Journal of the House of Delegates of the Commonwealth of Virginia; Begun and Holden in the City of Richmond, in the County of Henrico, on Monday, the Twentieth Day of October, in the Year of Our Lord One Thousand Seven Hundred and Eighty-Eight. Richmond: Thomas W. White, 1828.

Journal of the House of Delegates of the Commonwealth of Virginia, begun and held at the capitol, in the city of Richmond, on Monday, the fifth day of December, One Thousand Eight Hundred and Thirty-One. Richmond: Thomas Ritchie, 1831 [1832].

ADDITIONAL PRIMARY SOURCES

Address of the Board of Managers of the American Colonization Society, to the Auxiliary Societies and the people of the United States. Washington, DC: Davis & Force, 1820.

Address of the Colonization Society of Loudoun, Virginia. Annapolis: J. Green, 1819.

Address of the Managers of the American Colonization Society, to the People of the United States, Adopted at their Meeting, June 19, 1832. Washington, DC: James C. Dunn, 1832.

Ambler, Charles H. *The Life and Diary of John Floyd, Governor of Virginia, an Apostle of Secession, and the Father of the Oregon Country.* Richmond: Richmond Press, 1918.

[Appleton, Nathaniel]. *Considerations on Slavery, in a Letter to a Friend.* Boston: Edes & Gill, 1767.

Asbury, Francis. *Journal of Rev. Francis Asbury, Bishop of the Methodist Episcopal Church.* 3 vols. New York: Lane & Scott, 1852.

Benezet, Anthony. *Brief Considerations on Slavery, and the Expediency of its Abolition....* Burlington, NJ: Collins, 1773.

———. *A Caution and Warning to Great Britain and her Colonies, in a short Representation of the Calamitous State of the Enslaved Negroes in the British Dominions....* Philadelphia: Henry Miller, 1766.

———. *Observations on the Inslaving, importing, and purchasing of Negroes....* Germantown, PA: Christopher Sower, 1759.

Berry, Henry. *The Speech of Henry Berry (of Jefferson,) in the House of Delegates of Virginia, on the Abolition of Slavery.* Richmond: Thomas W. White, 1832.

Bolling, Philip A. *The Speeches of Philip A. Bolling (of Buckingham,) in the House of Delegates of Virginia, on the policy of the state in relation to her colored population: Delivered on the 11th and 25th of January, 1832.* 2nd ed. Richmond: Thomas W. White, 1832.

Brodnax, William H. *The Speech of William H. Brodnax on the policy of the state with respect to its colored population, delivered January 19, 1832.* Richmond: Thomas W. White, 1832.

Brookes, George S. *Friend Anthony Benezet*. Philadelphia: University of Pennsylvania Press, 1937.

Brown, John Thompson. *The Speech of John Thompson Brown . . . on the abolition of slavery, delivered Wednesday, January 18, 1832*. Richmond: T. W. White, 1832. Reprint, Richmond: Charles H. Wynne, 1860.

Carey, Mathew. *Letters on the Colonization Society; and of its probable results . . . Addressed to the Hon. C. F. Mercer, M.H.R.U.S.* 4th ed. Philadelphia, 1832.

Chandler, John A. *The Speech of John A. Chandler (of Norfolk County) in the House of Delegates of Virginia, on the Policy of the State with Respect to her Slave Population. Delivered January 17, 1832*. Richmond: Thomas W. White, 1832.

Coke, Thomas. *Extracts of the Journals of the Rev. Dr. Coke's Five Visits to America.* London: Paramore, 1793.

Colfax, Richard H. *Evidence against the views of the abolitionists, consisting of physical and moral proofs, of the natural inferiority of the negroes.* New York: James T. M. Bleakley, 1833.

Controversy between Caius Gracchus and Opimius in reference to the American Society for Colonizing the Free People of Colour of the United States, first published in the Richmond Enquirer. Georgetown, DC: James C. Dunn, 1827.

[Cooper, David]. *A Mite cast into the Treasury: or Observations on Slave-Keeping.* Philadelphia: Crukshank, [1772].

Dew, Thomas R. "Review of the Debate in the Virginia Legislature, 1831–32." In *The Pro-Slavery Argument; as maintained by the most distinguished writers of the southern states, containing the several essays on the subject, of Chancellor Harper, Governor Hammond, Dr. Simms, and Professor Dew,* 287–490. Charleston: Walker, Richards, 1852.

Faulkner, Charles. *The Speech of Charles Jas. Faulker (of Berkeley) in the House of Delegates of Virginia, on the Policy of the State with Respect to her Slave Population. Delivered January 20, 1832*. Richmond: Thomas W. White, 1832.

Fauquier County, Virginia Register of Free Negroes, 1817–1865. Abstracted and indexed by Karen King Ibrahim, Karen Hughes White, and Courtney Gaskins. 1993. Reprint, Lovettsville, VA: Willow Bend Books, 1993.

Gott, John K. *Fauquier County, Virginia Marriage Bonds, 1759–1854 and Marriage Returns, 1785–1848.* Bowie, MD: Heritage Books, 1989.

Jarratt, Devereux. *The Life of the Reverend Devereux Jarratt.* Foreword by David L. Holmes. Baltimore: Warner & Hanna, 1806. Reprint, Cleveland: Pilgrim Press, 1995.

Jefferson, Thomas. *Notes on the State of Virginia.* Introduction by Thomas Perkins Abernethy. New York: Harper & Row, Harper Torchbooks, 1964.

———. *A Summary View of the Rights of British America. Set forth in some Resolutions intended for the Inspection of the present Delegates of the People of Virginia, now in Convention.* Williamsburg: Clementina Rind, 1774. Facsimile reprint with an introduction by Thomas P. Abernethy, New York: Scholars' Facsimiles & Reprints, 1943.

Justice, Hilda, comp. *Life and Ancestry of Warner Mifflin.* Philadelphia: Ferris & Leach, 1905.

Lee, Arthur. *Extract from an Address in the Virginia Gazette, of March 19, 1767.* Philadelphia, 1770.

"Letters of Edward Coles—Second Instalment." *William and Mary Quarterly,* 2nd ser., 7 (1927): 97–113.

Littleton, Mark [John Pendleton Kennedy]. *Swallow Barn, or a Sojourn in the Old Dominion.* 2 vols. Philadelphia: Carey & Lea, 1832.

Madison, James. *The Writings of James Madison, comprising his public papers and his private correspondence, including numerous letters and documents now for the first time printed.* Edited by Gaillard Hunt. 9 vols. New York: G. P. Putnam's Sons, 1900–1910.

Marshall, Thomas. *The Speech of Thomas Marshall (of Fauquier) in the House of Delegates of Virginia, on the policy of the state with respect to its colored population, delivered January 14, 1832.* 2nd ed. Richmond: Thomas W. White, 1832.

McKitrick, Eric L. *Slavery Defended: The Views of the Old South.* Englewood Cliffs, NJ: Prentice Hall, 1963.

M'Dowell, James. *The Speech of James M'Dowell, Jr. (of Rockbridge,) in the House of Delegates of Virginia, on the Slave Question: Delivered Saturday, January 21, 1832.* Richmond: Thomas W. White, 1832.

Minutes of the Columbia Baptist Association, Held by Agreement, at the Grove Meetinghouse, Fauquier county, Va. September 7th, 8th and 9th, 1820. Alexandria: Samuel H. Davis, 1820.

Minutes of the Dover Baptist Association, held at Bestland Meeting House in Essex County, Virginia. October 14th, 1797. Richmond: John Dixon, n.d.

Minutes of the Dover Baptist Association, held at the Glebe-Landing Meeting House in Middlesex County, Virginia. October 12, 1793. Richmond: T. Nicolson, 1793.

Minutes of the Ketocton Baptist Association, Continued at Broad-Run Meeting-House, Fauquier County, Virginia, August 4, 1799 [actually 1798]. Winchester: Richard Bowen, n.d.

Minutes of the Ketockton Baptist Association, Held at Frying-Pan, Loudoun County, August 1797. N.p., n.d.

Minutes of the Ketockton Baptist Association, Held at Happy Creek Meeting House, in Frederick County, Virginia, August 1801. Winchester: G. Trisler, 1801.

Minutes of the Ketockton Baptist Association, Held at Little-River, Loudoun County, Virginia, August, 1794. N.p., n.d.

Minutes of the Ketocton Baptist Association, Held at Long-Branch in Fauquier County, August, 1792. N.p., n.d.

Minutes of the Ketocton Baptist Association, Holden at New Valley, Louden County, Virginia; August 17, and continued by adjournment till 20. Baltimore: Warner & Hanna, 1810.

Minutes of the Ketocton Baptist Association, Holden at Waterlick, Shenandoah County, Virginia, August 16, 1810 and continued by adjournment until the 19th inclusive. . . . Alexandria: Cottom & Stewart, 1810.

Minutes of the Ketocton Baptist Association. Thumb Run, Fauquier County, Virginia, August, 1796. N.p., n.d.

Minutes of the Middle District Association held at Tomahawk, Chesterfield, Saturday and Monday, August 27th and 29th, 1831. N.p., n.d.

Pleasants, Robert. "Some account of the first settlement of Friends in Virginia. . . . ," edited by Kenneth L. Carroll. In Carroll, "Robert Pleasants on Quakerism," *Virginia Magazine of History and Biography* 86 (1978): 3–15.

"Queries Relating to Slavery in Massachusetts," *Collections of the Massachusetts Historical Society*, 5th ser., 3 (1877).

Randolph, Thomas J. *The Speech of Thomas J. Randolph (of Albemarle) in the House of Delegates of Virginia, on the Abolition of Slavery: Delivered Saturday, January 21, 1832.* 2nd ed. Richmond: Thomas W. White, 1832.

Rutland, Robert A., ed. *The Papers of George Mason, 1725–1792.* 3 vols. Chapel Hill: University of North Carolina Press, 1970.

Somerset County, Maryland, Coventry Parish Church Record. 2 vols. Roanoke, TX: Jody Powell, 1993.

Stuart, C. *Remarks on the Colony of Liberia, and the American Colonization Society. With some account of the settlement of coloured people, at Wilberforce, Upper Canada.* London: J. Messeder, 1832.

Taylor, John. *Arator: Being a Series of Agricultural Essays, Practical and Political: in Sixty-Four Numbers.* Edited with an introduction by M. E. Bradford. Indianapolis: Liberty Classics, 1977. Originally published Petersburg, VA: Whitworth & Yancey, 1818.

Tucker, George. *Letter to a Member of the General Assembly of Virginia, on the subject of the Late Conspiracy of the Slaves; with a Proposal for their Colonization.* Baltimore: Bonsal & Niles, 1801.

[Tucker, George?]. *Letters from Virginia, translated from the French.* Baltimore: Fielding Lucas, jr., 1816.

Tucker, St. George. *A Dissertation on Slavery: with a Proposal for the Gradual Abolition of it in the State of Virginia.* Philadelphia: Mathew Carey, 1796. Reprint, Westport, CT: Negro Universities Press, 1970.

Turman, Nora Miller. *Marriage Records of Accomack County, Virginia, 1776–1854, Recorded in Bonds, Licenses and Ministers' Returns.* Bowie, MD: Heritage Books, 1994.

———. *St. James Church and St. George Parish, 1763–1990, Accomack County, Virginia.* Onancock, VA: Eastern Shore Printers, 1990.

A View of Exertions Lately Made for the purpose of Colonizing the Free People of Colour in the United States, in Africa, or elsewhere. Washington, DC: Jonathan Elliot, 1817.

Walker, Susie Wilkins, and Nora Miller Turman, comps. "Accomack County, Virginia, Soldiers and Sailors in America's War for Independence, April 1775 to December 1783." Onancock, VA: Eastern Shore Chapter of the Daughters of the American Revolution, 1975.

Walsh, Robert. *African Colonization. An enquiry into the origin, plan and prospects of the American Colonization Society.* Fredericksburg, VA: Arena Office, 1829.

Wesley, John. *The Works of the Rev. John Wesley.* Vol. 10. New York: J. & J. Harper, 1827.

Woolman, John. *Some considerations on the Keeping of Negroes.* Philadelphia: James Chattin, 1754.

SECONDARY SOURCES

Albert, Peter Joseph. "The Protean Institution: The Geography, Economy, and Ideology of Slavery in Post-Revolutionary Virginia." PhD diss., University of Maryland, 1976.

Ambler, Charles Henry. *Sectionalism in Virginia from 1776 to 1861.* Chicago: University of Chicago Press, 1910.

Andrews, Dee E. *The Methodists and Revolutionary America, 1760–1800: The Shaping of an Evangelical Culture.* Princeton, NJ: Princeton University Press, 2000.

Aptheker, Herbert. *American Negro Slave Revolts.* New York: Columbia University Press, 1943. 50th anniv. ed. New York: International Publishers, 1993.

———. *Nat Turner's Slave Rebellion, Together with the Full Text of the So-called "Confessions" Nat Turner Made in Prison in 1831.* New York: Humanities Press, 1966.

Babcock, Theodore Stoddard. "Manumission in Virginia, 1782–1806." Master's thesis, University of Virginia, 1973.

Bailyn, Bernard. *The Ideological Origins of the American Revolution.* Enl. ed. Cambridge, MA: Harvard University Press, Belknap Press, 1992.

Ballagh, James Curtis. "Introduction to Southern Economic History—the Land System—Part 1." In *Annual Report of the American Historical Association for the Year 1897*, 99–129. Washington, DC: American Historical Association, 1898.

Banner, James M., Jr. *To the Hartford Convention: The Federalists and the Origins of Party Politics in Massachusetts, 1789–1815.* New York: Knopf, 1970.

Barnes, Alton Brooks Parker. *John Cropper: A Life Fully Lived.* Onley, VA: A Lee Howard Book, 1989.

Bean, R. Bennett. *The Peopling of Virginia.* Boston: Chapman & Grimes, 1938.

Beeman, Richard R. *The Evolution of the Southern Backcountry: A Case Study of Lunenburg County, Virginia, 1746–1832.* Philadelphia: University of Pennsylvania Press, 1984.

———. *The Old Dominion and the New Nation, 1788–1801.* Lexington: University Press of Kentucky, 1972.

Bell, Derrick. "Racial Realism after We're Gone: Prudent Speculations on America in a Post-Racial Epoch." In *Critical Race Theory: the Cutting Edge,* edited by Richard Delgado. Philadelphia: Temple University Press, 1995.

Bennet, Hugh H. *Thomas Jefferson, Soil Conservationist.* Miscellaneous Publication No. 548. Washington, DC: United States Department of Agriculture Soil Conservation Service, April 1944.

Bennett, William W. *Memorials of Methodism in Virginia, from its Introduction into the State, in the year 1772, to the year 1829.* Richmond: privately published, 1871.

Berlin, Ira. *Many Thousands Gone: The First Two Centuries of Slavery in North America.* Cambridge, MA: Harvard University Press, Belknap Press, 1998.

———. *Slaves without Masters: The Free Negro in the Antebellum South.* New York: Pantheon Books, 1974.

Bogger, Tommy L. *Free Blacks in Norfolk, Virginia, 1790–1860: The Darker Side of Freedom.* Charlottesville: University Press of Virginia, 1997.

Breen, T. H., and Stephen Innes. *"Myne Owne Ground": Race and Freedom on Virginia's Eastern Shore, 1640–1676.* New York: Oxford University Press, 1980.

Breit, Frederick Emil. "The Anti-Slavery Sentiment of Virginia from 1830–1860." Master's thesis, University of Washington, 1934.

Brown, Kathleen M. *Good Wives, Nasty Wenches, and Anxious Patriarchs: Gender, Race, and Power in Colonial Virginia.* Chapel Hill: University of North Carolina Press for the Omohundro Institute of Early American History and Culture, 1996.

Brown, Robert E., and B. Katherine Brown. *Virginia, 1705–1786: Democracy or Aristocracy?* East Lansing: Michigan State University Press, 1964.

Bruce, Dickson D., Jr. *The Rhetoric of Conservatism: The Virginia Convention of 1829–30 and the Conservative Tradition in the South.* San Marino, CA: Huntington Library, 1982.

Bruce, Philip Alexander. *Economic History of Virginia in the Seventeenth Century: An Inquiry into the Material Condition of the People, Based upon Original and Contemporaneous Records.* New York: Macmillan, 1907.

Buckley, Thomas E. "Unfixing Race: Class, Power, and Identity in an Interracial Family." *Virginia Magazine of History and Biography* 102 (1994): 349–80.

Cassell, Frank A. "Slaves of the Chesapeake Bay Area and the War of 1812." *Journal of Negro History* 57 (1972): 144–55.
"Constructing Race." Special issue, *William and Mary Quarterly*, 3rd ser., 44 (1997).
Cover, Roger M. *Justice Accused: Antislavery and the Judicial Process*. New Haven, CT: Yale University Press, 1975.
Coyner, Martin Boyd, Jr. "John Hartwell Cocke of Bremo: Agriculture and Slavery in the Ante-Bellum South." PhD diss., University of Virginia, 1961.
Craven, Avery Odell. "Soil Exhaustion as a Factor in the Agricultural History of Virginia and Maryland, 1606–1860." *University of Illinois Studies in the Social Sciences* 13, no. 1 (1925): 9–172.
Crow, Jeffrey J., and Larry E. Tise, eds. *The Southern Experience in the American Revolution*. Chapel Hill: University of North Carolina Press, 1978.
Curtis, Christopher M. "Jefferson's Chosen People: Legal and Political Conceptions of the Freehold in the Old Dominion from Revolution to Reform." PhD diss., Emory University, 2002.
Dain, Bruce. *A Hideous Monster of the Mind: American Race Theory in the Early Republic*. Cambridge, MA: Harvard University Press, 2002.
Daniel, W. Harrison. "Virginia Baptists and the Negro in the Early Republic." *Virginia Magazine of History and Biography* 80 (1972): 60–69.
Davis, David Brion. *Challenging the Boundaries of Slavery*. Cambridge, MA: Harvard University Press, 2003.
———. *The Problem of Slavery in the Age of Revolution, 1770–1823*. Ithaca, NY: Cornell University Press, 1975. Reprint, New York: Oxford University Press, 1999.
———. *The Problem of Slavery in Western Culture*. Ithaca, NY: Cornell University Press, 1966. Reprint, New York: Oxford University Press, 1988.
Degler, Carl N. *Neither Black nor White: Slavery and Race Relations in Brazil and the United States*. Madison: University of Wisconsin Press, 1986.
Dillon, Merton L. *Slavery Attacked: Southern Slaves and Their Allies, 1619–1865*. Baton Rouge: Louisiana State University Press, 1990.
Dorsey, Bruce. *Reforming Men and Women: Gender in the Antebellum City*. Ithaca, NY: Cornell University Press, 2002.
Dunn, Richard S. "Black Society in the Chesapeake, 1776–1810." In *Slavery and Freedom in the Age of the American Revolution*, edited by Ira Berlin and Ronald Hoffman, 49–82. Urbana: University of Illinois Press, 1983.
Egerton, Douglas R. "Black Independence Struggles and the Tale of Two Revolutions: A Review Essay." *Journal of Southern History* 65 (1998): 95–116.
———. *Charles Fenton Mercer and the Trial of National Conservatism*. Jackson: University Press of Mississippi, 1989.

---. *Gabriel's Rebellion: The Virginia Slave Conspiracies of 1800 and 1802.* Chapel Hill: University of North Carolina Press, 1993.

---. *He Shall Go Out Free: The Lives of Denmark Vesey.* Madison, WI: Madison House, 1999.

Einhorn, Robin L. "Patrick Henry's Case against the Constitution: The Structural Problem with Slavery." *Journal of the Early Republic* 22 (2002): 549–73.

Elkins, Stanley, and Eric McKitrick. *The Age of Federalism.* New York: Oxford University Press, 1993.

Ely, Melvin Patrick. *Israel on the Appomattox: A Southern Experiment in Black Freedom from the 1790s through the Civil War.* New York: Knopf, 2004.

Ericson, David F. *Antislavery and Proslavery Liberalism in Antebellum America.* New York: New York University Press, 2000.

Essah, Patience. *A House Divided: Slavery and Emancipation in Delaware, 1638–1865.* Charlottesville: University Press of Virginia, 1996.

Essig, James D. *The Bonds of Wickedness: American Evangelicals against Slavery, 1770–1808.* Philadelphia: Temple University Press, 1982.

Evans, Paul Otis. "The Ideology of Inequality: Asbury, Methodism, and Slavery." PhD diss., Rutgers University, 1981.

Fauquier County Bicentennial Committee. *Fauquier County, Virginia, 1759–1959.* Warrenton, VA, 1959.

Faust, Drew Gilpin. *James Henry Hammond and the Old South: A Design for Mastery.* Baton Rouge: Louisiana State University Press, 1982.

---, ed. *The Ideology of Slavery: Proslavery Thought in the Antebellum South, 1830–1860.* Baton Rouge: Louisiana State University Press, 1981.

Fehrenbacher, Don E. *Constitutions and Constitutionalism in the Slaveholding South.* Athens: University of Georgia Press, 1989.

---. *The Slaveholding Republic: An Account of the United States Government's Relations to Slavery.* Completed and edited by Ward M. McAfee. New York: Oxford University Press, 2001.

Fields, Barbara J. "Slavery, Race, and Ideology in the United States of America." *New Left Review* 181 (May–June 1990), 95–118.

Finkelman, Paul. "Thomas Jefferson and Antislavery: The Myth Goes On." *Virginia Magazine of History and Biography* 104 (1994): 193–228.

Finnie, Gordon E. "The Antislavery Movement in the Upper South before 1840." *Journal of Southern History* 35 (1969): 319–42.

Fischer, David Hackett, and James C. Kelly. *Bound Away: Virginia and the Westward Movement.* Charlottesville: University Press of Virginia, 2000.

Foner, Eric. *Free Soil, Free Labor, Free Men: The Ideology of the Republican Party before the Civil War.* London: Oxford University Press, 1970.

Ford, Lacy K., Jr. *Origins of Southern Radicalism: The South Carolina Upcountry, 1800–1860.* New York: Oxford University Press, 1988.

Fredrickson, George M. *The Black Image in the White Mind: The Debate on Afro-American Character and Destiny, 1817–1914.* New York: Harper & Row, 1971. Reprint, Middletown, CT: Wesleyan University Press, 1987.

Freehling, Alison Goodyear. *Drift toward Dissolution: The Virginia Slavery Debate of 1831–1832.* Baton Rouge: Louisiana State University Press, 1982.

Freehling, William W. "The Founding Fathers and Slavery." *American Historical Review* 77 (1972): 81–93.

———. *The Road to Disunion: Secessionists at Bay, 1776–1854.* New York: Oxford University Press, 1990.

Frey, Sylvia R. *Water from the Rock: Black Resistance in a Revolutionary Age.* Princeton, NJ: Princeton University Press, 1991.

Genovese, Eugene D. *The Political Economy of Slavery: Studies in the Economy and Society of the Slave South.* 2nd ed. Middletown, CT: Wesleyan University Press, 1989.

Gragg, Larry Dale. *Migration in Early America: The Virginia Quaker Experience.* Ann Arbor, MI: UMI Research Press, 1980.

Gravely, William B. "Methodist Preachers, Slavery, and Caste: Types of Social Concern in Antebellum America." *Duke Divinity School Review* 34 (1969): 209–29.

Gray, Lewis Cecil. *History of Agriculture in the Southern United States to 1860.* New York: P. Smith, 1941.

Hadden, Sally E. *Slave Patrols: Law and Violence in Virginia and the Carolinas.* Cambridge, MA: Harvard University Press, 2001.

Hamilton, Phillip. "Revolutionary Principles and Family Loyalties: Slavery's Transformation in the St. George Tucker Household of Early National Virginia." *William and Mary Quarterly,* 3rd ser., 55 (1998): 531–56.

Handlin, Oscar, and Mary F. Handlin. "Origins of the Southern Labor System." *William and Mary Quarterly,* 3rd ser., 7 (1950): 199–222.

Henry, William Wirt. *Patrick Henry: Life Correspondence, and Speeches.* 3 vols. 1891. Reprint, New York: Burt Franklin, 1969.

Heyrman, Christine Leigh. *Southern Cross: The Beginnings of the Bible Belt.* New York: Knopf, 1997.

Hickin, Virginia P. "Antislavery in Virginia, 1831–1861." PhD diss., University of Virginia, 1968.

Hidden, Martha W. *How Justice Grew: Virginia Counties; An Abstract of Their Formation.* Jamestown 350th Anniversary Historical Booklet, no. 19. Williamsburg: Virginia 350th Anniversary Celebration Corporation, 1957.

Higginbotham, A. Leon, Jr. *In the Matter of Color: Race and the American Legal Process; The Colonial Period.* Oxford: Oxford University Press, 1978.

Hinshaw, William Wade. *Encyclopedia of American Quaker Genealogy.* 6 vols. Ann Arbor: Edwards Brothers, 1936–50.

Holton, Woody. *Forced Founders: Indians, Debtors, Slaves, and the Making of the American Revolution in Virginia.* Chapel Hill: University of North Carolina Press for the Omohundro Institute of Early American History and Culture, 1999.

Horsman, Reginald. *The Causes of the War of 1812.* Philadelphia: University of Pennsylvania Press, 1962.

Iaccarino, Anthony Alfred. "Virginia and the National Contest over Slavery in the Early Republic, 1780–1833." PhD diss., UCLA, 1999.

Isaac, Rhys. *The Transformation of Virginia, 1740–1790.* New York: Norton, 1982.

Isenberg, Nancy. *Sex and Citizenship in Antebellum America.* Chapel Hill: University of North Carolina Press, 1998.

Jackson, Luther Porter. *Free Negro Labor and Property Holding in Virginia, 1830–1860.* New York: Appleton-Century, 1942.

Jenkins, William Sumner. *Pro-Slavery Thought in the Old South.* Chapel Hill: University of North Carolina Press, 1935.

Johnston, James Hugo. *Race Relations in Virginia and Miscegenation in the South, 1776–1860.* Amherst: University of Massachusetts Press, 1970.

Jordan, Winthrop D. *White over Black: American Attitudes toward the Negro, 1550–1812.* New York: Norton, 1968.

Kettner, James H. "Persons or Property? The Pleasants Slaves in the Virginia Courts, 1792–1799." In *Launching the "Extended Republic": The Federalist Era,* edited by Ronald Hoffman and Peter J. Albert, 136–55. Charlottesville: University Press of Virginia, 1996.

Kulikoff, Allan. *Tobacco and Slaves: The Development of Southern Cultures in the Chesapeake, 1680–1800.* Chapel Hill: University of North Carolina Press, 1986.

Lebsock, Suzanne. *The Free Women of Petersburg: Status and Culture in a Southern Town, 1784–1860.* New York: Norton, 1984.

Ledbetter, Judith F. *In This Place I Delivered My Soul: The Methodists of Charles City, Virginia.* Charles City, VA: Memorial United Methodist Church, 1995.

Lewis, Jan. "The Problem of Slavery in Southern Political Discourse." In *Devising Liberty: Preserving and Creating Freedom in the New American Republic,* edited by David Thomas Konig, 268–97. Stanford, CA: Stanford University Press, 1995.

Locke, Mary Stoughton. *Anti-Slavery in America from the Introduction of African Slaves to the Prohibition of the Slave Trade (1619–1808).* Boston: Ginn, 1901. Reprint, Gloucester, MA: Peter Smith, 1965.

MacKethan, Lucinda H. Introduction to *Swallow Barn, or a Sojourn in the Old Dominion,* by John Pendleton Kennedy. Rev. ed. 1851. Reprint, 2 vols. in 1, Baton Rouge: Louisiana State University Press, 1986.

Macleod, Duncan J. *Slavery, Race, and the American Revolution.* London: Cambridge University Press, 1974.

MacMaster, Richard K. "Arthur Lee's 'Address on Slavery': An Aspect of Virginia's Struggle to End the Slave Trade, 1765–1774." *Virginia Magazine of History and Biography* 80 (1972): 141–57.

———. "Liberty or Property? The Methodists Petition for Emancipation in Virginia, 1785." *Methodist History* 10 (1971): 44–55.

Majewski, John. *A House Dividing: Economic Development in Pennsylvania and Virginia before the Civil War.* Cambridge: Cambridge University Press, 2000.

Mariner, Kirk. *Revival's Children: A Religious History of Virginia's Eastern Shore.* Salisbury, MD: Peninsula Press, 1979.

Mathews, Donald G. *Slavery and Methodism: A Chapter in American Morality, 1780–1845.* Princeton, NJ: Princeton University Press, 1965.

Matthews, Albert. "Notes on the Proposed Abolition of Slavery in Virginia in 1785." *Publications of the Colonial Society of Massachusetts* 6 (1904): 370–80.

McColley, Robert. *Slavery and Jeffersonian Virginia.* 2nd ed. Urbana: University of Illinois Press, 1978.

McCoy, Drew R. *The Elusive Republic.* Chapel Hill: University of North Carolina Press for the Institute of Early American History and Culture, 1980. Reprint, New York: Norton, 1982.

McCurry, Stephanie. *Masters of Small Worlds: Yeoman Households, Gender Relations, and the Political Culture of the Antebellum South Carolina Low Country.* New York: Oxford University Press, 1995.

McCusker, John J., and Russell R. Menard. *The Economy of British America, 1607–1789.* Chapel Hill: University of North Carolina Press for the Institute of Early American History and Culture, 1985.

McGraw, Marie Tyler. "The American Colonization Society in Virginia, 1816–1832: A Case Study in Southern Liberalism." PhD diss., George Washington University, 1980.

McPherson, James M. *The Negro's Civil War: How American Blacks Felt and Acted during the War for the Union.* New York: Ballantine Books, 1991. First published 1965 by Pantheon.

Melish, Joanne Pope. *Disowning Slavery: Gradual Emancipation and "Race" in New England, 1780–1860.* Ithaca, NY: Cornell University Press, 1998.

Miller, John Chester. *The Wolf by the Ears: Thomas Jefferson and Slavery.* New York: Free Press, 1977.

Moore, Glover. *The Missouri Controversy, 1819–1821.* Lexington: University of Kentucky Press, 1953.

Morgan, Edmund S. *American Slavery, American Freedom: The Ordeal of Colonial Virginia.* New York: Norton, 1975.

Morgan, Kenneth. "George Washington and the Problem of Slavery." *Journal of American Studies* 4 (2000): 279–301.

Morgan, Philip D. *Slave Counterpoint: Black Culture in the Eighteenth-Century Chesapeake and Lowcountry.* Chapel Hill: University of North Carolina Press for the Omohundro Institute of Early American History and Culture, 1998.

Morris, Thomas D. *Southern Slavery and the Law, 1619–1865.* Chapel Hill: University of North Carolina Press, 1996.

Moss, Roger W., Jr. "Isaac Zane, Jr., a 'Quaker for the Times.'" *Virginia Magazine of History and Biography* 77 (1969): 291–306.

Mullin, Gerald W. *Flight and Rebellion: Slave Resistance in Eighteenth-Century Virginia.* London: Oxford University Press, 1972.

Mullin, Michael. *Africa in America: Slave Acculturation and Resistance in the American South and the British Caribbean, 1736–1831.* Urbana: University of Illinois Press, 1994.

Najar, Monica. "'Meddling with Emancipation': Baptists, Authority, and the Rift over Slavery in the Upper South." *Journal of the Early Republic* 25 (2005): 157–86.

Nash, Gary B. *Forging Freedom: The Formation of Philadelphia's Black Community, 1720–1840.* Cambridge, MA: Harvard University Press, 1988.

———. *Race and Revolution.* Madison, WI: Madison House, 1990.

Nash, Gary B., and Jean Soderlund. *Freedom by Degrees: Emancipation in Pennsylvania and Its Aftermath.* New York: Oxford University Press, 1991.

Newman, Richard S. *The Transformation of American Abolitionism: Fighting Slavery in the Early Republic.* Chapel Hill: University of North Carolina Press, 2002.

Nicholls, Michael L. "'The squint of freedom': African-American Freedom Suits in Post-Revolutionary Virginia." *Slavery and Abolition* 20 (1999): 47–62.

Oakes, James. *The Ruling Race: A History of American Slaveholders.* New York: Knopf, 1982. Reprint, New York: Vintage Books, 1983.

Oates, Stephen B. *The Fires of Jubilee: Nat Turner's Fierce Rebellion.* New York: Harper & Row, 1975. Reprint, New York: HarperPerennial, 1990.

Ott, Thomas O. *The Haitian Revolution, 1789–1804.* Knoxville: University of Tennessee Press, 1973.

Patterson, Orlando. *Slavery and Social Death: A Comparative Study.* Cambridge, MA: Harvard University Press, 1982.

Peterson, Merrill D. *Thomas Jefferson and the New Nation.* New York: Oxford University Press, 1970.

Quarles, Benjamin. *The Negro in the American Revolution.* Chapel Hill: University of North Carolina Press for the Institute of Early American History and Culture, 1961. Reprint with a new foreword by Thad. W. Tate and a new intro. by Gary B. Nash, 1996.

Risjord, Norman K. "The Virginia Federalists." *Journal of Southern History* 33 (1967): 486–517.

Robarge, David. *A Chief Justice's Progress: John Marshall from Revolutionary Virginia to the Supreme Court.* Contributions in American History, ed. Jon L. Wakelyn, 185. Westport, CT: Greenwood, 2000.

Robert, Joseph Clarke. *The Road from Monticello: A Study of the Virginia Slavery Debate of 1832.* Historical Papers of the Trinity College Historical Society, ser. 24. Durham, NC: Duke University Press, 1941.

Roediger, David R. *The Wages of Whiteness: Race and the Making of the American Working Class.* London: Verso, 1991.

Rose, Willie Lee. "The Domestication of Domestic Slavery." In *Slavery and Freedom*, ed. William W. Freehling, 18–36. New York: Oxford University Press, 1982.

Rothman, Joshua D. *Notorious in the Neighborhood: Sex and Families across the Color Line in Virginia, 1782–1861.* Chapel Hill: University of North Carolina Press, 2003.

Rowland, Kate Mason. *The Life of George Mason, 1725–1792.* 2 vols. New York, 1892.

Russell, John H. *The Free Negro in Virginia.* Baltimore: John Hopkins Press, 1913. Reprint, New York: Negro Universities Press, 1969.

Rutman, Darrett B., and Anita H. Rutman. *A Place in Time: Middlesex County, Virginia, 1650–1750.* New York: Norton, 1984.

Salmon, Emily J., ed. *A Hornbook of Virginia History.* 3rd ed. Richmond: Virginia State Library, 1983.

Sayre, Robert Duane. "The Evolution of Early American Abolitionism: The American Convention for Promoting the Abolition of Slavery and Improving the Condition of the African Race, 1794–1837." PhD diss., Ohio State University, 1987.

Schmidt, Fredrika Teute, and Barbara Ripel Wilhelm. "Early Proslavery Petitions in Virginia." *William and Mary Quarterly*, 3rd ser., 30 (1973): 133–46.

Schwarz, Philip J. "Emancipators, Protectors, and Anomalies: Free Black Slaveowners in Virginia." *Virginia Magazine of History and Biography* 95 (1987): 317–38.

———. *Migrants against Slavery: Virginians and the Nation.* Charlottesville: University Press of Virginia, 2002.

———. *Twice Condemned: Slaves and the Criminal Laws of Virginia, 1795–1865.* Baton Rouge: Louisiana State University Press, 1988.

Scully, Randolph. "'Somewhat Liberated': Baptist Discourses over Race and Slavery in Nat Turner's Virginia, 1770–1840." *Explorations in Early American Culture* 5 (2001): 328–71.

Sellers, Charles. *The Market Revolution: Jacksonian America, 1815–1846.* New York: Oxford University Press, 1991.

Shade, William G. *Democratizing the Old Dominion: Virginia and the Second Party System, 1824–1861.* Charlottesville: University Press of Virginia, 1996.

Sidbury, James. *Ploughshares into Swords: Race, Rebellion, and Identity in Gabriel's Virginia, 1730–1810.* Cambridge: Cambridge University Press, 1997.

Smith, Jean Edward. *John Marshall: Definer of a Nation.* New York: Holt, 1996.

Soderlund, Jean R. *Quakers and Slavery: A Divided Spirit.* Princeton, NJ: Princeton University Press, 1985.

Spangler, Jewel L. "Becoming Baptists: Conversion in Colonial and Early National Virginia." *Journal of Southern History* 67 (2001): 243–86.

Spoede, Robert William. "William Allason: Merchant in an Emerging Nation." PhD diss., College of William and Mary, 1973.

Staudenraus, P. J. *The African Colonization Movement, 1816–1865.* New York: Columbia University Press, 1961.

Stevenson, Arthur L. *Natives of the Northern Neck of Virginia in the Methodist Ministry.* Brevard, NC: privately published, 1973.

Stevenson, Brenda E. *Life in Black and White: Family and Community in the Slave South.* Oxford: Oxford University Press, 1996.

Stoner, Robert Douthat. *A Seed-Bed of the Republic: A Study of the Pioneers in the Upper (Southern) Valley of Virginia.* Kingsport, TN: Kingsport Press for the Roanoke Historical Society, 1982.

Sutton, Robert P. *Revolution to Secession: Constitution Making in the Old Dominion.* Charlottesville: University Press of Virginia, 1989.

Sydnor, Charles S. *Gentlemen Freeholders: Political Practices in Washington's Virginia.* Chapel Hill: University of North Carolina Press, 1952.

Thomas, Arthur Dicken, Jr. "The Second Great Awakening in Virginia and Slavery Reform, 1785–1837." DTheol diss., Union Theological Seminary, Richmond, 1981.

Thompson, Edith E. B. "A Scottish Merchant in Falmouth in the Eighteenth Century." *Virginia Magazine of History and Biography* 39 (1931): 230–38.

Tise, Larry E. *Proslavery: A History of the Defense of Slavery in America, 1701–1840.* Athens: University of Georgia Press, 1987.

Turtle, Gordon Bruce. "Slave Manumission in Virginia, 1782–1806: The Jeffersonian Dilemma in the Age of Liberty." Master's thesis, University of Alberta, 1991.

U.S. Department of Agriculture. *Soil: The Yearbook of Agriculture, 1957.* Washington, DC: USGPO, 1957.

van Riemsdijk, Tatiana Ilona Maria. "Time and Property from Heaven: Wealth, Religion, and Reform in Chesapeake Society, 1790–1832." PhD diss., UCLA, 1999.

Varon, Elizabeth R. *We Mean to Be Counted: White Women and Politics in Antebellum Virginia.* Chapel Hill: University of North Carolina Press, 1998.

Vivian, Alfred. *First Principles of Soil Fertility.* New York: Orange Judd, 1908.

Watson, Harry L. *Liberty and Power: The Politics of Jacksonian America.* New York: Hill & Wang, 1990.

Weeks, Stephen B. *Southern Quakers and Slavery: A Study in Institutional History*. Baltimore: Johns Hopkins Press, 1896.
Wheeler, Robert Anthony. "Lancaster County, Virginia, 1650–1750: The Evolution of a Southern Tidewater Community." PhD diss., Brown University, 1972.
White, Blanche Sydnor. *History of the Baptists on the Eastern Shore of Virginia, 1776–1959*. Baltimore: Furst, 1959.
White, Shane. *Somewhat More Independent: The End of Slavery in New York City, 1770–1810*. Athens: University of Georgia Press, 1991.
Whitman, T. Stephen. *The Price of Freedom: Slavery and Manumission in Baltimore and Early National Maryland*. Lexington: University Press of Kentucky, 1997. Reprint, New York: Routledge, 2000.
Wiencek, Henry. *An Imperfect God: George Washington, His Slaves, and the Creation of America*. New York: Farrar, Straus & Giroux, 2003.
Wiethoff, William E. *A Peculiar Humanism: The Judicial Advocacy of Slavery in High Courts of the Old South, 1820–1850*. Athens: University of Georgia Press, 1996.
Williams, William H. *Slavery and Freedom in Delaware, 1639–1865*. Wilmington, DE: Scholarly Resources, 1996.
Wills, Garry. *Inventing America: Jefferson's Declaration of Independence*. Garden City, NY: Doubleday, 1978.
Wood, Gordon. *Creation of the American Republic, 1776–1787*. New York: Norton, 1969.
———. *The Radicalism of the American Revolution*. New York: Vintage Books, 1993.
Zilversmit, Arthur. *The First Emancipation: The Abolition of Slavery in the North*. Chicago: University of Chicago Press, 1967.

Index

Abba, Tom, 153–54
abolitionists: laws regarding, 118; in North, 197, 236
abolition of slavery: desire of in Virginia, xiii, 4, 14, 18, 87, 91–93, 214–15, 220–21, 225–27, 228, 230–31; lobbying for in Virginia, 9–10; in North, 6, 104; as northern goal, 174; proposals for in Virginia, xiii, 6, 101–6, 108–9, 199–202, 211, 213–14, 217–19; and race, 86–87, 103–4, 106–9, 225–27, 228; slave rebellion to be prevented by, 107, 115, 215–16. *See also* antislavery sentiment; emancipation of slaves
A.C., 108–9, 115
Accomack County: economy and history of, 40; free blacks in, 132–33, 136–39; freedom suits in, 69–70; manumission in, ix, 43, 46, 50, 54–56, 59–62, 68, 69, 75–80 passim, 83, 89, 131–33, 155, 239–41; manumission opposed by residents of, 62, 112; manumission supported by residents of, 65, 115–16; removal of free blacks attempted in, 136–39, 203
Adams, John Quincy, 134
Address on Slavery, An (Lee), 12
Africa: colonization of slaves to, 107, 164–71, 233, 247; slaves imported from, 2, 23, 24, 26, 107, 116
African Americans: laws regarding, 2–4, 34, 116–18, 119–21, 128, 134, 233; manumission by, 52, 66–69, 70, 73–75, 83, 132–33;

population of, xi, 3, 4, 6, 24, 40, 42, 43, 44–45, 78, 86, 110–11, 125, 127, 131, 135, 158, 163, 180, 182. *See also* free blacks; slaves
Albemarle County, 140, 180n26, 193, 200, 207n16, 222
Albert, William, 158
Amelia County, 94n13, 205n14, 243
American Colonization Society, xvi, 165–71, 195, 245. *See also* colonization of free blacks
American Revolution: antislavery sentiment promoted by, xi–xii, 3, 5–7, 9, 12, 18, 21, 23, 27, 29, 32, 36–38, 51, 60–62, 85, 92, 104, 116, 122, 123, 128, 163–64, 182, 198, 199, 225; meaning of, contested, 6, 185, 191–93; and proslavery sentiment, 20, 37, 93, 123, 190; race affected by, 7, 88, 126; slavery affected by, ix, x, xv, 35, 38; slaves in, 14–15, 35–37. *See also* War for Independence
Ames, Zorobabel, 132
Anderson, Hezekiah, 207n16
antiemancipation sentiment: in early national era, 86, 87, 90, 93–94, 97–98, 112–26; fear of slave rebellion as cause of, 115–21, 129; in petitions to the legislature, 85, 93–94; racial disorder as stimulus to, 112–13, 121; in Revolutionary era, 18–20, 86; in slavery debate of 1831–32, 214–17. *See also* defenses of slavery; manumission law of 1782: opposition to; proslavery sentiment

anti-importation law of 1778: amendments to, 26–27, 116, 128; freedom provision of, 25–26, 69, 128; legislative history of, 21–25; oath required by, 26n33; provisions of, 25–26; slaveholders' support of, 22–25

antislavery sentiment: in antebellum era, 164, 167–69, 170, 199–202, 210, 212–29; among Baptists, 10–12, 86, 96–101; change over time in, 163–64, 92, 181, 201–2; and colonization of African Americans, 101, 102–3, 106, 107, 163–64, 167–71, 206; in slavery debate of 1831–32, 212–29; in early national period, 85–86, 92–93, 97–99; among Federalists, 61; in free-labor ideology, 163, 225–27, 236; in laws, 35–36; in manumission, xi, xvi, 39, 43–46, 53–63, 79–80, 85; among Methodists, 10–12, 69, 83, 86, 88–93, 95–96, 100–101; in petitions to the legislature, 199–202, 208–9, 242; as political, xii, xvi, 86, 183–84, 234; among Quakers, 6–10, 12, 15–16, 18, 69, 86, 100–101, 199; and race, 87–88, 92–93, 101–8, 114, 128, 224, 225–27; in Revolutionary era, x, xv–xvi, 6–16, 17, 21, 53–62, 110; in Revolutionary ideology, xi, 85, 92, 97, 104, 175, 182, 199; among secular elite, 12–14, 101–9, 175; as self-interest, 220–21, 224–27; among slaves, 14–15; and slave trade, 21, 27; in western Virginia, 182, 195, 225–27, 228; among women, 168–69, 201. *See also* abolition of slavery; American Revolution: antislavery sentiment promoted by

Asbury, Francis, 60n25, 89, 91, 93, 96, 101, 109, 129

Augusta County, 201, 242

Bagwell, Jack, 136

Baptists: antislavery action a failure among, 86, 99, 127–28; as antislavery advocates, 6, 7, 10–11, 86, 127–28; black preachers among, 100; as compared to other denominations, 16, 95–96, 100–101; emancipation plan of, x; manumission by, 55, 57–58, 59, 239; policy toward free blacks among, 100; race among, 160–61; slavery debated among, x, 96–101; as threat to slavery, 11, 49, 91; and Virginia Baptist General Committee, 11, 57n21, 97–99

Barbour, Philip P., 173, 186, 190

Barrow, David, 11, 97

Bayly, Richard Drummond, 65–66, 68

Belknap, Jeremy, 104

Bell, Jane, 132, 139

Benezet, Anthony, 8, 10, 12n15

Berry, Henry, 215n29, 218–19, 224

Bias, Stephen, 140

Billy (slave), 119

Binford, Samuel, 158

Black Creek Church, 97

Bland, Richard, 14

Botetourt County: economy and history of, 42, 180–81; manumission in, 43, 46, 60, 62, 68, 76, 78, 89, 239–40; petition from, 244

Brodnax, William, 207n16, 208–9, 214n28, 217–19, 222

Brooke County, 207n16

Brown, John Thompson, 207n16, 211n23, 215–17

Brunswick County, 93, 94n14, 207n16

Bryan, Daniel, 175, 176, 182

Bryce, Archibald, Jr., 207n16, 229–31

Buckingham County, 199–200, 242, 243, 245

Burwell, John, 127, 181

Butterwood Nan, 147–49

Campbell, John, 207n16

Carey, Mathew, 165n3, 197n2

Caroline County, 23–24, 121n57, 202, 242

Carr, Judge, 156

Carter, Henry, 159

Carter, Priscilla, 159

Chandler, John, 215n29, 217

Charles City County: antislavery petition from, 199, 208, 242; economy and history of, 40; manumission in, 43, 46, 56n20, 57, 59, 68, 75, 76, 78, 239, 240; manumission law amendment supported in, 114n45; population of, 182

Charles v. Hunnicutt, 156
Chesterfield County: African Americans in, 71, 139; coal mined in, 181n27; economy and history of, 40; manumission in, 43, 46, 68, 75, 76, 77n46, 78, 131–32, 239; Tomahawk Baptist Church in, 160
citizenship: for free blacks, 5n5, 131, 139, 140, 169, 238; rights of, 149, 187, 189, 209; as white, xv, 5, 37
Clay, Henry, 176n21, 218
Cobb, Jeremiah, 207n16
Cochrane, Alexander, 133
Coke, Thomas, 89–91, 93, 95, 96, 100, 109
Coles, Edward, 211, 213
colonization of free blacks: advocation of, in citizens' petitions to the legislature, 199–206, 242–47; in antislavery plans, xiii, 101, 102–3, 106, 107, 163–64, 167–69, 170, 199–202, 206; discussion of, in slavery debate of 1831–32, 230–33; free blacks' rejection of, 171, 238; Lincoln as advocate of, 238; Mercer as advocate of, 165–66; Northampton County support of, 203–4; opposition to, 170, 235; and race, 171; slavery supported by, 165, 166, 170, 203, 206; State Rights ideology as barrier to, 172, 176, 178; women's support of, 168–69
Colonization Society of Virginia, 168, 170
Constitution of the United States, 13, 172, 173, 175, 176, 183n47, 245, 247
Corbin, George, 50n13, 60, 62
Cropper, John, Jr.: as manumitter, ix–xi, xv, 60, 62, 84, 241; Revolutionary war experience of, 60–61, 62; as slaveholder, 84
Cumberland County, 11

Daniel, William, 222
debate over slavery, 1831–32, x, xi, 197–98; abolition schemes proposed in, 2, 13, 217–19; final report of, 229–31; property rights discussed in, 213–17; race discussed in, 224; reasons for, 206–7, 208–9, 210–12; significance of, 212; slavery attacked in, 219, 220–21, 225–27, 228; slavery defended in, 220, 221–24, 227; structure of, 211–12; white safety discussed in, 215–17
Declaration of Independence, 1, 9, 13, 175, 190, 192, 214, 220
defenses of slavery: in antebellum era, 176–79, 185, 190–92, 213–29; based on law, 215; based on plantation ideal, 227; based on practicality, 17, 19–21, 209, 221–22; based on property rights, 93, 192, 214, 215, 217; based on race, 17, 19–20, 38, 224; based on republican ideals, 19, 20, 38, 222; based on Revolutionary principles, 93–94, 192; based on slavery's inevitability, 223–24; based on slaves' happiness, 177, 219, 222–23, 235; based on the Bible, 94, 100, 177; in early national era, 91, 93–94; in Revolutionary era, 16–21. *See also* antiemancipation sentiment, proslavery sentiment
Delaware, 9, 16, 55
Democratic Party, 236
demographic change in Virginia, xii, 86, 110–11, 163, 179–81, 194–95
Dew, Thomas, 235–36
Dinwiddie County, 123, 207n16, 209
Dover Association (Baptists), 98
Duck Creek Monthly Meeting (Quakers), 55
Dunmore, Earl of (John Murray), 15, 23
Dunmore's Proclamation of 1775, 15

Eastern Shore. *See* Accomack County; Northampton County
Elam, Richard, 160
emancipation of slaves: A.C. on, 108–9; attitudes toward, 29–31, 32, 33, 65, 72, 115–16, 118, 122, 123–25, 129, 130, 141, 146, 175–77, 230–31; Baptists on, x, 96–101; and colonization, xiii, 101, 102–3, 107, 163, 164–66, 168–69, 170, 195, 199–202, 206, 232–33, 242, 244, 245–47; Declaration of Rights as stimulus to, 32; discussion of, in Missouri Crisis, 173–75; discussion of, in slavery debate of 1831–32, 211–19, 227; discussion of, in Virginia Constitutional Convention of 1829–30, 187–89, 190–92; Fairfax on, 107;

emancipation of slaves (*continued*)
George Tucker on, 107; individual acts of (*see under* manumission; manumitters); Jefferson on, 102–3; laws regarding, 3, 34, 116, 125; by legislature, 30–31; Methodist petition advocating, 91–93, 94; Methodist rules promoting, 10–11, 83; in northern states, 6, 47n8; opposition to (*see* antiemancipation sentiment); petitions to the legislature in favor of, 199–202; among Quakers, 8–9, 10, 31–32, 34–35, 55–56; and race, xii, xiii, 83–84, 87, 102–3, 106, 109, 121, 125–26, 128, 171, 224, 238; in slave societies, 28; St. George Tucker on, 104–7; in War for Independence, 15, 35–36; in War of 1812, 135. *See also* abolition of slavery; manumission
environmentalism, xiv, 17
Episcopalians, 60, 167, 168, 241
Evans, Thomas, 115–16

Fairfax, Ferdinando, x, 107–8, 109, 165
Fairfax, George William, 13
Fairfax County, 23, 68, 205n14, 243
Faulkner, Charles, 215, 218–19
Fauquier, Governor, 24
Fauquier County: bill offered by delegate from, 123; division of Virginia decried in, 229; economy and history of, 40–42; manumission in, 43, 46, 68, 76, 78, 239; petitions to the legislature from, 158, 243, 244; property rights defended by delegate from, 214; race relations in, 131, 146–47
Federalists, 60–61, 118, 125n64, 172, 181n28
Fisher, Miers, 207n16
Fleming, William, 29, 156
Floyd, John, 197, 206, 210, 211–12
Fluvanna County, 207n16
Fox, George, 7
Frederick County, 182, 205n14, 207n16, 243, 245
free blacks: as citizens, 5n5, 131, 139, 140, 169; economic position of, 143; as illegal residents of Virginia, 135–38, 146; laws regarding, 2–4, 34, 116–18, 119–21, 134, 233; manumission by, 52, 64, 66, 67–69, 70, 73, 75, 83, 132–33; as members of the community, 139–47; petitions of, to the legislature, 138–41, 144–45; population of, 3–4, 43, 44–45, 77n46, 86, 110–11, 125, 131, 135, 158, 163, 180, 182; racial system threatened by, xiii, 3–4, 19, 83, 86, 87, 109–13, 117–21, 128–29, 158–61, 203–6, 219; relationship of, with former owners, 52, 69, 143; as scapegoats, 110, 129, 206; in seventeenth century, 62; social position of, 139–47, 158–61; in urban areas, 75, 111, 143; in War for Independence, 35; white ambivalence toward, 135–38, 146; white desire to remove, 29, 102–3, 104, 106, 125, 128, 135–38, 202–6, 207–8, 230–33, 237–38 (*see also* colonization of free blacks); white fear of, xiii, 114, 116, 123–24, 137–38, 203–6
freedom suits, 69–70, 118, 147–57
free-labor ideology, 163, 185–86, 224–26, 227, 236
Friend, Edward, 160
Friend to Liberty, 18, 21
Fry, Harry, 91

Gabriel, 118–19, 125
Gabriel's plot, xvi, 107, 109–10, 111, 118–19, 120, 121, 125, 129, 165, 206
Garrison, William Lloyd, 197
gender: in manumission, 67–69, 73–75; political participation defined by, 175, 189; and race, 2, 99, 105–6, 123–24, 160, 189
General Assembly of Virginia: Quakers' lobby of, 8–9, 33–34; views of, on manumission, 114–15. *See also* House of Delegates of Virginia, Senate of Virginia
Genovese, Eugene, 73
George, 28
Georgia, 26
Gholson, James, 207n16, 214, 216, 223–24
Golden Rule. *See under* Quakers
Goochland County, 205n14, 243
Goode, William, 209, 210–12
Green, John W., 153n39, 187

Griffith, John, 8
Grigsby, Hugh Blair, 186

Haiti, xvi. *See also* Saint Domingue
Halifax County, 89–90, 94n13, 95, 114n45, 214
Hall, Nancy Turner, 164n2, 169
Hamitic myth, 94n14
Hanover County, 23, 92n10, 112, 188, 202, 207n16, 208, 242, 245
Happy Creek church, 98
Harrison, Benjamin, 113
Hartford Convention, 172
Heaveningham, John, 67n34, 132
Henderson, Littleton, 137
Henderson, Richard, 136
Hening, William W., 168n8
Henrico County, 63n29, 67n34, 76n44, 92n10, 112–13, 114–15, 242, 245
Henry, Patrick, 10, 13, 24–25, 29, 193n47
Henry County, 127, 184
Holder of Slaves, 18–21, 38
Hook v. Nanny Pagee and her children, 150–51
House of Burgesses: colonial legislation of, 2–3, 23; manumission law considered by, 14; representation to, 126
House of Delegates of Virginia: colonization supported in, 165, 166; slavery debate of 1831–32 vote in, 229–31; manumission ban considered by, 123–25; manumission law amendments considered by, 113–14; manumission law considered by, 28–34; manumission law repeal considered by, 113; members of, 60, 61, 65; Methodist antislavery petition considered by, 94–95; and Nat Turner's rebellion committee, 207–8; petitions from African Americans considered by, 28, 139n15; representation to, 126, 181, 182, 184, 186–87; response of, to Missouri Crisis, 174–75; slave trade ban considered by, 24–25. *See also* debate over slavery, 1831–32; General Assembly of Virginia
Hudgins v. Wrights, 147–52

Indians, 2, 4, 19, 147, 148, 149, 151, 171
Isaac v. West, 155
Isle of Wight County, 205n14, 243

Jack, 169
James City County, 205n14, 243
Jefferson, Thomas: abolition proposal of, 4, 14, 102–3, 107, 108, 165, 200, 214; on African Americans, 103, 109; and colonization of African Americans, 102–3, 165–66; and Declaration of Independence, 1, 13, 214; and Enforcement Act, 172; influence of, 104–5, 213–14; and *Notes on the State of Virginia*, 101–3; on political reform in Virginia, 127, 184, 186; on race, 85, 103, 151; on slavery, x, xi, 13–14, 164, 170, 173–74, 178; and *Summary View of the Rights of British America*, 13–14
Johnson, Lucy, 142, 144–45, 146
Johnson, Patty, 142, 144
Johnson, Samuel, ix, xvi, 130–31, 138, 140–46, 158, 186
Johnston, Peter, 124
Joynes, John, 137
Justice, Robin, 133
Juveniles Vindex, 87
Juveniles Vindicis, 87, 88, 92

Kennedy, John Pendleton, 177
Kentucky, 26, 172
Ketocton Baptist Association, x, 98–100
King George County, 29
King William County, 114n45, 202, 242
Knox, Alexander, 222, 225, 227–28, 229

Lancaster County, 40; manumission in, 43, 46, 57, 62, 64, 68, 70, 76, 77, 78, 83, 240
Lee, Arthur, 12, 13
Lee, Henry, 23
Lee, Richard Henry, 22
Lee, Thomas Ludwell, 2n1, 7
Leigh, Benjamin Watkins: "inchoate freedom" coined by, 154; on slavery debate of 1831–32, 236; on Tom Abba case, 153–54;

Leigh, Benjamin Watkins (*continued*)
  in Virginia Constitutional Convention of 1829–30, 186, 187, 189–92
Liberia, 166, 169, 203, 204, 218, 232
liberty: as an American Revolutionary ideal, 1, 3–5, 7, 8, 18, 36, 62, 122, 124, 189–93, 220; as fragile, 227; limits on, 129, 155–56, 164, 190–92, 223, 238; as a natural right, 10, 51, 53, 55n, 58, 60, 92, 123, 154, 220; and property rights, 176, 192; and race (*see under* race); slavery as preserver of (*see under* slavery); slavery in tension with (*see under* slavery); slave trade not supported by, 8; suffrage as a measure of, 127, 188–89; as universal, 238; as white, xiii–xiv, 3–5, 120–21, 147–52, 171, 189, 226–27, 238
Lincoln, Abraham, 238
Littleton, Mark. *See* Kennedy, John Pendleton
Locke (pseudonym), 236
Locke, John, 8, 189
Loudoun County, 45n7, 131, 136, 139n15, 165, 180, 200–201, 202, 242, 244
Louisiana, 106
Love, John, 123–24, 142n20

Madison, James: and colonization of African Americans, 165; on manumission law, 94–95, 113; on political reform in Virginia, 184; on politics of slavery and emancipation, 5–6, 94–95, 113; and Robert Pleasants, 10; on slavery, x, 13; in Virginia Constitutional Convention of 1829–30, 186
Malvin, Rebecca, 145
Malvin, Sam, 145
Malvin, Spencer, 145
Malvin, Thomas T. Withers, 145, 146
manumission: age of slaves at, 71–72, 73; as antislavery act, 39, 43–44, 51, 53–62, 63; ban on, considered, 123–25; by Baptists, 55, 57–58, 59, 239; in cities, 74–75; and concubinage, 70–71; control of slaves through, 39, 44, 65–66, 81–82, 83–84, 128, 140, 146; in deeds, 47–49, 53, 63, 80; delay of, 53, 63, 72, 79–83, 152–55; economic factors regarding, 62, 72–80, 83; by Federalists, 60, 61; formal contractual mode of, 48n10; by free blacks, 52, 66, 67–69, 70, 73, 75, 83, 132–33; freedom suits as stimulus to, 69–70; gender in, 67–69, 73–75; and growth of free black population, 39, 44; and master-slave relations, 64–67, 70–72, 81–82; meanings of, to Virginians, 47–53; by Methodists, 55, 56–57, 59–60, 62, 77, 79–80, 83, 239–41; natural rights philosophy as influence on, 54–56, 59, 60–62, 84; opposition to, 62, 112–17, 118, 120–26; practice of, after 1806, 131–33, 157; practice of, in 1782–93, 39, 53–62; practice of, in 1794–1806, 39, 63–72; practice of, in 1805–6, 72; by Quakers, 9–10, 31–32, 34–35, 54, 55–56, 56n20, 59, 77; regional variations in, 73–78, 83; religion as influence on, 55–60, 62; as a reward, 63–66, 80, 131–33, 146; in rural areas, 73–74; as self-purchase, 66–68, 73, 74–75; sex as a factor in, 73–75; slave rebellion prevented by, 66; slavery's decline indicated by, 62; slaves' influence on, 64–67; surnames added after, 50, 58; two-race system threatened by, 47, 83–84; in wills, 53, 63, 80. *See also under* Accomack County; Botetourt County; Charles City County; Chesterfield County; Fauquier County; Lancaster County; Mecklenburg County; Piedmont region; Tidewater region; Trans-Allegheny region; Valley region; Wythe County
manumission law of 1691, 3, 29
manumission law of 1723, 3, 28, 29
manumission law of 1782, ix, 154–55; amending of, 116–17, 125, 134–35; amendments proposed to, 113–14, 122–25; assessment of, 34–35; effects of, 34–35, 39, 43, 47, 64–69, 83–84, 129; 1806 amendment to, 85, 125, 135, 137–38; legislative history of, 28–34; opposition to, 92–95, 113–14, 121–26; practice v. ideas of, 112, 128; provisions of, 34

manumitted slaves: Abraham, 55; Annes, 50; Arrow, Cyrus Rose, 69; Banks, George, 71; Banks, Thomas, 71; Barshaba, 80; Beck, William, 31; Bell, Jane, 132, 139; Bias, Stephen, 140; Bob, 156–57; Caleb, 68; Cary, Archy, 132; Cloe, 80; Cupid, 82; Davis, Fanny, 49; Davy, 68; Derry, 68; Downing, Solomon, 68; Duke, 64, 66, 68; Eliza, 64–65; Fanny, 68; Fraction, Nancy, 71; Frank (by Schwartz), 156–57; Frank (by Silverthorn and Wagonman), 68; George (by Chilton), 64; George (by Goode), 51; George (by Potter), 59–70; Hannah (by Hale), 68; Hannah (mother of Tom Abba), 153–54; Hannah (by West), 155; Hope, John (Barber Caesar), 31; Howard, Minta, 52, 69; Howard, Reubin (father), 51, 52, 57; Howard, Reubin (son), 52, 69; Isaac, 155; James (by Leatherbury), 68; James (by Ward), 48, 68; Jesop, Thomas, 70; Jessup, Tom, 68, 70; Juno, 80; Justice, Bowman, 133; Justice, Eve, 133; Justice, Peggy, 133; Kirk, Thomas, 68; Kitt, 30; Laws, Chriss, 68; Letty, 156–57; Lewis, 68; Liddia, 50; Lucy, 79; Luke (by Ames), 48; Luke (by Ball), 64–65; Major, 70; Mary, 154; Mathew, 52; Nancy, 69; Ned, 79; Parker, Betty, 68; Parris, 54; Patience, Judy, 64; Patty, 68, 75; Pegg, 31; Peter (by Ashby and Ashby), 54; Peter (by Spiers), 55; Pile, Nace, 68; Pleasant, 54; Polly, 156–57; Rachel, 79; Robin, 68; Sancho, 68; Sarah (by Graves), 81; Sarah (by Williams), 9; Sarah (by J. Withers), 71; Skurrey, Dick, 132; Solomon, 68; Teackle, 55; Wagnor, 80; Walles, James, 71; Westley, 68; William, 68

manumitters: Ames, Richard, 48; Ames, Zorobabel, 132; Andrews, Anna Maria, 70; Ashby, James and Matilda, 54; Ball, William, 64; Banks, Alexander, 71; Bayly, Richard Drummond, 68; Bell, John, 55; Bell, Levin, 55; Booth, John, 55; Bowry, John, 57, 240; Bradford, Caleb, 49–50; Branch, Benjamin, 51; Brent, Richard, 141; Buck, Cornelius, 68; Callahan, Griffin, 80, 240; Carter, Robert, 111; Chichester, Doddridge, 68; Chilton, Thomas, 68; Chilton, William, 50, 64; Corbin, George, 60; Crippen, Thomas, 49, 55; Cropper, John, Jr., 60–62; Dancy, Benjamin, 57, 79; Degges, John, 57; Digges, Edward, 141; Dix, Levin, 58; Dogget, John, 57; Downing, John, 68; Eustace, Anne and Hancock, 68; Evans, Thomas, 61, 115–16; Featherstone, Henry, 154; Foley, Enock, 49, 68; Gaskins, Thomas, 68; George Pickett, 68; Goode, Thomas, 51; Goodson, Samuel and William, 71; Graves, Nathaniel, 80; Griffin, Mary, 69; Hale, Joseph, 68; Hancock, George, 62; Herndon, George, 49, 68; Heveningham, John, 132; Holliday, William, 154; Holmes, Samuel, Jr., 79; Howard, Reubin, 51, 69; Irby, Hardyman, 64; James, Bridgett, 50; Jeffries, Swepson, 80; Jenkins, Frank, 52; Johnson, Gideon, 64; Justice, Robin, 132–33; Justice, William, 68; Ker, John S., 61, 62, 241; Layfield, George, 57–58; Leatherbury, Thomas, 68; Maddison, Caesar, 69; Madkins, Thomas Durham, 54; Mann, William, 68; Mayo, Joseph, 114; McEntire, John and Mary, 68; Michael, Adruaner, 55; Mifflin, Daniel, 55; Mifflin, Warner 9; Mitchell, Edward, 56; Muir, Ann, 82; Parker, George, 51, 52; Parker, Henry, 68; Parker, John, 58; Parramore, William, 60; Pickett, Martin, 68; Potter, Thomas Wood, 69–70; Savage, Robinson, 68; Schwartz, Mr., 156–57; Sévére Gallé, 64, 68; Silverthorn, William, 68; Spiers, William, 55; Stockly, Charles, 60; Sturman, Foxhall, 82; Tatham, Ezekiel, 52; Teackle, John, 60; Wagonman, Joseph, 68; Ward, Jesse, 48, 68; West, Abel, 155; Williams, James, 9; Withers, Jesse, 71

Maria v. Surbaugh, 154–55
Marshall, John, 167–68, 170, 186, 214
Marshall, Thomas, 214, 221, 226, 236
Maryland, 69, 74, 84, 134

Mason, George: and anti-importation law, 26; on expulsion of freed slaves, 114; and Fairfax County Resolves, 23; slavery opposed by, 12–13, 209; slave trade opposed by, 22–23, 26; and Virginia Declaration of Rights, 1–2, 4, 6
M'Dowell, James, 221, 223, 225–26, 228, 237
Mead, Stith, 56
Meade, William, 167, 168
Mecklenburg County: anti-Methodist petition from, 94n13; conservative views of delegate from, 209; economy and history of, 40, 77; manumission in, 40, 43, 46, 54, 56n20, 59–60, 68, 76, 77, 78, 239
Mercer, Charles Fenton, 165–66, 167, 170, 180
Methodists: in Accomack County, 59, 89; as antislavery advocates, 6, 7, 10–12, 69, 86, 88–96, 101, 127–28; antislavery rules of, 10–11, 79–80, 83, 95, 99; Baltimore Christmas Conference of, 10; colonization of African Americans supported by, 168; as compared to other denominations, 16, 95–96, 100–101; failure of antislavery action by, 16, 83, 91, 95–96, 127–28; in Gabriel's plot, 118, 119; manumission by, 55, 56–57, 60, 62, 77, 79–80, 83, 239–41; numbers of, in Virginia, 89n5; 1785 antislavery campaign of, 88–96, 109, 113, 177; as threat to slavery, 11, 91
Mifflin, Daniel, 9, 45n7, 55, 62, 239
Mifflin, Warner, 9, 16, 33–34, 55, 62
Minor, John, 125
Missouri Crisis, xi, xii, xvi, 162–63, 164, 171–79, 187, 197
Mitchell, Edward, 56
Monroe, James, x, 119, 165, 166, 186, 187, 190–91
Montesquieu, Baron de (Charles-Louis de Secondat), 8, 61n26
Montgomery County, 42, 78
Moore, Samuel, 207n16, 209, 220
Morgan, Edmund, xii
Morgan, Mr., 156–57
Morris, Richard, 188

Nansemond County, 23, 205n14, 243
Nat Turner's rebellion, x, xii, xvi, 196–97; debate on (see debate over slavery, 1831–32); petitions on, to the legislature, 198–206
negro, 157–60
Nelson County, 244
Newton, Willoughby, 207n16
New York, 47, 50, 214
Nicholas, Carter J., 168n8
Norfolk, 75n44, 111, 143
Northampton County, 61n26, 203–4, 232, 243
Northumberland County, 205, 243
Notes on the State of Virginia (Jefferson), 101–3, 105n33
Nottoway County, 207n16

Ohio, 101, 124, 140
Outten, Jim, 137

Page, Ann, 168–69
Page County, 244
Patrick County, 184
Patteson, William, 221
Pendleton, Edmund, 4, 14, 102
Pennsylvania, 16, 17–18, 42, 47, 180, 214
person of color, xvi, 157–60
Petersburg, 75n44, 111, 131, 132, 207n16, 215
Pharoah (slave), 119
Piedmont region: antislavery in, 242; history and economy of, 24, 40, 73, 110, 180, 221; manumission in, 40, 43, 73, 75, 77, 78, 83; political positions of inhabitants of, 181n28, 183n30, 214; slavery debated in, 98; slave trade supported in, 24; support for a constitutional convention in, 184; support for colonization in, 199–201, 205, 242–45
Pittsylvania County, 94n13, 207
Pleasants, Robert, 6n6, 9–10, 12n15, 32, 32n42, 113, 153
Pleasants v. Pleasants, 153, 154, 156
Powhatan County, 29, 139n15, 205n14, 243
Presbyterians, 95n15, 168
Preston, William, 212, 215, 220, 237
Preston amendment, 212, 220, 229, 231n57

Prince George County, 23
property rights in slaves: addressing of, in emancipation schemes, 105, 108, 213–14; emancipation prevented by, 123–24, 214; manumission as among, 123–24; protection of, in manumission, 31, 33, 34, 116; slavery defended through, 192–93, 215–16; versus liberty, 28, 116, 148–49; versus safety, 214–15, 216
proslavery sentiment: in antebellum era, 177, 185, 212–29, 235–36; as part of slave society, 127; racial arguments in, 17, 19–20, 235; in Revolutionary era, 6, 16–21; slaves portrayed as happy in, 20, 177, 222–23. *See also* antiemancipation sentiment; defenses of slavery

Quakers: as antislavery advocates, 9–10, 29–34, 45, 53, 62, 69, 86, 170, 199; as compared to other denominations, 16, 96, 100–101; in Gabriel's plot, 118; Golden Rule of, 7, 9, 16; manumission by, 9–10, 31–32, 34–35, 54, 55–56, 56n20, 59, 77; Methodists compared to, 91, 95, 101; presence of, in Virginia, 16, 59, 62, 83, 101; slavery opposed by, xv, 6, 7–10, 11, 12, 15–16, 20, 199, 201, 219
Quarles, Benjamin, 35

race: ambiguities in, 93, 101, 103, 146, 157–61; in antiemancipation sentiment, 18–20, 86–88, 115–21, 123–24; in antislavery sentiment, 87–88, 92–93, 101–8, 114, 128, 224, 225–27; and citizenship, xv, 4–5; and colonization, 205; in defenses of slavery, 16–21, 87, 224; definition of, xiv–xv, 3n2, 147, 150–51; as environmental, 17; and gender, 2, 105–6, 123–24, 189; and ideal society, 2, 19, 87, 107, 171, 189, 225–29; importance of, 128, 130, 160–61; Jefferson on, 103; legal distinctions according to, 2–4, 116–18, 119–20, 147–52; and liberty, x, xiii–xiv, 7, 84, 123, 126, 164, 193, 208; liberty defined by, 3–5, 35, 47, 127, 147–52, 162, 171; manumission as a challenge to, 39, 47, 54, 84, 88, 109, 121, 126, 158–60, 233; as a natural category, 17–20, 51n14, 88, 103, 150–51; operation of, in Virginia, xii–xiv, 130; rights limited by, 4–5, 37, 127, 189; and slavery, x, 5, 123, 126, 208; slavery defined by, 2–4, 5, 47, 149–51; as a social category, 2, 54, 86, 88, 117, 120, 127, 160, 162; as unimportant, 16, 148; versus class, 118–19, 125; white anxiety about, 88, 109, 119, 128
race war, white fear of, 103, 119, 123–24, 129, 166, 224
Randolph, Beverly, 168n8
Randolph, Edmund, 148–49
Randolph, George Wythe, 237
Randolph, Thomas Jefferson, 211–12, 213–14, 217, 218, 219, 220, 230, 232, 237
registers of free blacks, 71, 117, 120, 143
representation in Virginia legislature, 126–27, 163, 184; discussed in Virginia Constitutional Convention of 1829–30, 186–88; in Virginia Constitution of 1851, 237
Republican Party, 119, 172
Richmond, Virginia: colonization society in, 168, 170; economy of, 74, 111, 113; free blacks in, 111; Gabriel's plot in, 110–11, 118; manumission in, 63n29, 67n34, 75n44, 77n46; Virginia Constitutional Convention of 1829–30 held in, 186
Richmond Enquirer, 173, 175, 176, 178, 205n14, 210
Roane, Spencer, 150, 154
Roane, William, 207n16, 208, 212, 223–24, 227, 235
Roanoke Association (Baptists), 97
Robertson, Thomas, 123–24
Rockbridge County, 202, 207n16, 209, 220, 223, 242
Rockingham County, 175, 182
Roderick, 159
Rose, Willie Lee, 223

Saint Domingue, 26, 64, 109, 115–16, 124, 166
Scott, Jonathan, 146
Scribbler, 19–21, 38
Second Great Awakening, 166

sectionalism: in United States, 163, 172, 174, 237; in Virginia, xii, 24, 114, 127, 163, 179–85, 187–88, 192–95, 197, 228–29, 236–37

Senate of Virginia: colonization bill considered by, 232; manumission bill considered by, 30; representation to, 184, 185

Shenandoah Valley, 42, 182

Sierra Leone Company, 166

slaveholders: as minority, 187–88, 194; political power of, 37, 179, 187, 194; slavery supported by, 5, 18–21, 27–28, 37, 93; slave trade opposed by, 22–24. *See also* manumitters

slaveholding, frequency of, 6n6, 76nb

slave rebellion, white fear of, 12, 13, 24, 66, 108, 110, 111, 115–16, 118, 123–24, 199–200, 204–5, 212, 215–16

slavery: abolition of (*see* abolition of slavery); ambivalence toward, 5–7, 31, 35–37, 130, 137; American Revolution as challenge to, x, xv, 4, 8–9, 14–15, 21, 28, 35, 47, 61–62, 104, 112, 152, 175; ancient example of, cited, 13, 20; as beneficial, 19–20, 27, 219–20, 222–23, 227; defense of (*see* defenses of slavery; proslavery sentiment); definition of, in deeds of manumission, 49–51; as dehumanizing, ix, 17–18; as detrimental to whites, 12–14, 22–23, 115, 200–202, 209, 215, 217, 220–21, 226–27; diffusion of, 173–74; discussion of, in debate over slavery, 1831–32, xvi, 196–98, 212–29; discussion of, in Virginia Constitutional Convention of 1829–30, xi, xvi, 163–64, 170, 185, 187–88, 190–92, 233–34; economy of, 2, 72–75, 77, 111, 178–79, 182, 221; as a flexible institution, 47, 83; history of, in Virginia, 2–3; laws regarding, 2–3, 25–27, 35–37, 116–18, 119–21, 125, 128–29, 134–35, 149, 233; as legitimate, 19, 44, 51–52, 94, 100, 223–24; liberty in tension with, 1, 4–5, 7–10, 18, 51, 84, 104, 124, 163, 176, 190–91, 193–95, 220, 225, 238; liberty preserved by, 3–4, 20, 193, 195, 225, 238; manumission's effect on, 4, 34–35, 39, 62, 65–66, 80, 81–82, 84; meanings of, to Virginians, 29–30, 47–53, 65; metaphorical use of, 127; as a natural category, 51; opposition to (*see* antislavery sentiment); as a political issue, xvi, 162–63, 173–76, 178–79, 181, 183–85, 191, 193–95, 197, 233–34; practice versus theory of, 72, 82–83; property rights as central to, 5, 31, 36–37, 49, 123, 173, 176, 192, 216–17; as a racial institution, x, xii, 2–5, 17, 18–20, 38, 84, 88, 93, 147–52, 195, 205–6, 224; republicanism consonant with, 19, 20, 173; as a sectional issue, xii, 24, 86, 178–79, 181–82, 183, 185–95, 225–29; semicontractual form of, 82; white Virginians' commitment to, xi, 36–38, 52, 70, 96, 124, 232

slavery debate of 1831–32. *See* debate over slavery, 1831–32

slaves: hiring out of, 36, 111, 117; laws regarding, 2–3, 6, 25–27, 34, 36, 120, 125, 128–29, 233; manumission influenced by, 64–67; manumission of, by self-purchase, 35, 66–68, 73, 74–75; as persons and property, 31, 36–37; petitions of, to the legislature to remain in Virginia if freed, 130–31, 133, 134, 138–42, 144–45, 146, 159; population of, xi, 4, 6, 24, 40, 42, 43, 44–45, 78, 110–11, 127, 163, 180, 182; as property, 5–6, 13, 17–19, 21, 31, 48–49, 93, 105, 108, 121, 153, 156–57, 160; as runaways, 20, 36–37, 135; self-hire of, 67, 74–75, 111, 128, 133; in War of 1812, 133–34; in War of Independence, 14–15, 35–36; whites' view of, ix, xii, 4, 31, 37, 50–52, 54, 74, 84, 89, 108, 128–29

slave trade, opposition to, 22–25, 27

Smith, John B. D., 207n16

Society of Friends. *See* Quakers

Southampton County, 97, 196, 205n14, 207n16

South Carolina, 26, 27, 99, 183–84, 187, 204

Spotsylvania County, 125

Stamp Act, 8

State Rights ideology, 164, 172–73, 176, 178–79, 191, 192, 236, 237

Staunton, 184, 185

Sterling, 139, 159
Stillman, George, 207n16
Strawberry District Association (Baptists), 97–98
Sue, 160
suffrage requirements: debate over, in Virginia Constitutional Convention of 1829–30, 186–87, 188–91, 193; in 1830 constitution, 194, 225; in 1851 constitution, 237; in Jacksonian era, 163, 183; in 1776 constitution, 126–27, 182; westerners' desire for reform of, 183–85, 188–91
suits for freedom. *See* freedom suits
Summary View of the Rights of British America (Jefferson), 13–14
Summers, George, 216, 220
Surry County, 205n14, 243
Swallow Barn (Kennedy), 177

Taliaferro, John (1770s), 29
Taliaferro, John (1820s), 168, 169
Tallmadge, James, Jr., 173
Tallmadge amendment, 173, 174
Taylor, John, of Caroline, 121n57
Taylor, Richardson, 119
Thornton, John, 28
Tidewater region: colonization supported in, 202, 205, 232, 235–36, 243, 245; economy of, 22, 24, 83, 110, 182; emancipation opposed in, 121, 203; emancipation supported in, 98, 242; Federalists in, 181n28; history of, 24, 40; manumission in, 40, 43, 55, 57, 75–78, 83; political dominance of, 126, 181–84; population in, 24, 110, 126, 180, 182; slave trade opposed in, 24. *See also individual county names*
tobacco, economy of, 22–23, 110
Tomahawk Baptist Church, 160
Trans-Allegheny region: history and economy of, 42, 181; manumission in, 43, 75, 78; suffrage in, 183. *See also* Wythe County
Tucker, George: colonization plan of, 107, 108, 109, 202; on Missouri Crisis, 173

Tucker, St. George: abolition proposal of, 88n3, 104–7; on colonization of African Americans, 105–6, 165; and *Dissertation on Slavery*, 101, 104–7, 152; on free black population, 45; and *Hudgins v. Wrights*, 149–50, 151; on race, 106–7, 151–52; on slavery, x, 106, 164, 170, 178; on slaves' legal status, 49
Tucker, Thomas Tudor, 110
Turner, Nat, 196, 223. *See also* Nat Turner's rebellion
two-race system: as ideal, 126, 128–29, 130–31, 147, 158, 160–61, 203, 206, 233; threatening of, 39, 47, 119–21, 126, 128–29; in Virginia, 4
Tyler, John, 176, 186

Valley region: colonization supported in, 204n14, 243, 244, 245; economy and history of, 42, 110, 180–81; manumission in, 43, 75, 78; slavery opposed in, 175, 201, 202, 220, 242. *See also* Botetourt County
Virginia, 6; demographic change in (*see* demographic change in Virginia); economy of, 2, 8, 22–23, 40–42, 77, 110, 179–81, 219; population of, 42–43, 180–81; proposal to divide, 229; and secession from the Union, 237. *See also* sectionalism: in Virginia
Virginia Abolition Society. *See* Virginia Society for Promoting the Abolition of Slavery
Virginia and Kentucky Resolutions, 172
Virginia Constitutional Convention of 1829–30: outcome of, 194; as precedent for slavery debate of 1831–32, 220, 223, 229; representation discussed in, 186–88; Revolutionary ideals discussed in, 190, 193; sectionalism in Virginia as characteristic of, xi, xvi, 162–64, 179, 187–88, 197; slavery discussed in, xi, xvi, 163–64, 170, 185, 187–88, 190–92, 233–34; suffrage discussed in, 127, 186–87, 188–91, 193; vote to convene, 185
Virginia Constitution of 1776, 1, 126, 181, 182–83, 185, 186, 190
Virginia Constitution of 1851, 237

Virginia Declaration of Rights: discussion of, in Virginia Constitutional Convention of 1829–30, 186, 189, 190; draft of, 1, 4–5; emancipation justified by, 32; as radical, 6; slavery challenged by, 4–5, 16, 32, 190; slaves excluded from, 4–5, 190, 216, 149
Virginia Society for Promoting the Abolition of Slavery, 9, 10n12

Walker, David, 197
Wallace, James, 146
War for Independence: African Americans as soldiers in, 35–36; and antislavery sentiment, 62; as disruptive of society, 11, 86, 109; slaves in, 14–15
War of 1812: slaves gain freedom in, 133–34, 135
Warrenton, Virginia, 75n44, 142, 142n20, 144, 146
Warrenton Gazette, 229
Washington, Bushrod, 167
Washington, George, 10, 13, 61, 94, 175

Washington County, 244
Wesley, John, 10
West Indies, 26, 116. *See also* Saint Domingue
Westmoreland County, 205n14, 207n16, 243
West Virginia, 236, 237
Whig Party, 236, 237
"white negroes," 146, 147
Winn v. Bob and others, 156–57
Witcher, Vincent, 208–9
Withers, Thomas Thornton, 145, 146
Wood, Rice, 207n16, 222, 227
Woolman, John, 7
Wythe, George: and *Hudgins v. Wrights,* 148, 149; and *Pleasants v. Pleasants,* 154; as professor at College of William and Mary, 104; republican views of, 104, 148, 237; revisal of laws by, 4, 102
Wythe County, 42, 43, 46, 56, 68, 76, 77, 78

York County, 205n14, 243

Zane, Isaac, 24

Lightning Source UK Ltd.
Milton Keynes UK
UKHW020832300420
362523UK00015B/166

9 780807 134177